SARACINESCA

BY

F. Marion CRAWFORD

AUTHOR OF 'MR. ISAACS,' 'DR. CLAUDIUS,' 'A ROMAN SINGER,'
'ZOROASTER,' 'A TALE OF A LONELY PARISH,' ETC.

New York
MACMILLAN AND CO.
1887

NOTE

IT was at first feared that the name Saracinesca, as it is now printed, might be attached to an unused title in the possession of a Roman house. The name was therefore printed with an additional consonant— "Sarracinesca"—in the pages of 'Blackwood's Magazine.' After careful inquiry, the original spelling is now restored.

SORRENTO, *March* 1887.

124.4/4

SARACINESCA.

CHAPTER I.

In the year 1865 Rome was still in a great measure its old self. It had not then acquired that modern air which is now beginning to pervade it. The Corso had not been widened and whitewashed; the Villa Aldobrandini had not been cut through to make the Via Nazionale; the south wing of the Palazzo Colonna still looked upon a narrow lane through which men hesitated to pass after dark; the Tiber's course had not then been corrected below the Farnesina; the Farnesina itself was but just under repair; the iron bridge at the Ripetta was not dreamed of; and the Prati di Castello were still, as their name implies, a series of waste meadows. At the southern extremity of the city, the space between the fountain of Moses and the newly erected railway station, running past the Baths of Diocletian, was still an exercising-ground for the French cavalry. Even the people in the streets then presented an appearance very different from that which is now observed by the visitors and foreigners who come to Rome in the winter. French dragoons and hussars, French infantry and French officers, were everywhere to be seen in great numbers, mingled with a goodly sprinkling of the Papal Zouaves, whose grey Turco uniforms with bright red facings, red sashes, and

short yellow gaiters, gave colour to any crowd. A fine corps
of men they were, too, counting hundreds of gentlemen in
their ranks, and officered by some of the best blood in France
and Austria. In those days also were to be seen the great
coaches of the cardinals, with their gorgeous footmen and
magnificent black horses, the huge red umbrellas lying upon
the top, while from the open windows the stately princes of
the Church from time to time returned the salutations of the
pedestrians in the street. And often in the afternoon there
was heard the tramp of horse as a detachment of the noble
guards trotted down the Corso on their great chargers, escort-
ing the holy Father himself, while all who met him dropped
upon one knee and uncovered their heads to receive the benediction of the mild-eyed old man with the beautiful features,
the head of Church and State. Many a time, too, Pius IX.
would descend from his coach and walk upon the Pincio,
all clothed in white, stopping sometimes to talk with those
who accompanied him, or to lay his gentle hand on the
fair curls of some little English child that paused from its
play in awe and admiration as the Pope went by. For he
loved children well, and most of all, children with golden
hair—angels, not Angles, as Gregory said.

As for the fashions of those days, it is probable that most
of us would suffer severe penalties rather than return to them,
beautiful as they then appeared to us by contrast with the
exaggerated crinoline and flower-garden bonnet, which had
given way to the somewhat milder form of hoop-skirt madness, but had not yet flown to the opposite extreme in the invention of the close-fitting *princesse* garments of 1868. But,
to each other, people looked then as they look now. Fashion
in dress, concerning which nine-tenths of society gives itself
so much trouble, appears to exercise less influence upon
men and women in their relations towards each other than
does any other product of human ingenuity. Provided
every one is in the fashion, everything goes on in the age
of high heels and gowns tied back precisely as it did five-
and-twenty years ago, when people wore flat shoes, and
when gloves with three buttons had not been dreamed of—
when a woman of most moderate dimensions occupied three

or four square yards of space upon a ball-room floor, and men wore peg-top trousers. Human beings since the days of Adam seem to have retired like caterpillars into cocoons of dress, expecting constantly the wondrous hour when they shall emerge from their self-woven prison in the garb of the angelic butterfly, having entered into the chrysalis state as mere human grubs. But though they both toil and spin at their garments, and vie with Solomon in his glory to outshine the lily of the field, the humanity of the grub shows no signs of developing either in character or appearance in the direction of anything particularly angelic.

It was not the dress of the period which gave to the streets of Rome their distinctive feature. It would be hard to say, now that so much is changed, wherein the peculiar charm of the old-time city consisted; but it was there, nevertheless, and made itself felt so distinctly beyond the charm of any other place, that the very fascination of Rome was proverbial. Perhaps no spot in Europe has ever possessed such an attractive individuality. In those days there were many foreigners, too, as there are to-day, both residents and visitors; but they seemed to belong to a different class of humanity. They seemed less inharmonious to their surroundings then than now, less offensive to the general air of antiquity. Probably they were more in earnest; they came to Rome with the intention of liking the place, rather than of abusing the cookery in the hotels. They came with a certain knowledge of the history, the literature, and the manners of the ancients, derived from an education which in those days taught more through the classics and less through handy text-books and shallow treatises concerning the Renaissance; they came with preconceived notions which were often strongly dashed with old-fashioned prejudice, but which did not lack originality: they come now in the smattering mood, imbued with no genuine beliefs, but covered with exceeding thick varnish. Old gentlemen then visited the sights in the morning, and quoted Horace to each other, and in the evening endeavoured by associating with Romans to understand something of Rome; young gentlemen now spend

one or two mornings in finding fault with the architecture
of Bramante, and "in the evening," like David's enemies,
"they grin like a dog and run about the city:" young
women were content to find much beauty in the galleries
and in the museums, and were simple enough to admire
what they liked; young ladies of the present day can find
nothing to admire except their own perspicacity in detecting faults in Raphael's drawing or Michael Angelo's colouring. This is the age of incompetent criticism in matters
artistic, and no one is too ignorant to volunteer an opinion.
It is sufficient to have visited half-a-dozen Italian towns,
and to have read a few pages of fashionable æsthetic
literature—no other education is needed to fit the intelligent young critic for his easy task. The art of paradox
can be learned in five minutes, and practised by any
child; it consists chiefly in taking two expressions of
opinion from different authors, halving them, and uniting the first half of the one with the second half of the
other. The result is invariably startling, and generally
incomprehensible. When a young society critic knows
how to be startling and incomprehensible, his reputation
is soon made, for people readily believe that what they
cannot understand is profound, and anything which aston-
ishes is agreeable to a taste deadened by a surfeit of
spices. But in 1865 the taste of Europe was in a very
different state. The Second Empire was in its glory. M.
Emile Zola had not written his 'Assommoir.' Count Bis-
marck had only just brought to a successful termination
the first part of his trimachy; Sadowa and Sedan were
yet unfought. Garibaldi had won Naples, and Cavour had
said, "If we did for ourselves what we are doing for
Italy, we should be great scoundrels;" but Garibaldi had
not yet failed at Mentana, nor had Austria ceded Venice.
Cardinal Antonelli had yet ten years of life before him in
which to maintain his gallant struggle for the remnant of
the temporal power; Pius IX. was to live thirteen years
longer, just long enough to outlive by one month the
"honest king," Victor Emmanuel. Antonelli's influence
pervaded Rome, and to a great extent all the Catholic

Courts of Europe; yet he was far from popular with the Romans. The Jesuits, however, were even less popular than he, and certainly received a much larger share of abuse. For the Romans love faction more than party, and understand it better; so that popular opinion is too frequently represented by a transitory frenzy, violent and pestilent while it lasts, utterly insignificant when it has spent its fury.

But Rome in those days was peopled solely by Romans, whereas now a large proportion of the population consists of Italians from the north and south, who have been attracted to the capital by many interests—races as different from its former citizens as Germans or Spaniards, and unfortunately not disposed to show overmuch good-fellowship or loving-kindness to the original inhabitants. The Roman is a grumbler by nature, but he is also a "peace-at-any-price" man. Politicians and revolutionary agents have more than once been deceived by these traits, supposing that because the Roman grumbled he really desired change, but realising too late, when the change has been begun, that that same Roman is but a lukewarm partisan. The Papal Government repressed grumbling as a nuisance, and the people consequently took a delight in annoying the authorities by grumbling in secret places and calling themselves conspirators. The harmless whispering of petty discontent was mistaken by the Italian party for the low thunder of a smothered volcano; but, the change being brought about, the Italians find to their disgust that the Roman meant nothing by his murmurings, and that he now not only still grumbles at everything, but takes the trouble to fight the Government at every point which concerns the internal management of the city. In the days before the change, a paternal Government directed the affairs of the little State, and thought it best to remove all possibility of strife by giving the grumblers no voice in public or economic matters. The grumblers made a grievance of this; and then, as soon as the grievance had been redressed, they redoubled their complaints and retrenched themselves within the infallibility of inaction, on the prin-

ciple that men who persist in doing nothing cannot possibly
do wrong.

Those were the days, too, of the old school of artists—
men who, if their powers of creation were not always proportioned to their ambition for excellence, were as superior
to their more recent successors in their pure conceptions
of what art should be as Apelles was to the Pompeian
wall-painters, and as the Pompeians were to modern house-
decorators. The age of Overbeck and the last religious
painters was almost past, but the age of fashionable artistic debauchery had hardly begun. Water-colour was in
its infancy; wood-engraving was hardly yet a great profession; but the "Dirty Boy" had not yet taken a prize
at Paris, nor had indecency become a fine art. The French
school had not demonstrated the startling distinction between the nude and the naked, nor had the English school
dreamed nightmares of anatomical distortion.

Darwin's theories had been propagated, but had not yet
been passed into law, and very few Romans had heard of
them; still less had any one been found to assert that the
real truth of these theories would be soon demonstrated
retrogressively by the rapid degeneration of men into apes,
while apes would hereafter have cause to congratulate
themselves upon not having developed into men. Many
theories also were then enjoying vast popularity which
have since fallen low in the popular estimation. Prussia
was still, in theory, a Power of the second class, and the
empire of Louis Napoleon was supposed to possess elements of stability. The great civil war in the United
States had just been fought, and people still doubted
whether the republic would hold together. It is hard to
recall the common beliefs of those times. A great part
of the political creed of twenty years ago seems now a
mass of idiotic superstition, in no wise preferable, as
Macaulay would have said, to the Egyptian worship of
cats and onions. Nevertheless, then, as now, men met
together secretly in cellars and dens, as well as in drawing-
rooms and clubs, and whispered together, and said their
theories were worth something, and ought to be tried.

The word republic possessed then, as now, a delicious attraction for people who had grievances; and although, after the conquest of Naples, Garibaldi had made a sort of public abjuration of republican principles, so far as Italy was concerned, the plotters of all classes persisted in coupling his name with the idea of a commonwealth erected on the plan of "sois mon frère ou je te tue." Profound silence on the part of Governments, and a still more guarded secrecy on the part of conspiring bodies, were practised as the very first principle of all political operations. No copyist, at half-a-crown an hour, had yet betrayed the English Foreign Office; and it had not dawned upon the clouded intellects of European statesmen that deliberate national perjury, accompanied by public meetings of sovereigns, and much blare of many trumpets, could be practised with such triumphant success as events have since shown. In the beginning of the year 1865 people crossed the Alps in carriages; the Suez Canal had not been opened; the first Atlantic cable was not laid; German unity had not been invented; Pius IX. reigned in the Pontifical States; Louis Napoleon was the idol of the French; President Lincoln had not been murdered,— is anything needed to widen the gulf which separates those times from these? The difference between the States of the world in 1865 and in 1885 is nearly as great as that which divided the Europe of 1789 from the Europe of 1814.

But my business is with Rome, and not with Europe at large. I intend to tell the story of certain persons, of their good and bad fortune, their adventures, and the complications in which they found themselves placed during a period of about twenty years. The people of whom I tell this story are chiefly patricians; and in the first part of their history they have very little to do with any but their own class—a class peculiar and almost unique in the world.

Speaking broadly, there is no one at once so thoroughly Roman and so thoroughly non-Roman as the Roman noble. This is no paradox, no play on words. Roman nobles are Roman by education and tradition; by blood they are almost cosmopolitans. The practice of intermarrying with the great families of the rest of Europe is so general as to be almost a rule. One Roman prince is an English peer; most of the Roman princes are grandees of Spain; many of them have married daughters of great French houses, of reigning German princes, of ex-kings and ex-queens. In one princely house alone are found the following combinations: There are three brothers: the eldest married first the daughter of a great English peer, and secondly the daughter of an even greater peer of France; the second brother married first a German "serene highness," and secondly the daughter of a great Hungarian noble; the third brother married the daughter of a French house of royal Stuart descent. This is no solitary instance. A score of families might be cited who, by constant foreign marriages, have almost eliminated from their blood the original Italian element; and this great intermixture of races may account for the strangely un-Italian types that are found among them, for the undying vitality which seems to animate races already a thousand years old, and above all, for a very remarkable cosmopolitanism which pervades Roman society. A set of people whose near relations are socially prominent in every capital of Europe, could hardly be expected to have anything provincial about them in appearance or manners; still less can they be considered to be types of their own nation. And yet such is the force of tradition, of the patriarchal family life, of the early surroundings in which are placed these children of a mixed race, that they acquire from their earliest years the unmistakable outward manner of Romans, the broad Roman speech, and a sort of clannish and federative spirit, which has not its like in the same class anywhere in Europe. They grow up together, go to school together, go together into the world, and together discuss all the social affairs of their native city. Not a house is bought or sold, not a hundred francs won at écarté, not a marriage contract made, without being duly considered and commented upon by the whole of society. And yet, though there is much gossip, there is little scandal; there was even less twenty years

ago than there is now—not, perhaps, because the increment
of people attracted to the new capital have had any bad
influence, but simply because the city has grown much
larger, and in some respects has outgrown a certain simplicity of manners it once possessed, and which was its
chief safeguard. For, in spite of a vast number of writers
of all nations who have attempted to describe Italian life,
and who, from an imperfect acquaintance with the people,
have fallen into the error of supposing them to live perpetually in a highly complicated state of mind, the founda
tion of the Italian character is simple—far more so than
that of his hereditary antagonist, the northern European.
It is enough to notice that the Italian habitually expresses
what he feels, while it is the chief pride of Northern men
that whatever they may feel they express nothing. The
chief object of most Italians is to make life agreeable; the
chief object of the Teutonic races is to make it profitable.
Hence the Italian excels in the art of pleasing, and in
pleasing by means of the arts; whereas the Northern man
is pre-eminent in the faculty of producing wealth under
any circumstances, and when he has amassed enough possessions to think of enjoying his leisure, has generally been
under the necessity of employing Southern art as a means
to that end. But Southern simplicity carried to its ultimate expression leads not uncommonly to startling results;
for it is not generally a satisfaction to an Italian to be paid
a sum of money as damages for an injury done. When his
enemy has harmed him, he desires the simple retribution
afforded by putting his enemy to death, and he frequently
exacts it by any means that he finds ready to his hand.
Being simple, he reflects little, and often acts with violence.
The Northern mind, capable of vast intricacy of thought,
seeks to combine revenge of injury with personal profit,
and in a spirit of cold, far-sighted calculation, reckons up
the advantages to be got by sacrificing an innate desire for
blood to a civilised greed of money.

Dr Johnson would have liked the Romans—for in general they are good lovers and good haters, whatever faults
they may have. The patriarchal system, which was all

but universal twenty years ago, and is only now beginning
to yield to more modern institutions of life, tends to foster
the passions of love and hate.   Where father and mother
sit at the head and foot of the table, their sons with their
wives and their children each in his or her place, often to
the number of twenty souls—all living under one roof, one
name, and one bond of family unity—there is likely to be
a great similarity of feeling upon all questions of family
pride, especially among people who discuss everything with
vehemence, from European politics to the family cook.
They may bicker and squabble among themselves,—and
they frequently do,—but in their outward relations with
the world they act as one individual, and the enemy of one
is the enemy of all; for the pride of race and name is very
great.   There is a family in Rome who, since the memory
of man, have not failed to dine together twice every week,
and there are now more than thirty persons who take their
places at the patriarchal board.   No excuse can be pleaded
for absence, and no one would think of violating the rule.
Whether such a mode of life is good or not is a matter of
opinion; it is, at all events, a fact, and one not generally
understood or even known by persons who make studies
of Italian character.   Free and constant discussion of all
manner of topics should certainly tend to widen the intelligence; but, on the other hand, where the dialecticians
are all of one race, and name, and blood, the practice
may often merely lead to an undue development of prejudice.   In Rome, particularly, where so many families
take a distinct character from the influence of a foreign
mother, the opinions of a house are associated with its
mere name.   Casa Borghese thinks so and so, Casa Colonna
has diametrically opposite views, while Casa Altieri may dif-
fer wholly from both; and in connection with most subjects
the mere names Borghese, Altieri, Colonna are associated
in the minds of Romans of all classes with distinct sets of
principles and ideas, with distinct types of character, and
with distinctly different outward and visible signs of race.
Some of these conditions exist among the nobility of other
countries, but not, I believe, to the same extent.   In Ger-

many, the aristocratic body takes a certain uniform hue, so
to speak, from the army, in which it plays so important a
part, and the patriarchal system is broken up by the long
absences from the ancestral home of the soldier-sons. In
France, the main divisions of republicans, monarchists, and
imperialists have absorbed and unified the ideas and principles of large bodies of families into bodies politic. In
England, the practice of allowing younger sons to shift for
themselves, and the division of the whole aristocracy into
two main political parties, destroy the patriarchal spirit;
while it must also be remembered, that at a period when
in Italy the hand of every house was against its neighbour,
and the struggles of Guelph and Ghibelline were but an
excuse for the prosecution of private feuds, England was
engaged in great wars which enlisted vast bodies of men
under a common standard for a common principle. Whether
the principle involved chanced to be that of English domination in France, or whether men flocked to the standards
of the White Rose of York or the Red Rose of Lancaster,
was of little importance; the result was the same,—the
tendency of powerful families to maintain internecine traditional feuds was stamped out, or rather was absorbed in
the maintenance of the perpetual feud between the great
principles of Tory and Whig—of the party for the absolute
monarch, and the party for the freedom of the people.

Be the causes what they may, the Roman nobility has
many characteristics peculiar to it and to no other aristocracy. It is cosmopolitan by its foreign marriages, renewed
in every generation; it is patriarchal and feudal by its own
unbroken traditions of family life; and it is only essentially
Roman by its speech and social customs. It has undergone great vicissitudes during twenty years; but most of
these features remain in spite of new and larger parties,
new and bitter political hatreds, new ideas of domestic life,
and new fashions in dress and cookery.

In considering an account of the life of Giovanni Saracinesca from the time when, in 1865, he was thirty years
of age, down to the present day, it is therefore just that he
should be judged with a knowledge of some of these pecu-

liarities of his class. He is not a Roman of the people
like Giovañni Cardegna, the great tenor, and few of his
ideas have any connection with those of the singer; but he
has, in common with him, that singular simplicity of character which he derives from his Roman descent upon the
male side, and in which will be found the key to many of
his actions both good and bad—a simplicity which loves
peace, but cannot always refrain from sudden violence,
which loves and hates strongly and to some purpose.

CHAPTER II.

The hour was six o'clock, and the rooms of the Embassy
were as full as they were likely to be that day. There
would doubtless have been more people had the weather
been fine; but it was raining heavily, and below, in the
vast court that formed the centre of the palace, the lamps
of fifty carriages gleamed through the water and the darkness, and the coachmen, of all dimensions and characters,
sat beneath their huge umbrellas and growled to each
other, envying the lot of the footmen who were congregated in the ante - chamber up - stairs around the great
bronze braziers. But in the reception - rooms there was
much light and warmth; there were bright fires and softly
shaded lamps; velvet-footed servants stealing softly among
the guests, with immense burdens of tea and cake; men
of more or less celebrity chatting about politics in corners;
women of more or less beauty gossiping over their tea, or
flirting, or wishing they had somebody to flirt with; people
of many nations and ideas, with a goodly leaven of Romans.
They all seemed endeavouring to get away from the men
and women of their own nationality, in order to amuse
themselves with the difficulties of conversation in languages
not their own. Whether they amused themselves or not
is of small importance; but as they were all willing to
find themselves together twice a-day for the five months

of the Roman season—from the first improvised dance
before Christmas, to the last set ball in the warm April
weather after Easter—it may be argued that they did not
dislike each other's society. In case the afternoon should
seem dull, his Excellency had engaged the services of Signor
Strillone, the singer. From time to time he struck a few
chords upon the grand piano, and gave forth a song of his
own composition in loud and passionate tones, varied with
very sudden effects of extreme pianissimo, which occasionally surprised some one who was trying to make his conversation heard above the music.

There was a little knot of people standing about the door
of the great drawing-room. Some of them were watching
their opportunity to slip away unperceived; others had just
arrived, and were making a survey of the scene to ascertain the exact position of their Excellencies, and of the
persons they most desired to avoid, before coming forward.
Suddenly, just as Signor Strillone had reached a high note
and was preparing to bellow upon it before letting his voice
die away to a pathetic falsetto, the crowd at the door parted
a little. A lady entered the room alone, and stood out before the rest, pausing till the singer should have passed the
climax of his song, before she proceeded upon her way. She
was a very striking woman; every one knew who she was,
every one looked towards her, and the little murmur that
went round the room was due to her entrance rather than
to Signor Strillone's high note.

The Duchessa d'Astrardente stood still, and quietly
looked about her. A minister, two secretaries, and three
or four princes sprang towards her, each with a chair in
hand; but she declined each offer, nodding to one, thanking another by name, and exchanging a few words with a
third. She would not sit down; she had not yet spoken
to the ambassadress.

Two men followed her closely as she crossed the room
when the song was finished. One was a fair man of five-
and-thirty, rather stout, and elaborately dressed. He trod
softly and carried his hat behind him, while he leaned a
little forward in his walk. There was something unpleas-

ant about his face, caused perhaps by his pale complexion and almost colourless moustache; his blue eyes were small and near together, and had a watery, undecided look; his thin fair hair was parted in the middle over his low forehead; there was a scornful look about his mouth, though half concealed by the moustache; and his chin retreated rather abruptly from his lower lip. On the other hand, he was dressed with extreme care, and his manner showed no small confidence in himself as he pushed forwards, keeping as close as he could to the Duchessa. He had the air of being thoroughly at home in his surroundings.

Ugo del Ferice was indeed rarely disconcerted, and his self-reliance was most probably one chief cause of his success. He was a man who performed the daily miracle of creating everything for himself out of nothing. His father had barely been considered a member of the lower nobility, although he always called himself "dei conti del Ferice"— of the family of the counts of his name; but where or when the Conti del Ferice had lived, was a question he never was able to answer satisfactorily. He had made a little money, and had squandered most of it before he died, leaving the small remainder to his only son, who had spent every scudo of it in the first year. But to make up for the exiguity of his financial resources, Ugo had from his youth obtained social success. He had begun life by boldly calling himself "Il conte del Ferice." No one had ever thought it worth while to dispute him the title; and as he had hitherto not succeeded in conferring it upon any dowered damsel, the question of his countship was left unchallenged. He had made many acquaintances in the college where he had been educated; for his father had paid for his schooling in the Collegio dei Nobili, and that in itself was a passport—for as the lad grew to the young man, he zealously cultivated the society of his old schoolfellows, and by wisely avoiding all other company, acquired a right to be considered one of themselves. He was very civil and obliging in his youth, and had in that way acquired a certain reputation for being indispensable, which had stood him in good stead. No one asked whether he had paid his tailor's bill; or whether, upon certain conditions, his tailor supplied him with raiment gratis. He was always elaborately dressed, he was always ready to take a hand at cards, and he was always invited to every party in the season. He had cultivated with success the science of amusing, and people asked him to dinner in the winter, and to their country houses in the summer. He had been seen in Paris, and was often seen at Monte Carlo; but his real home and hunting-ground was Rome, where he knew every one, and every one knew him. He had made one or two fruitless attempts to marry young women of American extraction and large fortune; he had not succeeded in satisfying the paternal mind in regard to guarantees, and had consequently been worsted in his endeavours. Last summer, however, it appeared that he had been favoured with an increase of fortune. He gave out that an old uncle of his, who had settled in the south of Italy, had died, leaving him a modest competence; and while assuming a narrow band of *crêpe* upon his hat, he had adopted also a somewhat more luxurious mode of living. Instead of going about on foot or in cabs, he kept a very small coupé, with a very small horse and a diminutive coachman: the whole turn-out was very quiet in appearance, but very serviceable withal. Ugo sometimes wore too much jewellery; but his bad taste, if so it could be called, did not extend to the modest equipage. People accepted the story of the deceased uncle, and congratulated Ugo, whose pale face assumed on such occasions a somewhat deprecating smile. "A few scudi," he would answer —"a very small competence; but what would you have? I need so little—it is enough for me." Nevertheless people who knew him well warned him that he was growing stout.

The other man who followed the Duchessa d'Astrardente across the drawing-room was of a different type. Don Giovanni Saracinesca was neither very tall nor remarkably handsome, though in the matter of his beauty opinion varied greatly. He was very dark—almost as dark for a man as the Duchessa was for a woman. He was strongly

built, but very lean, and his features stood out in bold and
sharp relief from the setting of his short black hair and
pointed beard. His nose was perhaps a little large for his
face, and the unusual brilliancy of his eyes gave him an
expression of restless energy; there was something noble
in the shaping of his high square forehead and in the turn
of his sinewy throat. His hands were broad and brown,
but nervous and well knit, with straight long fingers and
squarely cut nails. Many women said Don Giovanni was
the handsomest man in Rome; others said he was too
dark or too thin, and that his face was hard and his
features ugly. There was a great difference of opinion
in regard to his appearance. Don Giovanni was not
married, but there were few marriageable women in Rome
who would not have been overjoyed to become his wife.
But hitherto he had hesitated—or, to speak more accurately,
he had not hesitated at all in his celibacy. His conduct
in refusing to marry had elicited much criticism, little of
which had reached his ears. He cared not much for what
his friends said to him, and not at all for the opinion of
the world at large, in consequence of which state of mind
people often said he was selfish—a view taken extensively
by elderly princesses with unmarried daughters, and even
by Don Giovanni's father and only near relation, the old
Prince Saracinesca, who earnestly desired to see his name
perpetuated. Indeed Giovanni would have made a good
husband, for he was honest and constant by nature, courteous by disposition, and considerate by habit and experience. His reputation for wildness rested rather upon his
taste for dangerous amusements than upon such scandalous
adventures as made up the lives of many of his contem-
poraries. But to all matrimonial proposals he answered
that he was barely thirty years of age, that he had plenty
of time before him, that he had not yet seen the woman
whom he would be willing to marry, and that he intended
to please himself.

The Duchessa d'Astrardente made her speech to her
hostess and passed on, still followed by the two men;
but they now approached her, one on each side, and

endeavoured to engage her attention. Apparently she intended to be impartial, for she sat down in the middle one of three chairs, and motioned to her two companions to seat themselves also, which they immediately did, whereby they became for the moment the two most important men in the room.

Corona d'Astrardente was a very dark woman. In all the Southern land there were no eyes so black as hers, no cheeks of such a warm dark-olive tint, no tresses of such raven hue. But if she was not fair, she was very beautiful; there was a delicacy in her regular features that artists said was matchless; her mouth, not small, but generous and nobly cut, showed perhaps more strength, more even determination, than most men like to see in women's faces; but in the exquisitely moulded nostrils there lurked much sensitiveness and the expression of much courage; and the level brow and straight-cut nose were in their clearness as an earnest of the noble thoughts that were within, and that so often spoke from the depths of her splendid eyes. She was not a scornful beauty, though her face could express scorn well enough. Where another woman would have shown disdain, she needed but to look grave, and her silence did the rest. She wielded magnificent weapons, and wielded them nobly, as she did all things. She needed all her strength, too, for her position from the first was not easy. She had few troubles, but they were great ones, and she bore them bravely.

One may well ask why Corona del Carmine had married the old man who was her husband—the broken-down and worn-out dandy of sixty, whose career was so well known, and whose doings had been as scandalous as his ancient name was famous in the history of his country. Her marriage was in itself almost a tragedy. It matters little to know how it came about; she accepted Astrardente with his dukedom, his great wealth, and his evil past, on the day when she left the convent where she had been educated; she did it to save her father from ruin, almost from starvation; she was seventeen years of age; she was told that the world was bad, and she resolved to begin her

B

life by a heroic sacrifice; she took the step heroically, and
no human being had ever heard her complain. Five years
had elapsed since then, and her father—for whom she had
given all she had, herself, her beauty, her brave heart, and
her hopes of happiness—her old father, whom she so loved,
was dead, the last of his race, saving only this beautiful
but childless daughter. What she suffered now—whether
she suffered at all—no man knew. There had been a wild
burst of enthusiasm when she appeared first in society, a
universal cry that it was a sin and a shame. But the
cynics who had said she would console herself had been
obliged to own their worldly wisdom at fault; the men
of all sorts who had lost their hearts to her were ignomini-
ously driven in course of time to find them again elsewhere. Amid all the excitement of the first two years
of her life in the world, Corona had moved calmly upon her
way, wrapped in the perfect dignity of her character; and
the old Duca d'Astrardente had smiled and played with
the curled locks of his wonderful wig, and had told every
one that his wife was the one woman in the universe who
was above suspicion. People had laughed incredulously at
first; but as time wore on they held their peace, tacitly
acknowledging that the aged fop was right as usual, but
swearing in their hearts that it was the shame of shames
to see the noblest woman in their midst tied to such a
wretched remnant of dissipated humanity as the Duca
d'Astrardente. Corona went everywhere, like other people;
she received in her own house a vast number of acquaintances; there were a few friends who came and went much
as they pleased, and some of them were young; but there
was never a breath of scandal breathed about the Duchessa.
She was indeed above suspicion.

She sat now between two men who were evidently
anxious to please her. The position was not new; she
was, as usual, to talk to both, and yet to show no preference for either. And yet she had a preference, and in her
heart she knew it was a strong one. It was by no means
indifferent to her which of those two men left her side and
which remained. She was above suspicion—yes, above the

suspicion of any human being besides herself, as she had been for five long years. She knew that had her husband entered the room and passed that way, he would have nodded to Giovanni Saracinesca as carelessly as though Giovanni had been his wife's brother—as carelessly as he would have noticed Ugo del Ferice upon her other side. But in her own heart she knew that there was but one face in all Rome she loved to see, but one voice she loved, and dreaded too, for it had the power to make her life seem unreal, till she wondered how long it would last, and whether there would ever be any change. The difference between Giovanni and other men had always been apparent. Others would sit beside her and make conversation, and then occasionally would make speeches she did not care to hear, would talk to her of love—some praising it as the only thing worth living for, some with affected cynicism scoffing at it as the greatest of unrealities, contradicting themselves a moment later in some passionate declaration to herself. When they were foolish, she laughed at them; when they went too far, she quietly rose and left them. Such experiences had grown rare of late, for she had earned the reputation of being cold and unmoved, and that protected her. But Giovanni had never talked like the rest of them. He never mentioned the old, worn subjects that the others harped upon. She would not have found it easy to say what he talked about, for he talked indifferently about many subjects. She was not sure whether he spent more time with her when in society than with other women; she reflected that he was not so brilliant as many men she knew, not so talkative as the majority of men she met; she knew only—and it was the thing she most bitterly reproached herself with—that she preferred his face above all other faces, and his voice beyond all voices. It never entered her head to think that she loved him; it was bad enough in her simple creed that there should be any man whom she would rather see than not, and whom she missed when he did not approach her. She was a very strong and loyal woman, who had sacrificed herself to a man who knew the world very thoroughly, who in the thoroughness of his knowledge was able to see that the world is not all bad, and who, in spite of all his evil deeds, was proud of his wife's loyalty. Astrardente had made a bargain when he married Corona; but he was a wise man in his generation, and he knew and valued her when he had got her. He knew the precise dangers to which she was exposed, and he was not so cruel as to expose her to them willingly. He had at first watched keenly the effect produced upon her by conversing with men of all sorts in the world, and among others he had noticed Giovanni; but he had come to the conclusion that his wife was equal to any situation in which she might be placed. Moreover, Giovanni was not an *habitué* at the Palazzo Astrardente, and showed none of the usual signs of anxiety to please the Duchessa.

From the time when Corona began to notice her own predilection for Saracinesca, she had been angry with herself for it, and she tried to avoid him; at all events, she gave him no idea that she liked him especially. Her husband, who at first had delivered many lectures on the subject of behaviour in the world, had especially warned her against showing any marked coldness to a man she wished to shun. "Men," said he, "are accustomed to that; they regard it as the first indication that a woman is really interested; when you want to get rid of a man, treat him systematically as you treat everybody, and he will be wounded at your indifference and go away." But Giovanni did not go, and Corona began to wonder whether she ought not to do something to break the interest she felt in him.

At the present moment she wanted a cup of tea. She would have liked to send Ugo del Ferice for it; she did what she thought least pleasant to herself, and she sent Giovanni. The servants who were serving the refreshments had all left the room, and Saracinesca went in pursuit of them. As soon as he was gone Del Ferice spoke. His voice was soft, and had an insinuating tone in it.

"They are saying that Don Giovanni is to be married," he remarked, watching the Duchessa from the corners of his eyes as he indifferently delivered himself of his news.

The Duchessa was too dark a woman to show emotion

easily. Perhaps she did not believe the story; her eyes fixed themselves on some distant object in the room, as though she were intensely interested in something she saw, and she paused before she answered.

"That is news indeed, if it is true. And whom is he going to marry?"

"Donna Tullia Mayer, the widow of the financier. She is immensely rich, and is some kind of cousin of the Saracinesca."

"How strange!" exclaimed Corona. "I was just looking at her. Is not that she over there, with the green feathers?"

"Yes," answered Del Ferice, looking in the direction the Duchessa indicated. "That is she. One may know her at a vast distance by her dress. But it is not all settled yet."

"Then one cannot congratulate Don Giovanni to-day?" asked the Duchessa, facing her interlocutor rather suddenly.

"No," he answered; "it is perhaps better not to speak to him about it."

"It is as well that you warned me, for I would certainly have spoken."

"I do not imagine that Saracinesca likes to talk of his affairs of the heart," said Del Ferice, with considerable gravity. "But here he comes. I had hoped he would have taken even longer to get that cup of tea."

"It was long enough for you to tell your news," answered Corona quietly, as Don Giovanni came up.

"What is the news?" asked he, as he sat down beside her.

"Only an engagement that is not yet announced," answered the Duchessa. "Del Ferice has the secret; perhaps he will tell you."

Giovanni glanced across her at the fair pale man, whose fat face, however, expressed nothing. Seeing he was not enlightened, Saracinesca civilly turned the subject.

"Are you going to the meet to-morrow, Duchessa?" he asked.

"That depends upon the weather and upon the Duke," she answered. "Are you going to follow?"

"Of course. What a pity it is that you do not ride!"

"It seems such an unnatural thing to see a woman hunting," remarked Del Ferice, who remembered to have heard the Duchessa say something of the kind, and was consequently sure that she would agree with him.

"You do not ride yourself," said Don Giovanni, shortly. "That is the reason you do not approve of it for ladies."

"I am not rich enough to hunt," said Ugo, modestly. "Besides, the other reason is a good one; for when ladies hunt I am deprived of their society."

The Duchessa laughed slightly. She never felt less like laughing in her life, and yet it was necessary to encourage the conversation. Giovanni did not abandon the subject.

"It will be a beautiful meet," he said. "Many people are going out for the first time this year. There is a man here who has brought his horses from England. I forget his name—a rich Englishman."

"I have met him," said Del Ferice, who was proud of knowing everybody. "He is a type—enormously rich— a lord—I cannot pronounce his name—not married either. He will make a sensation in society. He won races in Paris last year, and they say he will enter one of his hunters for the steeplechases here at Easter."

"That is a great inducement to go to the meet, to see this Englishman," said the Duchessa rather wearily, as she leaned back in her chair. Giovanni was silent, but showed no intention of going. Del Ferice, with an equal determination to stay, chattered vivaciously.

"Don Giovanni is quite right," he continued. "Every one is going. There will be two or three drags. Madame Mayer has induced Valdarno to have out his four-in-hand, and to take her and a large party."

The Duchessa did not hear the remainder of Del Ferice's speech, for at the mention of Donna Tullia—now commonly called Madame Mayer—she instinctively turned and looked at Giovanni. He, too, had caught the name, though he was not listening in the least to Ugo's chatter; and as he met Corona's eyes he moved uneasily, as much as to say he wished the fellow would stop talking. A moment later Del Ferice rose from his seat; he had seen Donna Tullia passing near, and thought the opportunity favourable for obtaining an invitation to join the party on the drag. With a murmured excuse which Corona did not hear, he went in pursuit of his game.

"I thought he was never going," said Giovanni, moodily. He was not in the habit of posing as the rival of any one who happened to be talking to the Duchessa. He had never said anything of the kind before, and Corona experienced a new sensation, not altogether unpleasant. She looked at him in some surprise.

"Do you not like Del Ferice?" she inquired, gravely.

"Do you like him yourself?" he asked in reply.

"What a question! Why should I like or dislike any one?" There was perhaps the smallest shade of bitterness in her voice as she asked the question she had so often asked herself. Why should she like Giovanni Saracinesca, for instance?

"I do not know what the world would be like if we had no likes and dislikes," said Giovanni, suddenly. "It would be a poor place; perhaps it is only a poor place at best. I merely wondered whether Del Ferice amused you as he amuses everybody."

"Well then, frankly, he has not amused me to-day," answered Corona, with a smile.

"Then you are glad he is gone?"

"I do not regret it."

"Duchessa," said Giovanni, suddenly changing his position, "I am glad he is gone, because I want to ask you a question. Do I know you well enough to ask you a question?"

"It depends——" Corona felt the blood rise suddenly to her dark forehead. Her hands burned intensely in her gloves. The anticipation of something she had never heard made her heart beat uncontrollably in her breast.

"It is only about myself," continued Giovanni, in low

tones. He had seen the blush, so rare a sight that there
was not another man in Rome who had seen it. He had
not time to think what it meant. "It is only about myself," he went on. "My father wants me to marry; he
insists that I should marry Donna Tullia — Madame
Mayer."

"Well?" asked Corona. She shivered; a moment before, she had been oppressed with the heat. Her mono-
syllabic question was low and indistinct. She wondered
whether Giovanni could hear the beatings of her heart, so
slow, so loud they almost deafened her.

"Simply this. Do you advise me to marry her?"

"Why do you ask me, of all people?" asked Corona,
faintly.

"I would like to have your advice," said Giovanni, twisting his brown hands together and fixing his bright eyes
upon her face.

"She is young yet. She is handsome—she is fabu-
lously rich. Why should you not marry her? Would she
make you happy?"

"Happy? Happy with her? No indeed. Do you think
life would be bearable with such a woman?"

"I do not know. Many men would marry her if they
could——"

"Then you think I should?" asked Giovanni. Corona
hesitated; she could not understand why she should care,
and yet she was conscious that there had been no such
struggle in her life since the day she had blindly resolved
to sacrifice herself to her father's wishes in accepting Astrardente. Still there could be no doubt what she should say:
how could she advise any one to marry without the prospect of the happiness she had never had?

"Will you not give me your counsel?" repeated Saracinesca. He had grown very pale, and spoke with such
earnestness that Corona hesitated no longer.

"I would certainly advise you to think no more about
it, if you are sure that you cannot be happy with her."

Giovanni drew a long breath, the blood returned to his
face, and his hands unlocked themselves.

"I will think no more about it," he said. "Heaven bless you for your advice, Duchessa!"

"Heaven grant I have advised you well!" said Corona, almost inaudibly. "How cold this house is! Will you put down my cup of tea? Let us go near the fire; Stril-lone is going to sing again."

"I would like him to sing a 'Nunc dimittis, Domine,' for me," murmured Giovanni, whose eyes were filled with a strange light.

Half an hour later Corona d'Astrardente went down the steps of the Embassy wrapped in her furs and preceded by her footman. As she reached the bottom Giovanni Saracinesca came swiftly down and joined her as her carriage drove up out of the dark courtyard. The footman opened the door, but Giovanni put out his hand to help Corona to mount the step. She laid her small gloved fingers upon the sleeve of his overcoat, and as she sprang lightly in she thought his arm trembled.

"Good night, Duchessa; I am very grateful to you," he said.

"Good night; why should you be grateful?" she asked, almost sadly.

Giovanni did not answer, but stood hat in hand as the great carriage rolled out under the arch. Then he buttoned his greatcoat, and went out alone into the dark and muddy streets. The rain had ceased, but everything was wet, and the broad pavements gleamed under the uncertain light of the flickering gas-lamps.

CHAPTER III.

The palace of the Saracinesca is in an ancient quarter of Rome, far removed from the broad white streets of mush-room dwelling-houses and machine-laid macadam; far from the foreigners' region, the varnish of the fashionable shops, the whirl of brilliant equipages, and the scream of the news-

vendor. The vast irregular buildings are built around
three courtyards, and face on all sides upon narrow streets.
The first sixteen feet, up to the heavily ironed windows of
the lower storey, consist of great blocks of stone, worn at
the corners and scored along their length by the battering
of ages, by the heavy carts that from time immemorial
have found the way too narrow and have ground their iron
axles against the massive masonry. Of the three enormous
arched gates that give access to the interior from different
sides, one is closed by an iron grating, another by huge
doors studded with iron bolts, and the third alone is usually
open as an entrance. A tall old porter used to stand there
in a long livery-coat and a cocked-hat; on holidays he appeared in the traditional garb of the Parisian "Suisse,"
magnificent in silk stockings and a heavily laced coat of
dark green, leaning upon his tall mace—a constant object
of wonder to the small boys of the quarter. He trimmed
his white beard in imitation of his master's—broad and
square—and his words were few and to the point.

No one was ever at home in the Palazzo Saracinesca in
those days; there were no ladies in the house; it was a man's
establishment, and there was something severely masculine
in the air of the gloomy courtyards surrounded by dark arch-
ways, where not a single plant or bit of colour relieved the
ancient stone. The pavement was clean and well kept, a new
flagstone here and there showing that some care was bestowed
upon maintaining it in good repair; but for any decoration
there was to be found in the courts, the place might have
been a fortress, as indeed it once was. The owners, father
and son, lived in their ancestral home in a sort of solemn
magnificence that savoured of feudal times. Giovanni was
the only son of five-and-twenty years of wedlock. His
mother had been older than his father, and had now been
dead some time. She had been a stern dark woman, and
had lent no feminine touch of grace to the palace while she
lived in it, her melancholic temper rather rejoicing in the
sepulchral gloom that hung over the house. The Saracinesca had always been a manly race, preferring strength to
beauty, and the reality of power to the amenities of comfort.

Giovanni walked home from the afternoon reception at the Embassy. His temper seemed to crave the bleak wet air of the cold streets, and he did not hurry himself. He intended to dine at home that evening, and he anticipated some kind of disagreement with his father. The two men were too much alike not to be congenial, but too combative by nature to care for eternal peace. On the present occasion it was likely that there would be a struggle, for Giovanni had made up his mind not to marry Madame Mayer, and his father was equally determined that he should marry her at once: both were singularly strong men, singularly tenacious of their opinions.

At precisely seven o'clock father and son entered from different doors the small sitting-room in which they generally met, and they had no sooner entered than dinner was announced. Two words might suffice for the description of old Prince Saracinesca—he was an elder edition of his son. Sixty years of life had not bent his strong frame nor dimmed the brilliancy of his eyes, but his hair and beard were snowy white. He was broader in the shoulder and deeper in the chest than Giovanni, but of the same height, and well proportioned still, with little tendency to stoutness. He was to all appearance precisely what his son would be at his age—keen and vigorous, the stern lines of his face grown deeper, and his very dark eyes and complexion made more noticeable by the dazzling whiteness of his hair and broad square beard—the same type in a different stage of development.

The dinner was served with a certain old-fashioned magnificence which has grown rare in Rome. There was old plate and old china upon the table, old cut glass of the diamond pattern, and an old butler who moved noiselessly about in the performance of the functions he had exercised in the same room for forty years, and which his father had exercised there before him. Prince Saracinesca and Don Giovanni sat on opposite sides of the round table, now and then exchanging a few words.

"I was caught in the rain this afternoon," remarked the Prince.

"I hope you will not have a cold," replied his son, civilly. "Why do you walk in such weather?"

"And you—why do you walk?" retorted his father. "Are you less likely to take cold than I am? I walk because I have always walked."

"That is an excellent reason. I walk because I do not keep a carriage."

"Why do not you keep one if you wish to?" asked the Prince.

"I will do as you wish. I will buy an equipage to-morrow, lest I should again walk in the rain and catch cold. Where did you see me on foot?"

"In the Orso, half an hour ago. Why do you talk about my wishes in that absurd way?"

"Since you say it is absurd, I will not do so," said Giovanni, quietly.

"You are always contradicting me," said the Prince. "Some wine, Pasquale."

"Contradicting you?" repeated Giovanni. "Nothing could be further from my intentions."

The old Prince slowly sipped a glass of wine before he answered.

"Why do not you set up an establishment for yourself and live like a gentleman?" he asked at length. "You are rich—why do you go about on foot and dine in cafés?"

"Do I ever dine at a café when you are dining alone?"

"You have got used to living in restaurants in Paris," retorted his father. "It is a bad habit. What was the use of your mother leaving you a fortune, unless you will live in a proper fashion?"

"I understand you very well," answered Giovanni, his dark eyes beginning to gleam. "You know all that is a pretence. I am the most home-staying man of your acquaintance. It is a mere pretence. You are going to talk about my marriage again."

"And has any one a more natural right to insist upon your marriage than I have?" asked the elder man, hotly. "Leave the wine on the table, Pasquale—and the fruit—

here. Give Don Giovanni his cheese. I will ring for the coffee—leave us." The butler and the footman left the room. "Has any one a more natural right, I ask?" repeated the Prince when they were alone.

"No one but myself, I should say," answered Giovanni, bitterly.

"Yourself—yourself indeed! What have you to say about it? This is a family matter. Would you have Saracinesca sold, to be distributed piecemeal among a herd of dogs of starving relations you never heard of, merely because you are such a vagabond, such a Bohemian, such a break-neck, crazy good-for-nothing, that you will not take the trouble to accept one of all the women who rush into your arms?"

"Your affectionate manner of speaking of your relatives is only surpassed by your good taste in describing the probabilities of my marriage," remarked Giovanni, scornfully.

"And you say you never contradict me!" exclaimed the Prince, angrily.

"If this is an instance, I can safely say so. Comment is not contradiction."

"Do you mean to say you have not repeatedly refused to marry?" inquired old Saracinesca.

"That would be untrue. I have refused, I do refuse, and I will refuse, just so long as it pleases me."

"That is definite, at all events. You will go on refusing until you have broken your silly neck in imitating Englishmen, and then—good night, Saracinesca! The last of the family will have come to a noble end!"

"If the only use of my existence is to become the father of heirs to your titles, I do not care to enjoy them myself."

"You will not enjoy them till my death, at all events. Did you ever reflect that I might marry again?"

"If you please to do so, do not hesitate on my account. Madame Mayer will accept you as soon as me. Marry by all means, and may you have a numerous progeny; and may they all marry in their turn, the day they are twenty. I wish you joy."

"You are intolerable, Giovanni. I should think you would have more respect for Donna Tullia——"

"Than to call her Madame Mayer," interrupted Giovanni.

"Than to suggest that she cares for nothing but a title and a fortune——"

"You showed much respect to her a moment ago, when you suggested that she was ready to rush into my arms."

"I! I never said such a thing. I said that any woman——"

"Including Madame Mayer, of course," interrupted Giovanni again.

"Can you not let me speak?" roared the Prince. Giovanni shrugged his shoulders a little, poured out a glass of wine, and helped himself to cheese, but said nothing. Seeing that his son said nothing, old Saracinesca was silent too; he was so angry that he had lost the thread of his ideas. Perhaps Giovanni regretted the quarrelsome tone he had taken, for he presently spoke to his father in a more conciliatory tone.

"Let us be just," he said. "I will listen to you, and I shall be glad if you will listen to me. In the first place, when I think of marriage I represent something to myself by the term——"

"I hope so," growled the old man.

"I look upon marriage as an important step in a man's life. I am not so old as to make my marriage an immediate necessity, nor so young as to be able wholly to disregard it. I do not desire to be hurried; for when I make up my mind, I intend to make a choice which, if it does not ensure happiness, will at least ensure peace. I do not wish to marry Madame Mayer. She is young, handsome, rich——"

"Very," ejaculated the Prince.

"Very. I also am young and rich, if not handsome."

"Certainly not handsome," said his father, who was nursing his wrath, and meanwhile spoke calmly. "You are the image of me."

"I am proud of the likeness," said Giovanni, gravely. "But to return to Madame Mayer. She is a widow——"

"Is that her fault?" inquired his father irrelevantly, his anger rising again.

"I trust not," said Giovanni, with a smile. "I trust she did not murder old Mayer. Nevertheless she is a widow. That is a strong objection. Have any of my ancestors married widows?"

"You show your ignorance at every turn," said the old Prince, with a scornful laugh. "Leone Saracinesca married the widow of the Elector of Limburger-Stinkenstein in 1581."

"It is probably the German blood in our veins which gives you your taste for argument," remarked Giovanni. "Because three hundred years ago an ancestor married a widow, I am to marry one now. Wait—do not be angry —there are other reasons why I do not care for Madame Mayer. She is too gay for me—too fond of the world."

The Prince burst into a loud ironical laugh. His white hair and beard bristled about his dark face, and he showed all his teeth, strong and white still.

"That is magnificent!" he cried; "it is superb, splendid, a piece of unpurchasable humour! Giovanni Saracinesca has found a woman who is too gay for him! Heaven be praised! We know his taste at last. We will give him a nun, a miracle of all the virtues, a little girl out of a convent, vowed to a life of sacrifice and self-renunciation. That will please him—he will be a model happy husband."

"I do not understand this extraordinary outburst," answered Giovanni, with cold scorn. "Your mirth is amazing, but I fail to understand its source."

His father ceased laughing, and looked at him curiously, his heavy brows bending with the intenseness of his gaze. Giovanni returned the look, and it seemed as though those two strong angry men were fencing across the table with their fiery glances. The son was the first to speak.

"Do you mean to imply that I am not the kind of man to be allowed to marry a young girl?" he asked, not taking his eyes from his father.

"Look you, boy," returned the Prince, "I will have no more nonsense. I insist upon this match, as I have told you before. It is the most suitable one that I can find for you; and instead of being grateful, you turn upon me and refuse to do your duty. Donna Tullia is twenty-three years of age. She is brilliant, rich. There is nothing against her. She is a distant cousin——"

"One of the flock of vultures you so tenderly referred to," remarked Giovanni.

"Silence!" cried old Saracinesca, striking his heavy hand upon the table so that the glasses shook together. "I will be heard; and what is more, I will be obeyed. Donna Tullia is a relation. The union of two such fortunes will be of immense advantage to your children. There is everything in favour of the match—nothing against it. You shall marry her a month from to-day. I will give you the title of Sant' Ilario, with the estate outright into the bargain, and the palace in the Corso to live in, if you do not care to live here."

"And if I refuse?" asked Giovanni, choking down his anger.

"If you refuse, you shall leave my house a month from to-day," said the Prince, savagely.

"Whereby I shall be fulfilling your previous commands, in setting up an establishment for myself and living like a gentleman," returned Giovanni, with a bitter laugh. "It is nothing to me—if you turn me out. I am rich, as you justly observed."

"You will have the more leisure to lead the life you like best," retorted the Prince; "to hang about in society, to go where you please, to make love to——" the old man stopped a moment. His son was watching him fiercely, his hand clenched upon the table, his face as white as death.

"To whom?" he asked, with a terrible effort to be calm.

"Do you think I am afraid of you? Do you think your father is less strong or less fierce than you? To whom?" cried the angry old man, his whole pent-up fury bursting out as he rose suddenly to his feet. "To whom but to Corona d'Astrardente—to whom else should you make love?—wasting your youth and life upon a mad passion! All Rome says it—I will say it too!"

"You have said it indeed," answered Giovanni, in a very low voice. He remained seated at the table, not moving a muscle, his face as the face of the dead. "You have said it, and in insulting that lady you have said a thing not worthy for one of our blood to say. God help me to remember that you are my father," he added, trembling suddenly.

"Hold!" said the Prince, who, with all his ambition for his son, and his hasty temper, was an honest gentleman. "I never insulted her—she is above suspicion. It is you who are wasting your life in a hopeless passion for her. See, I speak calmly——"

"What does 'all Rome say'?" asked Giovanni, interrupting him. He was still deadly pale, but his hand was unclenched, and as he spoke he rested his head upon it, looking down at the tablecloth.

"Everybody says that you are in love with the Astrardente, and that her husband is beginning to notice it."

"It is enough, sir," said Giovanni, in low tones. "I will consider this marriage you propose. Give me until the spring to decide."

"That is a long time," remarked the old Prince, resuming his seat and beginning to peel an orange, as though nothing had happened. He was far from being calm, but his son's sudden change of manner had disarmed his anger. He was passionate and impetuous, thoughtless in his language, and tyrannical in his determination; but he loved Giovanni dearly for all that.

"I do not think it long," said Giovanni, thoughtfully. "I give you my word that I will seriously consider the marriage. If it is possible for me to marry Donna Tullia, I will obey you, and I will give you my answer before Easter-day. I cannot do more."

"I sincerely hope you will take my advice," answered Saracinesca, now entirely pacified. "If you cannot make up your mind to the match, I may be able to find something else. There is Bianca Valdarno—she will have a quarter of the estate."

"She is so very ugly," objected Giovanni, quietly. He

c

was still much agitated, but he answered his father mechanically.

"That is true—they are all ugly, those Valdarni. Besides, they are of Tuscan origin. What do you say to the little Rocca girl? She has great *chic;* she was brought up in England. She is pretty enough."

"I am afraid she would be extravagant."

"She could spend her own money then; it will be sufficient."

"It is better to be on the safe side," said Giovanni. Suddenly he changed his position, and again looked at his father. "I am sorry we always quarrel about this question," he said. "I do not really want to marry, but I wish to oblige you, and I will try. Why do we always come to words over it?"

"I am sure I do not know," said the Prince, with a pleasant smile. "I have such a diabolical temper, I suppose."

"And I have inherited it," answered Don Giovanni, with a laugh that was meant to be cheerful. "But I quite see your point of view. I suppose I ought to settle in life by this time."

"Seriously, I think so, my son. Here is to your future happiness," said the old gentleman, touching his glass with his lips.

"And here is to our future peace," returned Giovanni, also drinking.

"We never really quarrel, Giovanni, do we?" said his father. Every trace of anger had vanished. His strong face beamed with an affectionate smile that was like the sun after a thunderstorm.

"No, indeed," answered his son, cordially. "We cannot afford to quarrel; there are only two of us left."

"That is what I always say," assented the Prince, beginning to eat the orange he had carefully peeled since he had grown calm. "If two men like you and me, my boy, can thoroughly agree, there is nothing we cannot accomplish; whereas if we go against each other——"

"Justitia non fit, cœlum vero ruet," suggested Giovanni, in parody of the proverb.

"I am a little rusty in my Latin, Giovannino," said the old gentleman.

"Heaven is turned upside down, but justice is not done."

"No; one is never just when one is angry. But storms clear the sky, as they say up at Saracinesca."

"By the bye, have you heard whether that question of the timber has been settled yet?" asked Giovanni.

"Of course—I had forgotten. I will tell you all about it," answered his father, cheerfully. So they chatted peacefully for another half-hour; and no one would have thought, in looking at them, that such fierce passions had been roused, nor that one of them felt as though his death-warrant had been signed. When they separated, Giovanni went to his own rooms, and locked himself in.

He had assumed an air of calmness which was not real before he left his father. In truth he was violently agitated. He was as fiery as his father, but his passions were of greater strength and of longer duration; for his mother had been a Spaniard, and something of the melancholy of her country had entered into his soul, giving depth and durability to the hot Italian character he inherited from his father. Nor did the latter suspect the cause of his son's sudden change of tone in regard to the marriage. It was precisely the difference in temperament which made Giovanni incomprehensible to the old Prince.

Giovanni had realised for more than a year past that he loved Corona d'Astrardente. Contrary to the custom of young men in his position, he determined from the first that he would never let her know it; and herein lay the key to all his actions. He had, as he thought, made a point of behaving to her on all occasions as he behaved to the other women he met in the world, and he believed that he had skilfully concealed his passion from the world and from the woman he loved. He had acted on all occasions with a circumspection which was not natural to him, and for which he undeniably deserved great credit. It had been a year of constant struggles, constant efforts at self-control, constant determination that, if possible, he

would overcome his instincts. It was true that, when
occasion offered, he had permitted himself the pleasure
of talking to Corona d'Astrardente — talking, he well
knew, upon the most general subjects, but finding at
each interview some new point of sympathy. Never, he
could honestly say, had he approached in that time the
subject of love, nor even the equally dangerous topic of
friendship, the discussion of which leads to so many
ruinous experiments. He had never by look or word
sought to interest the dark Duchessa in his doings nor in
himself; he had talked of books, of politics, of social
questions, but never of himself nor of herself. He had
faithfully kept the promise he had made in his heart,
that since he was so unfortunate as to love the wife of
another—a woman of such nobility that even in Rome
no breath had been breathed against her—he would keep
his unfortunate passion to himself. Astrardente was old,
almost decrepit, in spite of his magnificent wig; Corona
was but two-and-twenty years of age. If ever her husband died, Giovanni would present himself before the
world as her suitor; meanwhile he would do nothing to
injure her self-respect nor to disturb her peace—he hardly
flattered himself he could do that, for he loved her truly—
and above all, he would do nothing to compromise the
unsullied reputation she enjoyed. She might never love
him; but he was strong and patient, and would do her
the only honour it was in his power to do her, by waiting
patiently.

But Giovanni had not considered that he was the most
conspicuous man in society; that there were many who
watched his movements, in hopes he would come their
way; that when he entered a room, many had noticed
that, though he never went directly to Corona's side, he
always looked first towards her, and never omitted to speak
with her in the course of an evening. Keen observers,
the jays of society who hover about the eagle's nest, had
not failed to observe a look of annoyance on Giovanni's
face when he did not succeed in being alone by Corona's
side for at least a few minutes; and Del Ferice, who was

a sort of news-carrier in Rome, had now and then hinted that Giovanni was in love. People had repeated his hints, as he intended they should, with the illuminating wit peculiar to tale-bearers, and the story had gone abroad accordingly. True, there was not a man in Rome bold enough to allude to the matter in Giovanni's presence, even if any one had seen any advantage in so doing; but such things do not remain hidden. His own father had told him in a fit of anger, and the blow had produced its effect.

Giovanni sat down in a deep easy-chair in his own room, and thought over the situation. His first impulse had been to be furiously angry with his father; but the latter having instantly explained that there was nothing to be said against the Duchessa, Giovanni's anger against the Prince had turned against himself. It was bitter to think that all his self-denial, all his many and prolonged efforts to conceal his love, had been of no avail. He cursed his folly and imprudence, while wondering how it was possible that the story should have got abroad. He did not waver in his determination to hide his inclinations, to destroy the impression he had so unwillingly produced. The first means he found in his way seemed the best. To marry Donna Tullia at once, before the story of his affection for the Duchessa had gathered force, would, he thought, effectually shut the mouths of the gossips. From one point of view it was a noble thought, the determination to sacrifice himself wholly and for ever, rather than permit his name to be mentioned ever so innocently in connection with the woman he loved; to root out utterly his love for her by seriously engaging his faith to another, and keeping that engagement with all the strength of fidelity he knew himself to possess. He would save Corona from annoyance, and her name from the scandal-mongers; and if any one ever dared to mention the story——

Giovanni rose to his feet and mechanically took a fencing-foil from the wall, as he often did for practice. If any one mentioned the story, he thought, he had the

means to silence them, quickly and for ever. His eyes
flashed suddenly at the idea of action—any action, even
fighting, which might be distantly connected with Corona.
Then he tossed down the rapier and threw himself into
his chair, and sat quite still, staring at the trophies of
armour upon the wall opposite.

He could not do it. To wrong one woman for the sake
of shielding another was not in his power. People might
laugh at him and call him Quixotic, forsooth, because he
would not do like every one else and make a marriage of
convenience—of propriety. Propriety! when his heart was
breaking within him ; when every fibre of his strong frame
quivered with the strain of passion; when his aching eyes
saw only one face, and his ears echoed the words she had
spoken that very afternoon! Propriety indeed! Propriety
was good enough for cold-blooded dullards. Donna Tullia
had done him no harm that he should marry her for propriety's sake, and make her life miserable for thirty, forty,
fifty years. It would be propriety rather for him to go
away, to bury himself in the ends of the earth, until he
could forget Corona d'Astrardente, her splendid eyes, and
her deep sweet voice.

He had pledged his father his word that he would consider the marriage, and he was to give his answer before
Easter. That was a long time yet. He would consider it ;
and if by Eastertide he had forgotten Corona, he would——
he laughed aloud in his silent room, and the sound of his
voice startled him from his reverie.

Forget? Did such men as he forget? Other men did.
What were they made of? They did not love such women,
perhaps ; that was the reason they forgot. Any one could
forget poor Donna Tullia. And yet how was it possible to
forget if one loved truly?

Giovanni had never believed himself in love before. He
had known one or two women who had attracted him
strongly ; but he had soon found out that he had no real
sympathy with them, that though they amused him they
had no charm for him—most of all, that he could not
imagine himself tied to any one of them for life without

conceiving the situation horrible in the extreme. To his independent nature the idea of such ties was repugnant: he knew himself too courteous to break through the civilities of life with a wife he did not love ; but he knew also that in marrying a woman who was indifferent to him, he would be engaging to play a part for life in the most fearful of all plays—the part of a man who strives to bear bravely the galling of a chain he is too honourable to break.

It was four o'clock in the morning when Giovanni went to bed ; and even then he slept little, for his dreams were disturbed. Once he thought he stood upon a green lawn with a sword in his hand, and the blood upon its point, his opponent lying at his feet. Again, he thought he was alone in a vast drawing-room, and a dark woman came and spoke gently to him, saying, "Marry her for my sake." He awoke with a groan. The church clocks were striking eight, and the meet was at eleven, five miles beyond the Porta Pia. Giovanni started up and rang for his servant.

CHAPTER IV.

It was a beautiful day, and half Rome turned out to see the meet, not because it was in any way different from other meets, but because it chanced that society had a fancy to attend it. Society is very like a fever patient in a delirium ; it is rarely accountable for its actions ; it scarcely ever knows what it is saying ; and occasionally, without the least warning or premeditation, it leaps out of bed at an early hour of the morning and rushes frantically in pursuit of its last hallucination. The main difference is, that whereas a man in a fever has a nurse, society has none.

On the present occasion every one had suddenly conceived the idea of going to the meet, and the long road beyond the Porta Pia was dotted for miles with equipages of every description, from the four-in-hand of Prince Valdarno to the humble donkey-cart of the caterer who sells messes

of boiled beans, and bread and cheese, and salad to the
grooms—an institution not connected in the English mind
with hunting. One after another the vehicles rolled out
along the road, past Sant' Agnese, down the hill and across
the Ponte Nomentana, and far up beyond to a place where
three roads met and there was a broad open stretch of wet,
withered grass. Here the carriages turned in and ranged
themselves side by side, as though they were pausing in
the afternoon drive upon the Pincio, instead of being five
miles out upon the broad Campagna.

To describe the mountains to southward of Rome would
be an insult to nature; to describe a meet would be an
affront to civilised readers of the English language. The
one is too familiar to everybody: the pretty crowd of men
and women, dotted with pink and set off by the neutral
colour of the winter fields; the hunters of all ages, and
sizes, and breeds, led slowly up and down by the grooms;
while from time to time some rider gets into the saddle and
makes himself 'comfortable, assures himself of girth and
stirrup, and of the proper disposal of the sandwich-box and
sherry-flask, gives a final word of instruction to his groom,
and then moves slowly off. A Roman meet is a little
less business-like than the same thing elsewhere; there is
a little more dawdling, a little more conversation when
many ladies chance to have come to see the hounds throw
off; otherwise it is not different from other meets. As
for the Roman mountains, they are so totally unlike any
other hills in the world, and so extremely beautiful in their
own peculiar way, that to describe them would be an idle
and a useless task, which could only serve to exhibit the
vanity of the writer and the feebleness of his pen.

Don Giovanni arrived early in spite of his sleepless
night. He descended from his dogcart by the roadside,
instead of driving into the field, and he took a careful
survey of the carriages he saw before him. Conspicuous
in the distance he distinguished Donna Tullia Mayer
standing among a little crowd of men near Valdarno's
drag. She was easily known by her dress, as Del Ferice
had remarked on the previous evening. On this occasion

she wore a costume in which the principal colours were green and yellow, an enormous hat, with feathers in the same proportion surmounting her head, and she carried a yellow parasol. She was a rather handsome woman of middle height, with unnaturally blond hair, and a fairly good complexion, which as yet she had wisely abstained from attempting to improve by artificial means; her eyes were blue, but uncertain in their glance — of the kind which do not inspire confidence; and her mouth was much admired, being small and red, with full lips. She was rapid in her movements, and she spoke in a loud voice, easily collecting people about her wherever there were any to collect. Her conversation was not brilliant, but it was so abundant that its noisy vivacity passed current for cleverness; she had a remarkably keen judgment of people, and a remarkably bad taste in her opinions of things artistic, from beauty in nature to beauty in dress, but she maintained her point of view obstinately, and admitted no contradiction. It was a singular circumstance that whereas many of her attributes were distinctly vulgar, she nevertheless had an indescribable air of good breeding, the strange inimitable stamp of social superiority which cannot be acquired by any known process of education. A person seeing her might be surprised at her loud talking, amused at her eccentricities of dress, and shocked at her bold manner, but no one would ever think of classing her anywhere save in what calls itself "the best society."

Among the men who stood talking to Donna Tullia was the inevitable Del Ferice, a man of whom it might be said that he was never missed, because he was always present. Giovanni disliked Del Ferice without being able to define his aversion. He disliked generally men whom he suspected of duplicity; and he had no reason for supposing that truth, looking into her mirror, would have seen there the image of Ugo's fat pale face and colourless moustache. But if Ugo was a liar, he must have had a good memory, for he never got himself into trouble, and he had the reputation of being a useful member of society, an honour to which persons of doubtful veracity rarely attain. Giovanni, however, disliked him, and suspected him of many things; and although he had intended to go up to Donna Tullia, the sight of Del Ferice at her side very nearly prevented him. He strolled leisurely down the little slope, and as he neared the crowd, spoke to one or two acquaintances, mentally determining to avoid Madame Mayer, and to mount immediately. But he was disappointed in his intention. As he stood for a moment beside the carriage of the Marchesa Rocca, exchanging a few words with her, and looking with some interest at her daughter, the little Rocca girl whom his father had proposed as a possible wife for him, he forgot his proximity to the lady he wished to avoid; and when, a few seconds later, he proceeded in the direction of his horse, Madame Mayer stepped forward from the knot of her admirers and tapped him familiarly upon the shoulder with the handle of her parasol.

"So you were not going to speak to me to-day?" she said rather roughly, after her manner.

Giovanni turned sharply and faced her, bowing low. Donna Tullia laughed.

"Is there anything so amazingly ridiculous in my appearance?" he asked.

"*Altro!* when you make that tremendous salute——"

"It was intended to convey an apology as well as a greeting," answered Don Giovanni, politely.

"I would like more apology and less greeting."

"I am ready to apologise——"

"Humbly, without defending yourself," said Donna Tullia, beginning to walk slowly forward. Giovanni was obliged to follow her.

"My defence is, nevertheless, a very good one," he said.

"Well, if it is really good, I may listen to it; but you will not make me believe that you intended to behave properly."

"I am in a very bad humour. I would not inflict my cross temper upon you; therefore I avoided you."

Donna Tullia eyed him attentively. When she an-

swered she drew in her small red lips with an air of
annoyance.

"You look as though you were in bad humour," she
answered. "I am sorry I disturbed you. It is better to
leave sleeping dogs alone, as the proverb says."

"I have not snapped yet," said Giovanni. "I am not
dangerous, I assure you."

"Oh, I am not in the least afraid of you," replied his
companion, with a little scorn. "Do not flatter yourself
your little humours frighten me. I suppose you intend to
follow?"

"Yes," answered Saracinesca, shortly; he was beginning
to weary of Donna Tullia's manner of taking him to task.

"You had much better come with us, and leave the
poor foxes alone. Valdarno is going to drive us round by
the cross-roads to the Capannelle. We will have a picnic
lunch, and be home before three o'clock."

"Thanks very much. I cannot let my horse shirk his
work. I must beg you to excuse me———"

"Again?" exclaimed Donna Tullia. "You are always
making excuses." Then she suddenly changed her tone,
and looked down. "I wish you would come with us," she
said, gently. "It is not often I ask you to do anything."

Giovanni looked at her quickly. He knew that Donna
Tullia wished to marry him; he even suspected that his
father had discussed the matter with her—no uncommon
occurrence when a marriage has to be arranged with a
widow. But he did not know that Donna Tullia was in
love with him in her own odd fashion. He looked at her,
and he saw that as she spoke there were tears of vexation
in her bold blue eyes. He hesitated a moment, but natural courtesy won the day.

"I will go with you," he said, quietly. A blush of
pleasure rose to Madame Mayer's pink cheeks; she felt she
had made a point, but she was not willing to show her
satisfaction.

"You say it as though you were conferring a favour,"
she said, with a show of annoyance, which was belied by
the happy expression of her face.

"Pardon me; I myself am the favoured person," replied Giovanni, mechanically. He had yielded because he did not know how to refuse; but he already regretted it, and would have given much to escape from the party.

"You do not look as though you believed it," said Donna Tullia, eyeing him critically. "If you are going to be disagreeable, I release you." She said this well knowing, the while, that he would not accept of his liberty.

"If you are so ready to release me, as you call it, you do not really want me," said her companion. Donna Tullia bit her lip, and there was a moment's pause. "If you will excuse me a moment I will send my horse home—I will join you at once."

"There is your horse—right before us," said Madame Mayer. Even that short respite was not allowed him, and she waited while Don Giovanni ordered the astonished groom to take his hunter for an hour's exercise in a direction where he would not fall in with the hounds.

"I did not believe you would really do it," said Donna Tullia, as the two turned and sauntered back towards the carriages. Most of the men who meant to follow had already mounted, and the little crowd had thinned considerably. But while they had been talking another carriage had driven into the field, and had halted a few yards from Valdarno's drag. Astrardente had taken it into his head to come to the meet with his wife, and they had arrived late. Astrardente always arrived a little late, on principle. As Giovanni and Donna Tullia came back to their drag, they suddenly found themselves face to face with the Duchessa and her husband. It did not surprise Corona to see Giovanni walking with the woman he did not intend to marry, but it seemed to give the old Duke undisguised pleasure.

"Do you see, Corona, there is no doubt of it! It is just as I told you," exclaimed the aged dandy, in a voice so audible that Giovanni frowned and Donna Tullia blushed slightly. Both of them bowed as they passed the carriage. Don Giovanni looked straight into Corona's face as he took off his hat. He might very well have made her a little sign, the smallest gesture, imperceptible to Donna Tullia, whereby he could have given her the idea that his position was involuntary. But Don Giovanni was a gentleman, and he did nothing of the kind; he bowed and looked calmly at the woman he loved as he passed by. Astrardente watched him keenly, and as he noticed the indifference of Saracinesca's look, he gave a curious little snuffling snort that was peculiar to him. He could have sworn that neither his wife nor Giovanni had shown the smallest interest in each other. He was satisfied. His wife was above suspicion, as he always said; but he was an old man, and had seen the world, and he knew that however implicitly he might trust the noble woman who had sacrificed her youth to his old age, it was not beyond the bounds of possibility that she might become innocently interested, even unawares, in some younger man—in some such man as Giovanni Saracinesca—and he thought it worth his while to watch her. His little snort, however, was indicative of satisfaction. Corona had not winced at the mention of the marriage, and had nodded with the greatest unconcern to the man as he passed.

"Ah, Donna Tullia!" he cried, as he returned their greeting, "you are preventing Don Giovanni from mounting; the riders will be off in a moment."

Being thus directly addressed, there was nothing to be done but to stop and exchange a few words. The Duchessa was on the side nearest to the pair as they passed, and her husband rose and sat opposite her, so as to talk more at his ease. There were renewed greetings on both sides, and Giovanni naturally found himself talking to Corona, while her husband and Donna Tullia conversed together.

"What man could think of hunting when he could be talking to you instead?" said old Astrardente, whose painted face adjusted itself in a sort of leer that had once been a winning smile. Every one knew he painted, his teeth were a miracle of American dentistry, and his wig had deceived a great portrait-painter. The padding in his clothes was disposed with cunning wisdom, and in public he rarely removed the gloves from his small hands. Donna Tullia laughed at what he said.

"You should teach Don Giovanni to make pretty speeches," she said.· "He is as surly as a wolf this morning."

"I should think a man in his position would not need much teaching in order to be gallant to you," replied the old dandy, with a knowing look. Then lowering his voice, he added confidentially, "I hope that before very long I may be allowed to congrat——"

"I have prevailed upon him to give up following the hounds to-day," interrupted Donna Tullia, quickly. She spoke loud enough to be noticed by Corona. "He is coming with us to picnic at the Capannelle instead."

Giovanni could not help glancing quickly at Corona. She smiled faintly, and her face betrayed no emotion.

"I daresay it will be very pleasant," she said gently, looking far out over the Campagna. In the next field the pack was moving away, followed at a little distance by a score of riders in pink; one or two men who had stayed behind in conversation, mounted hastily and rode after the hunt; some of the carriages turned out of the field and began to follow slowly along the road, in hopes of seeing the hounds throw off; the party who were going with Valdarno gathered about the drag, waiting for Donna Tullia; the grooms who were left behind congregated around the men who sold boiled beans and salad; and in a few minutes the meet had practically dispersed.

"Why will you not join us, Duchessa?" asked Madame Mayer. "There is lunch enough for everybody, and the more people we are the pleasanter it will be." Donna Tullia made her suggestion with her usual frank manner, fixing her blue eyes upon Corona as she spoke. There was every appearance of cordiality in the invitation; but Donna Tullia knew well enough that there was a sting in her words, or at all events that she meant there should be. Corona, however, glanced quietly at her husband, and then courteously refused.

"You are most kind," she said, "but I fear we cannot

join you to-day. We are very regular people," she explained, with a slight smile, "and we are not prepared to go to-day. Many thanks; I wish we could accept your kind invitation."

"Well, I am sorry you will not come," said Donna Tullia, with a rather hard laugh. "We mean to enjoy ourselves immensely."

Giovanni said nothing. There was only one thing which could have rendered the prospect of Madame Mayer's picnic more disagreeable to him than it already was, and that would have been the presence of the Duchessa. He knew himself to be in a thoroughly false position in consequence of having yielded to Donna Tullia's half-tearful request that he would join the party. He remembered how he had spoken to Corona on the previous evening, assuring her that he would not marry Madame Mayer. Corona knew nothing of the change his plans had undergone during the stormy interview he had had with his father; he longed, indeed, to be able to make the Duchessa understand, but any attempt at explanation would be wholly impossible. Corona would think he was inconsistent, or at least that he was willing to flirt with the gay widow, while determined not to marry her. He reflected that it was part of his self-condemnation that he should appear unfavourably to the woman he loved, and whom he was determined to renounce; but he realised for the first time how bitter it would be to stand thus always in the appearance of weakness and self-contradiction in the eyes of the only human being whose good opinion he coveted, and for whose dear sake he was willing to do all things. As he stood by her, his hand rested upon the side of the carriage, and he stared blankly at the distant hounds and the retreating riders.

"Come, Don Giovanni, we must be going," said Donna Tullia. "What in the world are you thinking of? You look as though you had been turned into a statue!"

"I beg your pardon," returned Saracinesca, suddenly called back from the absorbing train of his unpleasant thoughts. "Good-bye, Duchessa; good-bye, Astrardente —a pleasant drive to you."

"You will always regret not having come, you know," cried Madame Mayer, shaking hands with both the occupants of the carriage. "We shall probably end by driving to Albano, and staying all night—just fancy! Immense fun—not even a comb in the whole party! Goodbye. I suppose we shall all meet to-night—that is, if we ever come back to Rome at all. Come along, Giovanni," she said, familiarly dropping the prefix from his name. After all, he was a sort of cousin, and people in Rome are very apt to call each other by their Christian names. But Donna Tullia knew what she was about; she knew that Corona d'Astrardente could never, under any circumstances whatever, call Saracinesca plain "Giovanni." But she had not the satisfaction of seeing that anything she said produced any change in Corona's proud dark face; she seemed of no more importance in the Duchessa's eyes than if she had been a fly buzzing in the sunshine.

So Giovanni and Madame Mayer joined their noisy party, and began to climb into their places upon the drag; but before they were prepared to start, the Astrardente carriage turned and drove rapidly out of the field. The laughter and loud talking came to Corona's ears, growing fainter and more distant every second, and the sound was very cruel to her; but she set her strong brave lips together, and leaned back, adjusting the blanket over her old husband's knees with one hand, and shading the sun from her eyes with the parasol she held in the other.

"Thank you, my dear; you are an angel of thoughtfulness," said the old dandy, stroking his wife's hand. "What a singularly vulgar woman Madame Mayer is! And yet she has a certain little *chic* of her own."

Corona did not withdraw her fingers from her husband's caress. She was used to it. After all, he was kind to her in his way. It would have been absurd to have been jealous of the grossly flattering speeches he made to other women; and indeed he was as fond of turning compliments to his wife as to any one. It was a singular relation that had grown up between the old man and the young girl he had married. Had he been less thoroughly a man of the world, or had Corona been less entirely honest and loyal and self-sacrificing, there would have been small peace in their wedlock. But Astrardente, decayed roué and worn-out dandy as he was, was in love with his wife; and she, in all the young magnificence of her beauty, submitted to be loved by him, because she had promised that she would do so, and because, having sworn, she regarded the breaking of her faith by the smallest act of unkindness as a thing beyond the bounds of possibility. It had been a terrible blow to her to discover that she cared for Don Giovanni even in the way she believed she did, as a man whose society she preferred to that of other men, and whose face it gave her pleasure to see. She, too, had spent a sleepless night; and when she had risen in the morning, she had determined to forget Giovanni, and if she could not forget him, she had sworn that more than ever she would be all things to her husband.

She wondered now, as Giovanni had known she would, why he had suddenly thrown over his day's hunting in order to spend his time with Donna Tullia; but she would not acknowledge, even to herself, that the dull pain she felt near her heart, and that seemed to oppress her breathing, bore any relation to the scene she had just witnessed. She shut her lips tightly, and arranged the blanket for her husband.

"Madame Mayer is vulgar," she answered. "I suppose she cannot help it."

"Women can always help being vulgar," returned Astrardente. "I believe she learned it from her husband. Women are not naturally like that. Nevertheless she is an excellent match for Giovanni Saracinesca. Rich, by millions. Undeniably handsome, gay—well, rather too gay; but Giovanni is so serious that the contrast will be to their mutual advantage."

Corona was silent. There was nothing the old man disliked so much as silence.

"Why do you not answer me?" he asked, rather petulantly.

"I do not know—I was thinking," said Corona, simply.

D

"I do not see that it is a great match after all, for the last of the Saracinesca."

"You think she will lead him a terrible dance, I daresay," returned the old man. "She is gay—very gay; and Giovanni is very, very solemn."

"I did not mean that she was too gay. I only think that Saracinesca might marry, for instance, the Rocca girl. Why should he take a widow?"

"Such a young widow. Old Mayer was as decrepit as any old statue in a museum. He was paralysed in one arm, and gouty—gouty, my dear; you do not know how gouty he was." The old fellow grinned scornfully; he had never had the gout. "Donna Tullia is a very young widow. Besides, think of the fortune. It would break old Saracinesca's heart to let so much money go out of the family. He is a miserly old wretch, Saracinesca!"

"I never heard that," said Corona.

"Oh, there are many things in Rome that one never hears, and that is one of them. I hate avarice—it is so extremely vulgar."

Indeed Astrardente was not himself avaricious, though he had all his life known how to protect his interests. He loved money, but he loved also to spend it, especially in such a way as to make a great show with it. It was not true, however, that Saracinesca was miserly. He spent a large income without the smallest ostentation.

"Really, I should hardly call Prince Saracinesca a miser," said Corona. "I cannot imagine, from what I know of him, why he should be so anxious to get Madame Mayer's fortune; but I do not think it is out of mere greediness."

"Then I do not know what you can call it," returned her husband, sharply. "They have always had that dismal black melancholy in that family—that detestable love of secretly piling up money, while their faces are as grave and sour as any Jew's in the Ghetto."

Corona glanced at her husband, and smiled faintly as she looked at his thin old features, where the lights and shadows were touched in with delicate colour more artfully than any actress's, superficially concealing the lines traced by years of affectation and refined egotism; and she thought of Giovanni's strong manly face, passionate indeed, but noble and bold. A moment later she resolutely put the comparison out of her mind, and finding that her husband was inclined to abuse the Saracinesca, she tried to turn the conversation.

"I suppose it will be a great ball at the Frangipani's," she said. "We will go, of course?" she added, interrogatively.

"Of course. I would not miss it for all the world. There has not been such a ball for years as that will be. Do I ever miss an opportunity of enjoying myself—I mean, of letting you enjoy yourself?"

"No, you are very good," said Corona, gently. "Indeed I sometimes think you give yourself trouble about going out on my account. Really, I am not so greedy of society. I would often gladly stay at home if you wished it."

"Do you think I am past enjoying the world, then?" asked the old man, sourly.

"No indeed," replied Corona, patiently. "Why should I think that? I see how much you like going out."

"Of course I like it. A rational man in the prime of life always likes to see his fellow-creatures. Why should not I?"

The Duchessa did not smile. She was used to hearing her aged husband speak of himself as young. It was a harmless fancy.

"I think it is quite natural," she said.

"What I cannot understand," said Astrardente, muffling his thin throat more closely against the keen bright *tramontana* wind, "is that such old fellows as Saracinesca should still want to play a part in the world."

Saracinesca was younger than Astrardente, and his iron constitution bade fair to outlast another generation, in spite of his white hair.

"You do not seem to be in a good humour with Saracinesca to-day," remarked Corona, by way of answer.

"Why do you defend him?" asked her husband, in a new fit of irritation. "He jars on my nerves, the sour old creature!"

"I fancy all Rome will go to the Frangipani ball," began Corona again, without heeding the old man's petulance.

"You seem to be interested in it," returned Astrardente.

Corona was silent; it was her only weapon when he became petulant. He hated silence, and generally returned to the conversation with more suavity. Perhaps, in his great experience, he really appreciated his wife's wonderful patience with his moods, and it is certain that he was exceedingly fond of her.

"You must have a new gown, my dear," he said presently, in a conciliatory tone.

His wife passed for the best-dressed woman in Rome, as she was undeniably the most remarkable in many other ways. She was not above taking an interest in dress, and her old husband had an admirable taste; moreover, he took a vast pride in her appearance, and if she had looked a whit less superior to other women, his smiling boast that she was above suspicion would have lost some of its force.

"I hardly think it is necessary," said Corona; "I have so many things, and it will be a great crowd."

"My dear, be economical of your beauty, but not in your adornment of it," said the old man, with one of his engaging grins. "I desire that you have a new gown for this ball which will be remembered by every one who goes to it. You must set about it at once."

"Well, that is an easy request for any woman to grant," answered Corona, with a little laugh; "though I do not believe my gown will be remembered so long as you think."

"Who knows—who knows?" said Astrardente, thoughtfully. "I remember gowns I saw "—he checked himself—"why, as many as ten years ago!" he added, laughing in his turn, perhaps at nearly having said forty for ten. "Gowns, my dear," he continued, "make a profound impression upon men's minds."

"For the matter of that," said the Duchessa, "I do not care to impress men at all, nor women either." She spoke lightly, pleased that the conversation should have taken a more pleasant turn.

"Not even to impress me, my dear?" asked old Astrardente, with a leer.

"That is different," answered Corona, quietly.

So they talked upon the subject of the gown and the ball until the carriage rolled under the archway of the Astrardente palace. But when it was three o'clock, and Corona was at liberty to go out upon her usual round of visits, she was glad that she could go alone; and as she sat among her cushions, driving from house to house and distributing cards, she had time to think seriously of her situation. It would seem a light thing to most wives of aged husbands to have taken a fancy to a man such as Giovanni Saracinesca. But the more Corona thought of it, the more certain it appeared to her that she was committing a great sin. It weighed heavily upon her mind, and took from her the innocent pleasure she was wont to feel in driving in the bright evening air in the Villa Borghese. It took the colour from the sky, and the softness from the cushions; it haunted her and made her miserably unhappy. At every turn she expected to see Giovanni's figure and face, and the constant recurrence of the thought seemed to add magnitude to the crime of which she accused herself,—the crime of even thinking of any man save her old husband—of wishing that Giovanni might not marry Donna Tullia after all.

"I will go to Padre Filippo," she said to herself as she reached home.

CHAPTER V.

Valdarno took Donna Tullia by his side upon the front seat of the drag; and as luck would have it, Giovanni and Del Ferice sat together behind them. Half-a-dozen other men found seats somewhere, and among them were the melancholy Spicca, who was a famous duellist, and a certain Casalverde, a man of rather doubtful reputation. The

others were members of what Donna Tullia called her
"corps de ballet." In those days Donna Tullia's conduct
was criticised, and she was thought to be emancipated, as
the phrase went. Old people opened their eyes at the
spectacle of the gay young widow going off into the Campagna to picnic with a party of men; but if any intimate
enemy had ventured to observe to her that she was giving
occasion for gossip, she would have raised her eyebrows,
explaining that they were all just like her brothers, and that
Giovanni was indeed a sort of cousin. She would perhaps
have condescended to say that she would not have done
such a thing in Paris, but that in dear old Rome one was
in the bosom of one's family, and might do anything. At
present she sat chatting with Valdarno, a tall and fair
young man, with a weak mouth and a good-natured disposition: she had secured Giovanni, and though he sat
sullenly smoking behind her, his presence gave her satisfaction. Del Ferice's smooth face wore an expression of
ineffable calm, and his watery blue eyes gazed languidly
on the broad stretch of brown grass which bordered the
highroad.

For some time the drag bowled along, and Giovanni was
left to his own reflections, which were not of a very pleasing kind. The other men talked of the chances of luck
with the hounds; and Spicca, who had been a great deal
in England, occasionally put in a remark not very com-
plimentary to the Roman hunt. Del Ferice listened in
silence, and Giovanni did not listen at all, but buttoned
his overcoat to the throat, half closed his eyes, and smoked
one cigarette after another, leaning back in his seat. Suddenly Donna Tullia's laugh was heard as she turned half
round to look at Valdarno.

"Do you really think so?" she cried. "How soon?
What a dance we will lead them then!"

Del Ferice pricked his ears in the direction of her voice,
like a terrier that suspects the presence of a rat. Valdarno's
answer was inaudible, but Donna Tullia ceased laughing
immediately.

"They are talking politics," said Del Ferice in a low

voice, leaning towards Giovanni as he spoke. The latter shrugged his shoulders and went on smoking. He did not care to be drawn into a conversation with Del Ferice.

Del Ferice was a man who was suspected of revolutionary sympathies by the authorities in Rome, but who was not feared. He was therefore allowed to live his life much as he pleased, though he was conscious from time to time that he was watched. Being a man, however, who under all circumstances pursued his own interests with more attention than he bestowed on those of any party, he did not pretend to attach any importance to the distinction of being occasionally followed by a spy, as a more foolish man might have done. If he was watched, he did not care to exhibit himself to his friends as a martyr, to tell stories of the *sbirro* who sometimes dogged his footsteps, nor to cry aloud that he was unjustly persecuted. He affected a character above suspicion, and rarely allowed himself to express an opinion. He was no propagator of new doctrines; that was too dangerous a trade for one of his temper. But he foresaw changes to come, and he determined that he would profit by them. He had little to lose, but he had everything to gain; and being a patient man, he resolved to gain all he could by circumspection—in other words, by acting according to his nature, rather than by risking himself in a bold course of action for which he was wholly unsuited. He was too wise to attempt wholly to deceive the authorities, knowing well that they were not easily deceived; and he accordingly steered a middle course, constantly speaking in favour of progress, of popular education, and of freedom of the press, but at the same time loudly proclaiming that all these things—that every benefit of civilisation, in fact —could be obtained without the slightest change in the form of government. He thus asserted his loyalty to the temporal power while affecting a belief in the possibility of useful reforms, and the position he thus acquired exactly suited his own ends; for he attracted to himself a certain amount of suspicion on account of his progressist professions, and then disarmed that suspicion by exhibiting a serene indifference to the espionage of which he was the object. The consequence was, that at the very time when he was most deeply implicated in much more serious matters—of which the object was invariably his own ultimate profit—at the time when he was receiving money for information he was able to obtain through his social position, he was regarded by the authorities, and by most of his acquaintances, as a harmless man, who might indeed injure himself by his foolish doctrines of progress, but who certainly could not injure any one else. Few guessed that his zealous attention to social duties, his occasional bursts of enthusiasm for liberal education and a free press, were but parts of his machinery for making money out of politics. He was so modest, so unostentatious, that no one suspected that the mainspring of his existence was the desire for money.

But, like many intelligent and bad men, Del Ferice had a weakness which was gradually gaining upon him and growing in force, and which was destined to hasten the course of the events which he had planned for himself. It is an extraordinary peculiarity in unbelievers that they are often more subject to petty superstitions than other men; and similarly, it often happens that the most cynical and coldly calculating of conspirators, who believe themselves proof against all outward influences, yield to some feeling of nervous dislike for an individual who has never harmed them, and are led on from dislike to hatred, until their soberest actions take colour from what in its earliest beginnings was nothing more than a senseless prejudice. Del Ferice's weakness was his unaccountable detestation of Giovanni Saracinesca; and he had so far suffered this abhorrence of the man to dominate his existence, that it had come to be one of his chiefest delights in life to thwart Giovanni wherever he could. How it had begun, or when, he no longer knew nor cared. He had perhaps thought Giovanni treated him superciliously, or even despised him; and his antagonism being roused by some fancied slight, he had shown a petty resentment, which, again, Saracinesca had treated with cold indifference. Little by little his fancied grievance had acquired great proportions in his own estimation, and he had learned to hate Giovanni more than any man living. At first it might have seemed an easy matter to ruin his adversary, or, at all event, to cause him great and serious injury; and but for that very indifference which Del Ferice so resented, his attempts might have been successful.

Giovanni belonged to a family who from the earliest times had been at swords-drawn with the Government. Their property had been more than once confiscated by the popes, had been seized again by force of arms, and had been ultimately left to them for the mere sake of peace. They seem to have quarrelled with everybody on every conceivable pretext, and to have generally got the best of the struggle. No pope had ever reckoned upon the friendship of Casa Saracinesca. For generations they had headed the opposition whenever there was one, and had plotted to form one when there was none ready to their hands. It seemed to Del Ferice that in the stirring times that followed the annexation of Naples to the Italian crown, when all Europe was watching the growth of the new Power, it should be an easy matter to draw a Saracinesca into any scheme for the subversion of a Government against which so many generations of Saracinesca had plotted and fought. To involve Giovanni in some Liberal conspiracy, and then by betraying him to cause him to be imprisoned or exiled from Rome, was a plan which pleased Del Ferice, and which he desired earnestly to put into execution. He had often tried to lead his enemy into conversation, repressing and hiding his dislike for the sake of his end; but at the first mention of political subjects Giovanni became impenetrable, shrugged his shoulders, and assumed an air of the utmost indifference. No paradox could draw him into argument, no flattery could loose his tongue. Indeed those were times when men hesitated to express an opinion, not only because any opinion they might express was liable to be exaggerated and distorted by willing enemies—a consideration which would not have greatly intimidated Giovanni Saracinesca—but also because it was impossible for the wisest man to form any satisfactory judgment upon the course of events

It was clear to every one that ever since 1848 the temporal
power had been sustained by France; and though no one
in 1865 foresaw the downfall of the Second Empire, no
one saw any reason for supposing that the military protec-
torate of Louis Napoleon in Rome could last for ever:
what would be likely to occur if that protection were
withdrawn was indeed a matter of doubt, but was not
looked upon by the Government as a legitimate matter for
speculation.

Del Ferice, however, did not desist from his attempts to
make Giovanni speak out his mind, and whenever an opportunity offered, tried to draw him into conversation. He
was destined on the present occasion to meet with greater
success than had hitherto attended his efforts. The picnic
was noisy, and Giovanni was in a bad humour; he did not
care for Donna Tullia's glances, nor for the remarks she constantly levelled at him; still less was he amused by the
shallow gaiety of her party of admirers, tempered as their
talk was by the occasional tonic of some outrageous cynicism from the melancholy Spicca. Del Ferice smiled, and
talked, and smiled again, seeking to flatter and please Donna
Tullia, as was his wont. By-and-by the clear north wind
and the bright sun dried the ground, and Madame Mayer
proposed that the party should walk a little on the road
towards Rome—a proposal of such startling originality that
it was carried by acclamation. Donna Tullia wanted to
walk with Giovanni; but on pretence of having left something upon the drag, he gave Valdarno time to take his
place. When Giovanni began to follow the rest, he found
that Del Ferice had lagged behind, and seemed to be waiting
for him.

Giovanni was in a bad humour that day. He had suffered
himself to be persuaded into joining in a species of amusement for which he cared nothing, by a mere word from a
woman for whom he cared less, but whom he had half determined to marry, and who had wholly determined to marry
him. He, who hated vacillation, had been dangling for
four-and-twenty hours like a pendulum, or, as he said to
himself, like an ass between two bundles of hay. At one

moment he meant to marry Donna Tullia, and at another
he loathed the thought; now he felt that he would make
any sacrifice to rid the Duchessa d'Astrardente of himself,
and now again he felt how futile such a sacrifice would be.
He was ashamed in his heart, for he was no boy of twenty
to be swayed by a woman's look or a fit of Quixotism; he
was a strong grown man who had seen the world. He had
been in the habit of supposing his impulses to be good,
and of following them naturally without much thought; it
seemed desperately perplexing to be forced into an analysis
of those impulses in order to decide what he should do.
He was in a thoroughly bad humour, and Del Ferice guessed
that if Giovanni could ever be induced to speak out, it
must be when his temper was not under control. In Rome,
in the club—there was only one club in those days—in
society, Ugo never got a chance to talk to his enemy; but
here upon the Appian Way, with the broad Campagna
stretching away to right and left and rear, while the remainder of the party walked three hundred yards in front,
and Giovanni showed an evident reluctance to join them,
it would go hard indeed if he could not be led into
conversation.

"I should think," Del Ferice began, "that if you had
your choice, you would walk anywhere rather than here."

"Why?" asked Giovanni, carelessly. "It is a very good
road."

"I should think that our Roman Campagna would be
anything but a source of satisfaction to its possessors—like
yourself," answered Del Ferice.

"It is a very good grazing ground."

"It might be something better. When one thinks that
in ancient times it was a vast series of villas——"

"The conditions were very different. We do not live in
ancient times," returned Giovanni, drily.

"Ah, the conditions!" ejaculated Del Ferice, with a
suave sigh. "Surely the conditions depend on man—not
on nature. What our proud forefathers accomplished by
law and energy, we could, we can accomplish, if we restore
law and energy in our midst."

"You are entirely mistaken," answered Saracinesca. "It would take five times the energy of the ancient Romans to turn the Campagna into a garden, or even into a fertile productive region. No one is five times as energetic as the ancients. As for the laws, they do well enough."

Del Ferice was delighted. For the first time, Giovanni seemed inclined to enter upon an argument with him.

"Why are the conditions so different? I do not see. Here is the same undulating country, the same climate——"

"And twice as much water," interrupted Giovanni. "You forget that the Campagna is very low, and that the rivers in it have risen very much. There are parts of ancient Rome now laid bare which lie below the present water-mark of the Tiber. If the city were built upon its old level, much of it would be constantly flooded. The rivers have risen and have swamped the country. Do you think any amount of law or energy could drain this fever-stricken plain into the sea? I do not. Do you think that if I could be persuaded that the land could be improved into fertility I would hesitate, at any expenditure in my power, to reclaim the miles of desert my father and I own here? The plain is a series of swamps and stone quarries. In one place you find the rock a foot below the surface, and the soil burns up in summer; a hundred yards farther you find a bog hundreds of feet deep, which even in summer is never dry."

"But," suggested Del Ferice, who listened patiently enough, "supposing the Government passed a law forcing all of you proprietors to plant trees and dig ditches, it would have some effect."

"The law cannot force us to sacrifice men's lives. The Trappist monks at the Tre Fontane are trying it, and dying by scores. Do you think I, or any other Roman, would send ᵖeasants to such a place, or could induce them to go?"

"Well, it is one of a great many questions which will be ‑‑some day," said Del Ferice. "You will not deny ‑ is room for much improvement in our country, ‑‑infusion of some progressist ideas would be whi‑

"Perhaps so; but you understand one thing by progress, and I understand quite another," replied Giovanni, eyeing in the bright distance the figures of Donna Tullia and her friends, and regulating his pace so as not to lessen the distance which separated them from him. He preferred talking political economy with a man he disliked, to being obliged to make conversation for Madame Mayer.

"I mean by progress, positive improvement without revolutionary change," explained Del Ferice, using the phrase he had long since constructed as his profession of faith to the world. Giovanni eyed him keenly for a moment. He cared nothing for Ugo or his ideas, but he suspected him of very different principles.

"You will pardon me," he said, civilly, "if I venture to doubt whether you have frankly expressed your views. I am under the impression that you really connect the idea of improvement with a very positive revolutionary change."

Del Ferice did not wince, but he involuntarily cast a glance behind him. Those were times when people were cautious of being overheard. But Del Ferice knew his man, and he knew that the only way in which he could continue the interview was to accept the imputation as though trusting implicitly to the discretion of his companion.

"Will you give me a fair answer to a fair question?" he asked, very gravely.

"Let me hear the question," returned Giovanni, indifferently. He also knew his man, and attached no more belief to anything he said than to the chattering of a parrot. And yet Del Ferice had not the reputation of a liar in the world at large.

"Certainly," answered Ugo. "You are the heir of a family which from immemorial time has opposed the popes. You cannot be supposed to feel any kind of loyal attachment to the temporal power. I do not know whether you individually would support it or not. But frankly, how would you regard such a revolutionary change as you suspect me of desiring?"

"I have no objection to telling you that. I would simply make the best of it."

Del Ferice laughed at the ambiguous answer, affecting to consider it as a mere evasion.

"We should all try to do that," he answered; "but what I mean to ask is, whether you would personally take up arms to fight for the temporal power, or whether you would allow events to take their course? I fancy that would be the ultimate test of loyalty."

"My instinct would certainly be to fight, whether fighting were of any use or not. But the propriety of fighting in such a case is a very nice question of judgment. So long as there is anything to fight for, no matter how hopeless the odds, a gentleman should go to the front—but no longer. The question must be to decide the precise point at which the position becomes untenable. So long as France makes our quarrels hers, every man should give his personal assistance to the cause; but it is absurd to suppose that if we were left alone, a handful of Romans against a great Power, we could do more, or should do more, than make a formal show of resistance. It has been a rule in all ages that a general, however brave, who sacrifices the lives of his soldiers in a perfectly hopeless resistance, rather than accept the terms of an honourable capitulation, is guilty of a military crime."

"In other words," answered Del Ferice, quietly, "if the French troops were withdrawn, and the Italians were besieging Rome, you would at once capitulate?"

"Certainly—after making a formal protest. It would be criminal to sacrifice our fellow-citizens' lives in such a case."

"And then?"

"Then, as I said before, I would make the best of it—not omitting to congratulate Del Ferice upon obtaining a post in the new Government," added Giovanni, with a laugh.

But Del Ferice took no notice of the jest.

"Do you not think that, aside from any question of sympathy or loyalty to the holy Father, the change of government would be an immense advantage to Rome?"

"No, I do not. To Italy the advantage would be inestimable; to Rome it would be an injury. Italy would consolidate the prestige she began to acquire when Cavour succeeded in sending a handful of troops to the Crimea eleven years ago; she would at once take a high position as a European Power—provided always that the smouldering republican element should not break out in opposition to the constitutional monarchy. But Rome would be ruined. She is no longer the geographical capital of Italy—she is not even the largest city; but in the course of a few years, violent efforts would be made to give her a fictitious modern grandeur, in the place of the moral importance she now enjoys as the headquarters of the Catholic world. Those efforts at a spurious growth would ruin her financially, and the hatred of Romans for Italians of the north would cause endless internal dissension. We should be subjected to a system of taxation which would fall more heavily on us than on other Italians, in proportion as our land is less productive. On the whole, we should grow rapidly poorer; for prices would rise, and we should have a paper currency instead of a metallic one. Especially we landed proprietors would suffer terribly by the Italian land system being suddenly thrust upon us. To be obliged to sell one's acres to any peasant who can scrape together enough to capitalise the pittance he now pays as rent, at five per cent, would scarcely be agreeable. Such a fellow, from whom I have the greatest difficulty in extracting his yearly bushel of grain, could borrow twenty bushels from a neighbour, or the value of them, and buy me out without my consent—acquiring land worth ten times the rent he and his father have paid for it, and his fathers before him. It would produce an extraordinary state of things, I can assure you. No—even putting aside what you call my sympathies and my loyalty to the Pope—I do not desire any change. Nobody who owns much property does; the revolutionary spirits are people who own nothing."

"On the other hand, those who own nothing, or next to nothing, are the great majority."

"Even if that is true, which I doubt, I do not see why

the intelligent few should be ruled by that same ignorant majority."

"But you forget that the majority is to be educated," objected Del Ferice.

"Education is a term few people can define," returned Giovanni. "Any good schoolmaster knows vastly more than you or I. Would you like to be governed by a majority of schoolmasters?"

"That is a plausible argument," laughed Del Ferice, "but it is not sound."

"It is not sound!" repeated Giovanni, impatiently. "People are so fond of exclaiming that what they do not like is not sound! Do you think that it would not be a fair case to put five hundred schoolmasters against five hundred gentlemen of average education? I think it would be very fair. The schoolmasters would certainly have the advantage in education: do you mean to say they would make better or wiser electors than the same number of gentlemen who cannot name all the cities and rivers in Italy, nor translate a page of Latin without a mistake, but who understand the conditions of property by practical experience as no schoolmaster can possibly understand them? I tell you it is nonsense. Education, of the kind which is of any practical value in the government of a nation, means the teaching of human motives, of humanising ideas, of some system whereby the majority of electors can distinguish the qualities of honesty and common-sense in the candidate they wish to elect. I do not pretend to say what that system may be, but I assert that no education which does not lead to that kind of knowledge is of any practical use to the voting majority of a constitutionally governed country."

Del Ferice sighed rather sadly.

"I am afraid you will not discover that system in Europe," he said. He was disappointed in Giovanni, and in his hopes of detecting in him some signs of a revolutionary spirit. Saracinesca was a gentleman of the old school, who evidently despised majorities and modern political science as a whole, who for the sake of his own interests desired no change

from the Government under which he lived, and who would
surely be the first to draw the sword for the temporal power,
and the last to sheathe it. His calm judgment concerning
the fallacy of holding a hopeless position would vanish like
smoke if his fiery blood were once roused. He was so
honest a man that even Del Ferice could not suspect him
of parading views he did not hold; and Ugo then and there
abandoned all idea of bringing him into political trouble
and disgrace, though he by no means gave up all hope of
being able to ruin him in some other way.

"I agree with you there at least," said Saracinesca. "The
only improvements worth having are certainly not to be
found in Europe. Donna Tullia is calling us. We had
better join that harmless flock of lambs, and give over
speculating on the advantages of allying ourselves with a
pack of wolves who will eat us up, house and home, bag
and baggage."

So the whole party climbed again to their seats upon
the drag, and Valdarno drove them back into Rome by
the Porta San Giovanni.

CHAPTER VI.

Corona d'Astrardente had been educated in a convent—
that is to say, she had been brought up in the strict practice of her religion; and during the five years which had
elapsed since she had come out into the world, she had
found no cause for forsaking the habits she had acquired
in her girlhood. Some people find religion a burden;
others regard it as an indifferently useless institution, in
which they desire no share, and concerning which they
never trouble themselves; others, again, look upon it as the
mainstay of their lives.

It is natural to suppose that the mode of thought and
the habits acquired by young girls in a religious institution
will not disappear without a trace when they first go into

E

the world, and it may even be expected that some memory of the early disposition thus cultivated will cling to them throughout their lives. But the multifarious interests of social existence do much to shake that young edifice of faith. The driving strength of stormy passions of all kinds undermines the walls of the fabric, and when at last the bolt of adversity strikes full upon the keystone of the arch, upon the self of man or woman, weakened and loosened by the tempests of years, the whole palace of the soul falls in, a hopeless wreck, wherein not even the memory of outline can be traced, nor the faint shadow of a beauty which is destroyed for ever.

But there are some whose interests in this world are not strong enough to shake their faith in the next; whose passions do not get the mastery, and whose self is sheltered from danger by something more than the feeble defence of an accomplished egotism. Corona was one of these, for her lot had not been happy, nor her path strewn with roses.

She was a friendless woman, destined to suffer much, and her suffering was the more intense that she seemed always upon the point of finding friends in the world where she played so conspicuous a part. There can be little happiness when a whole life has been placed upon a false foundation, even though so dire a mistake may have been committed willingly and from a sense of duty and obligation, such as drove Corona to marry old Astrardente. Consolation is not satisfaction; and though, when she reflected on what she had done, she knew that from her point of view she had done her best, she knew also that she had closed upon herself the gates of the earthly paradise, and that for her the prospect of happiness had been removed from the now to the hereafter—the dim and shadowy glass in which we love to see any reflection save that of our present lives. And to her, thus living in submission to the consequences of her choice, that faith in things better which had inspired her to sacrifice was the chief remaining source of consolation. There was a good man to whom she went for advice, as she had gone to him ever since she could remember. When she found herself in trouble she never hesitated. Padre Filippo was to her the living proof of the possibility of human goodness, as faith is to us all the evidence of things not seen.

Corona was in trouble now—in a trouble so new that she hardly understood it, so terrible and yet so vague that she felt her peril imminent. She did not hesitate, therefore, nor change her mind upon the morning following the day of the meet, but drove to the church of the Capuchins in the Piazza Barberini, and went up the broad steps with a beating heart, not knowing how she should tell what she meant to tell, yet knowing that there was for her no hope of peace unless she told it quickly, and got that advice and direction she so earnestly craved.

Padre Filippo had been a man of the world in his time —a man of great cultivation, full of refined tastes and understanding of tastes in others, gentle and courteous in his manners, and very kind of heart. No one knew whence he came. He spoke Italian correctly and with a keen scholarly use of words, but his slight accent betrayed his foreign birth. He had been a Capuchin monk for many years, perhaps for more than half his lifetime, and Corona could remember him from her childhood, for he had been a friend of her father's; but he had not been consulted about her marriage,—she even remembered that, though she had earnestly desired to see him before the wedding-day, her father had told her that he had left Rome for a time. For the old gentleman was in terrible earnest about the match, so that in his heart he feared lest Corona might waver and ask Padre Filippo's advice; and he knew the good monk too well to think that he would give his countenance to such a sacrifice as was contemplated in marrying the young girl to old Astrardente. Corona had known this later, but had hardly realised the selfishness of her father, nor indeed had desired to realise it. It was sufficient that he had died satisfied in seeing her married to a great noble, and that she had been able, in his last days, to relieve him from the distress of debt and embarrassment which had doubtless contributed to shorten his life.

The proud woman who had thus once humbled herself

for an object she thought good, had never referred to her
action again. She had never spoken of her position to
Padre Filippo, so that the monk wondered and admired
her steadfastness. If she suffered, it was in silence, without comment and without complaint, and so she would
have suffered to the end. But it had been ordered otherwise. For months she had known that the interest she felt
in Giovanni Saracinesca was increasing: she had choked it
down, had done all in her power to prove herself indifferent to him; but at last the crisis had come. When he
spoke to her of his marriage, she had felt—she knew now
that it was so—that she loved him. The very word, as
she repeated it to herself, rang like an awful, almost incomprehensible, accusation of evil in her ears. One moment
she stood at the top of the steps outside the church, looking down at the bare straggling trees below, and upward to
the grey sky, against which the lofty eaves of the Palazzo
Barberini stood out sharply defined. The weather had
changed again, and a soft southerly wind was blowing
the spray of the fountain half across the piazza. Corona
paused, her graceful figure half leaning against the stone
doorpost of the church, her hand upon the heavy leathern
curtain in the act to lift it; and as she stood there, a desperate temptation assailed her. It seemed desperate to her
—to many another woman it would have appeared only the
natural course to pursue—to turn her back upon the church,
to put off the hard moment of confession, to go down again
into the city, and to say to herself that there was no harm
in seeing Don Giovanni, provided she never let him speak
of love. Why should he speak of it? Had she any reason
to suppose there was danger to her in anything he meant
to say? Had he ever, by word or deed, betrayed that interest in her which she knew in herself was love for him?
Had he ever?—ah yes! It was only the night before last
that he had asked her advice, had besought her to advise
him not to marry another, had suffered his arm to tremble
when she laid her hand upon it. In the quick remembrance
that he too had shown some feeling, there was a sudden
burst of joy such as Corona had never felt, and a moment

later she knew it and was afraid. It was true, then. At the very time when she was most oppressed with the sense of her fault in loving him, there was an inward rejoicing in her heart at the bare thought that she loved him. Could a woman fall lower, she asked herself—lower than to delight in what she knew to be most bad? And yet it was such a poor little thrill of pleasure after all; but it was the first she had ever known. To turn away and reflect for a few days would be so easy! It would be so sweet to think of it, even though the excuse for thinking of Giovanni should be a good determination to root him from her life. It would be so sweet to drive again alone among the trees that very afternoon, and to weigh the salvation of her soul in the balance of her heart: her heart would know how to turn the scales, surely enough. Corona stood still, holding the curtain in her hand. She was a brave woman, but she turned pale—not hesitating, she said to herself, but pausing. Then, suddenly, a great scorn of herself arose in her. Was it worthy of her even to pause in doing right? The nobility of her courage cried loudly to her to go in and do the thing most worthy: her hand lifted the heavy leathern apron, and she entered the church.

The air within was heavy and moist, and the grey light fell coldly through the tall windows. Corona shuddered, and drew her furs more closely about her as she passed up the aisle to the door of the sacristy. She found the monk she sought, and she made her confession.

"Padre mio," she said at last, when the good man thought she had finished—"Padre mio, I am a very miserable woman." She hid her dark face in her ungloved hands, and one by one the crystal tears welled from her eyes and trickled down upon her small fingers and upon the worn black wood of the confessional.

"My daughter," said the good monk, " I will pray for you, others will pray for you—but before all things, you must pray for yourself. And let me advise you, my child, that as we are all led into temptation, we must not think that because we have been in temptation we have sinned hopelessly; nor, if we have fought against the thing that tempts us, should we at once imagine that we have overcome it, and have done altogether right. If there were no evil in ourselves, there could be no temptation from without, for nothing evil could seem pleasant. But with you I cannot find that you have done any great wrong as yet. You must take courage. We are all in the world, and do what we may, we cannot disregard it. The sin you see is real, but it is yet not very near you since you so abhor it; and if you pray that you may hate it, it will go further from you till you may hope not even to understand how it could once have been so near. Take courage—take comfort. Do not be morbid. Resist temptation, but do not analyse it nor yourself too closely; for it is one of the chief signs of evil in us that when we dwell too much upon ourselves and upon our temptations, we ourselves seem good in our own eyes, and our temptations not unpleasant, because the very resisting of them seems to make us appear better than we are."

But the tears still flowed from Corona's eyes in the dark corner of the church, and she could not be comforted.

"Padre mio," she repeated, "I am very unhappy. I have not a friend in the world to whom I can speak. I have never seen my life before as I see it now. God forgive me, I have never loved my husband. I never knew what it meant to love. I was a mere child, a very innocent child, when I was married to him. I would have sought your advice, but they told me you were away, and I thought I was doing right in obeying my father."

Padre Filippo sighed. He had long known and understood why Corona had not been allowed to come to him at the most important moment of her life.

"My husband is very kind to me," she continued in broken tones. "He loves me in his way, but I do not love him. That of itself is a great sin. It seems to me as though I saw but one half of life, and saw it from the window of a prison; and yet I am not imprisoned. I would that I were, for I should never have seen another man. I should never have heard his voice, nor seen his face, nor—nor loved him, as I do love him," she sobbed.

"Hush, my daughter," said the old monk, very gently.

"You told me you had never spoken of love; that you were interested in him, indeed, but that you did not know——"

"I know—I know now," cried Corona, losing all control as the passionate tears flowed down. "I could not say it —it seemed so dreadful—I love him with my whole self! I can never get it out—it burns me. O God, I am so wretched!"

Padre Filippo was silent for a while. It was a terrible case. He could not remember in all his experience to have known one more sad to contemplate, though his business was with the sins and the sorrows of the world. The beautiful woman kneeling outside his confessional was innocent—as innocent as a child, brave and faithful. She had sacrificed her whole life for her father, who had been little worthy of such devotion; she had borne for years the suffering of being tied to an old man whom she could not help despising, however honestly she tried to conceal the fact from herself, however effectually she hid it from others. It was a wonder the disaster had not occurred before: it showed how loyal and true a woman she was, that, living in the very centre and midst of the world, admired and assailed by many, she should never in five years have so much as thought of any man beside her husband. A woman made for love and happiness, in the glory of beauty and youth, capable of such unfaltering determination in her loyalty, so good, so noble, so generous,—it seemed unspeakably pathetic to hear her weeping her heart out, and confessing that, after so many struggles and efforts and sacrifices, she had at last met the common fate of all humanity, and was become subject to love. What might have been her happiness was turned to dishonour; what should have been the pride of her young life was made a reproach.

She would not fall. The grey-haired monk believed that, in his great knowledge of mankind. But she would suffer terribly, and it might be that others would suffer also. It was the consequence of an irretrievable error in the beginning, when it had seemed to the young girl just leaving the convent that the best protection against the

world of evil into which she was to go would be the un-
conditional sacrifice of herself.

Padre Filippo was silent.   He hoped that the passionate
outburst of grief and self-reproach would pass, though he
himself could find little enough to say.   It was all too
natural.   What was he, he thought, that he should explain
away nature, and bid a friendless woman defy a power that
has more than once overset the reckoning of the world?
He could bid her pray for help and strength, but he found
it hard to argue the case with her; for he had to allow that
his beautiful penitent was, after all, only experiencing
what it might have been foretold that she must feel, and
that, as far as he could see, she was struggling bravely against
the dangers of her situation.

Corona cried bitterly as she knelt there.   It was a great
relief to give way for a time to the whole violence of what
she felt.   It may be that in her tears there was a subtle
instinctive knowledge that she was weeping for her love as
well as for her sin in loving, but her grief was none the less
real.   She did not understand herself.   She did not know,
as Padre Filippo knew, that her woman's heart was breaking
for sympathy rather than for religious counsel.   She knew
many women, but her noble pride would not have let her
even contemplate the possibility of confiding in any one
of them, even if she could have done so in the certainty
of not being herself betrayed and of not betraying the
man she loved.   She had been accustomed to come to her
confessor for counsel, and she now came to him with her
troubles and craved sympathy for them, in the knowledge
that Padre Filippo could never know the name of the man
who had disturbed her peace.

But the monk understood well enough, and his kind heart
comprehended hers and felt for her.

"My daughter," he said at last, when she seemed to have
grown more calm, "it would be an inestimable advantage
if this man could go away for a time, but that is probably
not to be expected.   Meanwhile, you must not listen to him
if he speaks——"

"It is not that," interrupted Corona—"it is not that.

He never speaks of love. Oh, I really believe he does not love me at all!" But in her heart she felt that he must love her; and her hand, as it lay upon the hard wood of the confessional, seemed still to feel his trembling arm.

"That is so much the better, my child," said the monk, quietly. "For if he does not love you, your temptations will not grow stronger."

"And yet, perhaps—he may——" murmured Corona, feeling that it would be wrong even to conceal her faintest suspicions at such a time.

"Let there be no perhaps," answered Padre Filippo, almost sternly. "Let it never enter your mind that he might love you. Think that even from the worldly point there is small dignity in a woman who exhibits love for a man who has never mentioned love to her. You have no reason to suppose you are loved save that you desire to be. Let there be no perhaps."

The monk's keen insight into character had given him an unexpected weapon in Corona's defence. He knew how of all things a proud woman hates to know that where she has placed her heart there is no response, and that if she fails to awaken an affection akin to her own, what has been love may be turned to loathing, or at least to indifference. The strong character of the Duchessa d'Astrardente responded to his touch as he expected. Her tears ceased to flow, and her scorn rose haughtily against herself.

"It is true. I am despicable," she said, suddenly. "You have shown me myself. There shall be no perhaps. I loathe myself for thinking of it. Pray for me, lest I fall so low again."

A few minutes later Corona left the confessional and went and kneeled in the body of the church to collect her thoughts. She was in a very different frame of mind from that in which she had left home an hour ago. She hardly knew whether she felt herself a better woman, but she was sure that she was stronger. There was no desire left in her to meditate sadly upon her sorrow—to go over and over in her thoughts the feelings she experienced, the fears she felt, the half-formulated hope that Giovanni might love her after all. There was left only a haughty determination to have done with her folly quickly and surely, and to try and forget it for ever. The confessor's words had produced their effect. Henceforth she would never stoop so low again. She was ready to go out into the world now, and she felt no fear. It was more from habit than for the sake of saying a prayer that she knelt in the church after her confession, for she felt very strong. She rose to her feet presently, and moved towards the door: she had not gone half the length of the church when she came face to face with Donna Tullia Mayer.

It was a strange coincidence. The ladies of Rome frequently go to the church of the Capuchins, as Corona had done, to seek the aid and counsel of Padre Filippo, but Corona had never met Donna Tullia there. Madame Mayer did not profess to be very devout. As a matter of fact, she had not found it convenient to go to confession during the Christmas season, and she had been intending to make up for the deficiency for some time past; but it is improbable that she would have decided upon fulfilling her religious obligations before Lent if she had not chanced to see the Duchessa d'Astrardente's carriage standing at the foot of the church steps.

Donna Tullia had risen early because she was going to sit for her portrait to a young artist who lived in the neighbourhood of the Piazza Barberini, and as she passed in her brougham she caught sight of the Duchessa's liveries. The artist could wait half an hour; the opportunity was admirable. She was alone, and would not only do her duty in going to confession, but would have a chance of seeing how Corona looked when she had been at her devotions. It might also be possible to judge from Padre Filippo's manner whether the interview had been an interesting one. The Astrardente was so very devout that she probably had difficulty in inventing sins to confess. One might perhaps tell from her face whether she had felt any emotion. At all events the opportunity should not be lost. Besides, if Donna Tullia found that she herself was really not in a proper frame of mind for religious exercises, she could easily spend a few moments in the church and then proceed upon her way. She stopped her carriage and went in. She had just entered when she was aware of the tall figure of Corona d'Astrardente coming towards her, magnificent in the simplicity of her furs, a short veil just covering half her face, and an unwonted colour in her dark cheeks.

Corona was surprised at meeting Madame Mayer, but she did not show it. She nodded with a sufficiently pleasant smile, and would have passed on. This would not have suited Donna Tullia's intentions, however, for she meant to have a good look at her friend. It was not for nothing that she had made up her mind to go to confession at a moment's notice. She therefore stopped the Duchessa, and insisted upon shaking hands.

"What an extraordinary coincidence!" she exclaimed. "You must have been to see Padre Filippo too?"

"Yes," answered Corona. "You will find him in the sacristy." She noticed that Madame Mayer regarded her with great interest. Indeed she could hardly be aware how unlike her usual self she appeared. There were dark rings beneath her eyes, and her eyes themselves seemed to emit a strange light; while an unwonted colour illuminated her olive cheeks, and her voice had a curiously excited tone. Madame Mayer stared at her so hard that she noticed it.

"Why do you look at me like that?" asked the Duchessa, with a smile.

"I was wondering what in the world you could find to confess," replied Donna Tullia, sweetly. "You are so immensely good, you see; everybody wonders at you."

Corona's eyes flashed darkly. She suspected that Madame Mayer noticed something unusual in her appearance, and had made the awkward speech to conceal her curiosity. She was annoyed at the meeting, still more at being detained in conversation within the church.

"It is very kind of you to invest me with such virtues," she answered. "I assure you I am not half so good as you suppose. Good-bye—I must be going home."

"Stay!" exclaimed Donna Tullia; "I can go to confession another time. Will not you come with me to Gouache's studio? I am going to sit. It is such a bore to go alone."

"Thank you very much," said Corona, civilly. "I am afraid I cannot go. My husband expects me at home. I wish you a good sitting."

"Well, good-bye. Oh, I forgot to tell you, we had such a charming picnic yesterday. It was so fortunate—the only fine day this week. Giovanni was very amusing: he was completely *en train*, and kept us laughing the whole day. Good-bye; I do so wish you had come."

"I was very sorry," answered Corona, quietly, "but it was impossible. I am glad you all enjoyed it so much. Good-bye."

So they parted.

"How she wishes that same husband of hers would follow the example of my excellent old Mayer, of blessed memory, and take himself out of the world to-day or to-morrow!" thought Donna Tullia, as she walked up the church.

She was sure something unusual had occurred, and she longed to fathom the mystery. But she was not altogether a bad woman, and when she had collected her thoughts she made up her mind that even by the utmost stretch of moral indulgence, she could not consider herself in a proper state to undertake so serious a matter as confession. She therefore waited a few minutes, to give time for Corona to drive away, and then turned back. She cautiously pushed aside the curtain and looked out. The Astrardente carriage was just disappearing in the distance. Donna Tullia descended the steps, got into her brougham, and proceeded to the studio of Monsieur Anastase Gouache, the portrait-painter. She had not accomplished much, save to rouse her curiosity, and that parting thrust concerning Don Giovanni had been rather ill-timed.

She drove to the door of the studio and found Del Ferice waiting for her as usual. If Corona had accompanied her, she would have expressed astonishment at finding him; but, as a matter of fact, Ugo always met her there, and helped to pass the time while she was sitting. He was very amusing, and not altogether unsympathetic to her; and moreover, he professed for her the most profound devotion—genuine, perhaps, and certainly skilfully expressed. If any one had paid much attention to Del Ferice's doings, it would have been said that he was paying court to the rich young widow. But he was never looked upon by society from the point of view of matrimonial possibility, and no one thought of attaching any importance to his doings. Nevertheless Ugo, who had been gradually rising in the social scale for many years, saw no reason why he should not win the hand of Donna Tullia as well as any one else, if only Giovanni Saracinesca could be kept out of the way; and he devoted himself with becoming assiduity to the service of the widow, while doing his utmost to promote Giovanni's attachment for the Astrardente, which he had been the first to discover. Donna Tullia would probably have laughed to scorn the idea that Del Ferice could think of himself seriously as a suitor, but of all her admirers she found him the most constant and the most convenient.

"What are the news this morning?" she asked, as he opened her carriage-door for her before the studio.

"None, save that I am your faithful slave as ever," he answered.

"I have just seen the Astrardente," said Donna Tullia, still sitting in her seat. "I will let you guess where it was that we met."

"You met in the church of the Capuchins," replied Del Ferice promptly, with a smile of satisfaction.

"You are a sorcerer: how did you know? Did you guess it?"

"If you will look down this street from where I stand, you will perceive that I could distinctly see any carriage which turned out of the Piazza Barberini towards the Capuchins," replied Ugo. "She was there nearly an hour, and you only stayed five minutes."

"How dreadful it is to be watched like this!" exclaimed Donna Tullia, with a little laugh, half expressive of satisfaction and half of amusement at Del Ferice's devotion.

"How can I help watching you, as the earth watches the sun in its daily course?" said Ugo, with a sentimental intonation of his soft persuasive voice. Donna Tullia looked at his smooth face, and laughed again, half kindly.

"The Astrardente had been confessing her sins," she remarked.

"Again? She is always confessing."

"What do you suppose she finds to say?" asked Donna Tullia.

"That her husband is hideous, and that you are beautiful," answered Del Ferice, readily enough.

"Why?"

"Because she hates her husband and hates you."

"Why, again?"

"Because you took Giovanni Saracinesca to your picnic yesterday; because you are always taking him away from her. For the matter of that, I hate him as much as the Astrardente hates you," added Del Ferice, with an agreeable smile. Donna Tullia did not despise flattery, but Ugo made her thoughtful.

"Do you think she really cares——?" she asked.

"As surely as that he does not," replied Del Ferice.

"It would be strange," said Donna Tullia, meditatively. "I would like to know if it is true."

"You have only to watch them."

"Surely Giovanni cares more than she does," objected Madame Mayer. "Everybody says he loves her; nobody says she loves him."

"All the more reason. Popular report is always mistaken—except in regard to you."

"To me?"

"Since it ascribes to you so much that is good, it cannot be wrong," replied Del Ferice.

Donna Tullia laughed, and took his hand to descend from her carriage.

CHAPTER VII.

Monsieur Gouache's studio was on the second floor. The narrow flight of steps ended abruptly against a green door, perforated by a slit for the insertion of letters, by a shabby green cord which, being pulled, rang a feeble bell, and adorned by a visiting-card, whereon with many super-fluous flourishes and ornaments of caligraphy was inscribed the name of the artist—ANASTASE GOUACHE.

The door being opened by a string, Donna Tullia and Del Ferice entered, and mounting half-a-dozen more steps, found themselves in the studio, a spacious room with a window high above the floor, half shaded by a curtain of grey cotton. In one corner an iron stove gave out loud crackling sounds, pleasant to hear on the damp winter's morning, and the flame shone red through chinks of the rusty door. A dark-green carpet in passably good condi-tion covered the floor; three or four broad divans, spread with oriental rugs, and two very much dilapidated carved chairs with leathern seats, constituted the furniture; the walls were hung with sketches of heads and figures; half-finished portraits stood upon two easels, and others were leaning together in a corner; a couple of small tables were covered with colour-tubes, brushes, and palette-knives; mingled odours of paint, varnish, and cigarette-smoke per-vaded the air; and, lastly, upon a high stool before one of the easels, his sleeves turned up to the elbow, and his feet tucked in upon the rail beneath him, sat Anastase Gouache himself.

He was a man of not more than seven-and-twenty years, with delicate pale features, and an abundance of glossy black hair. A small and very much pointed moustache shaded his upper lip, and the extremities thereof rose short and perpendicular from the corners of his well-shaped mouth. His eyes were dark and singularly expressive, his forehead low and very broad; his hands were suffi-ciently nervous and well knit, but white as a woman's, and the fingers tapered delicately to the tips. He wore a brown velvet coat more or less daubed with paint, and his collar was low at the throat.

He sprang from his high stool as Donna Tullia and Del Ferice entered, his palette and mahl-stick in his hand, and made a most ceremonious bow; whereat Donna Tullia laughed gaily.

"Well, Gouache," she said familiarly, "what have you been doing?"

Anastase motioned to her to come before his canvas and contemplate the portrait of herself upon which he was working. It was undeniably good—a striking figure in full-length, life-size, and breathing with Donna Tullia's vitality, if also with something of her coarseness.

"Ah, my friend," remarked Del Ferice, "you will never be successful until you take my advice."

"I think it is very like," said Donna Tullia, thoughtfully.

"You are too modest," answered Del Ferice. "There is the foundation of likeness, but it lacks yet the soul."

"Oh, but that will come," returned Madame Mayer. Then turning to the artist, she added in a more doubtful voice, "Perhaps, as Del Ferice says, you might give it a little more expression—what shall I say?—more poetry."

Anastase Gouache smiled a fine smile. He was a man of immense talent; since he had won the Prix de Rome he had made great progress, and was already half famous with that young celebrity which young men easily mistake for fame itself. A new comet visible only through a good glass causes a deal of talk and speculation in the world; but unless it comes near enough to brush the earth with its tail, it is very soon forgotten. But Gouache seemed to understand this, and worked steadily on. When Madame Mayer expressed a wish for a little more poetry in her portrait, he smiled, well knowing that poetry was as far removed from her nature as dry champagne is different in quality from small beer.

"Yes," he said; "I know—I am only too conscious of that defect." As indeed he was—conscious of the defect of it in herself. But he had many reasons for not wishing

to quarrel with Donna Tullia, and he swallowed his artistic
convictions in a rash resolve to make her look like an
inspired prophetess rather than displease her.

"If you will sit down, I will work upon the head," he
said ; and moving one of the old carved chairs into position
for her, he adjusted the light and began to work without
any further words. Del Ferice installed himself upon a
divan whence he could see Donna Tullia and her portrait,
and the sitting began. It might have continued for some
time in a profound silence as far as the two men were
concerned, but silence was not bearable for long to Donna
Tullia.

"What were you and Saracinesca talking about yesterday ?" she asked suddenly, looking towards Del Ferice.

"Politics," he answered, and was silent.

"Well ?" inquired Madame Mayer, rather anxiously.

"I am sure you know his views as well as I," returned Del
Ferice, rather gloomily. "He is stupid and prejudiced."

"Really ?" ejaculated Gouache, with innocent surprise.
"A little more towards me, Madame. Thank you—so."
And he continued painting.

"You are absurd, Del Ferice !" exclaimed Donna Tullia,
colouring a little. "You think every one prejudiced and
stupid who does not agree with you."

"With me ? With you, with us, you should say.
Giovanni is a specimen of the furious Conservative, who
hates change and has a cold chill at the word 'republic.'
Do you call that intelligent ?"

"Giovanni is intelligent for all that," answered
Madame Mayer. "I am not sure that he is not more
intelligent than you—in some ways," she added, after
allowing her rebuke to take effect.

Del Ferice smiled blandly. It was not his business to
show that he was hurt.

"In one thing he is stupid compared with me," he
replied. "He is very far from doing justice to your
charms. It must be a singular lack of intelligence which
prevents him from seeing that you are as beautiful as you
are charming. Is it not so, Gouache ?"

"Does any one deny it?" asked the Frenchman, with an air of devotion.

Madame Mayer blushed with annoyance; both because she coveted Giovanni's admiration more than that of other men, and knew that she had not won it, and because she hated to feel that Del Ferice was able to wound her so easily. To cover her discomfiture she returned to the subject of politics.

"We talk a great deal of our convictions," she said; "but in the meanwhile we must acknowledge that we have accomplished nothing at all. What is the good of our meeting here two or three times a-week, meeting in society, whispering together, corresponding in cipher, and doing all manner of things, when everything goes on just the same as before?"

"Better give it up and join Don Giovanni and his party," returned Del Ferice, with a sneer. "He says if a change comes he will make the best of it. Of course, we could not do better."

"With us it is so easy," said Gouache, thoughtfully. "A handful of students, a few paving-stones, 'Vive la République!' and we have a tumult in no time."

That was not the kind of revolution in which Del Ferice proposed to have a hand. He meditated playing a very small part in some great movement; and when the fighting should be over, he meant to exaggerate the part he had played, and claim a substantial reward. For a good title and twenty thousand francs a-year he would have become as stanch for the temporal power as any canon of St Peter's. When he had begun talking of revolutions to Madame Mayer and to half-a-dozen hare-brained youths, of whom Gouache the painter was one, he had not really the slightest idea of accomplishing anything. He took advantage of the prevailing excitement in order to draw Donna Tullia into a closer confidence than he could otherwise have aspired to obtain. He wanted to marry her, and every new power he could obtain over her was a step towards his goal. Neither she nor her friends were of the stuff required for revolutionary work; but Del

Ferice had hopes that, by means of the knot of malcontents he was gradually drawing together, he might ruin Giovanni Saracinesca, and get the hand of Donna Tullia in marriage. He himself was indeed deeply implicated in the plots of the Italian party; but he was only employed as a spy, and in reality knew no more of the real intentions of those he served than did Donna Tullia herself. But the position was sufficiently lucrative; so much so that he had been obliged to account for his accession of fortune by saying that an uncle of his had died and left him money.

"If you expected Don Giovanni to join a mob of students in tearing up paving-stones and screaming 'Vive la République!' I am not surprised that you are disappointed in your expectations," said Donna Tullia, rather scornfully.

"That is only Gouache's idea of a popular movement," answered Del Ferice.

"And yours," returned Anastase, lowering his mahl-stick and brushes, and turning sharply upon the Italian—"yours would be to begin by stabbing Cardinal Antonelli in the back."

"You mistake me, my friend," returned Del Ferice, blandly. "If you volunteered to perform that service to Italy, I would certainly not dissuade you. But I would certainly not offer you my assistance."

"Fie! How can you talk like that of murder!" exclaimed Donna Tullia. "Go on with your painting, Gouache, and do not be ridiculous."

"The question of tyrannicide is marvellously interesting," answered Anastase in a meditative tone, as he resumed his work, and glanced critically from Madame Mayer to his canvas and back again.

"It belongs to a class of actions at which Del Ferice rejoices, but in which he desires no part," said Donna Tullia.

"It seems to me wiser to contemplate accomplishing the good result without any unnecessary and treacherous bloodshed," answered Del Ferice, sententiously. Again Gouache smiled in his delicate satirical fashion, and glanced at Madame Mayer, who burst into a laugh.

"Moral reflections never sound so especially and ridiculously moral as in your mouth, Ugo," she said.

"Why?" he asked, in an injured tone.

"I am sure I do not know. Of course, we all would like to see Victor Emmanuel in the Quirinal, and Rome the capital of a free Italy. Of course, we would all like to see it accomplished without murder or bloodshed; but somehow, when you put it into words, it sounds very absurd."

In her brutal fashion Madame Mayer had hit upon a great truth, and Del Ferice was very much annoyed. He knew himself to be a scoundrel; he knew Madame Mayer to be a woman of very commonplace intellect; he wondered why he was not able to deceive her more effectually. He was often able to direct her, he sometimes elicited from her some expression of admiration at his astuteness; but in spite of his best efforts, she saw through him and understood him better than he liked.

"I am sorry," he said, "that what is honourable should sound ridiculous when it comes from me. I like to think sometimes that you believe in me."

"Oh, I do," protested Donna Tullia, with a sudden change of manner. "I was only laughing. I think you are really in earnest. Only, you know, nowadays, it is not the fashion to utter moralities in a severe tone, with an air of conviction. A little dash of cynicism—you know, a sort of half sneer—is so much more *chic;* it gives a much higher idea of the morality, because it conveys the impression that it is utterly beyond you. Ask Gouache——"

"By all means," said the artist, squeezing a little more red from a tube upon his palette, "one should always sneer at what one cannot reach. The fox, you remember, called the grapes sour. He was probably right, for he is the most intelligent of animals."

"I would like to hear what Giovanni had to say about those grapes," remarked Donna Tullia.

"Oh, he sneered in the most fashionable way," answered Del Ferice. "He would have pleased you immensely. He said that he would be ruined by a change of government,

and that he thought it his duty to fight against it. He
talked a great deal about the level of the Tiber, and landed property, and the duties of gentlemen. And he ended
by saying he would make the best of any change that
happened to come about, like a thoroughgoing egotist,
as he is!"

"I would like to hear what you think of Don Giovanni
Saracinesca," said Gouache; "and then I would like to
hear what he thinks of you."

"I can tell you both," answered Del Ferice. "I think
of him that he is a thorough aristocrat, full of prejudices
and money, unwilling to sacrifice his convictions to his
wealth or his wealth to his· convictions, intelligent in regard to his own interests and blind to those of others, imbued with a thousand and one curious feudal notions, and
overcome with a sense of his own importance."

"And what does he think of you?" asked Anastase,
working busily.

"Oh, it is very simple," returned Del Ferice, with a
laugh. "He thinks I am a great scoundrel."

"Really! How strange! I should not have said that."

"What? That Del Ferice is a scoundrel?" asked
Donna Tullia, laughing.

"No; I should not have said it," repeated Anastase,
thoughtfully. "I should say that our friend Del Ferice
is a man of the most profound philanthropic convictions,
nobly devoting his life to the pursuit of liberty, fraternity,
and equality."

"Do you really think so?" asked Donna Tullia, with a
half-comic glance at Ugo, who looked uncommonly grave.

"Madame," returned Gouache, "I never permit myself
to think otherwise of any of my friends."

"Upon my word," remarked Del Ferice, "I am delighted
at the compliment, my dear fellow; but I must infer that
your judgment of your friends is singularly limited."

"Perhaps," answered Gouache. "But the number of
my friends is not large, and I myself am very enthusiastic.
I look forward to the day when 'liberty, equality, and
fraternity' shall be inscribed in letters of flame, in the

most expensive Bengal lights if you please, over the *porte cochère* of every palace in Rome, not to mention the churches. I look forward to that day, but I have not the slightest expectation of ever seeing it. Moreover, if it ever comes, I will pack up my palette and brushes and go somewhere else by the nearest route."

"Good heavens, Gouache!" exclaimed Donna Tullia; "how can you talk like that? It is really dreadfully irreverent to jest about our most sacred convictions, or to say that we desire to see those words written over the doors of our churches!"

"I am not jesting. I worship Victor Hugo. I love to dream of the universal republic—it has immense artistic attractions—the fierce yelling crowd, the savage faces, the red caps, the terrible mænad women urging the brawny ruffians on to shed more blood, the lurid light of burning churches, the pale and trembling victims dragged beneath the poised knife,—ah, it is superb, it has stupendous artistic capabilities! But for myself—bah! I am a good Catholic—I wish nobody any harm, for life is very gay after all."

At this remarkable exposition of Anastase Gouache's views in regard to the utility of revolutions, Del Ferice laughed loudly; but Anastase remained perfectly grave, for he was perfectly sincere. Del Ferice, to whom the daily whispered talk of revolution in Donna Tullia's circle was mere child's play, was utterly indifferent, and suffered himself to be amused by the young artist's vagaries. But Donna Tullia, who longed to see herself the centre of a real plot, thought that she was being laughed at, and pouted her red lips and frowned her displeasure.

"I believe you have no convictions!" she said angrily. "While we are risking our lives and fortunes for the good cause, you sit here in your studio dreaming of barricades and guillotines, merely as subjects for pictures—you even acknowledge that in case we produce a revolution you would go away."

"Not without finishing this portrait," returned Anastase, quite unmoved. "It is an exceedingly good likeness; and

in case you should ever disappear—you know people sometimes do in revolutions—or if by any unlucky accident
your beautiful neck should chance beneath that guillotine
you just mentioned,—why, then, this canvas would be the
most delightful souvenir of many pleasant mornings, would
it not?"

"You are incorrigible," said Donna Tullia, with a slight
laugh. "You cannot be serious for a moment."

"It is very hard to paint you when your expression
changes so often," replied Anastase, calmly.

"I am not in a good humour for sitting to you this
morning. I wish you would amuse me, Del Ferice. You
generally can."

"I thought politics amused you——"

"They interest me. But Gouache's ideas are detestable."

"Will you not give us some of your own, Madame?"
inquired the painter, stepping back from his canvas to get
a better view of his work.

"Oh, mine are very simple," answered Donna Tullia.
"Victor Emmanuel, Garibaldi, and a free press."

"A combination of monarchy, republicanism, and popular education—not very interesting," remarked Gouache,
still eyeing his picture.

"No; there would be nothing for you to paint, except
portraits of the liberators——"

"There is a great deal of that done. I have seen
them in every café in the north of Italy," interrupted
the artist. "I would like to paint Garibaldi. He has a
fine head."

"I will ask him to sit to you when he comes here."

"When he comes I shall be here no longer," answered
Gouache. "They will whitewash the Corso, they will
make a restaurant of the Colosseum, and they will hoist
the Italian flag on the cross of St Peter's. Then I will
go to Constantinople; there will still be some years before Turkey is modernised."

"Artists are hopeless people," said Del Ferice. "They
are utterly illogical, and it is impossible to deal with them.
If you like old cities, why do you not like old women?

Why would you not rather paint Donna Tullia's old Countess than Donna Tullia herself?"

"That is precisely the opposite case," replied Anastase,
quietly. "The works of man are never so beautiful as
when they are falling to decay; the works of God are most
beautiful when they are young. You might as well say
that because wine improves with age, therefore horses do
likewise. The faculty of comparison is lacking in your
mind, my dear Del Ferice, as it is generally lacking in the
minds of true patriots. Great reforms and great revolutions are generally brought about by people of fierce and
desperate convictions, like yours, who go to extreme
lengths, and never know when to stop. The quintessence
of an artist's talent is precisely that faculty of comparison,
that gift of knowing when the thing he is doing corre-
sponds as nearly as he can make it with the thing he has
imagined."

There was no tinge of sarcasm in Gouache's voice as he
imputed to Del Ferice the savage enthusiasm of a revolu-
tionist. But when Gouache, who was by no means calm
by nature, said anything in a particularly gentle tone, there
was generally a sting in it, and Del Ferice reflected upon
the mean traffic in stolen information by which he got his
livelihood, and was ashamed. Somehow, too, Donna Tullia
felt that the part she fancied herself playing was contemptible enough when compared with the hard work, the earnest purpose, and the remarkable talent of the young artist.
But though she felt her inferiority, she would have died
rather than own it, even to Del Ferice. She knew that
for months she had talked with Del Ferice, with Valdarno,
with Casalverde, even with the melancholy and ironical
Spicca, concerning conspiracies and deeds of darkness of all
kinds, and she knew that she and they might go on talking
for ever in the same strain without producing the smallest
effect on events; but she never to the very end relinquished
the illusion she cherished so dearly, that she was really and
truly a conspirator, and that if any one of her light-headed
acquaintance betrayed the rest, they might all be ordered
out of Rome in four-and-twenty hours, or might even dis-

appear into that long range of dark buildings to the left of
the colonnade of St Peter's, martyrs to the cause of their
own self - importance and semi - theatrical vanity. There
were many knots of such self-fancied conspirators in those
days, whose wildest deed of daring was to whisper across a
glass of champagne in a ball-room, or over a tumbler of
Velletri wine in a Trasteverine cellar, the magic and awe-
inspiring words, " Viva Garibaldi ! Viva Vittorio'!" They
accomplished nothing. The same men and women are now
grumbling and regretting the flesh-pots of the old Government, or whispering in impotent discontent "Viva la Re-
pubblica !" and they and their descendants will go on
whispering something to each other to the end of time,
while mightier hands than theirs are tearing down empires
and building up irresistible coalitions, and drawing red
pencil-marks through the geography of Europe.

The conspirators of those days accomplished nothing
after Pius IX. returned from Gaeta ; the only men who
were of any use at all were those who, like Del Ferice, had
sources of secret information, and basely sold their scraps
of news. But even they were of small importance. The
moment had not come, and all the talking and whispering
and tale-bearing in the world could not hasten events, nor
change their course. But Donna Tullia was puffed up with
a sense of her importance, and Del Ferice managed to
attract just as much attention to his harmless chatter about
progress as would permit him undisturbed to carry on his
lucrative traffic in secret information.

Donna Tullia, who was not in the least artistic, and
who by no means appreciated the merits of the portrait
Gouache was painting, was very far from comprehending
his definition of artistic comparison ; but Del Ferice understood it very well. Donna Tullia had much foreign blood
in her veins, like most of her class ; but Del Ferice's obscure
descent was in all probability purely Italian, and he had
inherited the common instinct in matters of art which is a
part of the Italian birthright. He had recognised Gouache's
wonderful talent, and had first brought Donna Tullia to his
studio—a matter of little difficulty when she had learned

that the young artist had already a reputation. It pleased her to fancy that by telling him to paint her portrait she might pose as his patroness, and hereafter reap the reputation of having influenced his career. For fashion, and the desire to be the representative of fashion, led Donna Tullia hither and thither as a lapdog is led by a string; and there is nothing more in the fashion than to patronise a fashionable portrait-painter.

But after Anastase Gouache had thus delivered himself of his views upon Del Ferice and the faculty of artistic comparison, the conversation languished, and Donna Tullia grew restless. "She had sat enough," she said; and as her expression was not favourable to the portrait, Anastase did not contradict her, but presently suffered her to depart in peace with her devoted adorer at her heels. And when they were gone, Anastase lighted a cigarette, and took a piece of charcoal and sketched a caricature of Donna Tullia in a liberty cap, in a fine theatrical attitude, invoking the aid of Del Ferice, who appeared as the Angel of Death, with the guillotine in the background. Having put the finishing touches to this work of art, Anastase locked his studio and went to breakfast, humming an air from the " Belle Hélène."

CHAPTER VIII.

When Corona reached home she went to her own small boudoir, with the intention of remaining there for an hour if she could do so without being disturbed. There was a prospect of this; for on inquiry she ascertained that her husband was not yet dressed, and his dressing took a very long time. He had a cosmopolitan valet, who alone of living men understood the art of fitting the artificial and the natural Astrardente together. Corona believed this man to be an accomplished scoundrel; but she never had any proof that he was anything worse than a very clever servant, thoroughly unscrupulous where his master's interests or his own were concerned. The old Duca believed in him sincerely and trusted him alone, feeling that since he could never be a hero in his valet's eyes, he might as well take advantage of that misfortune in order to gain a confidant.

Corona found three or four letters upon her table, and sat down to read them, letting her fur mantle drop to the floor, and putting her small feet out towards the fire, for the pavement of the church had been cold.

She was destined to pass an eventful day, it seemed. One of the letters was from Giovanni Saracinesca. It was the first time he had ever written to her, and she was greatly surprised on finding his name at the foot of the page. He wrote a strong clear handwriting, entirely without adornment of penmanship, close and regular and straight: there was an air of determination about it which was sympathetic, and a conciseness of expression which startled Corona, as though she had heard the man himself speaking to her.

"I write, dear Duchessa, because I covet your good opinion, and my motive is therefore before all things an interested one. I would not have you think that I had idly asked your advice about a thing so important to me as my marriage, in order to discard your counsel at the first opportunity. There was too much reason in the view you took of the matter to admit of my not giving your opinion all the weight I could, even if I had not already determined upon the very course you advised. Circumstances have occurred, however, which have almost induced me to change my mind. I have had an interview with my father, who has put the matter very plainly before me. I hardly know how to tell you this, but I feel that I owe it to you to explain myself, however much you may despise me for what I am going to say. It is very simple, nevertheless. My father has informed me that by my conduct I have caused my name to be coupled in the mouth of the gossips with that of a person very dear to me, but whom I am unfortunately prevented from marrying. He has convinced me that I owe to this lady, who, I confess, takes no interest whatever in me, the only reparation possible to be made—that of taking a wife, and thus publicly demonstrating that there was never any truth in what has been said. As a marriage will probably be forced upon me some day, it is as well to let things take their course at once, in order that a step so disagreeable to myself may at least distantly profit one whom I love in removing me from the appearance of being a factor in her life. The gossip about me has never reached your ears, but if it should, you will be the better able to understand my position.

"Do not think, therefore, that if I do not follow your advice I am altogether inconsistent, or that I wantonly presumed to consult you without any intention of being guided by you. Forgive me also this letter, which I am impelled to write from somewhat mean motives of vanity, in the hope of not altogether forfeiting your opinion; and especially I beg you to believe that I am at all times the most obedient of your servants,

"GIOVANNI SARACINESCA."

Of what use was it that she had that morning determined to forget Giovanni, since he had the power of thus bringing himself before her by means of a scrap of paper? Corona's hand closed upon the letter convulsively, and for a moment the room seemed to swim around her.

So there was some one whom he loved, some one for whose fair name he was willing to sacrifice himself even to the extent of marrying against his will. Some one, too, who not only did not love him, but took no interest whatever in him. Those were his own words, and they must be true, for he never lied. That accounted for his accompanying Donna Tullia to the picnic. He was going to marry her after all. To save the woman he loved so hopelessly from the mere suspicion of being loved by him, he was going to tie himself for life to the first who would marry him. That would never ·prevent the gossips from saying that he loved this other woman as much as ever. It could do her no great harm, since she took no interest whatever in him. Who could she be, this cold creature, whom even Giovanni could not move to interest? It was absurd — the letter was absurd — the whole thing was absurd! None but a madman would think of pursuing such a course; and why should he think it necessary to confide his plans—his very foolish plans—to her, Corona d'Astrardente,—why? Ah, Giovanni, how different things might have been!

Corona rose angrily from her seat and leaned against the broad chimney-piece, and looked at the clock—it was nearly mid-day. He might marry whom he pleased, and be welcome—what was it to her? He might marry and sacrifice himself if he pleased—what was it to her?

She thought of her own life. She, too, had sacrificed herself; she, too, had tied herself for life to a man she despised in her heart, and she had done it for an object she had thought good. She looked steadily at the clock, for she would not give way, nor bend her head and cry bitter tears again; but the tears were in her eyes, nevertheless.

"Giovanni, you must not do it—you must not do it!" Her lips formed the words without speaking them, and repeated the thought again and again. Her heart beat fast and her cheeks flushed darkly. She spread out the crumpled letter and read it once more. As she read, the most intense curiosity seized her to know who this woman might be whom Giovanni so loved; and with her curiosity there was a new feeling—an utterly hateful and hating passion—something so strong, that it suddenly dried her tears and sent the blood from her cheeks back to her heart. Her white hand was clenched, and her eyes were on fire. Ah, if she could only find that woman he loved! if she could only see her dead—dead with Giovanni Saracinesca there upon the floor before her! As she thought of it, she stamped her foot upon the thick carpet, and her face grew paler. She did not know what it was that she felt, but it completely overmastered her. Padre Filippo would be pleased, she thought, for she knew how in that moment she hated Giovanni Saracinesca.

With a sudden impulse she again sat down and opened the letter next to her hand. It was a gossiping epistle from a friend in Paris, full of stories of the day, exclamations upon fashion and all kinds of emptiness; she was about to throw it down impatiently and take up the next when her eyes caught Giovanni's name.

• "Of course it is not true that Saracinesca is to marry Madame Mayer, . . . " were the words she read. But that was all. There chanced to have been just room for the sentence at the foot of the page, and by the time her friend had turned over the leaf, she had already forgotten what she had written, and was running on with a different idea. It seemed as though Corona were haunted by Giovanni at every turn; but she had not reached the end yet, for one letter still remained. She tore open the envelope, and found that the contents consisted of a few lines penned in a small and irregular hand, without signature. There was an air of disguise about the whole, which was unpleasant; it was written upon a common sort of paper, and had come through the city post. It ran as follows :—

"The Duchessa d'Astrardente reminds us of the fable of the dog in the horse's manger, for she can neither eat herself nor let others eat. She will not accept Don Giovanni Saracinesca's devotion, but she effectually prevents him from fulfilling his engagements to others."

If Corona had been in her ordinary mood, she would very likely have laughed at the anonymous communication. She had formerly received more than one passionate declaration, not signed indeed, but accompanied always by some clue to the identity of the writer, and she had carelessly thrown them into the fire. But there was no such indication here whereby she might discover who it was who had undertaken to criticise her, to cast upon her so unjust an accusation. Moreover, she was very angry and altogether thrown out of her usually calm humour. Her first impulse was to go to her husband, and in the strength of her innocence to show him the letter. Then she laughed bitterly as she thought how the selfish old dandy would scoff at her sensitiveness, and how utterly incapable he would be of discovering the offender or of punishing the offence. Then again her face was grave, and she asked herself whether it was true that she was innocent; whether she were not really to be blamed, if perhaps she had really prevented Giovanni from marrying Donna Tullia.

But if that were true, she must herself be the woman he spoke of in his letter. Any other woman would have suspected as much. Corona went to the window, and for an instant there was a strange light of pleasure in her face. Then she grew very thoughtful, and her whole mood changed. She could not conceive it possible that Giovanni so loved her as to marry for her sake. Besides, no one could ever have breathed a word of him in connection with herself—until this abominable anonymous letter was written.

The thought that she might, after all, be the "person very dear to him," the one who "took no interest whatever in him," had nevertheless crossed her mind, and had given her for one moment a sense of wild and indescribable pleasure. Then she remembered what she had felt before; how angry, how utterly beside herself, she had been at the thought of another woman being loved by him, and she suddenly understood that she was jealous of her. The very thought revived in her the belief that it was not she herself who was thus influencing the life of Giovanni Saracinesca, but another, and she sat silent and pale.

Of course it was another! What had she done, what word had she spoken, whereby the world might pretend to believe that she controlled this man's actions? "Fulfilling his engagements," the letter said, too. It must have been written by an ignorant person—by some one who had no idea of what was passing, and who wrote at random, hoping to touch a sensitive chord, to do some harm, to inflict some pain, in petty vengeance for a fancied slight. But in her heart, though she crushed down the instinct, she would have believed the anonymous jest well founded, for the sake of believing, too, that Giovanni Saracinesca was ready to lay his life at her feet—although in that belief she would have felt that she was committing a mortal sin.

She went back to her interview that morning with Padre Filippo, and thought over all she had said and all he had answered; how she had been willing to admit the possibility of Giovanni's love, and how sternly the confessor had ruled down the clause, and told her there should never arise such a doubt in her mind; how she had scorned herself for being capable of seeking love where there was none, and how she had sworn that there should be no perhaps in the matter. It seemed very hard to do right, but she would try to see where the right lay. In the first place, she should burn the anonymous letter, and never condescend to think of it; and she should also burn Giovanni's, because it would be an injustice to him to keep it. She looked once more at the unsigned, ill-written page, and, with a little scornful laugh, threw it from where she sat into the fire with its envelope; then she took Giovanni's note, and would have done the same, but her hand trembled, and the crumpled bit of paper fell upon the hearth. She rose from her chair quickly, and took it up again, kneeling before the fire, like some beautiful dark priestess of old feeding the flames of a sacred altar. She smoothed the paper out once more, and once more read the even characters, and looked long at the signature, and back again to the writing.

"This lady, who, I confess, takes no interest whatever in me. . . ."

"How could he say it!" she exclaimed aloud. "Oh, if I knew who she was!" With an impatient movement she thrust the letter among the coals, and watched the fire curl it and burn it, from white to brown and from brown to black, till it was all gone. Then she rose to her feet and left the room.

Her husband certainly did not guess that the Duchessa d'Astrardente had spent so eventful a morning; and if any one had told him that his wife had been through a dozen stages of emotion, he would have laughed, and would have told his informant that Corona was not of the sort who experience violent passions. That evening they went to the opera together, and the old man was in an unusually cheerful humour. A new coat had just arrived from Paris, and the padding had attained a higher degree of scientific perfection than heretofore. Corona also looked more beautiful than even her husband ever remembered to have seen her; she wore a perfectly simple gown of black satin without the smallest relief of colour, and upon her neck the famous Astrardente necklace of pearls, three strings of even thickness, each jewel exquisitely white and just lighted in its shadow by a delicate pink tinge—such a necklace as an empress might have worn. In the raven masses of her hair there was not the least ornament, nor did any flower enhance the rich blackness of its silken coils. It would be impossible to imagine greater simplicity than Corona showed in her dress, but it would be hard to conceive of any woman who possessed by virtue of severe beauty a more indubitable right to dispense with ornament.

The theatre was crowded. There was a performance of " Norma," for which several celebrated artists had been engaged—an occurrence so rare in Rome, that the theatre was absolutely full. The Astrardente box was upon the second tier, just where the amphitheatre began to curve. There was room in it for four or five persons to see the stage.

The Duchessa and her husband arrived in the middle of the first act, and remained alone until it was over. Corona was extremely fond of " Norma," and after she was seated never took her eyes from the stage. Astrardente, on the other hand, maintained his character as a man of no illusions, and swept the house with his small opera-glass. The instrument itself was like him, and would have been appropriate for a fine lady of the First Empire; it was of mother-of-pearl, made very small and light, the metal-work upon it heavily gilt and ornamented with turquoises. The old man glanced from time to time at the stage, and then again settled himself to the study of the audience, which interested him far more than the opera.

G

"Every human being you ever heard of is here," he remarked at the end of the first act. "Really, I should think you would find it worth while to look at your magnificent fellow-creatures, my dear."

Corona looked slowly round the house. She had excellent eyes, and never used a glass. She saw the same faces she had seen for five years, the same occasional flash of beauty, the same average number of over-dressed women, the same paint, the same feathers, the same jewels. She saw opposite to her Madame Mayer, with the elderly countess whom she patronised for the sake of her deafness, and found convenient as a sort of flying chaperon. The countess could not hear much of the music, but she was fond of the world and liked to be seen, and she could not hear at all what Del Ferice said in an undertone to Madame Mayer. Sufficient to her were the good things of the day ; the rest was in no way her business. There was Valdarno in the club-box, with a knot of other men of his own stamp. There were the Rocca, mother and daughter and son—a boy of eighteen—and a couple of men in the back of the box. Everybody was there, as her husband had said ; and as she dropped her glance toward the stalls, she was aware of Giovanni Saracinesca's black eyes looking anxiously up to her. A faint smile crossed her serene face, and almost involuntarily she nodded to him and then looked away. Many men were watching her, and bowed as she glanced at them, and she bent her head to each ; but there was no smile for any save Giovanni, and when she looked again to where he had been standing with his back to the stage, he was gone from his place.

"They are the same old things," said Astrardente, "but they are still very amusing. Madame Mayer always seems to get the wrong man into her box. She would give all those diamonds to have Giovanni Saracinesca instead of that newsmonger fellow. If he comes here I will send him across."

"Perhaps she likes Del Ferice," suggested Corona.

"He is a good lapdog—a very good dog," answered her husband. "He cannot bite at all, and his bark is so soft that you would take it for the mewing of a kitten. He fetches and carries admirably."

"Those are good points, but not interesting ones. He is very tiresome with his eternal puns and insipid compliments, and his gossip."

"But he is so very harmless," answered Astrardente, with compassionate scorn. "He is incapable of doing an injury. Donna Tullia is wise in adopting him as her slave. She would not be so safe with Saracinesca, for instance. If you feel the need of an admirer, my dear, take Del Ferice. I have no objection to him."

"Why should I need admirers?" asked Corona, quietly.

"I was merely jesting, my love. Is not your own husband the greatest of your admirers, and your devoted slave into the bargain?" Old Astrardente's face twisted itself into the semblance of a smile, as he leaned towards his young wife, lowering his cracked voice to a thin whisper. He was genuinely in love with her, and lost no opportunity of telling her so. She smiled a little wearily.

"You are very good to me," she said. She had often wondered how it was that this aged creature, who had never been faithful to any attachment in his life for five months, did really seem to love her just as he had done for five years. It was perhaps the greatest triumph she could have attained, though she never thought of it in that light; but though she could not respect her husband very much, she could not think unkindly of him—for, as she said, he was very good to her. She often reproached herself because he wearied her; she believed that she should have taken more pleasure in his admiration.

"I cannot help being good to you, my angel," he said. "How could I be otherwise? Do I not love you most passionately?"

"Indeed I think so," Corona answered. As she spoke there was a knock at the door. Her heart leaped wildly, and she turned a little pale.

"The devil seize these visitors!" muttered old Astrardente, annoyed beyond measure at being interrupted when making love to his wife. "I suppose we must let them in?"

"I suppose so," assented the Duchessa, with forced calm. Her husband opened the door, and Giovanni Saracinesca entered, hat in hand.

"Sit down," said Astrardente, rather harshly.

"I trust I am not disturbing you," replied Giovanni, still standing. He was somewhat surprised at the old man's inhospitable tone.

"Oh no; not in the least," said the latter, quickly regaining his composure. "Pray sit down; the act will begin in a moment."

Giovanni established himself upon the chair immediately behind the Duchessa. He had come to talk, and he anticipated that during the second act he would have an excellent opportunity.

"I hear you enjoyed yourselves yesterday," said Corona, turning her head so as to speak more easily.

"Indeed!" Giovanni answered, and a shade of annoyance crossed his face. "And who was your informant, Duchessa?"

"Donna Tullia. I met her this morning. She said you amused them all—kept them laughing the whole day."

"What an extraordinary statement!" exclaimed Giovanni. "It shows how one may unconsciously furnish matter for mirth. I do not recollect having talked much to any one. It was a noisy party enough, however."

"Perhaps Donna Tullia spoke ironically," suggested Corona. "Do you like 'Norma'?"

"Oh yes; one opera is as good as another. There goes the curtain."

The act began, and for some minutes no one in the box spoke. Presently there was a burst of orchestral music. Giovanni leaned forward so that his face was close behind Corona. He could speak without being heard by Astrardente.

"Did you receive my letter?" he asked. Corona made an almost imperceptible inclination of her head, but did not speak.

"Do you understand my position?" he asked again. He could not see her face, and for some seconds she made no sign; at last she moved her head again, but this time to express a negative.

"It is simple enough, it seems to me," said Giovanni, bending his brows.

Corona found that by turning a little she could still look at the stage, and at the same time speak to the man behind her.

"How can I judge?" she said. "You have not told me all. Why do you ask me to judge whether you are right?"

"I could not do it if you thought me wrong," he answered shortly.

The Duchessa suddenly thought of that other woman for whom the man who asked her advice was willing to sacrifice his life.

"You attach an astonishing degree of importance to my opinion," she said very coldly, and turned her head from him.

"There is no one so well able to give an opinion," said Giovanni, insisting.

Corona was offended. She interpreted the speech to mean that since she had sacrificed her life to the old man on the opposite side of the box, she was able to judge whether Giovanni would do wisely in making a marriage of convenience, for the sake of an end which even to her mind seemed visionary. She turned quickly upon him, and there was an angry gleam in her eyes.

"Pray do not introduce the subject of my life," she said haughtily.

Giovanni was too much astonished to answer her at once. He had indeed not intended the least reference to her marriage.

"You have entirely misunderstood me," he said presently.

"Then you must express yourself more clearly," she replied. She would have felt very guilty to be thus talking to Giovanni, as she would not have talked before her husband, had she not felt that it was upon Giovanni's business, and that the matter discussed in no way concerned herself. As for Saracinesca, he was in a dangerous position, and was rapidly losing his self-control. He was too near to her, his heart was beating too fast, the blood was throbbing in his temples, and he was stung by being misunderstood.

"It is not possible for me to express myself more clearly," he answered. "I am suffering from having told you too little when I dare not tell you all. I make no reference to your marriage when I speak to you of my own. Forgive me; I will not refer to the matter again."

Corona felt again that strange thrill, half of pain, half of pleasure, and the lights of the theatre seemed moving before her uncertainly, as things look when one falls from a height. Almost unconsciously she spoke, hardly knowing that she turned her head, and that her dark eyes rested upon Giovanni's pale face.

"And yet there must be some reason why you tell me that little, and why you do not tell me more." When she had spoken, she would have given all the world to have taken back her words. It was too late. Giovanni answered in a low thick voice that sounded as though he were choking, his face grew white, and his teeth seemed almost to chatter as though he were cold, but his eyes shone like black stars in the shadow of the box.

"There is every reason. You are the woman I love."

Corona did not move for several seconds, as though not comprehending what he had said. Then she suddenly shivered, and her eyelids drooped as she leaned back in her chair. Her fingers relaxed their tight hold upon her fan, and the thing fell rattling upon the floor of the box.

Old Astrardente, who had taken no notice of the pair, being annoyed at Giovanni's visit, and much interested in the proceedings of Madame Mayer in the box opposite, heard the noise, and stooped with considerable alacrity to pick up the fan which lay at his feet.

"You are not well, my love," he said quickly, as he observed his wife's unusual pallor.

"It is nothing; it will pass," she murmured, with a terrible effort. Then, as though she had not said enough, she added, "There must be a draught here; I have a chill."

Giovanni had sat like a statue, utterly overcome by the sense of his own folly and rashness, as well as by the shock of having so miserably failed to keep the secret he dreaded to reveal. On hearing Corona's voice, he rose suddenly, as from a dream.

"Forgive me," he said hurriedly, "I have just remembered a most important engagement——"

"Do not mention it," said Astrardente, sourly. Giovanni bowed to the Duchessa and left the box. She did not look at him as he went away.

"We had better go home, my angel," said the old man. "You have got a bad chill."

"Oh no, I would rather stay. It is nothing, and the best part of the opera is to come." Corona spoke quietly enough. Her strong nerves had already recovered from the shock she had experienced, and she could command her voice. She did not want to go home; on the contrary, the brilliant lights and the music served for a time to soothe her. If there had been a ball that night she would have gone to it; she would have done anything that would take her thoughts from herself. Her husband looked at her curiously. The suspicion crossed his mind that Don Giovanni had said something which had either frightened or offended her, but on second thoughts the theory seemed absurd. He regarded Saracinesca as little more than a mere acquaintance of his wife's.

"As you please, my love," he answered, drawing his chair a little nearer to hers. "I am glad that fellow is gone. We can talk at our ease now."

"Yes; I am glad he is gone. We can talk now," repeated Corona, mechanically.

"I thought his excuse slightly conventional, to say the least of it," remarked Astrardente. "An important engagement!—just a little *banal*. However, any excuse was good enough which took him away."

"Did he say that?" asked Corona. "I did not hear. Of course, any excuse would do, as you say."

CHAPTER IX.

Giovanni left the theatre at once, alone, and on foot. He was very much agitated. He had done suddenly and unawares the thing of all others he had determined never to do; his resolutions had been broken down and carried away as an ineffectual barrier is swept to the sea by the floods of spring. His heart had spoken in spite of him, and in speaking had silenced every prompting of reason. He blamed himself bitterly, as he strode out across the deserted bridge of Sant' Angelo and into the broad gloom beyond, where the street widens from the fortress to the entrance of the three Borghi: he walked on and on, finding at every step fresh reason for self-reproach, and trying to understand what he had done. He paused at the end of the open piazza and looked down towards the black rushing river which he could hear, but hardly see; he turned into the silent Borgo Santo Spirito, and passed along the endless wall of the great hospital up to the colonnades, and still wandering on, he came to the broad steps of St Peter's and sat down, alone in the darkness, at the foot of the stupendous pile.

He was perhaps not so much to blame as he was willing to allow in his just anger against himself. Corona had tempted him sorely in that last question she had put to him. She had not known, she had not even faintly guessed what she was doing, for her own brain was intoxicated with a new and indescribable sensation which had left no room for reflection nor for weighing the force of words. But Giovanni, who had been willing to give up everything, even to his personal liberty, for the sake of concealing his love, would not allow himself any argument in extenuation of what he had done. He had had but very few affairs of the heart in his life, and they had been for the most part very insignificant, and his experience was limited. Even now it never entered his mind to imagine that Corona would condone his offence; he felt sure that she was deeply wounded, and that his next meeting with her would be a terrible ordeal—so terrible, indeed, that he doubted whether he had the courage to meet her at all. His love was so great, and its object so sacred to him, that he hesitated to conceive himself loved in return; perhaps if he had been able to understand that Corona loved him he would have left Rome for ever, rather than trouble her peace by his presence.

It would have been absolutely different if he had been paying court to Donna Tullia, for instance. The feeling that he should be justified would have lent him courage, and the coldness in his own heart would have left his judgment free play. He could have watched her calmly, and would have tried to take advantage of every mood in the prosecution of his suit. He was a very honourable man, but he did not consider marriages of propriety and convenience as being at all contrary to the ordinary standard of social honour, and would have thought himself justified in using every means of persuasion in order to win a woman whom, upon mature reflection, he had judged suitable to become his wife, even though he felt no real love for her. That is an idea inherent in most old countries, an idea for which Giovanni Saracinesca was certainly in no way responsible, seeing that it had been instilled into him from his boyhood. Personally he would have preferred to live and die unmarried, rather than to take a wife as a matter of obligation towards his family; but seeing that he had never seriously loved any woman, he had acquired the habit of contemplating such a marriage as a probability, perhaps as an ultimate necessity, to be put off as long as possible, but to which he would at last yield with a good grace.

But the current of his life had been turned. He was certainly not a romantic character, not a man who desired to experience the external sensations to be obtained by voluntarily creating dramatic events. He loved action, and he had a taste for danger, but he had sought both in a legitimate way; he never desired to implicate himself in adventures where the feelings were concerned, and hitherto such experiences had not fallen in his path. As is usual

with such men, when love came at last, it came with a
strength such as boys of twenty do not dream of. The
mature man of thirty years, with his strong and dominant
temper, his carelessness of danger, his high and untried
ideals of what a true affection should be, resisting the first
impressions of the master-passion with the indifference of
one accustomed to believe that love could not come near
his life, and was in general a thing to be avoided—a man,
moreover, who by his individual gifts and by his brilliant
position was able to command much that smaller men
would not dream of aspiring to,—such a man, in short, as
Giovanni Saracinesca,—was not likely to experience love-
sickness in a mild degree. Proud, despotic, and fiercely
unyielding by his inheritance of temper, he was out-
wardly gentle and courteous by acquired habit, a man
of·those whom women easily love and men very generally
fear.

He did not realise his own nature, he did not suspect
the extremes of feeling of which he was eminently capable.
He had at first felt Corona's influence, and her face and
voice seemed to awaken in him a memory, which was as
yet but an anticipation, and not a real remembrance.   It
was as the faint perfume of the spring wafted up to a
prisoner in some stern fortress, as the first gentle sweetness
that rose from the enchanted lakes of the cisalpine country
to the nostrils of the war-hardened Goths as they descended the last snow-slopes in their southern wandering
—an anticipation that seemed already a memory, a looking
forward again to something that had been already loved in
a former state.   Giovanni had laughed at himself for it
at first, then he had dreaded its growing charm, and at the
last he had fallen hopelessly under the spell, retaining only
enough of his former self to make him determined that the
harm which had come upon himself should not come near
this woman whom he so adored.

And behold, at the first provocation, the very first time
that by a careless word she had fired his blood and set his
brain throbbing, he had not only been unable to hide what
he felt, but had spoken such words as he would not have

believed he could speak—so bluntly, so roughly, that she had almost fainted before his very eyes.

She must have been very angry, he thought. Perhaps, too, she was frightened. It was so rude, so utterly contrary to all that was chivalrous to say thus at the first opportunity, "I love you"—just that and nothing more. Giovanni had never thought much about it, but he supposed that men in love, very seriously in love, must take a long time to express themselves, as is the manner in books; whereas he was horrified at his own bluntness in having blurted out rashly such words as could never be taken back, as could never even be explained now, he feared, because he had put himself beyond the pale of all explanation, perhaps beyond the reach of forgiveness.

Nobody ever yet explained away the distinct statement "I love you," upon any pretence of a mistake. Giovanni almost laughed at the idea, and yet he conceived that some kind of apology would be necessary, though he could not imagine how he was to frame one. He reflected that few women would consider a declaration, even as sudden as his had been, in the light of an insult; but he knew how little cause Corona had given him for speaking to her of love, and he judged from her manner that she had been either offended or frightened, or both, and that he was to blame for it. He was greatly disturbed, and the sweat stood in great drops upon his forehead as he sat there upon the steps of St Peter's in the cold night wind. He remained nearly an hour without changing his position, and then at last he rose and slowly retraced his steps, and went home by narrow streets, avoiding the theatre and the crowd of carriages that stood before it.

He had almost determined to go away for a time, and to let his absence speak for his contrition. But he had reckoned upon his former self, and he doubted now whether he had the strength to leave Rome. The most that seemed possible was that he should keep out of Corona's way for a few days, until she should have recovered from the shock of the scene in the theatre. After that he would go to her and tell her quite simply

that he was very sorry, but that he had been unable to
control himself. It would soon be over. She would not
refuse to speak to him, he argued, for fear of attracting the
attention of the gossips and making an open scandal. She
would perhaps tell him to avoid her, and her words would
be few and haughty, but she would speak to him, nevertheless.

Giovanni went to bed. The next day he gave out that
he had a touch of fever, and remained in his own apartments. His father, who was passionately attached to him,
in spite of his rough temper and hasty speeches, came and
spent most of the day with him, and in the intervals of
his kindly talk, marched up and down the room, swearing
that Giovanni was no more ill than he was himself, and
that he had acquired his accursed habit of staying in bed
upon his travels. As Giovanni had never before been
known to spend twenty-four hours in bed for any reason
whatsoever, the accusation was unjust; but he only smiled
and pretended to argue the case for the sake of pleasing
the old prince. He really felt exceedingly uncomfortable,
and would have been glad to be left alone at any price;
but there was nothing for it but to pretend to be ill in
body, when he was really sick at heart, and he remained
obstinately in bed the whole day. On the following
morning he declared his intention of going out of town,
and by an early train he left the city. No one saw
Giovanni again until the evening of the Frangipani ball.

Meanwhile it would have surprised him greatly to know
that Corona looked for him in vain wherever she went,
and that, not seeing him, she grew silent and pale, and
gave short answers to the pleasant speeches men made her.
Every one missed Giovanni. He wrote to Valdarno to
say that he had been suddenly obliged to visit Saracinesca
in order to see to some details connected with the timber
question; but everybody wondered why he should have
taken himself away in the height of the season for so
trivial a matter. He had last been seen in the Astrardente
box at the opera, where he had only stayed a few minutes,
as Del Ferice was able to testify, having sat immediately

opposite in the box of Madame Mayer. Del Ferice swore
secretly that he would find out what was the matter; and
Donna Tullia abused Giovanni in unmeasured terms to a
circle of intimate friends and admirers, because he had been
engaged to dance with her at the Valdarno cotillon, and
had not even sent word that he could not come. There-
upon all the men present immediately offered themselves
for the vacant dance, and Donna Tullia made them draw
lots by tossing a copper sou in the corner of the ball-room.
The man who won the toss recklessly threw over the partner he had already engaged, and almost had to fight a duel
in consequence; all of which was intensely amusing to
Donna Tullia. Nevertheless, in her heart, she was very
angry at Giovanni's departure.

But Corona sought him everywhere, and at last heard
that he had left town, two days after everybody else in
Rome had known it. She would probably have been very
much disturbed if she had actually met him within a day
or two of that fatal evening, but the desire to see him was
so great, that she entirely overlooked the consequences.
For the time being, her whole life seemed to have undergone a revolution—she trembled at the echo of the words
she had heard—she spent long hours in solitude, praying
with all her strength that she might be forgiven for having
heard him speak; but the moment she left her room, and
went out into the world, the dominant desire to see him
again returned. The secret longing of her soul was to
hear him speak again as he had spoken once. She would
have gone again to Padre Filippo and told him all; but
when she was alone in the solitude of her passionate prayers and self-accusation, she felt that she must fight this
fight alone, without help of any one; and when she was
in the world, she lacked courage to put altogether from her
what was so very sweet, and her eyes searched unceasingly
for the dark face she loved. But the stirring strength of
the mighty passion played upon her soul and body in spite
of her, as upon an instrument of strings; and sometimes
the music was gentle and full of sweet harmony, but often
there were crashes of discord, so that she trembled and felt

her heart wrung as by torture; then she set her strong
lips, and her white fingers wound themselves together, and
she could have cried aloud, but that her pride forbade
her.

The days came and went, but Giovanni did not return,
and Corona's face grew every morning more pale and her
eyes every night more wistful. Her husband did not understand, but he saw that something was the matter, as
others saw it, and in his quick suspicious humour he connected the trouble in his wife's face with the absence of
Giovanni and with the strange chill she had felt in the
theatre. But Corona d'Astrardente was a very brave and
strong woman, and she bore what seemed to her like the
agony of death renewed each day, so calmly that those
who knew her thought it was but a passing indisposition
or annoyance, unusual with her, who was never ill nor
troubled, but yet insignificant. She gave particular attention to the gown which her husband had desired she
should wear at the great ball, and the need she felt for
distracting her mind from her chief care made society
necessary to her.

The evening of the Frangipani ball came, and all Rome
was in a state of excitement and expectation. The great
old family had been in mourning for years, owing to three
successive deaths, and during all that time the ancient
stronghold which was called their palace had been closed
to the world. For some time, indeed, no one of the name
had been in Rome—the prince and princess preferring to
pass the time of mourning in the country and in travelling; while the eldest son, now just of age, was finishing
his academic career at an English University. But this
year the family had returned: there had been both dinners
and receptions at the palace, and the ball, which was to be
a sort of festival in honour of the coming of age of the
heir, was expected as the principal event of the year. It
was rumoured that there would be nearly thirty rooms
opened besides the great hall, which was set aside for dancing, and that the arrangements were on a scale worthy of
a household which had endured in its high position for up-

wards of a thousand years. It was understood that no distinction had been made, in issuing the invitations, between parties in politics or in society, and that there would be more people seen there than had been collected under one roof for many years.

The Frangipani did things magnificently, and no one was disappointed. The gardens and courts of the palace were brilliantly illuminated; vast suites of apartments were thrown open, and lavishly decorated with rare flowers; the grand staircase was lined with footmen in the liveries of the house, standing motionless as the guests passed up; the supper was a banquet such as is read of in the chronicles of medieval splendour; the enormous conservatory in the distant south wing was softly lit by shaded candles concealed among the tropical plants; and the ceilings and walls of the great hall itself had been newly decorated by famous painters; while the polished wooden floor presented an innovation upon the old-fashioned canvas - covered brick pavement, not hitherto seen in any Roman palace. A thousand candles, disposed in every variety of chandelier and candelabra, shed a soft rich light from far above, and high in the gallery at one end an orchestra of Viennese musicians played unceasingly.

As generally happens at very large balls, the dancing began late, but numbers of persons had come early in order to survey the wonders of the palace at their leisure. Among those who arrived soon after ten o'clock was Giovanni Saracinesca, who was greeted loudly by all who knew him. He looked pale and tired, if his tough nature could ever be said to seem weary; but he was in an unusually affable mood, and exchanged words with every one he met. Indeed he had been sad for so many days that he hardly understood why he felt gay, unless it was in the anticipation of once more seeing the woman he loved. He wandered through the rooms carelessly enough, but he was in reality devoured by impatience, and his quick eyes sought Corona's tall figure in every direction. But she was not yet there, and Giovanni at last came and took his station in one of the outer halls, waiting patiently for her arrival.

While he waited, leaning against one of the marble pillars of the door, the throng increased rapidly; but he hardly noticed the swelling crowd, until suddenly there was a lull in the unceasing talk, and the men and women parted to allow a cardinal to pass out from the inner rooms. With many gracious nods and winning looks, the great man moved on, his keen eyes embracing every one and everything within the range of his vision, his courteous smile seeming intended for each separate individual, and yet overlooking none, nor resting long on any, his high brow serene and unbent, his flowing robes falling back from his courtly figure, as with his red hat in his hand he bowed his way through the bowing crowd. His departure, which was quickly followed by that of several other cardinals and prelates, was the signal that the dancing would soon begin; and when he had passed out, the throng of men and women pressed more quickly in through the door on their way to the ball-room.

But as the great cardinal's eye rested on Giovanni Saracinesca, accompanied by that invariable smile that so many can remember well to this day, his delicate hand made a gesture as though beckoning to the young man to follow him. Giovanni obeyed the summons, and became for the moment the most notable man in the room. The two passed out together, and a moment later were standing in the outer hall. Already the torch-bearers were standing without upon the grand staircase, and the lackeys were mustering in long files to salute the Prime Minister. Just then the master of the house came running breathless from within. He had not seen that Cardinal Antonelli was taking his leave, and hastened to overtake him, lest any breach of etiquette on his part should attract the displeasure of the statesman.

"Your Eminence's pardon!" he exclaimed, hurriedly. "I had not seen that your Eminence was leaving us—so early too—the Princess feared——"

"Do not speak of it," answered the Cardinal, in suave tones. "I am not so strong as I used to be. We old fellows must to bed betimes, and leave you young ones to

enjoy yourselves.   No excuses—good night—a beautiful
ball—I congratulate you on the reopening of your house—
good night again.   I will have a word with Giovanni here
before I go down-stairs."

He extended his hand to Frangipani, who lifted it respectfully to his lips and withdrew, seeing that he was not
wanted.   He and many others speculated long upon the
business which engaged his Eminence in close conversation
with Giovanni Saracinesca, keeping him for more than a
quarter of an hour in the cold ante-chamber, where the
night wind blew in unhindered from the vast staircase of
the palace.   As a matter of fact, Giovanni was as much
surprised as any one.

"Where have you been, my friend?" inquired the Cardinal, when they were alone.

"To Saracinesca, your Eminence."

"And what have you been doing in Saracinesca at this
time of year?   I hope you are attending to the woods
there—you have not been cutting timber?"

"No one can be more anxious than we to see the woods
grow thick upon our hills," replied Giovanni.   "Your
Eminence need have no fear."

"Not for your estates," said the great Cardinal, his small
keen black eyes resting searchingly on Giovanni's face.
"But I confess I have some fears for yourself."

"For me, Eminence?" repeated Giovanni, in some astonishment.

"For you.   I have heard with considerable anxiety that
there is a question of marrying you to Madame Mayer.
Such a match would not meet with the Holy Father's approval, nor—if I may be permitted to mention my humble
self in the same breath with our august sovereign—would
it be wise in my own estimation."

"Permit me to remark to your Eminence," answered
Giovanni, proudly, "that in my house we have never been
in the habit of asking advice upon such subjects.   Donna
Tullia is a good Catholic.   There can therefore be no valid
objection to my asking her hand, if my father and I agree
that it is best."

H

"You are terrible fellows, you Saracinesca," returned the Cardinal, blandly. "I have read your family history with immense interest, and what you say is quite true. I cannot find an instance on record of your taking the advice of any one—certainly not of the Holy Church. It is with the utmost circumspection that I venture to approach the subject with you, and I am sure that you will believe me when I say that my words are not dictated by any officious or meddling spirit; I am addressing you by the direct desire of the Holy Father himself."

A soft answer turneth away wrath, and if the all-powerful statesman's answer to Giovanni seems to have been more soft than might have been expected, it must be remembered that he was speaking to the heir of one of the most powerful houses in the Roman State, at a time when the personal friendship of such men as the Saracinesca was of vastly greater importance than it is now. At that time some twenty noblemen owned a great part of the Pontifical States, and the influence they could exert upon their tenantry was very great, for the feudal system was not extinct, nor the feudal spirit. Moreover, though Cardinal Antonelli was far from popular with any party, Pius IX. was respected and beloved by a vast majority of the gentlemen as well as of the people. Giovanni's first impulse was to resist any interference whatsoever in his affairs; but on receiving the Cardinal's mild answer to his own somewhat arrogant assertion of independence, he bowed politely and professed himself willing to listen to reason.

"But," he said, "since his Holiness has mentioned the matter, I beg that your Eminence will inform him that, though the question of my marriage seems to be in everybody's mouth, it is as yet merely a project in which no active steps have been taken."

"I am glad of it, Giovanni," replied the Cardinal, familiarly taking his arm, and beginning to pace the hall; "I am glad of it. There are reasons why the match appears to be unworthy of you. If you will permit me, without any offence to Madame Mayer, I will tell you what those reasons are."

"I am at your service," said Giovanni, gravely, "provided only there is no offence to Donna Tullia."

"None whatever. The reasons are purely political. Madame Mayer—or Donna Tullia, since you prefer to call her so—is the centre of a sort of club of so-called Liberals, of whom the most active and the most foolish member is a certain Ugo del Ferice, a fellow who calls himself a count, but whose grandfather was a coachman in the Vatican under Leo XII. He will get himself into trouble some day. He is always in attendance upon Donna Tullia, and probably led her into this band of foolish young people for objects of his own. It is a very silly society; I daresay you have heard some of their talk?"

"Very little," replied Giovanni; "I do not trouble myself about politics. I did not even know that there was such a club as your Eminence speaks of."

Cardinal Antonelli glanced sharply at his companion as he proceeded.

"They affect solidarity and secrecy, these young people," he said, with a sneer, "and their solidarity betrays their secrecy, because it is unfortunately true in our dear Rome that wherever two or three are gathered together they are engaged in some mischief. But they may gather in peace at the studio of Monsieur Gouache, or anywhere else they please, for all I care. Gouache is a clever fellow; he is to paint my portrait. Do you know him? But, to return to my sheep in wolves' clothing—my amusing little conspirators. They can do no harm, for they know not even what they say, and their words are not followed by any kind of action whatsoever. But the principle of the thing is bad, Giovanni. Your brave old ancestors used to fight us Churchmen outright, and unless the Lord is especially merciful, their souls are in an evil case, for the devil knoweth his own, and is a particularly bad paymaster. But they fought outright, like gentlemen; whereas these people—*foderunt foveam ut caperent me*—they have digged a ditch, but they will certainly not catch me, nor any one else. Their conciliabules, as Rousseau would have called them, meet daily and talk great nonsense and do nothing;

which does not prove their principles to be good, while it demonstrates their intellect to be contemptible. No offence to the Signor Conte del Ferice, but I think ignorance has marked his little party for its own, and inanity waits on all his councils. If they believe in half the absurdities they utter, why do they not pack up their goods and chattels and cross the frontier? If they meant anything, they would do something."

"Evidently," replied Giovanni, half amused at his Eminence's tirade.

"Evidently. Therefore they mean nothing. Therefore our good friend Donna Tullia is dabbling in the emptiness of political dilettanteism for the satisfaction of a hollow vanity; no offence to her—it is the manner of her kind."

Giovanni was silent.

"Believe me, prince," said the Cardinal, suddenly changing his tone and speaking very seriously, "there is something better for strong men like you and me to do, in these times, than to dabble in conspiracy and to toss off glasses of champagne to Italian unity and Victor Emmanuel. The condition of our lives is battle, and battle against terrible odds. Neither you nor I should be content to waste our strength in fighting shadows, in waging war on petty troubles of our own raising, knowing all the while that the powers of evil are marshalled in a deadly array against the powers of good. *Sed non prævalebunt!*"

The Cardinal's thin face assumed a strange look of determination, and his delicate fingers grasped Giovanni's arm with a force that startled him.

"You speak bravely," answered the young man. "You are more sanguine than we men of the world. You believe that disaster impossible which to me seems growing daily more imminent."

Cardinal Antonelli turned his gleaming black eyes full on his companion.

"*O generatio incredula!* If you have not faith, you have not courage, and if you have not courage you will waste your life in the pursuit of emptiness! It is for men like you, for men of ancient race, of broad acres, of iron body and healthy mind, to put your hand to the good work and help us who have struggled for many years and whose strength is already failing. Every action of your life, every thought of your waking hours, should be for the good end, lest we all perish together and expiate our luke-warm indifference. *Timidi nunquam statuerunt tropæum* —if we would divide the spoil we must gird on the sword and use it boldly; we must not allow the possibility of failure; we must be vigilant; we must be united as one man. You tell me that you men of the world already regard a disaster as imminent—to expect defeat is nine-tenths of a defeat itself. Ah, if we could count upon such men as you to the very death, our case would be far from desperate."

"For the matter of that, your Eminence can count upon us well enough," replied Giovanni, quietly.

"Upon you, Giovanni—yes, for you are a brave gentle-man. But upon your friends, even upon your class—no. Can I count upon the Valdarno, even? You know as well as I that they are in sympathy with the Liberals—that they have neither the courage to support us nor the audacity to renounce us; and, what is worse, they represent a large class, of whom, I regret to say, Donna Tullia Mayer is one of the most prominent members. With her wealth, her youth, her effervescent spirits, and her early widowhood, she leads men after her; they talk, they chatter, they set up an opinion and gloat over it, while they lack the spirit to support it. They are all alike—*non tantum ovum ovo simile*—one egg is not more like another than they are. *Non tali auxilio*—we want no such help. We ask for bread, not for stones; we want men, not empty-headed dandies. We have both at present; but if the Emperor fails us, we shall have too many dandies and too few men —too few men like you, Don Giovanni. Instead of armed battalions we shall have polite societies for mutual assur-ance against political risks,—instead of the support of the greatest military power in Europe, we shall have to rely on a parcel of young gentlemen whose opinions are guided by Donna Tullia Mayer."

Giovanni laughed and glanced at his Eminence, who
chose to refer all the imminent disasters of the State to
the lady whom he did not wish to see married to his companion.

"Is her influence really so great?" asked Saracinesca,
incredulously.

"She is agreeable, she is pretty, she is rich—her influence is a type of the whole influence which is abroad in
Rome—a reflection of the life of Paris. There, at least,
the women play a real part—very often a great one : here,
when they have got command of a drawing-room full of
fops, they do not know where to lead them; they change
their minds twenty times a-day; they have an access of
religious enthusiasm in Advent, followed by an attack of
Liberal fever in Carnival, and their season is brought to
a fitting termination by the prostration which overtakes
them in Lent. By that time all their principles are upset,
and they go to Paris for the month of May—*pour se re-
tremper dans les idées idéalistes,* as they express it. Do
you think one could construct a party out of such elements,
especially when you reflect that this mass of uncertainty is
certain always to yield to the ultimate consideration of self-
interest? Half of them keep an Italian flag with the
Papal one, ready to thrust either of them out of their window as occasion may require. Good night, Giovanni. I
have talked enough, and all Rome will set upon you to find
out what secrets of State I have been confiding. You had
better prepare an answer, for you can hardly inform Donna
Tullia and her set that I have been calling them a parcel
of—weak and ill-advised people. They might take offence
—they might even call me by bad names,—fancy how very
terribly that would afflict me! Good night, Giovanni—my
greetings to your father."

The Cardinal nodded, but did not offer his hand. He
knew that Giovanni hated to kiss his ring, and he had too
much tact to press the ceremonial etiquette upon any one
whom he desired to influence. But he nodded graciously,
and receiving his cloak from the gentleman who accompanied him and who had waited at a respectful distance,

the statesman passed out of the great doorway, where the double line of torch-bearers stood ready to accompany him down the grand staircase to his carriage, in accordance with the custom of those days.

CHAPTER X.

When he was alone, Giovanni retraced his steps, and again took up his position near the entrance to the reception-rooms. He had matter for reflection in the interview which had just ended; and, having nothing better to do while he waited for Corona, he thought about what had happened. He was not altogether pleased at the interest his marriage excited in high quarters; he hated interference, and he regarded Cardinal Antonelli's advice in such a matter as an interference of the most unwarrantable kind. Neither he himself nor his father were men who sought counsel from without, for independence in action was with them a family tradition, as independence of thought was in their race a hereditary quality. To think that if he, Giovanni Saracinesca, chose to marry any woman whatsoever, any one, no matter how exalted in station, should dare to express approval or disapproval, was a shock to every inborn and cultivated prejudice in his nature. He had nearly quarrelled with his own father for seeking to influence his matrimonial projects; it was not likely that he would suffer Cardinal Antonelli to interfere with them. If Giovanni had really made up his mind—had firmly determined to ask the hand of Donna Tullia—it is more than probable that the statesman's advice would not only have failed signally in preventing the match, but by the very opposition it would have aroused in Giovanni's heart it would have had the effect of throwing him into the arms of a party which already desired his adhesion, and which, under his guidance, might have become as formidable as it was previously insignificant. But the great Cardinal was probably well informed, and his words had not fallen upon a barren soil. Giovanni had vacillated sadly in trying to come to a decision. His first Quixotic impulse to marry Madame Mayer, in order to show the world that he cared nothing for Corona d'Astrardente, had proved itself absurd, even to his impetuous intelligence. The growing antipathy he felt for Donna Tullia had made his marriage with her appear in the light of a disagreeable duty, and his rashness in confessing his love for Corona had so disturbed his previous conceptions that marriage no longer seemed a duty at all. What had been but a few days before almost a fixed resolution, had dwindled till it seemed an impracticable and even a useless scheme. When he had arrived at the Palazzo Frangipani that evening, he had very nearly forgotten Donna Tullia, and had quite determined that whatever his father might say he would not give the promised answer before Easter. By the time the Cardinal had left him, he had decided that no power on earth should induce him to marry Madame Mayer. He did not take the trouble of saying to himself that he would marry no one else.

The Cardinal's words had struck deep, in a deep nature. Giovanni had given Del Ferice a very fair exposition of the views he believed himself to hold, on the day when they had walked together after Donna Tullia's picnic. He believed himself a practical man, loyal to the temporal power by principle rather than by any sort of enthusiastic devotion; not desirous of any great change, because any change that might reasonably be expected would be bad for his own vested interests; not prejudiced for any policy save that of peace—preferring, indeed, with Cicero, the most unjust peace to the most just war; tenacious of old customs, and not particularly inquisitive concerning ideas of progress,—on the whole, Giovanni thought himself what his father had been in his youth, and more or less what he hoped his sons, if he ever had any, would be after him.

But there was more in him than all this, and at the first distant sound of battle he felt the spirit stir within him, for his real nature was brave and loyal, unselfish and

devoted, instinctively sympathising with the weak and
hating the lukewarm. He had told Del Ferice that he
believed he would fight as a matter of principle: as he
leaned against the marble pillar of the door in the Palazzo
Frangipani, he wished the fight had already begun.

Waiting there, and staring into the moving crowd, he
was aware of a young man with pale and delicate features
and black hair, who stood quietly by his side, and seemed
like himself an idle though not uninterested spectator of
the scene. Giovanni glanced once at the young fellow, and
thought he recognised him, and glancing again, he met his
earnest look, and saw that it was Anastase Gouache, the
painter. Giovanni knew him slightly, for Gouache was
regarded as a rising celebrity, and, thanks to Donna Tullia,
was invited to most of the great receptions and balls of that
season, though he was not yet anywhere on a footing of intimacy. Gouache was proud, and would perhaps have stood
aloof altogether rather than be treated as one of the herd
who are asked "with everybody," as the phrase goes; but
he was of an observing turn of mind, and it amused him
immensely to stand unnoticed, following the movements of
society's planets, comets, and satellites, and studying the
many types of the cosmopolitan Roman world.

"Good evening, Monsieur Gouache," said Giovanni.

"Good evening, prince," replied the artist, with a somewhat formal bow — after which both men relapsed into
silence, and continued to watch the crowd.

"And what do you think of our Roman world?" asked
Giovanni, presently.

"I cannot compare it to any other world," answered
Gouache, simply. "I never went into society till I came
to Rome. I think it is at once brilliant and sedate—it has
a magnificent air of historical antiquity, and it is a little
paradoxical."

"Where is the paradox?" inquired Giovanni.

> "'Es-tu libre? Les lois sont-elles respectées?
> Crains-tu de voir ton champ pillé par le voisin?
> Le maître a-t-il son toit, et l'ouvrier son pain?'"

A smile flickered over the young artist's face as he quoted

Musset's lines in answer to Giovanni's question. Giovanni himself laughed, and looked at Anastase with somewhat increased interest.

" Do you mean that we are revelling under the sword of Damocles—dancing on the eve of our execution ? "

" Not precisely. A delicate flavour of uncertainty about to-morrow gives zest to the appetite of to-day. It is impossible that such a large society should be wholly unconscious of its own imminent danger—and yet these men and women go about to-night as if they were Romans of old, rulers of the world, only less sure of themselves than of the stability of their empire."

" Why not ? " asked Giovanni, glancing curiously at the pale young man beside him. " In answer to your quotation, I can say that I am as free as I care to be; that the laws are sufficiently respected; that no one has hitherto thought it worth while to plunder my acres; that I have a modest roof of my own; and that, as far as I am aware, there are no workmen starving in the streets at present. You are answered, it seems to me, Monsieur Gouache."

" Is that really your belief ? " asked the artist, quietly.

" Yes. As for my freedom, I am as free as air; no one thinks of hindering my movements. As for the laws, they are made for good citizens, and good citizens will respect them; if bad citizens do not, that is their loss. My acres are safe, possibly because they are not worth taking, though they yield me a modest competence sufficient for my needs and for the needs of those who cultivate them for me."

" And yet there is a great deal of talk in Rome about misery and injustice and oppression——"

" There will be a great deal more talk about those evils, with much better cause, if people who think like you succeed in bringing about a revolution, Monsieur Gouache," answered Giovanni, coldly.

" If many people think like you, prince, a revolution is not to be thought of. As for me, I am a foreigner, and I see what I can, and listen to what I hear."

. " A revolution is not to be thought of. It was tried here and failed. If we are overcome by a great power from without, we shall have no choice but to yield, if any of us survive—for we would fight. But we have nothing to fear from within."

"Perhaps not," returned Gouache, thoughtfully. "I hear such opposite opinions that I hardly know what to think."

"I hear that you are to paint Cardinal Antonelli's portrait," said Giovanni. "Perhaps his Eminence will help you to decide."

"Yes; they say he is the cleverest man in Europe."

"In that opinion they — whoever they may be — are mistaken," replied Giovanni. "But he is a man of immense intellect, nevertheless."

"I am not sure whether I will paint his portrait after all," said Gouache.

"You do not wish to be persuaded?"

"No. My own ideas please me very well for the present. I would not exchange them for those of any one else."

"May I ask what those ideas are?" inquired Giovanni, with a show of interest.

"I am a republican," answered Gouache, quietly. "I am also a good Catholic."

"Then you are yourself much more paradoxical than the whole of our Roman society put together," answered Giovanni, with a dry laugh.

"Perhaps. There comes the most beautiful woman in the world."

It was nearly twelve o'clock when Corona arrived, old Astrardente sauntering jauntily by her side, his face arranged with more than usual care, and his glossy wig curled cunningly to represent nature. He was said to possess a number of wigs of different lengths, which he wore in rotation, thus sustaining the impression that his hair was cut from time to time. In his eye a single eyeglass was adjusted, and as he walked he swung his hat delicately in his tightly gloved fingers. He wore the plainest of collars and the simplest of gold studs; no chain dangled showily from his waistcoat-pocket, and his small

feet were encased in little patent-leather shoes. But for
his painted face, he might have passed for the very incarnation of fashionable simplicity. But his face betrayed
him.

As for Corona, she was dazzlingly beautiful. Not that
any colour or material she wore could greatly enhance her
beauty, for all who saw her on that memorable night remembered the wonderful light in her face, and the strange
look in her splendid eyes; but the thick soft fall of the
white velvet made as it were a pedestal for her loveliness,
and the Astrardente jewels that clasped her waist and
throat and crowned her black hair, collected the radiance
of the many candles, and made the light cling to her and
follow her as she walked. Giovanni saw her enter, and
his whole adoration came upon him as a madness upon a
sick man in a fever, so that he would have sprung forward
to meet her, and fallen at her feet and worshipped her,
had he not suddenly felt that he was watched by more
than one of the many who paused to see her go by. He
moved from his place and waited near the door where she
would have to pass, and for a moment his heart stood
still.

He hardly knew how it was. He found himself speaking to her. He asked her for a dance, he asked boldly for
the cotillon—he never knew how he had dared; she assented, let her eyes rest upon him for one moment with an
indescribable expression, then grew very calm and cold,
and passed on.

It was all over in an instant. Giovanni moved back
to his place as she went by, and stood still like a man
stunned. It was well that there were yet nearly two hours
before the preliminary dancing would be over; he needed
some time to collect himself. The air seemed full of
strange voices, and he watched the moving faces as in a
dream, unable to concentrate his attention upon anything
he saw.

"He looks as though he had a stroke of paralysis," said
a woman's voice near him. It did not strike him, in his
strange bewilderment, that it was Donna Tullia who had

spoken, still less that she was speaking of him, almost to him.

"Something very like it, I should say," answered Del Ferice's oily voice. "He has probably been ill since you saw him. Saracinesca is an unhealthy place."

Giovanni turned sharply round.

"Yes; we were speaking of you, Don Giovanni," said Donna Tullia, with some scorn. ."Does it strike you that you were exceedingly rude in not letting me know that you were going out of town when you had promised to dance with me at the Valdarno ball?" She curled her small lip and showed her sharp white teeth. Giovanni was a man of the world, however, and was equal to the occasion.

"I apologise most humbly," he said. "It was indeed very rude; but in the urgency of the case, I forgot all other engagements. I really beg your pardon. Will you honour me with a dance this evening?"

"I have every dance engaged," answered Madame Mayer, coldly staring at him.

"I am very sorry," said Giovanni, inwardly thanking heaven for his good fortune, and wishing she would go away.

"Wait a moment," said Donna Tullia, judging that she had produced the desired effect upon him. "Let me look. I believe I have one waltz left. Let me see. Yes, the one before the last—you can have it if you like."

"Thank you," murmured Giovanni, greatly annoyed. "I will remember."

Madame Mayer laid her hand upon Del Ferice's arm, and moved away. She was a vain woman, and being in love with Saracinesca after her own fashion, could not understand that he should be wholly indifferent to her. She thought that in telling him she had no dances she had given him a little wholesome punishment, and that in giving one after all she had conferred a favour upon him. She also believed that she had annoyed Del Ferice, which always amused her. But Del Ferice was more than a match for her, with his quiet ways and smooth tongue.

They went into the ball-room together and danced a few
minutes. When the music ceased, Ugo excused himself
on the plea that he was engaged for the quadrille that
followed. He at once set out in search of the Duchessa
d'Astrardente, and did not lose sight of her again. She
did not dance before the cotillon, she said; and she sat
down in a high chair in the picture-gallery, while three or
four men, among whom was Valdarno, sat and stood near
her, doing their best to amuse her. Others came, and
some went away, but Corona did not move, and sat
amongst her little court, glad to have the time pass in any
way until the cotillon. When Del Ferice had ascertained
her position, he went about his business, which was manifold—dancing frequently, and making a point of speaking
to every one in the room. At the end of an hour, he
joined the group of men around the Duchessa and took
part in the conversation.

In was an easy matter to make the talk turn upon
Giovanni Saracinesca. Every one was more or less curious
about the journey he had made, and especially about the
cause of his absence. Each of the men had something to
say, and each, knowing the popular report that Giovanni
was in love with Corona, said his say with as much wit as
he could command. Corona herself was interested, for she
alone understood his sudden absence, and was anxious to
hear the common opinion concerning it.

The theories advanced were various. Some said he had
been quarrelling with the local authorities of Saracinesca,
who interfered with his developments and improvements
upon the estate, and they gave laughable portraits of the
village sages with whom he had been engaged. Others
said he had only stopped there a day, and had been in
Naples. One said he had been boar-hunting; another,
that the Saracinesca woods had been infested by a band of
robbers, who were terrorising the country.

"And what do you say, Del Ferice?" asked Corona,
seeing a cunning smile upon the man's pale fat face.

"It is very simple," said Ugo; "it is a very simple
matter indeed. If the Duchessa will permit me, I will

call him, and we will ask him directly what he has been
doing. There he stands with old Cantalorgano at the
other end of the room. Public curiosity demands to be
satisfied. May I call him, Duchessa ? "

" By no means," said Corona, quickly. But before she
had spoken, Valdarno, who was always sanguine and im-
pulsive, had rapidly crossed the gallery and was already
speaking to Giovanni. The latter bowed his head as
though obeying an order, and came quietly back with the
young man who had called him. The crowd of men
parted before him as he advanced to the Duchessa's chair,
and stood waiting in some surprise.

" What are your commands, Duchessa ? " he asked, in
somewhat formal tones.

" Valdarno is too quick," answered Corona, who was
greatly annoyed. " Some one suggested calling you to
settle a dispute, and he went before I could stop him. I
fear it is very impertinent of us."

" I am entirely at your service," said Giovanni, who was
delighted at having been called, and had found time to
recover from his first excitement on seeing her. " What
is the question ? "

" We were all talking about you," said Valdarno.

" We were wondering where you had been," said another.

" They said you had gone boar-hunting."

" Or to Naples."

" Or even to Paris." Three or four spoke in one breath.

" I am exceedingly flattered at the interest you all show
in me," said Giovanni, quietly. " There is very little to
tell. I have been in Saracinesca upon a matter of business, spending my days in the woods with my steward,
and my nights in keeping away the cold and the ghosts.
I would have invited you all to join the festivity, had I
known how much you were interested. The beef up there
is monstrously tough, and the rats are abominably noisy,
but the mountain air is said to be very healthy."

Most of the men present felt that they had not only
behaved foolishly, but had spoiled the little circle around

the Duchessa by introducing a man who had the power to interest her, whereas they could only afford her a little amusement. Valdarno was still standing, and his chair beside Corona was vacant. Giovanni calmly installed himself upon it, and began to talk as though nothing had happened.

"You are not dancing, Duchessa," he remarked. "I suppose you have been in the ball-room?"

"Yes—but I am rather tired this evening. I will wait."

"You were here at the last great ball, before the old prince died, were you not?" asked Giovanni, remembering that he had first seen her on that occasion.

"Yes," she answered; "and I remember that we danced together; and the accident to the window, and the story of the ghost."

So they fell into conversation, and though one or two of the men ventured an ineffectual remark, the little circle dropped away, and Giovanni was left alone by the side of the Duchessa. The distant opening strains of a waltz came floating down the gallery, but neither of the two heard, nor cared.

"It is strange," Giovanni said. "They say it has always happened, since the memory of man. No one has ever seen anything, but whenever there is a great ball, there is a crash of broken glass some time in the course of the evening. Nobody could ever explain why that window fell in, five years ago—five years ago this month,—this very day, I believe," he continued suddenly, in the act of recollection. "Yes—the nineteenth of January, I remember very well—it was my mother's birthday."

"It is not so extraordinary," said Corona, "for it chances to be the name-day of the present prince. That was probably the reason why it was chosen this year." She spoke a little nervously, as though still ill at ease.

"But it is very strange," said Giovanni, in a low voice. "It is strange that we should have met here the first time, and that we should not have met here since, until —to-day."

He looked towards her as he spoke, and their eyes met and lingered in each other's gaze. Suddenly the blood mounted to Corona's cheeks, her eyelids drooped, she leaned back in her seat and was silent.

Far off, at the entrance to the ball-room, Del Ferice found Donna Tullia alone. She was very angry. The dance for which she was engaged to Giovanni Saracinesca had begun, and was already half over, and still he did not come. Her pink face was unusually flushed, and there was a disagreeable look in her blue eyes.

"Ah!—I see Don Giovanni has again forgotten his engagement," said Ugo, in smooth tones. He well knew that he himself had brought about the omission, but none could have guessed it from his manner. "May I have the honour of a turn before your cavalier arrives?" he asked.

"No," said Donna Tullia, angrily. "Give me your arm. We will go and find him." She almost hissed the words through her closed teeth.

She hardly knew that Del Ferice was leading her as they moved towards the picture-gallery, passing through the crowded rooms that lay between. She never spoke; but her movement was impetuous, and she resented being delayed by the hosts of men and women who filled the way. As they entered the long apartment, where the portraits of the Frangipani lined the walls from end to end, Del Ferice uttered a well-feigned exclamation.

"Oh, there he is!" he cried. "Do you see him?—his back is turned—he is alone with the Astrardente."

"Come," said Donna Tullia, shortly. Del Ferice would have preferred to have let her go alone, and to have witnessed from a distance the scene he had brought about. But he could not refuse to accompany Madame Mayer.

Neither Corona, who was facing the pair, but was talking with Giovanni, nor Giovanni himself, who was turned away from them, noticed their approach until they came and stood still beside them. Saracinesca looked up and started. The Duchessa d'Astrardente raised her black eyebrows in surprise.

I

"Our dance!" exclaimed Giovanni, in considerable agitation. "It is the one after this——"

"On the contrary," said Donna Tullia, in tones trembling with rage, "it is already over. It is the most unparalleled insolence!"

Giovanni was profoundly disgusted at himself and Donna Tullia. He cared not so much for the humiliation itself, which was bad enough, as for the annoyance the scene caused Corona, who looked from one to the other in angry astonishment, but of course could have nothing to say.

"I can only assure you that I thought——"

"You need not assure me!" cried Donna Tullia, losing all self-control. "There is no excuse, nor pardon—it is the second time. Do not insult me further, by inventing untruths for your apology."

"Nevertheless——" began Giovanni, who was sincerely sorry for his great rudeness, and would gladly have attempted to explain his conduct, seeing that Donna Tullia was so justly angry.

"There is no nevertheless!" she interrupted. "You may stay where you are," she added, with a scornful glance at the Duchessa d'Astrardente. Then she laid her hand upon Del Ferice's arm, and swept angrily past, so that the train of her red silk gown brushed sharply against Corona's soft white velvet.

Giovanni remained standing a moment, with a puzzled expression upon his face.

"How could you do anything so rude?" asked Corona, very gravely. "She will never forgive you, and she will be quite right."

"I do not know how I forgot," he answered, seating himself again. "It is dreadful—unpardonable—but perhaps the consequences will be good."

CHAPTER XI.

Corona was ill at ease. In the first few moments of being alone with Giovanni the pleasure she felt outweighed all other thoughts. But as the minutes lengthened to a quarter of an hour, then to half an hour, she grew nervous, and her answers came more and more shortly. She said to herself that she should never have given him the cotillon, and she wondered how the remainder of the time would pass. The realisation of what had occurred came upon her, and the hot blood rose to her face and ebbed away again, and rose once more. Yet she could not speak out what her pride prompted her to say, because she pitied Giovanni a little, and was willing to think for a moment that it was only compassion she felt, lest she should feel that she must send him away.

But Giovanni sat beside her, and knew that the spell was working upon him, and that there was no salvation. He had taken her unawares, though he hardly knew it, when she first entered, and he asked her suddenly for a dance. He had wondered vaguely why she had so freely consented; but, in the wild delight of being by her side, he completely lost all hold upon himself, and yielded to the exquisite charm of her presence, as a man who has struggled for a moment against a powerful opiate sinks under its influence, and involuntarily acknowledges his weakness. Strong as he was, his strength was all gone, and he knew not where he should find it.

"You will have to make her some further apology," said Corona, as Madame Mayer's red train disappeared through the doorway at the other end of the room.

"Of course—I must do something about it," said Giovanni, absently. "After all, I do not wonder—it is amazing that I should have recognised her at all. I should forget anything to-night, except that I am to dance with you."

The Duchessa looked away, and fanned herself slowly; but she sighed, and checked the deep-drawn breath as by a great effort. The waltz was over, and the dancers streamed through the intervening rooms towards the gallery in quest of fresher air and freer space. Two and two they came, quickly following each other and passing on, some filling the high seats along the walls, others hastening towards the supper-rooms beyond. A few minutes earlier Saracinesca and Corona had been almost alone in the great apartment; now they were surrounded on all sides by a chattering crowd of men and women, with flushed faces or unnaturally pale, according as the effort of dancing affected each, and the indistinguishable din of hundreds of voices so filled the air that Giovanni and the Duchessa could hardly hear each other speak.

"This is intolerable," said Giovanni, suddenly. "You are not engaged for the last quadrille? Shall we not go away until the cotillon begins?"

Corona hesitated a moment, and was silent. She glanced once at Giovanni, and again surveyed the moving crowd.

"Yes," she said at last; "let us go away."

"You are very good," answered Giovanni in a low voice, as he offered her his arm. She looked at him inquiringly, and her face grew grave, as they slowly made their way out of the room.

At last they came to the conservatory, and went in among the great plants and the soft lights. There was no one there, and they slowly paced the broad walk that was left clear all round the glass-covered chamber, and up and down the middle. The plants were disposed so thickly as to form almost impenetrable walls of green on either side; and at one end there was an open space where a little marble fountain played, around which were disposed seats of carved wood. But Giovanni and Corona continued to walk slowly along the tiled path.

"Why did you say I was good just now?" asked Corona at last. Her voice sounded cold.

"I should not have said it, perhaps," answered Giovanni. "I say many things which I cannot help saying. I am very sorry."

"I am very sorry too," answered the Duchessa, quietly.

"Ah! if you knew, you would forgive me. If you could guess half the truth, you would forgive me."

"I would rather not guess it."

"Of course; but you have already—you know it all. Have I not told you?" Giovanni spoke in despairing tones. He was utterly weak and spellbound; he could hardly find any words at all.

"Don Giovanni," said Corona, speaking very proudly and calmly, but not unkindly, "I have known you so long, I believe you to be so honourable a man, that I am willing to suppose that you said—what you said—in a moment of madness."

"Madness! It was madness; but it is more sweet to remember than all the other doings of my life," said Saracinesca, his tongue unloosed at last. "If it is madness to love you, I am mad past all cure. There is no healing for me now; I shall never find my senses again, for they are lost in you, and lost for ever. Drive me away, crush me, trample on me if you will; you cannot kill me nor kill my madness, for I live in you and for you, and I cannot die. That is all. I am not eloquent as other men are, to use smooth words and twist phrases. I love you——"

"You have said too much already—too much, far too much," murmured Corona, in broken tones. She had withdrawn her hand from his during his passionate speech, and stood back from him against the dark wall of green plants, her head drooping upon her breast, her fingers clasped fast together. His short rude words were terribly sweet to hear; it was fearful to think that she was alone with him, that one step would bring her to his side, that with one passionate impulse she might throw her white arms about his neck, that one faltering sigh of overwhelming love might bring her queenly head down upon his shoulder. Ah, God! how gladly she would let her tears flow and speak for her! how unutterably sweet it would be to rest for one instant in his arms, to love and be loved as she longed to be!

"You are so cold," he cried, passionately. "You cannot understand. All spoken words are not too much, are not enough to move you, to make you see that I do really worship and adore you; you, the whole of you — your glorious face, your sweet small hands, your queenly ways, the light of your eyes, and the words of your lips—all of you, body and soul, I love. I would I might die now, for your know it, even if you will not understand——"

He moved a step nearer to her, stretching out his hands as he spoke. Corona trembled convulsively, and her lips turned white in the torture of temptation; she leaned far back against the green leaves, staring wildly at Giovanni, held as in a vice by the mighty passions of love and fear. Having yielded her ears to his words, they fascinated her horribly. He, poor man, had long lost all control of himself. His resolutions, long pondered in the solitude of Saracinesca, had vanished like unsubstantial vapours before a strong fire, and his heart and soul were ablaze.

"Do not look at me so," he said, almost tenderly. "Do not look at me as though you feared me, as though you hated me. Can you not see that it is I who fear you as well as love you, who tremble at your coldness, who watch for your slightest kind look? Ah, Corona, you have made me so happy !—there is no angel in all heaven but would give up his Paradise to change for mine !"

He had taken her hand and pressed it wildly to his lips. Her eyelids drooped, and her head fell back for one moment. They stood so very near that his arm had almost stolen about her slender waist, he almost thought he was supporting her.

Suddenly, without the least warning, she drew herself up to her full height, and thrust Giovanni back to her arm's length, strongly, almost roughly.

"Never !" she said. "I am a weak woman, but not so weak as that. I am miserable, but not so miserable as to listen to you. Giovanni Saracinesca, you say you love me —God grant it is not true ! but you say it. Then, have you no honour, no courage, no strength ? Is there nothing of the man left in you ? Is there no truth in your love,

no generosity in your heart? If you so love me as you
say you do, do you care so little what becomes of me as to
tempt me to love you?"

She spoke very earnestly, not scornfully nor angrily, but
in the certainty of strength and right, and in the strong
persuasion that the headstrong man would hear and be
convinced. She was weak no longer; for one desperate
moment her fate had trembled in the balance, but she had
not hesitated even then; she had struggled bravely, and
her brave soul had won the great battle. She had been
weak the other day at the theatre, in letting herself ask
the question to which she knew the answer; she had been
miserably weak that very night in so abandoning herself
to the influence she loved and dreaded; but at the great
moment, when heaven and earth swam before her as in a
wild and unreal mirage, with the voice of the man she
loved ringing in her ears, speaking such words as it was
an ecstasy to hear, she had been no longer weak—the
reality of danger had brought forth the sincerity of her
goodness, and her heart had found courage to do a great
deed. She had overcome, and she knew it.

Giovanni stood back from her, and hung his head. In
a moment the force of his passion was checked, and from
the supreme verge of unspeakable and rapturous delight,
he was cast suddenly into the depths of his own remorse.
He stood silent before her, trembling and awestruck.

"You cannot understand me," she said, "I do not understand myself. But this I know, that you are not what
you have seemed to-night—that there is enough manliness
and nobility in you to respect a woman, and that you will
hereafter prove that I am right. I pray that I may not
see you any more; but if I must see you, I will trust you
thus much—say that I may trust you," she added, her
strong smooth voice sinking in a trembling cadence, half
beseeching, and yet wholly commanding.

Saracinesca bent his heavy brows, and was silent for a
moment. Then he looked up, and his eyes met hers, and
seemed to gather strength from her.

"If you will let me see you sometimes, you may trust

me. I would I were as noble and good as you—I am not. I will try to be. Ah, Corona!" he cried suddenly, "forgive me, forgive me! I hardly knew what I said."

"Hush!" said the Duchessa, gently; "you must not speak like that, nor call me Corona. Perhaps I am wrong to forgive you wholly, but I believe in you. I believe you will understand, and that you will be worthy of the trust I place in you."

"Indeed, Duchessa, none shall say that they have trusted me in vain," answered Giovanni very proudly— "neither man nor woman—and, least of all women, you."

"That is well," said she, with the faint shadow of a smile. "I would rather see you proud than reckless. See that you remain so—that neither by word nor deed you ever remind me that I have had anything to forgive. It is the only way in which any intercourse between us can be possible after this—this dreadful night."

Giovanni bowed his head. He was still pale, but he had regained control of himself.

"I solemnly promise that I will not recall it to your memory, and I implore your forgiveness, even though you cannot forget."

"I cannot forget," said Corona, almost under her breath. Giovanni's eyes flashed for a moment. "Shall we go back to the ball-room? I will go home soon."

As they turned to go, a loud crash, as of broken glass, with the fall of some heavy body, startled them, and made them stand still in the middle of the walk. The noisy concussion was followed by a complete silence. Corona, whose nerves had been severely tried, trembled slightly.

"It is strange," she said; "they say it always happens."

There was nothing to be seen. The thick web of plants hid the cause of the noise from view, whatever it might be. Giovanni hesitated a moment, looking about to see how he could get behind the banks of flower-pots. Then he left Corona without a word, and striding to the end of the walk, disappeared into the depths of the conservatory. He had noticed that there was a narrow entrance at the end nearest the fountain, intended probably to ad-

mit the gardener for the purpose of watering the plants.
Corona could hear his quick steps; she thought she heard
a low groan and a voice whispering,—but she might have
been mistaken, for the place was large, and her heart was
beating fast.

Giovanni had not gone far in the narrow way, which
was sufficiently lighted by the soft light of the many
candles concealed in various parts of the conservatory,
when he came upon the figure of a man sitting, as he had
apparently fallen, across the small passage. The fragments of a heavy earthenware vase lay beyond him, with
a heap of earth and roots; and the tall india-rubber plant
which grew in it had fallen against the sloping glass roof
and shattered several panes. As Giovanni came suddenly
upon him, the man struggled to rise, and in the dim light
Saracinesca recognised Del Ferice. The truth flashed
upon him at once. The fellow had been listening, and
had probably heard all. Giovanni instantly resolved to
conceal the fact from the Duchessa, to whom the knowledge
that the painful scene had been overheard would be a
bitter mortification. Giovanni could undertake to silence
the eavesdropper.

Quick as thought his strong brown hands gripped the
throat of Ugo del Ferice, stifling his breath like a collar
of iron.

"Dog!" he whispered fiercely in the wretch's ear, "if
you breathe, I will kill you now! You will find me in
my own house in an hour. Be silent now!" Giovanni
whispered, with such a terrible grip on the fellow's throat
that his eyeballs seemed starting from his head. Then he
turned and went out by the way he had entered, leaving
Del Férice writhing with pain and gasping for breath. As
he joined Corona, his face betrayed no emotion—he had
been so pale before that he could not turn whiter in his
anger—but his eyes gleamed fiercely at the thought of fight.
The Duchessa stood where he had left her, still much
agitated.

"It is nothing," said Giovanni, with a forced laugh, as
he offered her his arm and led her quickly away. "Im-

agine. A great vase with one of Frangipani's favourite
plants in it had been badly propped, and had fallen right
through the glass, outward."

"It is strange," said Corona. "I was almost sure I
heard a groan."

"It was the wind. The glass was broken, and it is a
stormy night."

"That was just the way that window fell in five years
ago," said Corona. "Something always happens here. I
think I will go home—let us find my husband."

No one would have guessed, from Corona's face, that
anything extraordinary had occurred in the half-hour she
had spent in the conservatory. She walked calmly by
Giovanni's side, not a trace of excitement on her pale
proud face, not a sign of uneasiness in the quiet glance of
her splendid eyes. She had conquered, and she knew it,
never to be tempted again; she had conquered herself and
she had overcome the man beside her. Giovanni glanced
at her in wondering admiration.

"You are the bravest woman in the world, as I am
the most contemptible of men," he said suddenly, as they
entered the picture-gallery.

"I am not brave," she answered calmly, "neither are
you contemptible, my friend. We have both been very
near to our destruction, but it has pleased God to save us."

"By you," said Saracinesca, very solemnly. He knew
that within six hours he might be lying dead upon some
plot of wet grass without the city, and he grew very grave,
after the manner of brave men when death is abroad.

"You have saved my soul to-night," he said earnestly.
"Will you give me your blessing and whole forgiveness?
Do not laugh at me, nor think me foolish. The blessing
of such women as you should make men braver and better."

The gallery was again deserted. The cotillon had begun, and those who were not dancing were at supper.
Corona stood still for one moment by the very chair
where they had sat so long.

"I forgive you wholly. I pray that all blessings may
be upon you always, in life and in death, for ever."

Giovanni bowed his head reverently. It seemed as though the woman he so loved were speaking a benediction upon his death, a last *in pace* which should follow him for all eternity.

"In life and in death, I will honour you truly and serve you faithfully for ever," he answered. As he raised his head, Corona saw that there were tears in his eyes, and she felt that there were tears in her own.

"Come," she said, and they passed on in silence.

She found her husband at last in the supper-room. He was leisurely discussing the wing of a chicken and a small glass of claret-and-water, with a gouty ambassador whose wife had insisted upon dancing the cotillon, and who was revenging himself upon a Strasbourg *pâté* and a bottle of dry champagne.

"Ah, my dear," said Astrardente, looking up from his modest fare, "you have been dancing? You have come to supper? You are very wise. I have danced a great deal myself, but I have not seen you—the room was so crowded. Here—this small table will hold us all, just a quartet."

"Thanks—I am not hungry. Will you take me home when you have finished supper? Or are you going to stay? Do not wait, Don Giovanni; I know you are busy in the cotillon. My husband will take care of me. Good night."

Giovanni bowed, and went away, glad to be alone at last. He had to be at home in half an hour according to his engagement, and he had to look about him for a friend. All Rome was at the ball; but the men upon whom he could call for such service as he required, were all dancing. Moreover, he reflected that in such a matter it was necessary to have some one especially trustworthy. It would not do to have the real cause of the duel known, and the choice of a second was a very important matter. He never doubted that Del Ferice would send some one with a challenge at the appointed time. Del Ferice was a scoundrel, doubtless; but he was quick with the foils, and had often appeared as second in affairs of honour.

Giovanni stood by the door of the ball-room, looking at the many familiar faces, and wondering how he could induce any one to leave his partner at that hour, and go home with him. Suddenly he was aware that his father was standing beside him and eyeing him curiously.

"What is the matter, Giovannino?" inquired the old Prince. "Why are you not dancing?"

"The fact is——" began Giovanni, and then stopped suddenly. An idea struck him. He went close to his father, and spoke in a low voice.

"The fact is, that I have just taken a man by the throat and otherwise insulted him, by calling him a dog. The fellow seemed annoyed, and so I told him he might send to our house in an hour for an explanation. I cannot find a friend, because everybody is dancing this abominable cotillon. Perhaps you can help me," he added, looking at his father rather doubtfully. To his surprise and considerable relief the old Prince burst into a hearty laugh.

"Of course," he cried. "What do you take me for? Do you think I would desert my boy in a fight? Go and call my carriage, and wait for me while I pick up somebody for a witness; we can talk on the way home."

The old Prince had been a duellist in his day, and he would no more have thought of advising his son not to fight than of refusing a challenge himself. He was, moreover, exceedingly bored at the ball, and not in the least sleepy. The prospect of an exciting night was novel and delightful. He knew Giovanni's extraordinary skill, and feared nothing for him. He knew everybody in the ballroom was engaged, and he went straight to the supper-table, expecting to find some one there. Astrardente, the Duchessa, and the gouty ambassador were still together, as Giovanni had left them a moment before. The Prince did not like Astrardente, but he knew the ambassador very well. He called him aside, with an apology to the Duchessa.

"I want a young man immediately," said old Saracinesca, stroking his white beard with his broad brown hand. "Can you tell of any one who is not dancing?"

"There is Astrardente," answered his Excellency, with an ironical smile. "A duel?" he asked.

Saracinesca nodded.

"I am too old," said the diplomatist, thoughtfully; "but it would be infinitely amusing. I cannot give you one of my secretaries either. It always makes such a scandal. Oh, there goes the very man! Catch him before it is too late!"

Old Saracinesca glanced in the direction the ambassador indicated, and darted away. He was as active as a boy, in spite of his sixty years.

"Eh!" he cried. "Hi! you! Come here! Spicca! Stop! Excuse me—I am in a great hurry!"

Count Spicca, whom he thus addressed, paused and looked round through his single eyeglass in some surprise. He was an immensely tall and cadaverous-looking man, with a black beard and searching grey eyes.

"I really beg your pardon," said the Prince hurriedly, in a low voice, as he came up, "but I am in a great hurry —an affair of honour—will you be witness? My carriage is at the door."

"With pleasure," said Count Spicca, quietly; and without further comment he accompanied the Prince to the outer hall. Giovanni was waiting, and the Prince's footman stood at the head of the stairs. In three minutes the father and son and the melancholy Spicca were seated in the carriage, on their way to the Palazzo Saracinesca.

"Now then, Giovannino," said the Prince, as he lit a cigarette in the darkness, "tell us all about it."

"There is not much to tell," said Giovanni. "If the challenge arrives, there is nothing to be done but to fight. I took him by the throat and nearly strangled him."

"Whom?" asked Spicca, mournfully.

"Oh! it is Del Ferice," answered Giovanni, who had forgotten that he had not mentioned the name of his probable antagonist. The Prince laughed.

"Del Ferice! Who would have thought it? He is a dead man. What was it all about?"

"That is unnecessary to say here," said Giovanni, quietly.

"He insulted me grossly. I half-strangled him, and told him he was a dog. I suppose he will fight."

"Ah yes; he will probably fight," repeated Spicca, thoughtfully. "What are your weapons, Don Giovanni?"

"Anything he likes."

"But the choice is yours if he challenges," returned the Count.

"As you please. Arrange all that — foils, swords, or pistols."

"You do not seem to take much interest in this affair," remarked Spicca, sadly.

"He is best with foils," said the old Prince.

"Foils or pistols, of course," said the Count. "Swords are child's play."

Satisfied that his seconds meant business, Giovanni sank back in his corner of the carriage, and was silent.

"We had better have the meeting in my villa," said his father. "If it rains, they can fight indoors. I will send for the surgeon at once."

In a few moments they reached the Palazzo Saracinesca. The Prince left word at the porter's lodge that any gentlemen who arrived were to be admitted, and all three went up-stairs. It was half-past two o'clock.

As they entered the apartments, they heard a carriage drive under the great archway below.

"Go to your rooms, Giovannino," said the old Prince. "These fellows are punctual. I will call you when they are gone. I suppose you mean business seriously?"

"I care nothing about him. I will give him any satisfaction he pleases," answered Giovanni. "It is very kind of you to undertake the matter—I am very grateful."

"I would not leave it to anybody else," muttered the old Prince, as he hurried away to meet Del Ferice's seconds.

Giovanni entered his own rooms, and went straight to his writing-table. He took a pen and a sheet of paper and began writing. His face was very grave, but his hand was steady. For more than an hour he wrote without pausing. Then his father entered the room.

"Well?" said Giovanni, looking up.

"It is all settled," said the old gentleman, seriously. "I was afraid they might make some objection to me as a second. You know there is an old clause about near relations acting in such cases. But they declared that they considered my co-operation an honour—so that is all right. You must do your best, my boy. This rascal means to hurt you if he can. Seven o'clock is the time. We must leave here at half-past six. You can sleep two hours and a half. I will sit up and call you. Spicca has gone home to change his clothes, and is coming back immediately. Now lie down. I will see to your foils——"

"It is foils, then?" asked Giovanni, quietly.

"Yes. They made no objection. You had better lie down."

"I will. Father, if anything should happen to me—it may, you know—you will find my keys in this drawer, and this letter, which I beg you will read. It is to yourself."

"Nonsense, my dear boy! Nothing will happen to you—you will just run him through the arm and come home to breakfast."

The old Prince spoke in his rough cheerful way; but his voice trembled, and he turned aside to hide two great tears that had fallen upon his dark cheeks and were losing themselves in his white beard.

CHAPTER XII.

Giovanni slept soundly for two hours. He was very tired with the many emotions of the night, and the arrangements for the meeting being completed, it seemed as though work were over and the pressure removed. It is said that men will sleep for hours when their trial is over and the sentence of death has been passed; and though it was more likely that Del Ferice would be killed than that Giovanni

would be hurt, the latter felt not unlike a man who has
been tried for his life. He had suffered in a couple of
hours almost every emotion of which he was capable—his
love for Corona, long controlled and choked down, had
broken bounds at last, and found expression for itself; he
had in a moment suffered the severest humiliation and the
most sincere sorrow at her reproaches; he had known the
fear of seeing her no more, and the sweetness of pardon
from her own lips; he had found himself on a sudden in
a frenzy of righteous wrath against Del Ferice, and a
moment later he had been forced to hide his anger under
a calm face; and at last, when the night was far spent, he
had received the assurance that in less than four hours he
would have ample opportunity for taking vengeance upon
the cowardly eavesdropper who had so foully got possession
of the one secret he held dear. Worn out with all he had
suffered, and calm in the expectation of the morning's
struggle, Giovanni lay down upon his bed and slept.

Del Ferice, on the contrary, was very wakeful. He had
an unpleasant sensation about his throat as though he had
been hanged, and cut down before he was dead; and he
suffered the unutterable mortification of knowing that, after
a long and successful social career, he had been detected by
his worst enemy in a piece of disgraceful villany. In the
first place, Giovanni might kill him. Del Ferice was a
very good fencer, but Saracinesca was stronger and more
active; there was certainly considerable danger in the duel.
On the other hand, if he survived, Giovanni had him in
his power for the rest of his life, and there was no escape
possible. He had been caught listening—caught in a
flagrantly dishonest trick—and he well knew that if the
matter had been brought before a jury of honour, he would
have been declared incompetent to claim any satisfaction.

It was not the first time Del Ferice had done such
things, but it was the first time he had been caught. He
cursed his awkwardness in oversetting the vase just at the
moment when his game was successfully played to the end
—just when he thought that he began to see land, in having
discovered beyond all doubt that Giovanni was devoted

body and soul to Corona d'Astrardente. The information had been necessary to him, for he was beginning seriously to press his suit with Donna Tullia, and he needed to be sure that Giovanni was not a rival to be feared. He had long suspected Saracinesca's devotion to the dark Duchessa, and by constantly putting himself in his way, he had done his best to excite his jealousy and to stimulate his passion. Giovanni never could have considered Del Ferice as a rival; the idea would have been ridiculous. But the constant annoyance of finding the man by Corona's side, when he desired to be alone with her, had in some measure heightened the effect Del Ferice desired, though it had not actually produced it. Being a good judge of character, he had sensibly reckoned his chances against Giovanni, and he had formed so just an opinion of the man's bold and devoted character as to be absolutely sure that if Saracinesca loved Corona he would not seriously think of marrying Donna Tullia. He had done all he could to strengthen the passion when he guessed it was already growing, and at the very moment when he had received circumstantial evidence of it which placed it beyond all doubt, he had allowed himself to be discovered, through his own unpardonable carelessness.

Evidently the only satisfactory way out of the difficulty was to kill Giovanni outright, if he could do it. In that way he would rid himself of an enemy, and at the same time of the evidence against himself. The question was, how this could be accomplished; for Giovanni was a man of courage, strength, and experience, and he himself—Ugo del Ferice—possessed none of those qualities in any great degree. The result was, that he slept not at all, but passed the night in a state of nervous anxiety by no means conducive to steadiness of hand or calmness of the nerves. He was less pleased than ever when he heard that Giovanni's seconds were his own father and the melancholy Spicca, who was the most celebrated duellist in Italy, in spite of his cadaverous long body, his sad voice, and his expression of mournful resignation to the course of eve

In the event of his neither killing Don Giovanni nor

K

being himself killed, what he most dreaded was the certainty that for the rest of his life he must be in his enemy's power. He knew that, for Corona's sake, Giovanni would not mention the cause of the duel, and no one could have induced him to speak of it himself; but it would be a terrible hindrance in his life to feel at every turn that the man he hated had the power to expose him to the world as a scoundrel of the first water. What he had heard gave him but small influence over Saracinesca, though it was of great value in determining his own action. To say aloud to the world that Giovanni loved the Duchessa d'Astrardente would be of little use. Del Ferice could not, for very shame, tell how he had found it out; and there was no other proof but his evidence, for he guessed that from that time forward the open relations between the two would be even more formal than before—and the most credulous people do not believe in a great fire unless they can see a little smoke. He had not even the advantage of turning the duel to account in his interest with Donna Tullia, since Giovanni could force him to deny that she was implicated in the question, on pain of exposing his treachery. There was palpably no satisfactory way out of the matter unless he could kill his adversary. He would have to leave the country for a while; but Giovanni once dead, it would be easy to make Donna Tullia believe they had fought on her account, and to derive all the advantage there was to be gained from posing before the world as her defender.

But though Del Ferice's rest was disturbed by the contemplation of his difficulties, he did not neglect any precaution which might save his strength for the morrow He lay down upon his bed, stretching himself at full length, and carefully keeping his right arm free, lest, by letting his weight fall upon it as he lay, he should benumb the muscles or stiffen the joints; from time to time he rubbed a little strengthening ointment upon his wrist, and he was careful that the light should not shine in his eyes and weary them. At six o'clock his seconds appeared with the surgeon they had engaged, and the four men were soon driving rapidly down the Corso towards the gate.

So punctual were the two parties that they arrived simultaneously at the gate of the villa which had been selected for the encounter. The old Prince took a key from his pocket and himself opened the great iron gate. The carriages drove in, and the gates were closed by the astonished porter, who came running out as they creaked upon their hinges. The light was already sufficient for the purpose of fencing, as the eight men descended simultaneously before the house. The morning was cloudy, but the ground was dry. The principals and seconds saluted each other formally. Giovanni withdrew to a little distance on one side with his surgeon, and Del Ferice stood aside with his.

The melancholy Spicca, who looked like the shadow of death in the dim morning light, was the first to speak.

"Of course you know the best spot in the villa?" he said to the old Prince.

"As there is no sun, I suggest that they fight upon the ground behind the house. It is hard and dry."

The whole party followed old Saracinesca. Spicca had the foils in a green bag. The place suggested by the Prince seemed in every way adapted, and Del Ferice's seconds made no objection. There was absolutely no choice of position upon the ground, which was an open space about twenty yards square, hard and well rolled, preferable in every way to a grass lawn.

Without further comment, Giovanni took off his coat and waistcoat, and Del Ferice, who looked paler and more unhealthy than usual, followed his example. The seconds crossed sides to examine the principals' shirts, and to assure themselves that they wore no flannel underneath the unstarched linen. This formality being accomplished, the foils were carefully compared, and Giovanni was offered the first choice. He took the one nearest his hand, and the other was carried to Del Ferice. They were simple fencing foils, the buttons being removed and the points sharpened—there was nothing to choose between them. The seconds then each took a sword, and stationed the combatants some seven or eight paces apart, while they

themselves stood a little aside, each upon the right hand
of his principal, and the witnesses placed themselves at
opposite corners of the ground, the surgeons remaining at
the ends behind the antagonists. There was a moment's
pause. When all was ready, old Saracinesca came close
to Giovanni, while Del Ferice's second approached his
principal in like manner.

"Giovanni," said the old Prince, gravely, "as your
second I am bound to recommend you to make any advance in your power towards a friendly understanding.
Can you do so?"

"No, father, I cannot," answered Giovanni, with a
slight smile. His face was perfectly calm, and of a
natural colour. Old Saracinesca crossed the ground, and
met Casalverde, the opposite second, half-way. Each
formally expressed to the other his great regret that no
arrangement would be possible, and then retired again to
the right hand of his principal.

"Gentlemen," said the Prince, in a loud voice, "are you
ready?" As both men bowed their assent, he added
immediately, in a sharp tone of command, "In guard!"

Giovanni and Del Ferice each made a step forward,
saluted each other with their foils, repeated the salute to
the seconds and witnesses, and then came face to face and
fell into position. Each made one thrust in tierce at the
other, in the usual fashion of compliment, each parrying in
the same way.

"Halt!" cried Saracinesca and Casalverde, in the same
breath.

"In guard!" shouted the Prince again, and the duel
commenced.

In a moment the difference between the two men was
apparent. Del Ferice fenced in the Neapolitan style—
his arm straight before him, never bending from the elbow,
making all his play with his wrist, his back straight, and
his knees so much bent that he seemed not more than half
his height. He made his movements short and quick, and
relatively few, in evident fear of tiring himself at the start.
To a casual observer his fence was less graceful than his

antagonist's, his lunges less daring, his parries less brilliant.
But as the old Prince watched him he saw that the point
of his foil advanced and retreated in a perfectly straight
line, and in parrying described the smallest circle possible,
while his cold watery blue eye was fixed steadily upon his
antagonist; old Saracinesca ground his teeth, for he saw
that the man was a most accomplished swordsman.

Giovanni fought with the air of one who defended himself, without much thought of attack. He did not bend so
low as Del Ferice, his arm doubled a little before his lunge,
and his foil occasionally made a wide circle in the air.
He seemed careless, but in strength and elasticity he was
far superior to his enemy, and could perhaps afford to
trust to these advantages, when a man like Del Ferice was
obliged to employ his whole skill and science.

They had been fencing for more than two minutes,
without any apparent result, when Giovanni seemed suddenly to change his tactics. He lowered the point of his
weapon a little, and, keeping it straight before him, began
to press more closely upon his antagonist. Del Ferice
kept his arm at full length, and broke ground for a yard
or two, making clever feints in carte at Giovanni's body,
with the object of stopping his advance. But Giovanni
pressed him, and suddenly made a peculiar movement with
his foil, bringing it in contact with his enemy's along its
length.

"Halt!" cried Casalverde. Both men lowered their
weapons instantly, and the seconds sprang forward and
touched their swords between them. Giovanni bit his lip
angrily.

"Why 'halt'?" asked the Prince, sharply. "Neither
is touched."

"My principal's shoe-string is untied," answered Casalverde, calmly. It was true. "He might easily trip and
fall," explained Del Ferice's friend, bending down and pro
ceeding to tie the silk ribbon. The Prince shrugged his
shoulders, and retired with Giovanni a few steps back.

"Giovanni," he said, in a voice trembling with emotion,
"if you are not more careful, he will do you a mischief.

For heaven's sake run him through the arm and let us be done with it."

"I should have disarmed him that time if his second had not stopped us," said Giovanni, calmly. "He is ready again," he added, "come on."

"In guard!"

Again the two men advanced, and again the foils crossed and recrossed and rang loudly in the cold morning air. Once more Giovanni pressed upon Del Ferice, and Del Ferice broke ground. In answer to a quick feint, Giovanni made a round parry and a sharp short lunge in tierce.

"Halt!" yelled Casalverde. Old Saracinesca sprang in, and Giovanni lowered his weapon. But Casalverde did not interpose his sword. A full two seconds after the cry to halt, Del Ferice lunged right forward. Giovanni thrust out his arm to save his body from the foul attempt—he had not time to raise his weapon. Del Ferice's sharp rapier entered his wrist and tore a long wound nearly to the elbow.

Giovanni said nothing, but his sword dropped from his hand and he turned upon his father, white with rage. The blood streamed down his sleeve, and his surgeon came running towards him.

The old man had understood at a glance the foul play that had been practised, and going forward laid his hand upon the arm of Del Ferice's second.

"Why did you stop them, sir? And where was your sword?" he said in great anger. Del Ferice was leaning upon his friend; a greenish pallor had overspread his face, but there was a smile under his colourless moustache.

"My principal was touched," said Casalverde, pointing to a tiny scratch upon Del Ferice's neck, from which a single drop of blood was slowly oozing.

"Then why did you not prevent your principal from thrusting after you cried the halt?" asked Saracinesca, severely. "You have singularly misunderstood your duties, sir, and when these gentlemen are satisfied, you will be answerable to me."

Casalverde was silent.

"I protest myself wholly satisfied," said Ugo, with a disagreeable smile, as he glanced to where the surgeon was binding up Giovanni's arm.

"Sir," said old Saracinesca, fiercely addressing the second, "I am not here to bandy words with your principal. He may express himself satisfied through you, if he pleases. My principal, through me, expresses his entire dissatisfaction."

"Your principal, Prince," answered Casalverde, coldly, "is unable to proceed, seeing that his right arm is injured."

"My son, sir, fences as readily with his left hand as with his right," returned old Saracinesca.

Del Ferice's face fell, and his smile vanished instantly.

"In that case we are ready," returned Casalverde, unable, however, to conceal his annoyance. He was a friend of Del Ferice's, and would gladly have seen Giovanni run through the body by the foul thrust.

There was a moment's consultation on the other side.

"I will give myself the pleasure of killing that gentleman to-morrow morning," remarked Spicca, as he mournfully watched the surgeon's operations.

"Unless I kill him myself to-day," returned the Prince savagely, in his white beard. "Are you ready, Giovannino?" It never occurred to him to ask his son if he was too badly hurt to proceed.

Giovanni never spoke, but the hot blood had mounted to his temples, and he was dangerously angry. He took the foil they gave him, and felt the point quietly. It was sharp as a needle. He nodded to his father's question, and they resumed their places, the old Prince this time standing on the left, as his son had changed hands. Del Ferice came forward rather timidly. His courage had sustained him so far, but the consciousness of having done a foul deed, and the sight of the angry man before him, were beginning to make him nervous. He felt uncomfortable, too, at the idea of fencing against a left-handed antagonist.

Giovanni made one or two lunges, and then, with a strange movement unlike anything any one present was acquainted with, seemed to wind his blade round Del

Ferice's, and, with a violent jerk of the wrist, sent the weapon flying across the open space. It struck a window of the house, and crashed through the panes.

"More broken glass!" said Giovanni scornfully, as he lowered his point and stepped back two paces. "Take another sword, sir," he said; "I will not kill you defenceless."

"Good heavens, Giovannino!" exclaimed his father in the greatest excitement; "where on earth did you learn that trick?"

"On my travels, father," returned Giovanni, with a smile; "where you tell me I learned so much that was bad. He looks frightened," he added in a low voice, as he glanced at Del Ferice's livid face.

"He has cause," returned the Prince, "if he ever had in his life!"

Casalverde and his witness advanced from the other side with a fresh pair of foils; for the one that had gone through the window could not be recovered at once, and was probably badly bent by the twist it had received. The gentlemen offered Giovanni his choice.

"If there is no objection I will keep the one I have," said he to his father. The foils were measured, and were found to be alike. The two gentlemen retired, and Del Ferice chose a weapon.

"That is right," said Spicca, as he slowly went back to his place. "You should never part with an old friend."

"We are ready!" was called from the opposite side.

"In guard, then!" cried the Prince. The angry flush had not subsided from Giovanni's forehead, as he again went forward. Del Ferice came up like a man who has suddenly made up his mind to meet death, with a look of extraordinary determination on his pale face.

Before they had made half-a-dozen passes Ugo slipped, or pretended to slip, and fell upon his right knee; but as he came to the ground, he made a sharp thrust upwards under Giovanni's extended left arm.

"The old Prince uttered a fearful oath, that rang and echoed along the walls of the ancient villa. Del Ferice had executed the celebrated feint known long ago as the "Colpo del Tancredi," "Tancred's lunge," from the supposed name of its inventor. It is now no longer permitted in duelling. But the deadly thrust loses half its danger, against a left-handed man. The foil grazed the flesh on Giovanni's left side, and the blood again stained his white shirt. In the moment when Del Ferice slipped, Giovanni had made a straight and deadly lunge at his body, and the sword, instead of passing through Ugo's lungs, ran swift and sure through his throat, with such force that the iron guard struck the falling man's jaw with tremendous impetus, before the oath the old Prince had uttered was fairly out of his mouth.

Seconds and witnesses and surgeons sprang forward hastily. Del Ferice lay upon his side; he had fallen so heavily and suddenly as to wrench the sword from Giovanni's grip. The old Prince gave one look, and dragged his son away.

"He is as dead as a stone," he muttered, with a savage gleam in his eyes.

Giovanni hastily began to dress, without paying any attention to the fresh wound he had received in the last encounter. In the general excitement, his surgeon had joined the group about the fallen man. Before Giovanni had got his overcoat on he came back with Spicca, who looked crestfallen and disappointed.

"He is not dead at all," said the surgeon. "You did the thing with a master's hand—you ran his throat through without touching the jugular artery or the spine."

"Does he want to go on?" asked Giovanni, so savagely that the three men stared at him.

"Do not be so bloodthirsty, Giovannino," said the old Prince, reproachfully.

"I should be justified in going back and killing him as he lies there," said the younger Saracinesca, fiercely. "He nearly murdered me twice this morning."

"That is true," said the Prince, "the dastardly brute!"

"By the bye," said Spicca, lighting a cigarette, "I am afraid I have deprived you of the pleasure of dealing with the man who called himself Del Ferice's second. I just took the opportunity of having a moment's private conversation with him—wé disagreed a little."

"Oh, very well," growled the Prince; "as you please. I daresay I shall have enough to do in taking care of Giovanni to-morrow. That is a villanous bad scratch on his arm."

"Bah! it is nothing to mention, save for the foul way it was given," said Giovanni between his teeth.

Once more old Saracinesca and Spicca crossed the ground. There was a word of formality exchanged, to the effect that both combatants were satisfied, and then Giovanni and his party moved off, Spicca carrying his green bag of foils under his arm, and puffing clouds of smoke into the damp morning air. They had been nearly an hour on the ground, and were chilled with cold, and exhausted for want of sleep. They entered their carriage and drove rapidly homewards.

"Come in and breakfast with us," said the old Prince to Spicca, as they reached the Palazzo Saracinesca.

"Thank you, no," answered the melancholy man. "I have much to do, as I shall go to Paris to-morrow morning by the ten o'clock train. Can I do anything for you there? I shall be absent some months."

"I thought you were going to fight to-morrow," objected the Prince.

"Exactly. It will be convenient for me to leave the country immediately afterwards."

The old man shuddered. With all his fierce blood and headstrong passion, he could not comprehend the fearful calm of this strange man, whose skill was such that he regarded his adversary's death as a matter of course whenever he so pleased. As for Giovanni, he was still so angry that he cared little for the issue of the second duel.

"I am sincerely grateful for your kind offices," he said, as Spicca took leave of him.

"You shall be amply revenged of the two attempts to murder you," said Spicca, quietly; and so, having shaken hands with all, he again entered the carriage. It was the last they saw of him for a long time. He faithfully fulfilled his programme. He met Casalverde on the following morning at seven o'clock, and at precisely a quarter past, he left him dead on the field. He breakfasted with his seconds at half-past eight, and left Rome with them for Paris at ten o'clock. He had selected two French officers who were about to return to their home, in order not to inconvenience any of his friends by obliging them to leave the country; which showed that, even in moments of great excitement, Count Spicca was thoughtful of others.

When the surgeon had dressed Giovanni's wounds, he left the father and son together. Giovanni lay upon a couch in his own sitting-room, eating his breakfast as best he could with one hand. The old Prince paced the floor, commenting from time to time upon the events of the morning.

"It is just as well that you did not kill him, Giovannino," he remarked; "it would have been a nuisance to have been obliged to go away just now."

Giovanni did not answer.

"Of course, duelling is a great sin, and is strictly forbidden by our religion," said the Prince suddenly. "But then——"

"Precisely," returned Giovanni. "We nevertheless cannot always help ourselves."

"I was going to say," continued his father, "that it is, of course, very wicked, and if one is killed in a duel, one probably goes straight into hell. But then—it was worth something to see how you sent that fellow's foil flying through the window!"

"It is a very simple trick. If you will take a foil, I will teach it to you."

"Presently, presently; when you have finished your breakfast. Tell me, why did you say, 'more broken glass'?"

Giovanni bit his lip, remembering his imprudence.

"I hardly know. I believe it suggested something to my mind. One says all sorts of foolish things in moments of excitement."

"It struck me as a very odd remark," answered the Prince, still walking about. "By the bye," he added, pausing before the writing-table, "here is that letter you wrote for me. Do you want me to read it?"

"No," said Giovanni, with a laugh. "It is of no use now. It would seem absurd, since I am alive and well. It was only a word of farewell."

The Prince laughed too, and threw the sealed letter into the fire.

"The last of the Saracinesca is not dead yet," he said. "Giovanni, what are we to say to the gossips? All Rome will be ringing with this affair before night. Of course, you must stay at home for a few days, or you will catch cold in your arm. I will go out and carry the news of our victory."

"Better to say nothing about it—better to refer people to Del Ferice, and tell them he challenged me. Come in!" cried Giovanni, in answer to a knock at the door. Pasquale, the old butler, entered the room.

"The Duca d'Astrardente has sent to inquire after the health of his Excellency Don Giovanni," said the old man, respectfully.

The elder Saracinesca paused in his walk, and broke out into a loud laugh.

"Already! You see, Giovannino," he said. "Tell him, Pasquale, that Don Giovanni caught a severe cold at the ball last night—or no—wait! What shall we say, Giovannino?"

"Tell the servant," said Giovanni, sternly, "that I am much obliged for the kind inquiry, that I am perfectly well, and that you have just seen me eating my breakfast."

Pasquale bowed and left the room.

"I suppose you do not want her to know——" said the Prince, who had suddenly recovered his gravity.

Giovanni bowed his head silently.

"Quite right, my boy," said the old man, gravely. "I do not want to know anything about it either. How the devil could they have found out?"

The question was addressed more to himself than to his

son, and the latter volunteered no answer. He was grateful to his father for his considerate silence.

CHAPTER XIII.

When Astrardente saw the elder Saracinesca's face during his short interview with the diplomatist, his curiosity was immediately aroused. He perceived that there was something the matter, and he proceeded to try and ascertain the circumstances from his acquaintance. The ambassador returned to his *pâté* and his champagne with an air of amused interest, but vouchsafed no information whatever.

"What a singularly amusing fellow old Saracinesca is!" remarked Astrardente.

"When he likes to be," returned his Excellency, with his mouth full.

"On the contrary—when he least meditates it. I never knew a man better suited for a successful caricature. Indeed he is not a bad caricature of his own son, or his own son of him—I am not sure which."

The ambassador laughed a little and took a large mouthful.

"Ha! ha! very good," he mumbled as he ate. "He would appreciate that. He loves his own race. He would rather feel that he is a comic misrepresentation of the most hideous Saracinesca who ever lived, than possess all the beauty of the Astrardente and be called by another name."

The diplomatist paused for a second after this speech, and then bowed a little to the Duchessa; but the hit had touched her husband in a sensitive spot. The old dandy had been handsome once, in a certain way, and he did his best, by artificial means, to preserve some trace of his good looks. The Duchessa smiled faintly.

"I would wager," said Astrardente, sourly, "that his excited manner just now was due to one of two things—

either his vanity or his money is in danger. As for the way he yelled after Spicca, it looked as though there were a duel in the air—fancy the old fellow fighting a duel! Too ridiculous!"

"A duel!" repeated Corona in a low voice.

"I do not see anything so very ridiculous in it," said the diplomatist, slowly twisting his glass of champagne in his fingers, and then sipping it. "Besides," he added deliberately, glancing at the Duchessa from the corner of his eyes, "he has a son."

Corona started very slightly.

"Why should there be a duel?" she asked.

"It was your husband who suggested the idea," returned the diplomatist.

"But you said there was nothing ridiculous in it," objected the Duchessa.

"But I did not say there was any truth in it, either," answered his Excellency with a reassuring smile. "What made you think of duelling?" he asked, turning to Astrardente.

"Spicca," said the latter. "Wherever Spicca is concerned there is a duel. He is a terrible fellow, with his death's-head and dangling bones—one of those extraordinary phenomena—bah! it makes one shiver to think of him!" The old fellow made the sign of the horns with his forefinger and little finger, hiding his thumb in the palm of his hand, as though to protect himself against the evil eye—the sinister influence invoked by the mention of Spicca. Old Astrardente was very superstitious. The ambassador laughed, and even Corona smiled a little.

"Yes," said the diplomatist, "Spicca is a living *memento mori;* he occasionally reminds men of death by killing them."

"How horrible!" exclaimed Corona.

"Ah, my dear lady, the world is full of horrible things."

"That is not a reason for making jests of them."

"It is better to make light of the inevitable," said Astrardente. "Are you ready to go home, my dear?"

"Quite—I was only waiting for you," answered Corona, who longed to be at home and alone.

"Let me know the result of old Saracinesca's warlike undertakings," said Astrardente, with a cunning smile on his painted face. "Of course, as he consulted you, he will send you word in the morning."

"You seem so anxious that there should be a duel, that I should almost be tempted to invent an account of one, lest you should be too grievously disappointed," returned the diplomatist.

"You know very well that no invention will be necessary," said the Duca, pressing him, for his curiosity was roused.

"Well—as you please to consider it. Good night," replied the ambassador. It had amused him to annoy Astrardente a little, and he left him with the pleasant consciousness of having excited the inquisitive faculty of his friend to its highest pitch, without giving it anything to feed upon.

Men who have to do with men, rather than with things, frequently take a profound and seemingly cruel delight in playing upon the feelings and petty vanities of their fellow-creatures. The habit is as strong with them as the constant practice of conjuring becomes with a juggler; even when he is not performing, he will for hours pass coins, perform little tricks of sleight-of-hand with cards, or toss balls in the air in marvellously rapid succession, unable to lay aside his profession even for a day, because it has grown to be the only natural expression of his faculties. With men whose business it is to understand other men, it is the same. They cannot be in a man's company for a quarter of an hour without attempting to discover the peculiar weaknesses of his character—his vanities, his tastes, his vices, his curiosity, his love of money or of reputation; so that the operation of such men's minds may be compared to the process of auscultation—for their ears are always upon their neighbours' hearts—and their conversation to the percutations of a physician to ascertain the seat of disease in a pair of consumptive lungs.

But, with all his failings, Astrardente was a man of considerable acuteness of moral vision. He had made a

shrewd guess at Saracinesca's business, and had further
gathered from a remark dropped by his diplomatic friend,
that if there was to be a duel at all, it would be fought by
Giovanni. As a matter of fact, the ambassador himself knew
nothing certainly concerning the matter, or it is possible
that, for the sake of observing the effect of the news upon
the Duchessa, he would have told the whole truth; for he
had of course heard the current gossip concerning Giovanni's
passion for her, and the experiment would have been too
attractive and interesting to be missed. As it was, she had
started at the mention of Saracinesca's son. The diplomatist
only did what every one else who came near Corona attempted to do at that time, in endeavouring to ascertain
whether she herself entertained any feeling for the man whom
the gossips had set down as her most devoted admirer.

Poor Duchessa! It was no wonder that she had started
at the idea that Giovanni was in trouble. He had played
a great part in her life that day, and she could not forget
him. She had hardly as yet had time to think of what
she felt, for it was only by a supreme effort that she had
been able to bear the great strain upon her strength. If
she had not loved him, it would have been different; and
in the strange medley of emotions through which she was
passing, she wished that she might never have loved—that,
loving, she might be allowed wholly to forget her love,
and to return by some sudden miracle to that cold dreamy
state of indifference to all other men, and of unfailing
thoughtfulness for her husband, from which she had been
so cruelly awakened. She would have given anything to
have not loved, now that the great struggle was over; but
until the supreme moment had come, she had not been
willing to put the dangerous thought from her, saving in
those hours of prayer and solitary suffering, when the
whole truth rose up clearly before her in its undisguised
nakedness. So soon as she had gone into the world, she
had recklessly longed for Giovanni Saracinesca's presence.

But now it was all changed. She had not deceived
herself when she had told him that she would rather not
see him any more. It was true; not only did she wish

not to see him, but she earnestly desired that the love of
him might pass from her heart. With a sudden longing,
her thoughts went back to the old convent-life of her girlhood, with its regular occupations, its constant religious
exercises, its narrowness of view, and its unchanging simplicity. What mattered narrowness, when all beyond that
close limitation was filled with evil? Was it not better
that the lips should be busy with singing litanies than
that the heart should be tormented by temptation? Were
not those simple tasks, that had seemed so all-important
then, more sweet in the performance than the manifold
duties of this complicated social existence, this vast web
and woof of life's loom, this great machinery that worked
and groaned and rolled endlessly upon its wheels without
producing any more result than the ceaseless turning of a
prison treadmill? But there was no way out of life now;
there was no escape, as there was also no prospect of relief,
from care and anxiety. There was no reason why Giovanni
should go away—no reason either why Corona should ever
love him less. She belonged to a class of women, if there
are enough of them to be called a class, who, where love is
concerned, can feel but one impression, which becomes in
their hearts the distinctive seal and mark of their lives, for
good or for evil. Corona was indeed so loyal and good a
woman, that the strong pressure of her love could not
abase her nobility, nor put untruth where all was so true;
but the sign of her love for Giovanni was upon her for
ever. The vacant place in her heart had been filled, and
filled wholly; the bulwark she had reared against the love
of man was broken down and swept away, and the waters
flowed softly over its place and remembered it not. She
would never be the same woman again, and it was bitter
to her to feel it: for ever the face of Giovanni would
haunt her waking hours and visit her dreams unbidden,—
a perpetual reproach to her, a perpetual memory of the
most desperate struggle of her life, and more than a memory
—the undying present of an unchanging love.

She was quite sure of herself in future, as she also
trusted sincerely in Giovanni's promise. There should be

no moment of weakness, no word should ever fall from her
lips to tempt him to a fresh outbreak of passionate words
and acts; her life should be measured in the future by the
account of the dangers past, and there should be no instant
of unguarded conduct, no hour wherein even to herself she
would say it was sweet to love and to be loved.   It was
indeed not sweet, but bitter as death itself, to feel that
weight at her heart, that constant toiling effort in her mind
to keep down the passion in her breast.   But Corona had
sacrificed much; she would sacrifice this also; she would
get strength by her prayers and courage from her high
pride, and she would smile to all the world as she had
never smiled before.   She could trust herself, for she was
doing the right and trampling upon the wrong.   But the
suffering would be none the less for all her pride; there
was no concealing it—it would be horrible.   To meet him
daily in the world, to speak to him and to hear his voice,
perhaps to touch his hand, and all the while to smile
coldly, and to be still and for ever above suspicion, while
her own burning consciousness accused her of the past,
and seemed to make the dangers of mere living yawn
beside her path at every step,—all this would be terrible
to bear, but by God's help she would bear it to the end.

But now a new horror seized her, and terrified her
beyond measure.   This rumour of a duel—a mere word
dropped carelessly in conversation by a thoughtless acquaintance—called up to her sudden visions of evil to
come.   Surely, howsoever she might struggle against love
and beat it roughly to silence in her breast, it was not
wrong to fear danger for Giovanni,—it could not be a sin
to dread the issue of peril when it was all so very near to
her.   It might perhaps not be true, for people in the world
are willing to amuse their empty minds with empty tales,
acknowledging the emptiness.   It could not be true; she
had seen Giovanni but a moment before—he would have
given some hint, some sign.

Why—after all?   Was it not the boast of such men
that they could face the world and wear an indifferent
look, at times of the greatest anxiety and danger?   But,

again, if Giovanni had been involved in a quarrel so serious as to require the arbitrament of blood, some rumour of it would have reached her. She had talked with many men that night, and with some women— gossips all, whose tongues wagged merrily over the troubles of friend or foe, and who would have battened upon any- thing so novel as a society duel, as a herd of jackals upon the dead body of one of their fellows, to make their feast off it with a light heart. Some one of all these would have told her; the quarrel would have been common property in half an hour, for somebody must have wit- nessed it.

It was a consolation to Corona to reflect upon the extreme improbability of the story; for when the diplo- matist was gone, her husband dwelt upon it—whether because he could not conceal his unsatisfied curiosity, or from other motives, it was hard to tell.

Astrardente led his wife from the supper-table through the great rooms, now almost deserted, and past the wide doors of the hall where the cotillon was at its height. They paused a moment and looked in, as Giovanni had done a quarter of an hour earlier. It was a magnificent scene; the lights flashed back from the jewels of fair women, and surged in the dance as starlight upon rippling waves. The air was heavy with the odour of the countless flowers that filled the deep recesses of the windows, and were distributed in hundreds of nosegays for the figures of the cotillon; enchanting strains of waltz music seemed to float down from above and inspire the crowd of men and women with harmonious motion, so that sound was made visible by translation into graceful movement. As Corona looked there was a pause, and the crowd parted, while a huge tiger, the heraldic beast of the Frangipani family, was drawn into the hall by the young prince and Bianca Valdarno. The magnificent skin had been so artfully stuffed as to convey a startling impression of life, and in the creature's huge jaws hung a great basket filled with tiny tigers, which were to be distributed as badges for the dance by the leaders. A wild burst of applause greeted this novel figure, and every one ran forward to obtain a nearer view.

"Ah!" exclaimed old Astrardente, "I envy them that invention, my dear; it is perfectly magnificent. You must have a tiger to take home. How fortunate we were to be in time!" He forced his way into the crowd, leaving his wife alone for a moment by the door; and he managed to catch Valdarno, who was distributing the little emblems to right and left. Madame Mayer's quick eyes had caught sight of Corona and her husband, and from some instinct of curiosity she made towards the Duchessa. She was still angry, as she had never been in her short life, at Giovanni's rudeness in forgetting her dance, and she longed to inflict some wound upon the beautiful woman who had led him into such forgetfulness. When Astrardente left his wife's side, Donna Tullia pressed forward with her partner in the general confusion that followed upon the entrance of the tiger, and she managed to pass close to Corona. She looked up suddenly with an air of surprise.

"What! not dancing, Duchessa?" she asked. "Has your partner gone home?"

With the look that accompanied the question, it was an insulting speech enough. Had Donna Tullia seen old Astrardente close behind her, she would not have made it. The old dandy was returning in triumph in possession of the little tiger-badge for Corona. He heard the words, and observed with inward pleasure his wife's calm look of indifference.

"Madam," he said, placing himself suddenly in Madame Mayer's way, "my wife's partners do not go home while she remains."

"Oh, I see," returned Donna Tullia, flushing quickly; "the Duchessa is dancing the cotillon with you. I beg your pardon—I had forgotten that you still danced."

"Indeed it is long since I did myself the honour of asking you for a quadrille, madam," answered Astrardente with a polite smile; and so saying, he turned and presented the little tiger to his wife with a courtly bow. There was good blood in the old *roué*.

Corona was touched by his thoughtfulness in wishing to get her the little keepsake of the dance, and she was still more affected by his ready defence of her. He was indeed sometimes a little ridiculous, with his paint and his artificial smile—he was often petulant and unreasonable in little things; but he was never unkind to her, nor discourteous. In spite of her cold and indifferent stare at Donna Tullia, she had keenly felt the insult, and she was grateful to the old man for taking her part. Knowing what she knew of herself that night, she was deeply sensible to his kindness. She took the little gift, and laid her hand upon his arm.

"Forgive me," she said, as they moved away, "if I am ever ungrateful to you. You are so very good to me. I know no one so courteous and kind as you are."

Her husband looked at her in delight. He loved her sincerely with all that remained of him. There was something sad in the thought of a man like him finding the only real passion of his life when worn out with age and dissipation. Her little speech raised him to the seventh heaven of joy.

"I am the happiest man in all Rome," he said, assuming his most jaunty walk, and swinging his hat gaily between his thumb and finger. But a current of deep thought was stirring in him as he went down the broad staircase by his wife's side. He was thinking what life might have been to him had he found Corona del Carmine—how could he? she was not born then—had he found her, or her counterpart, thirty years ago. He was wondering what conceivable sacrifice there could be which he would not make to regain his youth—even to have his life lived out and behind him, if he could only have looked back to thirty years of marriage with Corona. How differently he would have lived, how very differently he would have thought! how his whole memory would be full of the sweet past, and would be common with her own past life, which, to her too, would be sweet to ponder on! He would have been such a good man—so true to her in all those years! But they were gone, and he had not found her until his foot was on the edge of the grave—until he could hardly count on one year more of a pitiful artificial life, painted, bewigged, stuffed to the semblance of a man by a clever tailor—and she in the bloom of her glory beside him! What he would have given to have old Saracinesca's strength and fresh vitality — old Saracinesca whom he hated! Yes, with all that hair—it was white, but a little dye would change it. What was a little dye compared with the profound artificiality of his own outer man? How the old fellow's deep voice rang, loud and clear, from his broad chest! How strong he was, with his firm step, and his broad brown hands, and his fiery black eyes! He hated him for the greenness of his age—he hated him for his stalwart son, another of those long-lived fierce Sara-cinesca, who seemed destined to outlive time. He himself had no children, no relations, no one to bear his name—he had only a beautiful young wife and much wealth, with just enough strength left to affect a gay walk when he was with her, and to totter unsteadily to his couch when he was alone, worn out with the effort of trying to seem young.

As they sat in their carriage he thought bitterly of all these things, and never spoke. Corona herself was weary, and glad to be silent. They went up-stairs, and as she took his arm, she gently tried to help him rather than be helped. He noticed it, and made an effort, but he was very tired. He paused upon the landing, and looked at her, and a gentle and sad smile stole over his face, such as Corona had never seen there.

"Shall we go into your boudoir for ten minutes, my love?" he said; "or will you come into my smoking-room? I would like to smoke a little before going to bed."

"You may smoke in my boudoir, of course," she answered kindly, though she was surprised at the request. It was half-past three o'clock. They went into the softly lighted little room, where the embers of the fire were still glowing upon the hearth. Corona dropped her furs upon a chair, and sat down upon one side of the chimneypiece.

Astrardente sank wearily into a deep easy-chair opposite her, and having found a cigarette, lighted it, and began to smoke. He seemed in a mood which Corona had never seen. After a short silence he spoke.

"Corona," he said, "I love you." His wife looked up with a gentle smile, and in her determination to be loyal to him she almost forgot that other man who had said those words but two hours before, so differently.

"Yes," he said, with a sigh, "you have heard it before —it is not new to you. I think you believe it. You are good, but you do not love me—no, do not interrupt me, my dear; I know what you would say. How should you love me? I am an old man—very old, older than my years." Again he sighed, more bitterly, as he confessed what he had never owned before. The Duchessa was too much astonished to answer him.

"Corona," he said again, "I shall not live much longer."

"Ah, do not speak like that," she cried suddenly. "I trust and pray that you have yet many years to live." Her husband looked keenly at her.

"You are so good," he answered, "that you are really capable of uttering such a prayer, absurd as it would seem."

"Why absurd? It is unkind of you to say it——"

"No, my dear; I know the world very well. That is all. I suppose it is impossible for me to make you understand how I love you. It must seem incredible to you, in the magnificence of your strength and beautiful youth, that a man like me—an artificial man"—he laughed scornfully —"a creature of paint and dye—let me be honest—a creature with a wig, should be capable of a mad passion. And yet, Corona," he added, his thin cracked voice trembling with a real emotion, "I do love you—very dearly. There are two things that make my life bitter: the regret that I did not meet you, that you were not born, when I was young; and worse than that, the knowledge that I must leave you very soon—I, the exhausted dandy, the shadow of what I was, tottering to my grave in a last vain effort to be young for your sake—for your sake, Corona dear. Ah, it is contemptible!" he almost moaned.

Corona hid her eyes in her hand. She was taken off her
guard by his strange speech.

"Oh, do not speak like that—do not!" she cried. "You
make me very unhappy. Do I reproach you? Do I ever
make you feel that you are—older than I? I will lead a
new life; you shall never think of it again. You are too
kind—too good for me."

"No one ever said I was too good before," replied the old
man with a shade of sadness. "I am glad the one person
who finds me good, should be the only one for whose sake
I ever cultivated goodness. I could have been different,
Corona, if I had had you for my wife for thirty years, instead of five. But it is too late now. Before long I shall
be dead, and you will be free."

"What makes you say such things to me?" asked
Corona. "Can you think I am so vile, so ungrateful, so
unloving, as to wish your death?"

"Not unloving; no, my dear child. But not loving,
either. I do not ask impossibilities. You will mourn for
me a while—my poor soul will rest in peace if you feel one
moment of real regret for me, for your old husband, before
you take another. Do not cry, Corona, dearest; it is the
way of the world. We waste our youth in scoffing at
reality, and in the unrealness of our old age the present no
longer avails us much. You know me, perhaps you despise
me. You would not have scorned me when I was young—
oh, how young I was! how strong and vain of my youth,
thirty years ago!"

"Indeed, indeed, no such thought ever crossed my mind.
I give you all I have," cried Corona, in great distress; "I
will give you more—I will devote my whole life to you——"

"You do, my dear. I am sensible of it," said Astrardente,
quietly. "You cannot do more, if you will; you cannot
make me young again, nor take away the bitterness of death
—of a death that leaves you behind."

Corona leaned forward; staring into the dying embers of
the fire, one hand supporting her chin. The tears stood in
her eyes and on her cheeks. The old dandy in his genuine
misery had excited her compassion.

"I would mourn you long," she said. "You may have wasted your life; you say so. I would love you more if I could, God knows. You have always been to me a courteous gentleman and a faithful husband."

The old man rose with difficulty from his deep chair, and came and stood by her, and took the hand that lay idle on her knees. She looked up at him.

"If I thought my blessing were worth anything, I would bless you for what you say. But I would not have you waste your youth. Youth is that which, being wasted, is like water poured out upon the ground. You must marry again, and marry soon—do not start. You will inherit all my fortune; you will have my title. It must descend to your children. It has come to an unworthy end in me; it must be revived in you."

"How can you think of it? Are you ill?" asked Corona kindly, pressing gently his thin hand in hers. "Why do you dwell on the idea of death to-night?"

"I am ill; yes, past all cure, my dear," said the old man, gently raising her hand to his lips, and kissing it.

"What do you mean?" asked Corona, suddenly rising to her feet and laying her hand affectionately upon his shoulder. "Why have you never told me?"

"Why should I tell you—except that it is near, and you must be prepared? Why should I burden you with anxiety? But you were so gentle and kind to-night, upon the stairs," he said, with some hesitation, "that I thought perhaps it would be a relief to you to know—to know that it is not for long."

There was something so gentle in his tone, so infinitely pathetic in his thought that possibly he might lighten the burden his wife bore so bravely, there was something at last so human in the loving regret with which he spoke, that Corona forgot all his foolish ways, his wig and his false teeth and his petty vanities, and letting her head fall upon his shoulder, burst into passionate tears.

"Oh no, no!" she sobbed. "It must be a long time yet; you must not die!"

"It may be a year, not more," he said gently. "God

bless you for those tears, Corona—the tears you have shed
for me. Good night, my dearest."

He let her sink upon her chair, and his hand rested for
one moment upon her raven hair. Then with a last remnant of energy he quickly left the room.

CHAPTER XIV.

Such affairs as the encounter between Giovanni and Del
Ferice were very rare in Rome. There were many duels
fought; but, as a general rule, they were not very serious,
and the first slight wound decided the matter in hand to
the satisfaction of both parties. But here there had been
a fight for life and death. One of the combatants had
received two such wounds as would have been sufficient to
terminate an ordinary meeting, and the other was lying at
death's door stabbed through the throat. Society was
frantic with excitement. Giovanni was visited by scores
of acquaintances, whom he allowed to be admitted, and he
talked with them cheerfully, in order to have it thoroughly
known that he was not badly hurt. Del Ferice's lodging
was besieged by the same young gentlemen of leisure, who
went directly from one to the other, anxious to get all the
news in their power. But Del Ferice's door was guarded
jealously from intruders by his faithful Neapolitan servant
—a fellow who knew more about his master than all the
rest of Rome together, but who had such a dazzlingly
brilliant talent for lying as to make him a safe repository
for any secret committed to his keeping. On the present
occasion, however, he had small use for duplicity. He sat
all day long by the open door, for he had removed the
bell-handle, lest the ringing should disturb his master. He
had a basket into which he dropped the cards of the visitors
who called, answering each inquiry with the same unchanging words:

"He is very ill, the signorino. Do not make any noise."

"Where is he hurt?" the visitor would ask. Whereupon Temistocle pointed to his throat.

"Will he live?" was the next question; to which the
man answered by raising his shoulders to his ears, elevating
his eyebrows, and at the same time shutting his eyes, while
he spread out the palms of his hands over his basket of
cards—whereby he meant to signify that he did not know,
but doubted greatly. It being impossible to extract any
further information from him, the visitor had nothing left
but to leave his card and turn away. Within, the wounded
man was watched by a Sister of Mercy. The surgeon
had pronounced his recovery probable if he had proper
care: the wound was a dangerous one, but not likely to
prove mortal unless the patient died of the fever or of
exhaustion.

The young gentlemen of leisure who thus obtained the
news of the two duellists, lost no time in carrying it from
house to house. Giovanni himself sent twice in the course
of the day to inquire after his antagonist, and received by
his servant the answer which was given to everybody. By
the time the early winter night was descending upon Rome,
there were two perfectly well-authenticated stories circulated
in regard to the cause of the quarrel—neither of which, of
course, contained a grain of truth. In the first place, it
was confidently asserted by one party, represented by Valdarno and his set, that Giovanni had taken offence at Del
Ferice for having proposed to call him to be examined
before the Duchessa d'Astrardente in regard to his absence
from town: that this was a palpable excuse for picking a
quarrel, because it was well known that Saracinesca loved
the Astrardente, and that Del Ferice was always in his
way.

"Giovanni is a rough fellow," remarked Valdarno, "and
will not stand any opposition, so he took the first opportunity of getting the man out of the way. Do you see?
The old story—jealous of the wrong man. Can one be
jealous of Del Ferice? Bah!"

"And who would have been the right man to attack?"
was asked.

"Her husband, of course," returned Valdarno with a sneer. "That angel of beauty has the ineffably eccentric idea that she loves that old transparency, that old magic-lantern slide of a man!"

On the other hand, there was a party of people who affirmed, as beyond all doubt, that the duel had been brought about by Giovanni's forgetting his dance with Donna Tullia. Del Ferice was naturally willing to put himself forward in her defence, reckoning on the favour he would gain in her eyes. He had spoken sharply to Giovanni about it, and told him he had behaved in an un-gentlemanly manner—whereupon Giovanni had answered that it was none of his business; an altercation had ensued in a remote room in the Frangipani palace, and Giovanni had lost his temper and taken Del Ferice by the throat, and otherwise greatly insulted him. The result had been the duel in which Del Ferice had been nearly killed. There was a show of truth about this story, and it was told in such a manner as to make Del Ferice appear as the injured party. Indeed, whichever tale were true, there was no doubt that the two men had disliked each other for a long time, and that they were both looking out for the oppor-tunity of an open disagreement.

Old Saracinesca appeared in the afternoon, and was sur-rounded by eager questioners of all sorts. The fact of his having served his own son in the capacity of second excited general astonishment. Such a thing had not been heard of in the annals of Roman society, and many ancient wisdom-mongers severely censured the course he had pursued. Could anything be more abominably unnatural? Was it possible to conceive of the hard-heartedness of a man who could stand quietly and see his son risk his life? Disgraceful!

The old Prince either would not tell what he knew, or had no information to give. The latter theory was im-probable. Some one made a remark to that effect.

"But, Prince," the man said, "would you second your own son in an affair without knowing the cause of the quarrel?"

"Sir," returned the old man, proudly, "my son asked my assistance; I did not sell it to him for his confidence." People knew the old man's obstinacy, and had to be satisfied with his short answers, for he was himself as quarrelsome as a Berserker or as one of his own irascible ancestors.

He met Donna Tullia in the street. She stopped her carriage, and beckoned him to come to her. She looked paler than Saracinesca had ever seen her, and was much excited.

"How could you let them fight?" were her first words.

"It could not be helped. The quarrel was too serious. No one would more gladly have prevented it than I; but as my son had so desperately insulted Del Ferice, he was bound to give him satisfaction."

"Satisfaction!" cried Donna Tullia. "Do you call it satisfaction to cut a man's throat? What was the real cause of the quarrel?"

"I do not know."

"Do not tell me that—I do not believe you," answered Donna Tullia, angrily.

"I give you my word of honour that I do not know," returned the Prince.

"That is different. Will you get in and drive with me for a few minutes?"

"At your commands." Saracinesca opened the carriage-door and got in.

"We shall astonish the world; but I do not care," said Donna Tullia. "Tell me, is Don Giovanni seriously hurt?"

"No—a couple of scratches that will heal in a week. Del Ferice is very seriously wounded."

"I know," answered Donna Tullia, sadly. "It is dreadful—I am afraid it was my fault."

"How so?" asked Saracinesca, quickly. He had not heard the story of the forgotten waltz, and was really ignorant of the original cause of disagreement. He guessed, however, that Donna Tullia was not so much concerned in it as the Duchessa d'Astrardente.

"Your son was very rude to me," said Madame Mayer. "Perhaps I ought not to tell you, but it is best you should know. He was engaged to dance with me the last waltz but one before the cotillon. He forgot me, and I found him with that—with a lady—talking quietly."

"With whom did you say?" asked Saracinesca, very gravely.

"With the Astrardente—if you will know," returned Donna Tullia, her anger at the memory of the insult bringing the blood suddenly to her face.

"My dear lady," said the old Prince, "in the name of my son I offer you the humble apologies which he will make in person when he is well enough to ask your forgiveness."

"I do not want apologies," answered Madame Mayer, turning her face away.

"Nevertheless they shall be offered. But, pardon my curiosity, how did Del Ferice come to be concerned in that incident?"

"He was with me when I found Don Giovanni with the Duchessa. It is very simple. I was very angry— I am very angry still; but I would not have had Don Giovanni risk his life on my account for anything, nor poor Del Ferice either. I am horribly upset about it all."

Old Saracinesca wondered whether Donna Tullia's vanity would suffer if he told her that the duel had not been fought for anything which concerned her. But he reflected that her supposition was very plausible, and that he himself had no evidence. Furthermore, and in spite of his good-natured treatment of Giovanni, he was very angry at the thought that his son had quarrelled about the Duchessa. When Giovanni should be recovered from his wounds he intended to speak his mind to him. But he was sorry for Donna Tullia, for he liked her in spite of her eccentricities, and would have been satisfied to see her married to his son. He was a practical man, and he took a prosaic view of the world. Donna Tullia was rich, and good-looking enough to be called handsome. She had the talent to make herself a sort of centre in her world. She was a little noisy; but noise was fashionable, and there was no harm in her—no one had ever said anything against her. Besides, she was one of the few relations still left to the Saracinesca. The daughter of a cousin of the Prince, she would make a good wife for Giovanni, and would bring sunshine into the house. There was a tinge of vulgarity in her manner; but, like many elderly men of his type, Saracinesca pardoned her this fault in consideration of her noisy good spirits and general good-nature. He was very much annoyed at hearing that his son had offended her so· grossly by his forgetfulness; especially it was unfortunate that since she believed herself the cause of the duel, she should have the impression that it had been provoked by Del Ferice to obtain satisfaction for the insult Giovanni had offered her. There would be small chance of making the match contemplated after such an affair.

"I am sincerely sorry," said the Prince, stroking his white beard and trying to get a sight of his companion's face, which she obstinately turned away from him. "Perhaps it is better not to think too much of the matter until the exact circumstances are known. Some one is sure to tell the story one of these days."

"How coldly you speak of it! One would think it had happened in Peru, instead of here, this very morning."

Saracinesca was at his wits' end. He wanted to smooth the matter over, or at least to soften the unfavourable impression against Giovanni. He had not the· remotest idea how to do it. He was not a very diplomatic man.

"No, no; you misunderstand me. I am not cold. I quite appreciate your situation. You are very justly annoyed."

"Of course I am," said Donna Tullia, impatiently. She was beginning to regret that she had made him get into her carriage.

"Precisely; of course you are. Now, so soon as Giovanni is quite recovered, I will send him to explain his conduct to you if he can, or to———"

"Explain it? How can he explain it? I do not want

you to send him, if he will not come of his own accord.
Why should I?"

"Well, well, as you please, my dear cousin," said old
Saracinesca, smiling to cover his perplexity. "I am not a
good ambassador; but you know I am a good friend, and
I really want to do something to restore Giovanni to your
graces."

"That will be difficult," answered Donna Tullia, although
she knew very well that she would receive Giovanni
kindly enough when she had once had an opportunity of
speaking her mind to him.

"Do not be hard-hearted," urged the Prince. "I am
sure he is very penitent."

"Then let him say so."

"That is exactly what I ask."

"Is it? Oh, very well. If he chooses to call I will
receive him, since you desire it. Where shall I put you
down?"

"Anywhere, thank you. Here, if you wish — at the
corner. Good-bye. Do not be too hard on the boy."

"We shall see," answered Donna Tullia, unwilling to
show too much indulgence. The old Prince bowed, and
walked away into the gloom of the dusky streets.

"That is over," he muttered to himself. "I wonder
how the Astrardente takes it." He would have liked to
see her; but he recognised that, as he so very rarely called
upon her, it would seem strange to choose such a time for his
visit. It would not do—it would be hardly decent, seeing
that he believed her to be the cause of the catastrophe.
His steps, however, led him almost unconsciously in the
direction of the Astrardente palace; he found himself in
front of the arched entrance almost before he knew where
he was. The temptation to see Corona was more than he
could resist. He asked the porter if the Duchessa was at
home, and on being answered in the affirmative, he boldly
entered and ascended the marble staircase—boldly, but
with an odd sensation, like that of a schoolboy who is getting himself into trouble.

Corona had just come home, and was sitting by the fire

in her great drawing-room, alone, with a book in her hand, which she was not reading. She rarely remained in the reception-rooms; but to-day she had rather capriciously taken a fancy to the broad solitude of the place, and had accordingly installed herself there. She was very much surprised when the doors were suddenly opened wide and the servant announced Prince Saracinesca. For a moment she thought it must be Giovanni, for his father rarely entered her house, and when the old man's stalwart figure advanced towards her, she dropped her book in astonishment, and rose from her deep chair to meet him. She was very pale, and there were dark rings under her eyes that spoke of pain and want of sleep. She was so utterly different from Donna Tullia, whom he had just left, that the Prince was almost awed by her stateliness, and felt more than ever like a boy in a bad scrape. Corona bowed rather coldly, but extended her hand, which the old gentleman raised to his lips respectfully, in the manner of the old school.

"I trust you are not exhausted after the ball?" he began, not knowing what to say.

"Not in the least. We did not stay late," replied Corona, secretly wondering why he had come.

"It was really magnificent," he answered. "There has been no such ball for years. Very unfortunate that it should have terminated in such an unpleasant way," he added, making a bold dash at the subject of which he wished to speak.

"Very. You did a bad morning's work," said the Duchessa, severely. "I wonder that you should speak of it."

"No one speaks of anything else," returned the Prince, apologetically. "Besides, I do not see what was to be done."

"You should have stopped it," answered Corona, her dark eyes gleaming with righteous indignation. "You should have prevented it at any price, if not in the name of religion, which forbids it as a crime, at least in the name of decency—as being Don Giovanni's father."

"You speak strong words, Duchessa," said the Prince, evidently annoyed at her tone.

M

"If I speak strongly, it is because I think you acted shamefully in permitting this disgraceful butchery."

Saracinesca suddenly lost his temper, as he frequently did.

"Madam," he said, " it is certainly not for you to accuse me of crime, lack of decency, and what you are pleased to call disgraceful butchery, seeing who was the probable cause of the honourable encounter which you characterise in such tasteful language."

"Honourable indeed!" said Corona, very scornfully. "Let that pass. Who, pray, is more to blame than you? Who is the probable cause?"

"Need I tell you?" asked the old man, fixing his flashing eyes upon her.

"What do you mean?" inquired Corona, turning white, and her voice trembling between her anger and her emotion.

"I may be wrong," said the Prince, "but I believe I am right. I believe that the duel was fought on your account."

"On my account!" repeated Corona, half rising from her chair in her indignation. Then she sank back again, and added, very coldly, "If you have come here to insult me, Prince, I will send for my husband."

"I beg your pardon, Duchessa," said old Saracinesca. "It is very far from my intention to insult you."

"And who has told you this abominable lie?" asked Corona, still very angry.

"No one, upon my word."

"Then how dare you——"

"Because I have reason to believe that you are the only woman alive for whom my son would engage in a quarrel."

"It is impossible," cried Corona. "I will never believe that Don Giovanni could——" She checked herself.

"Don Giovanni Saracinesca is a gentleman, madam," said the old Prince, proudly. "He keeps his own counsel. I have come by the information without any evidence of it from his lips."

"Then I am at a loss to understand you," returned the Duchessa. "I must beg you either to explain your extraordinary language, or else to leave me."

Corona d'Astrardente was a match for any man when she

was angry. But old Saracinesca, though no diplomatist, was a formidable adversary, from his boldness and determination to discover the truth at any price.

"It is precisely because, at the risk of offending you, I desired an explanation, that I have intruded myself upon you to-day," he answered. "Will you permit me one question before I leave you?"

"Provided it is not an insulting one, I will answer it," replied Corona.

"Do you know anything of the circumstances which led to this morning's encounter?"

"Certainly not," Corona answered, hotly. "I assure you most solemnly," she continued in calmer tones, "that I am wholly ignorant of it. I suppose you have a right to be told that."

"I, on my part, assure you, upon my word, that I know no more than you yourself, excepting this: on some provocation, concerning which he will not speak, my son seized Del Ferice by the throat and used strong words to him. No one witnessed the scene. Del Ferice sent the challenge. My son could find no one to act for him and applied to me, as was quite right that he should. There was no apology possible—Giovanni had to give the man satisfaction. You know as much as I know now."

"That does not help me to understand why you accuse me of having caused the quarrel," said Corona. "What have I to do with Del Ferice, poor man?"

"This—any one can see that you are as indifferent to my son as to any other man. Every one knows that the Duchessa d'Astrardente is above suspicion."

Corona raised her head proudly and stared at Saracinesca.

"But, on the other hand, every one knows that my son loves you madly—can you yourself deny it?"

"Who dares to say it?" asked Corona, her anger rising afresh.

"Who sees, dares. Can you deny it?"

"You have no right to repeat such hearsay tales to me," answered Corona. But the blush rose to her pale dark cheeks, and she suddenly dropped her eyes.

"Can you deny it, Duchessa?" asked the Prince a third time, insisting roughly.

"Since you are so certain, why need you care for my denial?" inquired Corona.

"Duchessa, you must forgive me," answered Saracinesca, his tone suddenly softening. "I am rough, probably rude; but I love my son dearly. I cannot bear to see him running into a dangerous and hopeless passion, from which he may issue only to find himself grown suddenly old and bitter, disappointed and miserable for the rest of his life. I believe you to be a very good woman; I cannot look at you and doubt the truth of anything you tell me. If he loves you, you have influence over him. If you have influence, use it for his good; use it to break down this mad love of his, to show him his own folly — to save him, in short, from his fate. Do you understand me? Do I ask too much?"

Corona understood well enough — far too well. She knew the whole extent of Giovanni's love for her, and, what old Saracinesca never guessed, the strength of her own love for him, for the sake of which she would do all that a woman could do. There was a long pause after the old Prince had spoken. He waited patiently for an answer.

"I understand you—yes," she said at last. "If you are right in your surmises, I should have some influence over your son. If I can advise him, and he will take my advice, I will give him the best counsel I can. You have placed me in a very embarrassing position, and you have shown little courtesy in the way you have spoken to me; but I will try to do as you request me, if the opportunity offers, for the sake of—of turning what is very bad into something which may at last be good."

"Thank you, thank you, Duchessa!" cried the Prince. "I will never forget——"

"Do not thank me," said Corona, coldly. "I am not in a mood to appreciate your gratitude. There is too much blood of those honest gentlemen upon your hands."

"Pardon me, Duchessa, I wish there were on my hands

and head the blood of that gentleman you call honest—the gentleman who twice tried to murder my son this morning, and twice nearly succeeded."

"What!" cried Corona, in sudden terror.

"That fellow thrust at Giovanni once to kill him while they were halting and his sword was hanging lowered in his hand; and once again he threw himself upon his knee and tried to stab him in the body—which is a dastardly trick not permitted in any country. Even in duelling, such things are called murder; and it is their right name."

Corona was very pale. Giovanni's danger had been suddenly brought before her in a very vivid light, and she was horror-struck at the thought of it.

"Is—is Don Giovanni very badly wounded?" she asked.

"No, thank heaven; he will be well in a week. But either one of those attempts might have killed him; and he would have died, I think—pardon me, no insult this time—I think, on your account. Do you see why for him I dread this attachment to you, which leads him to risk his life at every turn for a word about you? Do you see why I implore you to take the matter into your serious consideration, and to use your influence to bring him to his senses?"

"I see; but in this question of the duel you have no proof that I was concerned."

"No,—no proof, perhaps. I will not weary you with surmises; but even if it was not for you this time, you see that it might have been."

"Perhaps," said Corona, very sadly.

"I have to thank you, even if you will not listen to me," said the Prince, rising. "You have understood me. It was all I asked. Good night."

"Good night," answered Corona, who did not move from her seat nor extend her hand this time. She was too much agitated to think of formalities. Saracinesca bowed low and left the room.

It was characteristic of him that he had come to see the Duchessa not knowing what he should say, and that he had blurted out the whole truth, and then lost his temper in support of it. He was a hasty man, of noble instincts, but always inclined rather to cut a knot than to unloose it —to do by force what another man would do by skill— angry at opposition, and yet craving it by his combative nature.

His first impulse on leaving Corona was to go to Giovanni and tell him what he had done; but he reflected as he went home that his son was ill with his wounds, and that it would be bad for him to be angry, as of course he would be if he were told of his father's doings. Moreover, as old Saracinesca thought more seriously of the matter, he wisely concluded that it would be better not to speak of the visit; and when he entered the room where Giovanni was lying on his couch with a novel and a cigarette, he had determined to conceal the whole matter.

"Well, Giovanni," he said, "we are the talk of the town, of course."

"It was to be expected. Whom have you seen?"

"In the first place, I have seen Madame Mayer. She is in a state of anger against you which borders on madness— not because you have wounded Del Ferice, but because you forgot to dance with her. I cannot conceive how you could be so foolish."

"Nor I. It was idiotic in the last degree," replied Giovanni, annoyed that his father should have learned the story.

"You must go and see her at once—as soon as you can go out. It is a disagreeable business."

"Of course. What else did she say?"

"She thought that Del Ferice had challenged you on her account, because you had not danced with her."

"How silly! As if I should fight duels about her."

"Since there was probably a woman in the case, she might have been the one," remarked his father.

"There was no woman in the case, practically speaking," said Giovanni, shortly.

"Oh, I supposed there was. However, I told Donna Tullia that I advised her not to think anything more of the matter until the whole story came out."

"When is that likely to occur ? " asked Giovanni, laughing. "No one alive knows the cause of the quarrel but Del Ferice and I myself. He will certainly not tell the world, as the thing was even more disgraceful to him than his behaviour this morning. There is no reason why I should speak of it either."

"How reticent you are, Giovanni!" exclaimed the old gentleman.

"Believe me, if I could tell you the whole story without injuring any one but Del Ferice, I would."

"Then there was really a woman in the case ? "

"There was a woman outside the case, who caused us to be in it," returned Giovanni.

"Always your detestable riddles," cried the old man, petulantly ; and presently, seeing that his son was obstinately silent, he left the room to dress for dinner.

CHAPTER XV.

It may be that when Astrardente spoke so tenderly to his wife after the Frangipani ball, he felt some warning that told him his strength was failing. His heart was in a dangerous condition, the family doctor had said, and it was necessary that he should take care of himself. He had been very tired after that long evening, and perhaps some sudden sinking had shaken his courage. He awoke from an unusually heavy sleep with a strange sense of astonishment, as though he had not expected to awake again in life. He felt weaker than he had felt for a long time, and even his accustomed beverage of chocolate mixed with coffee failed to give him the support he needed in the norning. He rose very late, and his servant found him more than usually petulant, nor did the message brought back from Giovanni seem to improve his temper. He met his wife at the midday breakfast, and was strangely silent, and in the afternoon he shut himself up in his own rooms and would see nobody. But at dinner he appeared again, seemingly revived, and declared his intention of accompanying his wife to a reception given at the Austrian embassy. He seemed so unlike his usual self, that Corona did not venture to speak of the duel which had taken place in the morning; for she feared anything which might excite him, well knowing that excitement might prove fatal. She did what she could to dissuade him from going out; but he grew petulant, and she unwillingly yielded.

At the embassy he soon heard all the details, for no one talked of anything else; but Astrardente was ashamed of not having heard it all before, and affected a cynical indifference to the tale which the military attaché of the embassy repeated for his benefit. He vouchsafed some remark to the effect that fighting duels was the natural amusement of young gentlemen, and that if one of them killed another there was at least one fool the less in society; after which he looked about him for some young beauty to whom he might reel off a score of compliments. He knew all the time that he was making a great effort, that he felt unaccountably ill, and that he wished he had taken his wife's advice and stayed quietly at home. But at the end of the evening he chanced to overhear a remark that Valdarno was making to Casalverde, who looked exceedingly pale and ill at ease.

"You had better make your will, my dear fellow," said Valdarno. "Spicca is a terrible man with the foils."

Astrardente turned quickly and looked at the speaker. But both men were suddenly silent, and seemed absorbed in gazing at the crowd. It was enough, however. Astrardente had gathered that Casalverde was to fight Spicca the next day, and that the affair begun that morning had not yet reached its termination. He determined that he would not again be guilty of not knowing what was going on in society; and with the intention of rising early on the following morning, he found Corona, and rather unceremoniously told her it was time to go home.

On the next day the Duca d'Astrardente walked into the club soon after ten o'clock. On ordinary occasions that resort of his fellows was entirely empty until a much later hour; but Astrardente was not disappointed to-day. Twenty or thirty men were congregated in the large hall which served as a smoking-room, and all of them were talking together excitedly. As the door swung on its hinges and the old dandy entered, a sudden silence fell upon the assembly. Astrardente naturally judged that the conversation had turned upon himself, and had been checked by his appearance; but he affected to take no notice of the occurrence, adjusting his single eyeglass in his eye and serenely surveying the men in the room. He could see that, although they had been talking loudly, the matter in hand was serious enough, for there was no trace of mirth on any of the faces before him. He at once assumed an air of gravity, and going up to Valdarno, who seemed to have occupied the most prominent place in the recent discussion, he put his question in an undertone.

"I suppose Spicca killed him?"

Valdarno nodded, and looked grave. He was a thoughtless young fellow enough, but the news of the tragedy had sobered him. Astrardente had anticipated the death of Casalverde, and was not surprised. But he was not without human feeling, and showed a becoming regret at the sad end of a man he had been accustomed to see so frequently.

"How was it?" he asked.

"A simple 'un, deux,' tierce and carte at the first bout. Spicca is as quick as lightning. Come away from this crowd," added Valdarno, in a low voice, "and I will tell you all about it."

In spite of his sorrow at his friend's death, Valdarno felt a certain sense of importance at being able to tell the story to Astrardente. Valdarno was vain in a small way, though his vanity was to that of the old Duca as the humble violet to the full-blown cabbage-rose. Astrardente enjoyed a considerable importance in society as the husband of Corona, and was an object of especial interest to Valdarno, who supported the incredible theory of Corona's devotion to the old man. Valdarno's stables were near the club, and on pretence of showing a new horse to

Astrardente, he nodded to his friends, and left the room
with the aged dandy. It was a clear, bright winter's
morning, and the two men strolled slowly down the Corso
towards Valdarno's palace.

"You know, of course, how the affair began?" asked
the young man.

"The first duel? Nobody knows—certainly not I."

"Well—perhaps not," returned Valdarno, doubtfully.
"At all events, you know that Spicca flew into a passion
because poor Casalverde forgot to step in after he cried
halt; and then Del Ferice ran Giovanni through the arm."

"That was highly improper—most reprehensible," said
Astrardente, putting up his eyeglass to look at a pretty
little sempstress who hurried past on her way to her work.

"I suppose so. But Casalverde certainly meant no
harm; and if Del Ferice had not been so unlucky as to
forget himself in the excitement of the moment, no one
would have thought anything of it."

"Ah yes, I suppose not," murmured Astrardente, still
looking after the girl. When he could see her face no
longer, he turned sharply back to Valdarno.

"This is exceedingly interesting," he said. "Tell me
more about it."

"Well, when it was over, old Saracinesca was for killing
Casalverde himself."

"The old fire-eater! He ought to be ashamed of himself!"

"However, Spicca was before him, and challenged Casalverde then and there. As both the principals in the first
duel were so badly wounded, it had to be put off until this
morning."

"They went out, and—piff, paff! Spicca ran him
through," interrupted Astrardente. "What a horrible
tragedy!"

"Ah yes; and what is worse——"

"What surprises me most," interrupted the Duca again,
"is that in this delightfully peaceful and paternally governed little nest of ours, the authorities should not have
been able to prevent either of these duels. It is perfectly

amazing! I cannot remember a parallel instance. Do you mean to say that there was not a *sbirro* or a *gendarme* in the neighbourhood to-day nor yesterday?"

"That is not so surprising," answered Valdarno, with a knowing look. "There would have been few tears in high quarters if Del Ferice had been killed yesterday; there will be few to-day over the death of poor Casalverde."

"Bah!" ejaculated Astrardente. "If Antonelli had heard of these affairs he would have stopped them soon enough."

Valdarno glanced behind him, and, bending a little, whispered in Astrardente's ear—

"They were both Liberals, you must know."

"Liberals?" repeated the old dandy, with a cynical sneer. "Nonsense, I say! Liberals? Yes, in the way you are a Liberal, and Donna Tullia Mayer, and Spicca himself, who has just killed that other Liberal, Casalverde. Liberals indeed! Do you flatter yourself for a moment that Antonelli is afraid of such Liberals as you are? Do you think the life of Del Ferice is of any more importance to politics than the life of that dog there?"

It was Astrardente's habit to scoff mercilessly at all the petty manifestations of political feeling he saw about him in the world. He represented a class distinct both from the Valdarno set and from the men represented by the Saracinesca—a class who despised everything political as unworthy of the attention of gentlemen, who took everything for granted, and believed that all was for the best, provided that society moved upon rollers and so long as no one meddled with old institutions. To question the wisdom of the municipal regulations was to attack the Government itself; to attack the Government was to cast a slight upon his Holiness the Pope, which was rank heresy, and very vulgar into the bargain. Astrardente had seen a great deal of the world, but his ideas of politics were almost childishly simple—whereas many people said that his principles in relation to his fellows were fiendishly cynical. He was certainly not a very good man; and if he pretended to no reputation for devoutness, it was probable that he recognised the absurdity of his attempting such a pose.   But politically he believed in Cardinal Antonelli's ability to defy Europe with or without the aid of France, and laughed as loudly at Louis Napoleon's old idea of putting the sovereign Pontiff at the head of an Italian federation, as he jeered at Cavour's favourite phrase concerning a free Church in a free State.   He had good blood in him, and the hereditary courage often found with it.   He had a certain skill in matters worldly; but his wit in things political seemed to belong to an earlier generation, and to be incapable of receiving new impressions.

But Valdarno, who was vain and set great value on his opinions, was deeply offended at the way Astrardente spoke of him and his friends.   In his eyes he was risking much for what he considered a good object, and he resented any contemptuous mention of Liberal principles, whenever he dared.   No one cared much for Astrardente, and certainly no one feared him; nevertheless in those times men hesitated to defend anything which came under the general head of Liberalism, when they were likely to be overheard, or when they could not trust the man to whom they were speaking.   If no one feared Astrardente, no one trusted him either.   Valdarno consequently judged it best to smother his annoyance at the old man's words, and to retaliate by striking him in a weak spot.

"If you despise Del Ferice as much as you say," he remarked, "I wonder that you tolerate him as you do."

"I tolerate him.   Toleration is the very word—it delightfully expresses my feelings towards him.   He is a perfectly harmless creature, who affects immense depth of insight into human affairs, and who cannot see an inch before his face.   Dear me! yes, I shall always tolerate Del Ferice, poor fellow!"

"You may not be called upon to do so much longer," replied Valdarno.   "They say he is in a very dangerous condition."

"Ah!" ejaculated Astrardente, putting up his eyeglass at his companion.   "Ah, you don't say so!"

There was something so insolent in the old man's affected stare that even the foolish and good-natured Valdarno lost his temper, being already somewhat irritated.

"It is a pity that you should be so indifferent. It is hardly becoming. If you had not tolerated him as you have, he might not be lying there at the point of death."

Astrardente stared harder than ever.

"My dear young friend," he said, "your language is the most extraordinary I ever heard. How in the world can my treatment of that unfortunate man have had anything to do with his being wounded in a duel?"

"My dear old friend," replied Valdarno, impudently mimicking the old man's tone, "your simplicity surpasses anything I ever knew. Is it possible that you do not know that this duel was fought for your wife?"

Astrardente looked fixedly at Valdarno; his eyeglass dropped from his eye, and he turned ashy pale beneath his paint. He staggered a moment, and steadied himself against the door of a shop. They were just passing the corner of the Piazza di Sciarra, the most crowded crossing of the Corso.

"Valdarno," said the old man, his cracked voice dropping to a hoarser and deeper tone, "you must explain yourself or answer for this."

"What! Another duel!" cried Valdarno, in some scorn. Then, seeing that his companion looked ill, he took him by the arm and led him rapidly through the crowd, across the Arco dei Carbognani. Entering the Caffè Aragno, a new institution in those days, both men sat down at a small marble table. The old dandy was white with emotion; Valdarno felt that he was enjoying his revenge.

"A glass of cognac, Duke?" he said, as the waiter came up. Astrardente nodded, and there was silence while the man brought the cordial. The Duca lived by an invariable rule, seeking to balance the follies of his youth by excessive care in his old age; it was long, indeed, since he had taken a glass of brandy in the morning. He swallowed it quickly, and the stimulant produced its effect immediately; he readjusted his eyeglass, and faced Valdarno sternly.

"And now," he said, "that we are at our ease, may I inquire what the devil you mean by your insinuations about my wife?"

"Oh," replied Valdarno, affecting great indifference, "I only say what everybody says. There is no offence to the Duchessa."

"I should suppose not, indeed. Go on."

"Do you really care to hear the story?" asked the young man.

"I intend to hear it, and at once," replied Astrardente.

"You will not have to employ force to extract it from me, I can assure you," said Valdarno, settling himself in his chair, but avoiding the angry glance of the old man. "Everybody has been repeating it since the day before yesterday, when it occurred. You were at the Frangipani ball—you might have seen it all. In the first place, you must know that there exists another of those beings to whom you extend your merciful toleration—a certain Giovanni Saracinesca—you may have noticed him?"

"What of him?" asked Astrardente, fiercely.

"Among other things, he is the man who wounded Del Ferice, as I daresay you have heard. Among other things concerning him, he has done himself the honour of falling desperately, madly in love with the Duchessa d'Astrardente, who——"

"What?" cried the old man in a cracked voice, as Valdarno paused.

"Who does you the honour of ignoring his existence on most occasions, but who was so unfortunate as to recall him to her memory on the night of the Frangipani ball. We were all sitting in a circle round the Duchessa's chair that night, when the conversation chanced to turn upon this same Giovanni Saracinesca, a fire-eating fellow with a bad temper. He had been away for some days; indeed he was last seen at the Apollo in your box, when they gave 'Norma'——"

"I remember," interrupted Astrardente. The mention of that evening was but a random shot. Valdarno had been in the club-box, and had seen Giovanni when he

made his visit to the Astrardente; he had not seen him
again till the Frangipani ball.

"Well, as I was saying, we spoke of Giovanni, and
every one had something to say about his absence. The
Duchessa expressed her curiosity, and Del Ferice, who was
with us, proposed calling him—he was at the other end of
the room, you see—that he might answer for himself. So
I went and brought him up. He was in a very bad
humour——"

"What has all this absurd story got to do with the
matter?" asked the old man, impatiently.

"It is the matter itself. The irascible Giovanni is angry
at being questioned, treats us all like mud under his feet,
sits down by the Duchessa and forces us to go away. The
Duchessa tells him the story, with a laugh no doubt, and
Giovanni's wrath overflows. He goes in search of Del
Ferice, and nearly strangles him. The result of these
eccentricities is the first duel, leading to the second."

Astrardente was very angry, and his thin gloved hands
twitched nervously at the handle of his stick.

"And this," he said—"this string of trivial ball-room
incident, seems to you a sufficient pretext for stating that
the duel was about my wife?"

"Certainly," replied Valdarno, coolly. "If Saracinesca
had not been for months openly devoting himself to the
Duchessa—who, I assure you, takes no kind of notice of
him——"

"You need not waste words——"

"I do not,—and if Giovanni had not thought it worth
while to be jealous of Del Ferice, there would have been
no fighting."

"Have you been telling your young friends that my
wife was the cause of all this?" asked Astrardente, trembling with a genuine rage which lent a certain momentary
dignity to his feeble frame and painted face.

"Why not?"

"Have you or have you not?"

"Certainly—if you please," returned Valdarno inso-
lently, enjoying the old man's fury.

"Then permit me to tell you that you have taken upon yourself an outrageous liberty, that you have lied, and that you do not deserve to be treated like a gentleman."

Astrardente got upon his feet and left the café without further words. Valdarno had indeed wounded him in a weak spot, and the wound was mortal. His blood was up, and at that moment he would have faced Valdarno sword in hand, and might have proved himself no mean adversary, so great is the power of anger to revive in the most decrepit the energies of youth. He believed in his wife with a rare sincerity, and his blood boiled at the idea of her being rudely spoken of as the cause of a scandalous quarrel, however much Valdarno insisted upon it that she was as indifferent to Giovanni as to Del Ferice. The story was a shallow invention upon the face of it. But though the old man told himself so again and again as he almost ran through the narrow streets towards his house, there was one thought suggested by Valdarno which rankled deep. It was true that Giovanni had last been seen in the Astrardente box at the opera; that he had not remained five minutes seated by the Duchessa before he had suddenly invented a shallow excuse for leaving; and finally, there was no doubt that at that very moment Corona had seemed violently agitated. Giovanni had not reappeared till the night of the Frangipani ball, and the duel had taken place on the very next morning. Astrardente could not reason—his mind was too much disturbed by his anger against Valdarno; but a vague impression that there was something wrong in it all, drove him homewards in wild excitement. He was ill, too, and had he been in a frame of mind to reflect upon himself, he would have noticed that his heart was beating with ominous irregularity. He did not even think of taking a cab, but hurried along on foot, finding, perhaps, a momentary relief in violent exertion. The old blood rushed to his face in good earnest, and shamed the delicately painted lights and shadows touched in by the master-hand of Monsieur Isidore, the cosmopolitan valet.

Valdarno remained seated in the café, rather disturbed at what he had done. He certainly had had no intention of raising such a storm; he was a weak and good-natured fellow, whose vanity was easily wounded, but who was not otherwise very sensitive, and was certainly not very intelligent. Astrardente had laughed at him and his friends in a way which touched him to the quick, and with childish petulance he had retaliated in the easiest way which presented itself. Indeed there was more foundation for his tale than Astrardente would allow. At least it was true that the story was in the mouths of all the gossips that morning, and Valdarno had only repeated what he had heard. He had meant to annoy the old man; he had certainly not intended to make him so furiously angry. As for the deliberate insult he had received, it was undoubtedly very shocking to be told that one lied in such very plain terms; but on the other hand, to demand satisfaction of such an old wreck as Astrardente would be ridiculous in the extreme. Valdarno was incapable of very violent passion, and was easily persuaded that he was in the wrong when any one contradicted him flatly; not that he was altogether devoid of a certain physical courage if hard pushed, but because he was not very strong, not very confident of himself, not very combative, and not very truthful. When Astrardente was gone, he waited a few minutes, and then sauntered up the Corso again towards the club, debating in his mind how he should turn a good story out of his morning's adventure without making himself appear either foolish or pusillanimous. It was also necessary so to turn his narrative that in case any one repeated it to Giovanni, the latter might not propose to cut his throat, though it was not probable that any one would be bold enough to desire a conversation with the younger Saracinesca on such a subject.

When he again entered the smoking-room of the club, he was greeted by a chorus of inquiries concerning his interview with Astrardente.

"What did he ask? What did he say? Where is he? What did you tell him? Did he drop his eyeglass? Did he blush through his paint?"

Everybody spoke together in the same breath. Val-

darno's vanity rose to the occasion. Weak and insignificant by nature, he particularly delighted in being the centre
of general interest, if even for a moment only.

"He really dropped his eyeglass," he answered, with a
gay laugh, "and he really changed colour in spite of his
paint."

"It must have been a terrible interview, then," remarked one or two of the loungers.

"I shall be happy to offer you my services in case you
wish to cut each other's throats," said a French officer of
the Papal Zouaves who stood by the fireplace rolling a
cigarette. Whereupon everybody laughed loudly.

"Thanks," answered Valdarno; "I am expecting a
challenge every minute. If he proposes a powder-puff and
a box of rouge for the weapons, I accept without hesitation.
Well, it was very amusing. He wanted to know all about
it, and so I told him about the scene in Casa Frangipani.
He did not seem to understand at all. He is a very obtuse
old gentleman."

"I hope you explained the connection of events," said
some one.

"Indeed I did. It was delightful to witness his fury.
It was then that he dropped his eyeglass and turned as red
as a boiled lobster. He swore that his wife was above
suspicion, as usual."

"That is true," said a young man who had attempted to
make love to Corona during the previous year.

"Of course it is true," echoed all the rest, with a unan-
imity rare indeed where a woman's reputation is concerned.

"Yes," continued Valdarno, "of course. But he goes
so far as to say it is absurd that any one should admire his
wife, who is nevertheless a most admirable woman. He
stamped, he screamed, he turned red in the face, and he
went off without taking leave of me, flourishing his stick,
and swearing eternal hatred and vengeance against the
entire civilised society of the world. He was delightfully
amusing. Will anybody play baccarat? I will start a
bank."

The majority were for the game, and in a few minutes

were seated at a large green table, drawing cards and betting with a good will, and interspersing their play with stray remarks on the events of the morning.

CHAPTER XVI.

Corona was fast coming to a state of mind in which a kind of passive expectation—a sort of blind submission to fate—was the chief feature. She had shed tears when her husband spoke of his approaching end, because her gentle heart was grateful to him, and by its own sacrifices had grown used to his presence, and because she suddenly felt that she had comprehended the depth of his love for her, as she had never understood it before. In the five years of married life she had spent with him, she had not allowed herself to think of his selfishness, of his small daily egotism; for, though it was at no great expense to himself, he had been uniformly generous and considerate to her. But she had been conscious that if she should ever remove from her conscience the pressure of a self-imposed censorship, so that her judgment might speak boldly, the verdict of her heart would not have been so indulgent to her husband as was that formal opinion of him which she forced herself to hold. Now, however, it seemed as though the best things she had desired to believe of him were true; and with the conviction that he was not only not selfish, but absolutely devoted to herself, there had come upon her a fear of desolation, a dread of being left alone—of finding herself abandoned by this strange companion, the only person in the world with whom she had the habit of familiarity and the bond of a common past. Astrardente had thought, and had told her too, that the knowledge of his impending death might lighten her burden—might make the days of self-sacrifice that yet remained seem shorter; he had spoken kindly of her marrying again when he should be dead, deeming per- haps, in his sudden burst of generosity, that she would be

capable of looking beyond the unhappy present to the
possibilities of a more brilliant future, or at least that the
certainty of his consent to such a second union would
momentarily please her. It was hard to say why he had
spoken. It had been an impulse such as the most selfish
people sometimes yield to when their failing strength brings
upon them suddenly the sense of their inability to resist
any longer the course of events. The vanity of man is so
amazing, that when he is past arrogating to himself the
attention which is necessary to him as his daily bread, he
is capable of so demeaning his manhood as to excite interest
in his weaknesses rather than that he should cease to be the
object of any interest whatever. The analysis of the feelings of old and selfish persons is the most difficult of all
studies; for in proportion as the strength of the dominant
passion or passions is quenched in the bitter still waters of
the harbour of superannuation, the small influences of life
grow in importance. As when, from the breaking surge of
an angry ocean, the water is dashed high among the re-
echoing rocks, leaving little pools of limpid clearness in the
hollows of the storm-beaten cliffs; and as when the anger
of the tossing waves has subsided, the hot sun shines upon
the mimic seas, and the clear waters that were so trans-
parent grow thick and foul with the motion of a tiny and
insignificant insect-life undreamed of before in such crystal
purity: so also the clear strong sea of youth is left to dry
in the pools and puddles of old age, and in the motionless
calm of the still places where the ocean of life has washed
it, it is dried up and consumed by myriads of tiny parasites
—lives within lives, passions within passions—tiny efforts
at mimic greatness,—a restless little world, the very parody
and infinitesimal reproduction of the mighty flood whence
it came, wherein great monsters have their being, and things
of unspeakable beauty grow free in the large depths of an
unfathomed ocean.

To Corona d'Astrardente in the freshness of her youth
the study of her husband's strange littleness had grown to
be a second nature from the habit of her devotion to him.
But she could not understand him; she could not explain

to herself the sudden confession of old age, the quiet anticipation of death, the inexplicable generosity towards herself. She only knew that he must be at heart a man more kindly and of better impulse than he had generally been considered, and she resolved to do her utmost to repay him, and to soothe the misery of his last years.

Since he had told her so plainly, it must be true. It was natural, perhaps — for he was growing more feeble every day—but it was very sad. Five years ago, when she had choked down her loathing for the old man to whom she had sold herself for her father's sake, she would not have believed that she should one day feel the tears rise fast at the thought of his dying and leaving her free. He had said it; she would be free. They say that men who have been long confined in a dungeon become indifferent, and when turned out upon the world would at first gladly return to their prison walls. Liberty is in the first place an instinct, but it will easily grow to be a habit. Corona had renounced all thought of freedom five years ago, and in the patient bowing of her noble nature to the path she had chosen, she had attained to a state of renunciation like that of a man who has buried himself for ever in an order of Trappists, and neither dreams of the freedom of the outer world, nor desires to dream of it. And she had grown fond of the aged dandy and his foolish ways—ways which seemed foolish because they were those of youth grafted upon senility. She had not known that she was fond of him, it is true; but now that he spoke of dying, she felt that she would weep his loss. He was her only companion, her only friend. In the loyal determination to be faithful to him, she had so shut herself from all intimacy with the world that she had not a friend. She kept women at a distance from her, instinctively dreading lest in their careless talk some hint or comment should remind her that she had married a man ridiculous in their eyes; and with men she could have but little intercourse, for their society was dangerous. No man save Giovanni Saracinesca had for years put himself in the light of a mere acquaintance, always ready to talk to her upon general subjects, studiously avoiding himself in all discussions, and delicately flattering her vanity by his deference to her judgment. The other men had generally spoken of love at the second meeting, and declared themselves devoted to her for life at the end of a week: she had quietly repulsed them, and they had dropped back into the position of indifferent acquaintances, going in search of other game, after the manner of young gentlemen of leisure. Giovanni alone had sternly maintained his air of calmness, had never offended her simple pride of loyalty to Astrardente by word or deed; so that, although she felt and dreaded her growing interest in him, she had actually believed that he was nothing in her life, until at last she had been undeceived and awakened to the knowledge of his fierce passion, and being taken unawares, had nearly been carried off her feet by the tempest his words had roused in her own breast. But her strength had not utterly deserted her. Years of supreme devotion to the right, of honest and unwavering loyalty, neither deceiving her conscience on the one hand with the morbid food of a fictitious religious exaltation, nor, upon the other, sinking to a cynical indifference to inevitable misery; days of quiet and constant effort; long hours of thoughtful meditation upon the one resolution of her life,—all this had strengthened the natural force of her character, so that, when at last the great trial had come, she had not yielded, but had conquered once and for ever, in the very moment of sorest temptation. And with her there would be no return of the danger. Having found strength to resist, she knew that there would be no more weakness; her love for Giovanni was deep and sincere, but it had become now the chief cause of suffering in her life; it had utterly ceased to be the chief element of joy, as it had been for a few short days. It was one thing more to be borne, and it outweighed all other cares.

The news of the duel had given her great distress. She believed honestly that she was in no way concerned in it, and she had bitterly resented old Saracinesca's imputation. In the hot words that had passed between them, she had felt her anger rise justly against the old Prince; but when he appealed to her on account of his son, her love for Giovanni had vanquished h·r wrath against the old man. Come what might, she would do what was best for him. If possible, she would induce him to leave Rome at once, and thus free herself from the pain of constantly meeting him. Perhaps she could make him marry—anything would be better than to allow things to go on in their present course, to have to face him at every turn, and to know that at any moment he might be quarrelling with somebody and fighting duels on her account.

She went boldly into the world that night, not knowing whether she should meet Giovanni or not, but resolved upon her course if he appeared. Many people looked curiously at her, and smiled cunningly as they thought they detected traces of care upon her proud face; but though they studied her, and lost no opportunity of talking to her upon the one topic which absorbed the general conversation, no one had the satisfaction of moving her even so much as to blush a little, or to lower the gaze of her eyes that looked them all indifferently through and through.

Giovanni, however, did not appear, and people told her he would not leave his room for several days, so that she returned to her home without having accomplished anything in the matter. Her husband was very silent, but looked at her with an expression of uncertainty, as though hesitating to speak to her upon some subject that absorbed his interest. Neither of them referred to the strange interview of the previous night. They went home early, as has been already recorded, seeing it was only a great and formal reception to which the world went that night; and even the toughest old society jades were weary from the ball of the day before, which had not broken up until half-past six in the morning.

On the next day, at about twelve o'clock, Corona was sitting in her boudoir writing a number of invitations which were to be distributed in the afternoon, when the door opened and her husband entered the room.

"My dear," he cried in great excitement, "it is perfectly horrible! Have you heard?"

"What?" asked Corona, laying down her pen.

"Spicca has killed Casalverde—the man who seconded Del Ferice yesterday,—killed him on the spot——"

Corona uttered an exclamation of horror.

"And they say Del Ferice is dead, or just dying"—his cracked voice rose at every word; "and they say," he almost screamed, laying his withered hand roughly upon his wife's shoulder,—"they say that the duel was about you—you, do you understand?"

"That is not true," said Corona, firmly. "Calm yourself—I beseech you to be calm. Tell me connectedly what has happened—who told you this story."

"What right has any man to drag your name into a quarrel?" cried the old man, hoarsely. "Everybody is saying it—it is outrageous, abominable——"

Corona quietly pushed her husband into a chair, and sat down beside him.

"You are excited—you will harm yourself,—remember your health," she said, endeavouring to soothe him. "Tell me, in the first place, who told you that it was about me."

"Valdarno told me; he told me that every one was saying it—that it was the talk of the town."

"But why?" insisted Corona. "You allow yourself to be furious for the sake of a piece of gossip which has no foundation whatever. What is the story they tell?"

"Some nonsense about Giovanni Saracinesca's going away last week. Del Ferice proposed to call him before you, and Giovanni was angry."

"That is absurd," said Corona. "Don Giovanni was not the least annoyed. He was with me afterwards——"

"Always Giovanni! Always Giovanni! Wherever you go, it is Giovanni!" cried the old man, in unreasonable petulance—unreasonable from his point of view, reasonable enough had he known the truth. But he struck unconsciously upon the key-note of all Corona's troubles, and she turned pale to the lips.

"You say it is not true," he began again. "How do

you know? How can you tell what may have been said? How can you guess it? Giovanni Saracinesca is about you in society more than any one. He has quarrelled about you, and two men have lost their lives in consequence. He is in love with you, I tell you. Can you not see it? You must be blind!"

Corona leaned back in her chair, utterly overcome by the suddenness of the situation, unable to answer, her hands folded tightly together, her pale lips compressed. Angry at her silence, old Astrardente continued, his rage gradually getting the mastery of his sense, and his passion working itself up to the pitch of madness.

"Blind—yes—positively blind!" he cried. "Do you think that I am blind too? Do you think I will overlook all this? Do you not see that your reputation is injured —that people associate your name with his—that no woman can be mentioned in the same breath with Giovanni Saracinesca and hope to maintain a fair fame? A fellow whose adventures are in everybody's mouth, whose doings are notorious; who has but to look at a woman to destroy her; who is a duellist, a libertine——"

"That is not true," interrupted Corona, unable to listen calmly to the abuse thus heaped upon the man she so dearly loved. "You are mad——"

"You defend him!" screamed Astrardente, leaning far forward in his chair and clenching his hands. "You dare to support him—you acknowledge that you care for him! Does he not pursue you everywhere, so that the town rings with it? You ought to long to be rid of him, to wish he were dead, rather than allow his name to be breathed with yours; and instead, you defend him to me—you say he is right, that you prefer his odious devotion to your good name, to my good name! Oh, it is not to be believed! If you loved him yourself you could not do worse!"

"If half you say were true——" said Corona, in terrible distress.

"True?" cried Astrardente, who would not brook interruption. "It is all true—and more also. It is true that he loves you, true that all the world says it, true—by all

that is holy, from your face I would almost believe that
you do love him! Why do you not deny it? · Miserable
woman!" he screamed, springing towards her and seizing
her roughly by the arm, as she hid her face in her hands.
" Miserable.woman! you have betrayed me——"

In the paroxysm of his rage the feeble old man became
almost strong; his grip tightened upon his wife's wrist, and
he dragged her violently from her seat.

"Betrayed! And by you!" he cried again, shaking
with passion. "You whom I have loved! This is your
gratitude, your sanctified devotion, your cunning pretence
at patience! All to hide your love for such a man as
that! You hypocrite, you——"

By a sudden effort Corona shook off his grasp, and drew
herself up to her full height in magnificent anger.

"You shall hear me," she said, in deep commanding tones.
"I have deserved much, but I have not deserved this."

"Ha!" he hissed, standing back from her a step, "you
can speak now—I have touched you! You have found
words. It was time!"

Corona was as white as death, and her black eyes shone
like coals of fire. Her words came slowly, every accent
clear and strong with concentrated passion.

" I have not betrayed you. I have spoken no word of
love to any man alive, and you know that I speak the
truth. If any one has said to me what should not be said,
I have rebuked him to silence. You know, while you
accuse me, that I have done my best to honour and love
you; you know well that I would die by my own hand,
your loyal and true wife, rather than let my lips utter one
syllable of love for any other man."

Corona possessed a supreme power over her husband.
She was so true a woman that the truth blazed visibly
from her clear eyes; and what she said was nothing but
the truth. She had doubted it herself for one dreadful
moment; she knew it now beyond all doubting. In a
moment the old man's wrath broke and vanished before the
strong assertion of her perfect innocence. He turned pale
under his paint, and his limbs trembled. He made a step

forward, and fell upon his knees before her, and tried to take her hands.

"Oh, Corona, forgive me," he moaned—"forgive me! I so love you!"

Suddenly his grasp relaxed from her hands, and with a groan he fell forward against her knees.

"God knows I forgive you!" cried Corona, the tears starting to her eyes in sudden pity. She bent down to support him; but as she moved, he fell prostrate upon his face before her. With a cry of terror she kneeled beside him; with her strong arms she turned his body and raised his head upon her knees. His face was ghastly white, save where the tinges of paint made a hideous mockery of colour upon his livid skin. His parted lips were faintly purple, and his hollow eyes stared wide open at his wife's face, while the curled wig was thrust far back upon his bald and wrinkled forehead.

Corona supported his weight upon one knee, and took his nerveless hand in hers. An agony of terror seized her.

"Onofrio!" she cried — she rarely called him by his name — "Onofrio! speak to me! My husband!" She clasped him wildly in her arms. "O God, have mercy!"

Onofrio d'Astrardente was dead. The poor old dandy, in his paint and his wig and his padding, had died at his wife's feet, protesting his love for her to the last. The long-averted blow had fallen. For years he had guarded himself against sudden emotions, for he was warned of the disease at his heart, and knew his danger; but his anger had killed him. He might have lived another hour while his rage lasted; but the revulsion of feeling, the sudden repentance for the violence he had done his wife, had sent the blood back to its source too quickly, and with his last cry of love upon his lips he was dead.

Corona had hardly ever seen death. She gently lowered the dead man's weight till he lay at full length upon the floor. Then she started to her feet, and drew back against the fireplace, and gazed at the body of her husband.

For fully five minutes she stood motionless, scarcely daring to draw breath, dazed and stupefied with horror,

trying to realise what had happened. There he lay, her
only friend, the companion of her life since she had known
life ; the man who in that very room, but two nights since,
had spoken such kind words to her that her tears had
flowed—the tears that would not flow now ; the man who
but a moment since was railing at her in a paroxysm
of rage—whose anger had melted at her first word of
defence, who had fallen at her feet to ask forgiveness, and
to declare once more, for the last time, that he loved
her ! Her friend, her companion, her husband—had he
heard her answer, that she forgave him freely ? He could
not be dead—it was impossible. A moment ago he had
been speaking to her. She went forward again and kneeled
beside him.

" Onofrio," she said very gently, " you are not dead—
you heard me ? "

She gazed down for a moment at the motionless features.
Womanly thoughtful, she moved his head a little, and
straightened the wig upon his poor forehead. Then, in an
instant, she realised all, and with a wild cry of despair fell
prostrate upon his body in an agony of passionate weeping.
How long she lay, she knew not. A knock at the door did
not reach her ears, nor another and another, at short intervals ; and then some one entered. It was the butler, who
had come to announce the mid-day breakfast. He uttered
an exclamation and started back, holding the handle of the
door in his hand.

Corona raised herself slowly to her knees, gazing down
once more upon the dead man's face. Then she lifted her
streaming eyes and saw the servant.

" Your master is dead," she said, solemnly.

The man grew pale and trembled, hesitated, and then
turned and fled down the hall without, after the manner
of Italian servants, who fear death, and even the sight of
it, as they fear nothing else in the world.

Corona rose to her feet and brushed the tears from her
eyes. Then she turned and rang the bell. No one answered the summons for some time. The news had spread
all over the house in an instant, and everything was dis-

organised. At last a woman came and stood timidly at
the door. She was a lower servant, a simple strong creature
from the mountains. Seeing the others terrified and
paralysed, it had struck her common-sense that her mistress was alone. Corona understood.

"Help me to carry him," she said, quietly; and the
peasant and the noble lady stooped and lifted the dead
duke, and bore him to his chamber without a word, and
laid him tenderly upon his bed.

"Send for the doctor," said Corona; "I will watch
beside him."

"But, Excellency, are you not afraid?" asked the
woman.

Corona's lip curled a little.

"I am not afraid," she answered. "Send at once."
When the woman was gone, she sat down by the bedside
and waited. Her tears were dry now, but she could not
think. She waited motionless for an hour. Then the old
physician entered softly, while a crowd of servants stood
without, peering timidly through the open door. Corona
crossed the room and quietly shut it. The physician
stood by the bedside.

"It is simple enough, Signora Duchessa," he said,
gently. "He is quite dead. It was only the day before
yesterday that I warned him that the heart disease was
worse. Can you tell me how it happened?"

"Yes, exactly," answered Corona, in a low voice. She
was calm enough now. "He came into my room two
hours ago, and suddenly, in conversation, he became very
angry. Then his anger subsided in a moment, and he fell
at my feet."

"It is just as I expected," answered the physician,
quietly. "They always die in this way. I entreat you to
be calm—to consider that all men are mortal——"

"I am calm now," interrupted Corona. "I am alone.
Will you see that what is necessary is done quickly? I
will leave you for a moment. There are people outside."

As she opened the door the gaping crowd of servants
slunk out of her way. With bent head she passed be-

tween them, and went out into the great reception-rooms, and sat down alone in her grief.

It was genuine, of its kind. The poor man's soul might rest in peace, for she felt the real sorrow at his death which he had longed for, which he had perhaps scarcely dared to hope she would feel. Had it not been real, in those first moments some thought would have crossed her mind—some faint, repressed satisfaction at being free at last—free to marry Giovanni Saracinesca. But it was not so. She did not feel free—she felt alone, intensely alone. She longed for the familiar sound of his querulous voice—for the expression of his thousand little wants and interests; she remembered tenderly his harmless little vanities. She thought of his wig, and she wept. So true it is that what is most ridiculous in life is most sorrowfully pathetic in death. There was not one of the small things about him she did not recall with a pang of regret. It was all over now. His vanity was dead with him; his tender love for her was dead too. It was the only love she had known, until that other love—that dark and stirring passion—had been roused in her. But that did not trouble her now. Perhaps the unconscious sense that henceforth she was free to love whom she pleased had suddenly made insignificant a feeling which had before borne in her mind the terrible name of crime. The struggle for loyalty was no more, but the memory of what she had borne for the dead man made him dearer than before. The follies of his life had been many, but many of them had been for her, and there was the true ring in his last words. "To be young for your sake, Corona—for your sake!" The phrase echoed again and again in her remembrance, and her silent tears flowed afresh. The follies of his life had been many, but to her he had been true. The very violence of his last moments, the tenderness of his passionate appeal for forgiveness, spoke for the honesty of his heart, even though his heart had never been honest before.

She needed never to think again of pleasing him, of helping him, of foregoing for his sake any intimacy with the world which she might desire. But the thought brought no relief. He had become so much a part of her life that she could not conceive of living without him, and she would miss him at every turn. The new exist- ence before her seemed dismal and empty beyond all ex- pression. She wondered vaguely what she should do with her time. For one moment a strange longing came over her to return to the dear old convent, to lay aside for ever her coronet and state, and in a simple garb to do simple and good things to the honour of God.

She roused herself at last, and went to her own rooms, dragging her steps slowly as though weighed down by a heavy burden. She entered the room where he had died, and a cold shudder passed over her. The afternoon sun was streaming through the window upon the writing-table where yet lay the unfinished invitation she had been writing, and upon the plants and the rich ornaments, upon the heavy carpet—the very spot where he had breathed his last word of love and died at her feet.

Upon that spot Corona d'Astrardente knelt down rever- ently and prayed,—prayed that she might be forgiven for all her shortcomings to the dear dead man; that she might have strength to bear her sorrow and to honour his memory; above all, that his soul might rest in peace and find for- giveness, and that he might know that she had been truly innocent—she prayed for that too, for she had a dreadful doubt. But surely he knew all now: how she had striven to be loyal, and how truly—yes, how truly—she mourned his death.

At last she rose to her feet, and lingered still a moment, her hands clasped as they had been in her prayer. Glanc- ing down, something glistened on the carpet. She stooped and picked it up. It was her husband's seal-ring, engraven with the ancient arms of the Astrardente. She looked long at the jewel, and then put it upon her finger.

"God give me grace to honour his memory as he would have me honour it," she said, solemnly.

Truly, she had deserved the love the poor old dandy had so deeply felt for her.

CHAPTER XVII.

That night Giovanni insisted on going out. His wounds no longer pained him, he said; there was no danger whatever, and he was tired of staying at home. But he would dine with his father as usual. He loved his father's company, and when the two omitted to quarrel over trifles they were very congenial. To tell the truth, the differences between them arose generally from the petulant quickness of the Prince; for in his son his own irascible character was joined with the melancholy gravity which Giovanni inherited from his mother, and in virtue of which, being taciturn, he was sometimes thought long-suffering.

As usual, they sat opposite each other, and the ancient butler Pasquale served them. As the man deposited Giovanni's soup before him, he spoke. A certain liberty was always granted to Pasquale; Italian servants are members of the family, even in princely houses. Never assuming that confidence implies familiarity, they enjoy the one without ever approaching the latter. Nevertheless it was very rarely that Pasquale spoke to his masters when they were at table.

"I beg your Excellencies' pardon——" he began, as he put down the soup-plate.

"Well, Pasquale?" asked old Saracinesca, looking sharply at the old servant from under his heavy brows.

"Have your Excellencies heard the news?"

"What news? No," returned the Prince.

"The Duca d'Astrardente——"

"Well, what of him?"

"Is dead."

"Dead!" repeated Giovanni in a loud voice, that echoed to the vaulted roof of the dining-room.

"It is not true," said old Saracinesca; "I saw him in the street this morning."

"Nevertheless, your Excellency," replied Pasquale, "it is quite true. The gates of the palace were already draped with black before the Ave Maria this evening; and the

porter, who is a nephew of mine, had *crêpe* upon his hat
and arm. He told me that the Duca fell down dead of a
stroke in the Signora Duchessa's room at half-past twelve
to-day."

"Is that all you could learn?" asked the Prince.

"Except that the Signora Duchessa was overcome with
grief," returned the servant, gravely.

"I should think so—her husband dead of an apoplexy!
It is natural," said the Prince, looking at Giovanni. The
latter was silent, and tried to eat as though nothing had
happened—inwardly endeavouring not to rejoice too madly
at the terrible catastrophe. In his effort to control his
features, the blood rushed to his forehead, and his hand
trembled violently. His father saw it, but made no
remark.

"Poor Astrardente!" he said. "He was not so bad as
people thought him."

"No," replied Giovanni, with a great effort; "he was a
very good man."

"I should hardly say that," returned his father, with
a grim smile of amusement. "I do not think that by
the greatest stretch of indulgence he could be called
good."

"And why not?" asked the younger man, sharply
snatching at any possible discussion in order to conceal
his embarrassment.

"Why not, indeed! Why, because he had a goodly
share of original sin, to which he added others of his own
originating but having an equal claim to originality."

"I say I think he was a very good man," repeated Giovanni, maintaining his point with an air of conviction.

"If that is your conception of goodness, it is no wonder
that you have not attained to sanctity," said the old man,
with a sneer.

"It pleases you to be witty," answered his son. "Astrardente did not gamble; he had no vices of late. He
was kind to his wife."

"No vices—no. He did not steal like a fraudulent
bank-clerk, nor try to do murder like Del Ferice. He did

not deceive his wife, nor starve her to death. He had therefore no vices. He was a good man."

"Let us leave poor Del Ferice alone," said Giovanni.

"I suppose you will pity him now," replied the Prince, sarcastically. "You will talk differently if he dies and you have to leave the country at a moment's notice, like Spicca this morning."

"I should be very sorry if Del Ferice died. I should never recover from it. I am not a professional duellist like Spicca. And yet Casalverde deserved his death. I can quite understand that Del Ferice might in the excitement of the moment have lunged at me after the halt was cried, but I cannot understand how Casalverde could be so infamous as not to cross his sword when he himself called. It looked very much like a preconcerted arrangement. Casalverde deserved to die, for the safety of society. I should think that Rome had had enough of duelling for a while."

"Yes; but after all, Casalverde did not count for much. I am not sure I ever saw the fellow before in my life. And I suppose Del Ferice will recover. There was a story this morning that he was dead; but I went and inquired myself, and found that he was better. People are much shocked at this second duel. Well, it could not be helped. Poor old Astrardente! So we shall never see his wig again at every ball and theatre and supper-party! There was a man who enjoyed his life to the very end!"

"I should not call it enjoyment to be built up every day by one's valet, like a card-house, merely to tumble to pieces again when the pins are taken out," said Giovanni.

"You do not seem so enthusiastic in his defence as you were a few minutes ago," said the Prince, with a smile.

Giovanni was so much disturbed at the surprising news that he hardly knew what he said. He made a desperate attempt to be sensible.

"It appears to me that moral goodness and personal appearance are two things," he said, oracularly. The Prince burst into a loud laugh.

"Most people would say that! Eat your dinner, Giovanni, and do not talk such arrant nonsense."

"Why is it nonsense? Because you do not agree with me?"

"Because you are too much excited to talk sensibly," said his father. "Do you think I cannot see it?"

Giovanni was silent for a time. He was angry at his father for detecting the cause of his vagueness, but he supposed there was no help for it. At last Pasquale left the room. Old Saracinesca gave a sigh of relief.

"And now, Giovannino," he said familiarly, "what have you got to say for yourself?"

"I?" asked his son, in some surprise.

"You! What are you going to do?"

"I will stay at home," said Giovanni, shortly.

"That is not the question. You are wise to stay at home, because you ought to get yourself healed of that scratch. Giovanni, the Astrardente is now a widow."

"Seeing that her husband is dead—of course. There is vast ingenuity in your deduction," returned the younger man, eyeing his father suspiciously.

"Do not be an idiot, Giovannino. I mean, that as she is a widow, I have no objection to your marrying her."

"Good God, sir!" cried Giovanni, "what do you mean?"

"What I say. She is the most beautiful woman in Rome. She is one of the best women I know. She will have a sufficient jointure. Marry her. You will never be happy with a silly little girl just out of a convent. You are not that sort of man. The Astrardente is not three-and-twenty, but she has had five years of the world, and she has stood the test well. I shall be proud to call her my daughter."

In his excitement Giovanni sprang from his seat, and rushing to his father's side, threw his arms round his neck and embraced him. He had never done such a thing in his life. Then he remained standing, and grew suddenly thoughtful.

"It is heartless of us to talk in this way," he said. "The poor man is not buried yet."

"My dear boy," said the old Prince, "Astrardente is

dead. He hated me, and was beginning to hate you, I
fancy. We were neither of us his friends, at any rate.
We do not rejoice at his death; we merely regard it in
the light of an event which modifies our immediate future.
He is dead, and his wife is free. So long as he was alive,
the fact of your loving her was exceedingly unfortunate:
it was injuring you and doing a wrong to her. Now, on
the contrary, the greatest good fortune that can happen to
you both is that you should marry each other."

"That is true," returned Giovanni. In the suddenness
of the news, it had not struck him that his father would
ever look favourably upon the match, although the immediate possibility of the marriage had burst upon him as a
great light suddenly rising in a thick darkness. But his
nature, as strong as his father's, was a little more delicate,
a shade less rough; and even in the midst of his great joy,
it struck him as heartless to be discussing the chances of
marrying a woman whose husband was not yet buried. No
such scruple disturbed the geniality of the old Prince. He
was an honest and straightforward man—a man easily possessed by a single idea—and he was capable of profound
affections. He had loved his Spanish wife strongly in his
own fashion, and she had loved him; but there was no one
left to him now but his son, whom he delighted in, and
he regarded the rest of the world merely as pawns to be
moved into position for the honour and glory of the Saracinesca. He thought no more of a man's life than of the
end of a cigar, smoked out and fit to be thrown away.
Astrardente had been nothing to him but an obstacle. It
had not struck him that he could ever be removed; but
since it had pleased Providence to take him out of the way,
there was no earthly reason for mourning his death. All
men must die—it was better that death should come to
those who stood in the way of their fellow-creatures.

"I am not at all sure that she will consent," said
Giovanni, beginning to walk up and down the room.

"Bah!" ejaculated his father. "You are the best match
in Italy. Why should any woman refuse you?"

"I am not so sure. She is not like other women. Let

us not talk of it now. It will not be possible to do any-thing for a year, I suppose. A year is a long time. Mean-while I will go to that poor man's funeral."

"Of course. So will I."

And they both went, and found themselves in a vast crowd of acquaintances. No one had believed that Astrardente could ever die, that the day would ever come when society should know his place no more; and with one consent everybody sent their carriages to the funeral, and went themselves a day or two later to the great requiem Mass in the parish church. There was nothing to be seen but the great black catafalque, with Corona's household of servants in deep mourning liveries kneeling behind it. Relations she had none, and the dead man was the last of his race—she was utterly alone.

"She need not have made it so terribly impressive," said Madame Mayer to Valdarno when the Mass was over. Madame Mayer paused beside the holy-water basin, and dipping one gloved finger, she presented it to Valdarno with an engaging smile. Both crossed themselves.

"She need not have got it up so terribly impressively, after all," she repeated.

"I daresay she will miss him at first," returned Val-darno, who was a kind-hearted fellow enough, and was very far from realising how much he had contributed to the sudden death of the old dandy. "She is a strange woman. I believe she had grown fond of him."

"Oh, I know all that," said Donna Tullia, as they left the church.

"Yes," answered her companion, with a significant smile, "I presume you do." Donna Tullia laughed harshly as she got into her carriage.

"You are detestable, Valdarno—you always misunder-stand me. Are you going to the ball to-night ?"

"Of course. May I have the pleasure of the cotillon ?"

"If you are very good—if you will go and ask the news of Del Ferice."

"I sent this morning. He is quite out of danger, they believe."

"Is he? Oh, I am very glad—I felt so very badly, you know. Ah, Don Giovanni, are you recovered?" she asked coldly, as Saracinesca approached the other side of the carriage. Valdarno retired to a distance, and pretended to be buttoning his greatcoat; he wanted to see what would happen.

"Thank you, yes; I was not much hurt. This is the first time I have been out, and I am glad to find an opportunity of speaking to you. Let me say again how profoundly I regret my forgetfulness at the ball the other night——"

Donna Tullia was a clever woman, and though she had been very angry at the time, she was in love with Giovanni. She therefore looked at him suddenly with a gentle smile, and just for one moment her fingers touched his hand as it rested upon the side of the carriage.

"Do you think it was kind?" she asked, in a low voice.

"It was abominable. I shall never forgive myself," answered Giovanni.

"I will forgive you," answered Donna Tullia, softly. She really loved him. It was the best thing in her nature, but it was more than balanced by the jealousy she had conceived for the Duchessa d'Astrardente.

"Was it on that account that you quarrelled with poor Del Ferice?" she asked, after a moment's pause. "I have feared it——"

"Certainly not," answered Giovanni, quickly. "Pray set your mind at rest. Del Ferice or any other man would have been quite justified in calling me out for it— but it was not for that. It was not on account of you."

It would have been hard to say whether Donna Tullia's face expressed more clearly her surprise or her disappointment at the intelligence. Perhaps she had both really believed herself the cause of the duel, and had been flattered at the thought that men would fight for her.

"Oh, I am very glad—it is a great relief," she said, rather coldly. "Are you going to the ball to-night?"

"No; I cannot dance. My right arm is bound up in a sling, as you see."

"I am sorry you are not coming. Good-bye, then."

"Good-bye; I am very grateful for your forgiveness." Giovanni bowed low, and Donna Tullia's brilliant equipage dashed away.

Giovanni was well satisfied at having made his peace so easily, but he nevertheless apprehended danger from Donna Tullia.

The next thing which interested Roman society was Astrardente's will, but no one was much surprised when the terms of it were known. As there were no relations, everything was left to his wife. The palace in Rome, the town and castle in the Sabines, the broad lands in the low hill-country towards Ceprano, and what surprised even the family lawyer, a goodly sum in solid English securities, —a splendid fortune in all, according to Roman ideas. Astrardente abhorred the name of money in his conversation—it had been one of his affectations; but he had an excellent understanding of business, and was exceedingly methodical in the management of his affairs. The inheritance, the lawyer thought, might be estimated at three millions of scudi.

"Is all this wealth mine, then?" asked Corona, when the solicitor had explained the situation.

"All, Signora Duchessa. You are enormously rich."

Enormously rich! And alone in the world. Corona asked herself if she was the same woman, the same Corona del Carmine who five years before had suffered in the old convent the humiliation of having no pocket-money, whose wedding-gown had been provided from the proceeds of a little sale of the last relics of her father's once splendid collection of old china and pictures. She had never thought of money since she had been married; her husband was generous, but methodical; she never bought anything without consulting him, and the bills all went through his hands. Now and then she had rather timidly asked for a small sum for some charity; she had lacked nothing that money could buy, but she never remembered to have had more than a hundred francs in her purse. Astrardente had once offered to give her an allowance, and had seemed pleased that she refused it.

He liked to manage things himself, being a man of detail.

And now she was enormously rich, and alone. It was a strange sensation. She felt it to be so new that she innocently said so to the lawyer.

"What shall I do with it all?"

"Signora Duchessa," returned the old man, "with regard to money the question is, not what to do with it, but how to do without it. You are very young, Signora Duchessa."

"I shall be twenty-three in August," said Corona, simply.

"Precisely. I would beg to be allowed to observe that by the terms of the will, and by the laws of this country, you are not the dowager-duchess, but you are in your own right and person the sole and only feudal mistress and holder of the title."

"Am I?"

"Certainly, with all the privileges thereto attached. It may be—I beg pardon for being so bold as to suggest it—it may be that in years to come, when time has soothed your sorrow, you may wish, you may consent, to renew the marriage tie."

"I doubt it—but the thing is possible," said Corona, quietly.

"In that case, and should you prefer to contract a marriage of inclination, you will have no difficulty in conferring your title upon your husband, with any reservations you please. Your children will then inherit from you, and become in their turn Dukes of Astrardente. This I conceive to have been the purpose and spirit of the late Duke's will. The estate, magnificent as it is, will not be too large for the foundation of a new race. If you desire any distinctive title, you can call yourself Duchessa del Carmine d'Astrardente—it would sound very well," remarked the lawyer, contemplating the beautiful woman before him.

"It is of little importance what I call myself," said Corona. "At present I shall certainly make no change. It is very unlikely that I shall ever marry."

"I trust, Signora Duchessa, that in any case you will always command my most humble services."

With this protestation of fidelity the lawyer left the Palazzo Astrardente, and Corona remained in her boudoir in meditation of what it would be like to be the feudal mistress of a great title and estate. She was very sad, but she was growing used to her solitude. Her liberty was strange to her, but little by little she was beginning to enjoy it. At first she had missed the constant care of the poor man who for five years had been her companion; she had missed his presence and the burden of thinking for him at every turn of the day. But it was not for long. Her memory of him was kind and tender, and for months after his death the occasional sight of some object associated with him brought the tears to her eyes. She often wished he could walk into the room in his old way, and begin talking of the thousand and one bits of town gossip that interested him. But the first feeling of desolation soon passed, for he had not been more than a companion; she could analyse every memory she had of him to its source and reason. There was not in her that passionate unformulated yearning for him that comes upon a loving heart when its fellow is taken away, and which alone is a proof that love has been real and true. She soon grew accustomed to his absence.

To marry again—every one would say she would be right —to marry and to be the mother of children, of brave sons and noble girls,—ah yes! that was a new thought, a wonderful thought, one of many that were wonderful.

Then, again, her strong nature suddenly rose in a new sense of strength, and she paced the room slowly with a strange expression of sternness upon her beautiful features.

"I am a power in the world," she said to herself, almost starting at the truth of the thought, and yet taking delight in it. "I am what men call rich and powerful; I have money, estates, castles, and palaces; I am young, I am strong. What shall I do with it all?"

As she walked, she dreamed of raising some great institution of charity; she knew not for what precise object, but there was room enough for charity in Rome. The great Torlonia had built churches, and hospitals, and asylums. She would do likewise; she would make for herself an interest in doing good, a satisfaction in the exercise of her power to combat evil. It would be magnificent to feel that she had done it herself, alone and unaided; that she had built the walls from the foundation and the corner-stone to the eaves; that she had entered herself into the study of each detail, and herself peopled the great institution with such as most needed help in the world—with little children, perhaps. She would visit them every day, and herself provide for their wants and care for their sufferings. She would give the place her husband's name, and the good she would accomplish with his earthly portion might perhaps profit his soul. She would go to Padre Filippo and ask his advice. He would know what was best to be done, for he knew more of the misery in Rome than any one, and had a greater mind to relieve it. She had seen him since her husband's death, but she had not yet conceived this scheme.

And Giovanni—she thought of him too; but the habit of putting him out of her heart was strong. She dimly fancied that in the far future a day might come when she would be justified in thinking of him if she so pleased; but for the present, her loyalty to her dead husband seemed more than ever a sacred duty. She would not permit herself to think of Giovanni, even though, from a general point of view, she might contemplate the possibility of a second marriage. She would go to Padre Filippo and talk over everything with him; he would advise her well.

Then a wild longing seized her to leave Rome for a while, to breathe the air of the country, to get away from the scene of all her troubles, of all the terrible emotions that had swept over her life in the last three weeks, to be alone in the hills or by the sea. It seemed dreadful to be tied to her great house in the city, in her mourning, shut off suddenly from the world, and bound down by the chain of conventionality to a fixed method of existence. She would give anything to go away. Why not? She suddenly realised what was so hard to understand, that she was free to go where she pleased—if only, by accident, she could chance to meet Giovanni Saracinesca before she left. No—the thought was unworthy. She would leave town at once—surely she could have nothing to say to Giovanni—she would leave to-morrow morning.

CHAPTER XVIII.

Corona found it impossible to leave town so soon as she had wished. She had indeed sent out great cart-loads of furniture, servants, horses, and all the paraphernalia of an establishment in the country, and she believed herself ready to move at once, when she received an exceedingly courteous note from Cardinal Antonelli requesting the honour of being received by her the next day at twelve o'clock. It was impossible to refuse, and to her great annoyance she was obliged to postpone her departure another twenty-four hours. She guessed that the great man was the bearer of some message from the Holy Father himself; and in her present frame of mind, such words of comfort could not fail to be acceptable from one whom she reverenced and loved, as all who knew Pius IX. did sincerely revere and love him. She did not like the Cardinal, it is true; but she did not confound the ambassador with him who sent the embassy. The Cardinal was a most courteous and accomplished man of the world, and Corona could not easily have explained the aversion she felt for him. It is very likely that if she could have understood the part he was sustaining in the great European struggle of those days, she would have accorded him at least the admiration he deserved as a statesman. He had his faults, and they were faults little becoming a cardinal of the Holy Roman Church. But few are willing to consider that, though a cardinal, he was not a priest— that he was practically a layman who, by his own unaided

genius, had attained to great power, and that those faults
which have been charged against him with such virulence
would have passed, nay, actually pass, unnoticed and un-
censured in many a great statesman of those days and of
these.   He was a brave man, who fought a desperate and
hopeless fight to his last breath, and who fought almost
alone—a man most bitterly hated by many, at whose death
many rejoiced loudly and few mourned; and to the shame
of many be it said, that his most obstinate adversaries,
those who unsparingly heaped abuse upon him during his
lifetime, and most unseemingly exulted over his end, were
the very men among whom he should have found the most
willing supporters and the firmest friends.   But in 1865
he was feared, and those who reckoned without him in the
game of politics reckoned badly.

Corona was a woman, and very young.   She had not
the knowledge or the experience to understand his value,
and she had taken a personal dislike to him when she first
appeared in society.   He was too smooth for her; she
thought him false.   She preferred a rougher type.   Her
husband, on the other hand, had a boundless admiration
for the cardinal-statesman; and perhaps the way in which
Astrardente constantly tried to impress his wife with a
sense of the great man's virtues, indirectly contributed to
increase her aversion.   Nevertheless, when he sent word
that he desired to be received by her, she did not hesitate
a moment, but expressed her willingness at once.   Punctu-
ally as the gun of Sant' Angelo roared out the news that
the sun was on the meridian, Cardinal Antonelli entered
Corona's house.   She received him in the great drawing-
room.   There was an air of solemnity about the meeting.
The room itself, divested of a thousand trifles which had
already been sent into the country, looked desolate and
formal; the heavy curtains admitted but little light; there
was no fire on the hearth; Corona stood all in black—a
very incarnation of mourning—as her visitor trod softly
across the dark carpet towards her.

The Cardinal's expressive face was softened by a look of
gentle sympathy, as he came forward and took her hand

in both of his, and gazed for a moment into her beautiful eyes.

"I am an ambassador, Duchessa," he said, softly. "I come to tell you how deeply our Holy Father sympathises in your great sorrow."

Corona bent her head respectfully, and motioned to the Cardinal to be seated.

"I beg that your Eminence will convey to his Holiness my most sincere gratitude for this expression of his paternal kindness to one so unhappy."

"Indeed I will not fail to deliver your message, Duchessa," answered the Cardinal, seating himself by her side in one of the great arm-chairs which had been placed together in the middle of the room. "His Holiness has promised to remember you in his august prayers; and I also, for my own part, entreat you to believe that my poor sympathy is wholly with you in your distress."

"Your Eminence is most kind," replied Corona, gravely.

It seemed as though there were little more to be said in such a case. There was no friendship between the two, no bond of union or fellowship: it was simply a formal visit of condolence, entailed as a necessity by Corona's high position. The Pope had sent her a gift at her wedding; he sent her a message of sympathy at her husband's death. Half-a-dozen phrases would be exchanged, and the Cardinal would take his leave, accompanied by a file of the Duchessa's lackeys—and so it would all be over. But the Cardinal was a statesman, a diplomatist, and one of the best talkers in Europe; moreover, he never allowed an opportunity of pursuing his ends to pass unimproved.

"Ah, Duchessa!" he said, folding his hands upon his knee and looking down, "there is but one Consoler in sorrow such as yours. It is vain for us mortals to talk of any such thing as alleviating real mental suffering. There are consolations—many of them—for some people, but they are not for you. To many the accidents of wealth, of youth, of beauty, seem to open the perspective of a brilliant future at the very moment when all the present appears to be shrouded in darkness; but if you will permit

me, who know you so little, to say it frankly, I do not
believe that any of these things which you possess in such
plentiful abundance will lessen the measure of your grief.
It is not right that they should, I suppose. It is not
fitting that noble minds should even possess the faculty of
forgetting real suffering in the unreal trifles of a great
worldly possession, which so easily restore the weak to
courage, and flatter the vulgar into the forgetfulness of
honourable sorrow. I am no moraliser, no pedantic phil-
osopher. The stoic may have shrugged his heavy shoulders
in sullen indifference to fate; the epicurean may have
found such bodily ease in his excessive refinement of moderate enjoyment as to overlook the deepest afflictions in
anticipating the animal pleasure of the next meal. I cannot conceive of such men as those philosophising diners;
nor can I imagine by what arguments the wisest of mankind could induce a fellow-creature in distress to forget
his sufferings. Sorrow is sorrow still to all finely organised natures. The capacity for feeling sorrow is one of the
highest tests of nobility—a nobility of nature not found
always in those of high blood and birth, but existing in
the people, wherever the people are good."

The Cardinal's voice became even more gentle as he
spoke. He was himself of very humble origin, and spoke
feelingly. Corona listened, though she only heard half of
what he said; but his soft tone soothed her almost unconsciously.

"There is little consolation for me—I am quite alone,"
she said.

"You are not of those who find relief in worldly greatness," continued the Cardinal. "But I have seen women,
young, rich, and beautiful, wear their mourning with wonderful composure. Youth is so much, wealth is so much
more, beauty is such a power in the world—all three together are resistless. Many a young widow is not ashamed
to think of marriage before her husband has been dead a
month. Indeed they do not always make bad wives. A
woman who has been married young and is early deprived
of her husband, has great experience, great knowledge of

the world. Many feel that they have no right to waste
the goods given them in a life of solitary mourning.
Wealth is given to be used, and perhaps many a rich
young widow thinks she can use it more wisely in the
company of a husband young as herself. It may be; I
cannot tell. These are days when power of any sort
should be used, and perhaps no one should even for a
moment think of withdrawing from the scene where such
great battles are being fought. But one may choose wisely
a way of using power, or one may choose unwisely. There
is much to be done."

"How?" asked Corona, catching at his expression of an
idea which pursued her. "Here am I, rich, alone, idle—
above all, very unhappy. What can I do? I wish I knew,
for I would try and do it."

"Ah! I was not speaking of you, Duchessa," answered
the statesman. "You are too noble a woman to be easily
consoled. And yet, though you may not find relief from
your great sorrow, there are many things within your reach
which you might do, and feel that in your mourning you
have done honour to your departed husband as well as to
yourself. You have great estates—you can improve them,
and especially you can improve the condition of your
peasants, and strengthen their loyalty to you and to the
State. You can find many a village on your lands where a
school might be established, an asylum built, a road opened
—anything which shall give employment to the poor, and
which, when finished, shall benefit their condition. Especially about Astrardente they are very poor; I know the
country well. In six months you might change many things;
and then you might return to Rome next winter. If it
pleases you, you can do anything with society. You can
make your house a centre for a new party—the oldest of
all parties it is, but it would now be thought new here.
We have no centre. There is no *salon* in the good old
sense of the word—no house where all that is intelligent,
all that is powerful, all that is influential, is irresistibly
drawn. To make a centre of that kind would be a worthy
object, it seems to me. You would surround yourself with

men of genius; you would bring those together who cannot
meet elsewhere; you would give a vigorous tone to a society
which is fast falling to decay from inanition; you could
become a power, a real power, not only in Rome, but in
Europe; you could make your house famous as the point
from which, in Rome, all that is good and great should
radiate to the very ends of the earth. You could do all
this in your young widowhood, and you would not dishonour the memory of him you loved so dearly."

Corona looked earnestly at the Cardinal as he enlarged
upon the possibilities of her life. What he said seemed
true and good. It opened to her a larger field than she
had dreamed of half an hour ago. Especially the plan of
working for the improvement of her estates and people
attracted her. She wanted to do something at once—
something good, and something worth doing.

"I believe you are right," she said. "I shall die if I
am idle."

"I know I am right," returned the Cardinal in a tone of
conviction. "Not that I propose all this as an unalterable
plan for you. I would not have you think I mean to lay
down any system, or even to advise you at all. I was
merely thinking aloud. I am too happy if my thoughts
please you—if anything I say can even for a moment
relieve your mind from the pressure of this sudden grief.
It is not consolation I offer you. I am not a priest, but a
man of action; and it is action I propose to you, not as an
anodyne for sorrow, but simply because it is right that in
these days we should all strive with a good will. Your
peasants are many of them in an evil case: you can save
them and make them happy, even though you find no
happiness for yourself. Our social world here is falling to
pieces, going astray after strange gods, and especially after
Madame Mayer and her *lares* and *penates*, young Valdarno
and Del Ferice: it is in your power to create a new life
here, or at least to contribute greatly towards re-establishing
the social balance. I say, do this thing, if you will, for it
is a good thing to do. At all events, while you are building
roads—and perhaps schools—at Astrardente, you can think

over the course you will afterwards pursue. And now, my dear Duchessa, I have detained you far too long. Forgive me if I have wearied you, for I have great things at heart, and must sometimes speak of them, though I speak feebly. Count on me always for any assistance you may require. Bear with me if I weary you, for I was a good friend of him we both mourn."

"Thank you—you have given me good thoughts," said Corona, simply.

So the courtly Cardinal rose and took his leave, and once more Corona was left alone. It was a strange thing that, while he disclaimed all power to comfort her, and denied that consolation was possible in her case, she had nevertheless listened to him with interest, and now found herself thinking seriously of what he had said. He seemed to have put her thoughts into shape, and to have given direction to that sense of power she had already begun to feel. For the first time in her life she felt something like sympathy for the Cardinal, and she lingered for some minutes alone in the great reception-room, wondering whether she could accomplish any of the things he had proposed to her. At all events, there was nothing now to hinder her departure; and she thought with something like pleasure of the rocky Sabines, the solitude of the mountains, the simple faces of the people about her place, and of the quiet life she intended to lead there during the next six months.

But the Cardinal went on his way, rolling along through the narrow streets in his great coach. Leaning far back in his cushioned seat, he could just catch a glimpse of the people as he passed, and his quick eyes recognised many, both high and low. But he did not care to show himself, for he felt himself disliked, and deep in his finely organised nature there lay a sensitiveness which was wounded by the popular hatred. It hurt him to see the lowering glances of the poor man, and to return the forced bow of the rich man who feared him. He often longed to be able to explain many things to them both, to the rich and to the poor; and then, knowing how impossible it was that he should be understood by either,

P

he sighed somewhat bitterly, and hid himself still deeper in his carriage. Few men in the midst of the world have stood so wholly alone as Cardinal Antonelli.

To-day, however, he had an appointment which he anticipated with a sort of interest quite new to him. Anastase Gouache was coming to begin his portrait, and Anastase was an object of curiosity to him. It would have surprised the young Frenchman had he guessed how carefully he was watched, for he was a modest fellow, and did not think himself of very much importance. He allowed Donna Tullia and her friends to come to his studio whenever they pleased, and he listened to their shallow talk, and joined occasionally in the conversation, letting them believe that he sympathised with them, simply because his own ideas were unsettled. It was a good thing for him to paint a portrait of Donna Tullia, for it made him the fashion, and he had small scruple in agreeing with her views so long as he had no fixed convictions of his own. She and her set regarded him as a harmless boy, and looked upon his little studio as a convenience, in payment whereof they pushed him into society, and spread abroad the rumour that he was the rising artist of the day. But the great Cardinal had seen him more than once, and had conceived a liking for his delicate intellectual face and unobtrusive manner. He had watched him and caused him to be watched, and his interest had increased, and finally he had taken a fancy to have a portrait of himself painted by the young fellow. This was the day appointed for the first sitting; and when the Cardinal reached his lodgings, high up in the Vatican pile, he found Anastase Gouache waiting for him in the small ante-chamber.

The prime minister was not luxuriously lodged. Four rooms sufficed him—to wit, the said ante-chamber, bare and uncarpeted, and furnished with three painted wooden box benches; a comfortable study lined throughout with shelves and lockers, furnished with half-a-dozen large chairs and a single writing-table, whereon stood a crucifix and an inkstand; beyond this a bedroom and a small dining-room: that was all. The drawers of the lockers and bookcases contained a correspondence which would have astonished Europe, and a collection of gems and precious stones unrivalled in the world; but there was nothing in the shape of ornament visible to the eye, unless one were to class under that head a fairly good bust of Pius IX., which stood upon a plain marble pedestal in one corner. Gouache followed the great man into this study. He was surprised by the simplicity of the apartment; but he felt in sympathy with it, and with the Cardinal himself; and with the intuitive knowledge of a true artist, he foresaw that he was to paint a successful portrait.

The Cardinal busied himself with some papers while the painter silently made his preparations.

"If your Eminence is ready?" suggested Gouache.

"At your service, my friend," replied the Cardinal, blandly. "How shall I sit? The portrait must be taken in full face, I think."

"By all means. Here, I think—so; the light is very good at this hour, but a little later we shall have the sun. If your Eminence will look at me—a little more to the left —I think that will do. I will draw it in in charcoal, and your Eminence can judge."

"Precisely," returned the Cardinal. "You will paint the devil even blacker than he is."

"The devil?" repeated Gouache, raising his eyebrows with a slight smile. "I was not aware——"

"And yet you have been in Rome four years!"

"I am very careful," returned Gouache. "I never by any chance hear any evil of those whom I am to paint."

"You have very well-bred ears, Monsieur Gouache. I fear that if I had attended some of the meetings in your studio while Donna Tullia was having her portrait painted, I should have heard strange things. Have they all escaped you?"

Gouache was silent for a moment. It did not surprise him to learn that the omniscient Cardinal was fully acquainted with the doings in his studio, but he looked curiously at the great man before he answered. The Cardinal's small gleaming eyes met his with the fearlessness of superiority.

"I remember nothing but good of your Eminence," the painter replied at last, with a laugh; and applying himself to his work, he began to draw in the outline of the Cardinal's head. The words he had just heard, implying as they did a thorough knowledge of the minutest details of social life, would have terrified Madame Mayer, and would perhaps have driven Del Ferice out of the Papal States in fear of his life. Even the good-natured and foolish Valdarno might reasonably have been startled; but Anastase was made of different stuff. His grandfather had helped to storm the Bastille, his father had been among the men of 1848; there was revolutionary blood in his veins, and he distinguished between real and imaginary conspiracy with the unerring certainty of instinct, as the bloodhound knows the track of man from the slot of meaner game. He laughed at Donna Tullia, he distrusted Del Ferice, and to some extent he understood the Cardinal. And the statesman understood him, too, and was interested by him.

"You may as well forget their chatter. It does me no harm, and it amuses them. It does not seem to surprise you that I should know all about it, however. You have good nerves, Monsieur Gouache."

"Of course your Eminence can send me out of Rome to-morrow, if you please," answered Gouache, with perfect unconcern. "But the portrait will not be finished so soon."

"No—that would be a pity. You shall stay. But the others—what would you advise me to do with them?" asked the Cardinal, his bright eyes twinkling with amusement.

"If by the others your Eminence means my friends," replied Gouache, quietly, "I can assure you that none of them will ever cause you the slightest inconvenience."

"I believe you are right—their ability to annoy me is considerably inferior to their inclination. Is it not so?"

"If your Eminence will allow me," said Gouache, rising suddenly and laying down his charcoal pencil, "I will pin this curtain across the window. The sun is beginning to come in."

He had no intention of answering any questions. If the Cardinal knew of the meetings in the Via San Basilio, that was not Gouache's fault; Gouache would certainly not give any further information. The statesman had expected as much, and was not at all surprised at the young man's silence.

"One of those young gentlemen seems to have met his match, at all events," he remarked, presently. "I am sorry it should have come about in that way."

"Your Eminence might easily have prevented the duel."

"I knew nothing about it," answered the Cardinal, glancing keenly at Anastase.

"Nor I," said the artist, simply.

"You see my information is not always so good as people imagine, my friend."

"It is a pity," remarked Gouache. "It would have been better had poor Del Ferice been killed outright. The matter would have terminated there."

"Whereas——"

"Whereas Del Ferice will naturally seek an occasion for revenge."

"You speak as though you were a friend of Don Giovanni's," said the Cardinal.

"No; I have a very slight acquaintance with him. I admire him, he has such a fine head. I should be sorry if anything happened to him."

"Do you think Del Ferice is capable of murdering him?"

"Oh no! He might annoy him a great deal."

"I think not," answered the Cardinal, thoughtfully. "Del Ferice was afraid that Don Giovanni would marry Donna Tullia and spoil his own projects. But Giovanni will not think of that again."

"No; I suppose Don Giovanni will marry the Duchessa d'Astrardente."

"Of course," replied the Cardinal. For some minutes there was silence. Gouache, while busy with his pencil, was wondering at the interest the great man took in such details of the Roman social life. The Cardinal was thinking of Corona, whom he had seen but half an hour ago, and was revolving in his mind the advantages that might be got by allying her to Giovanni. He had in view for her a certain Serene Highness whom he wished to conciliate, and whose circumstances were not so splendid as to make Corona's fortune seem insignificant to him. But on the other hand, the Cardinal had no Serene Highness ready for Giovanni, and feared lest he should after all marry Donna Tullia, and get into the opposite camp.

"You are from Paris, Monsieur Gouache, I believe," said the Cardinal at last.

"Parisian of the Parisians, your Eminence."

"How can you bear to live in exile so long? You have not been to your home these four years, I think."

"I would rather live in Rome for the present. I will go to Paris some day. It will always be a pleasant recollection to have seen Rome in these days. My friends write me that Paris is gay, but not pleasant."

"You think there will soon be nothing of this time left but the recollection of it?" suggested the Cardinal.

"I do not know what to think. The times seem unsettled, and so are my ideas. I was told that your Eminence would help me to decide what to believe." Gouache smiled pleasantly, and looked up.

"And who told you that?"

"Don Giovanni Saràcinesca."

"But I must have some clue to what your ideas are," said the Cardinal. "When did Don Giovanni say that?"

"At Prince Frangipani's. He had been talking with your Eminence—perhaps he had come to some conclusion in consequence," suggested Gouache.

"Perhaps so," answered the great man, with a look of considerable satisfaction. "At all events I am flattered by the opinion he gave you of me. Perhaps I may help you to decide. What are your opinions? or rather, what would you like your opinions to be?"

"I am an ardent republican," said Gouache, boldly. It needed no ordinary courage to make such a statement to

the incarnate chief of reactionary politics in those days—
within the walls of the Vatican, not a hundred yards from
the private apartments of the Holy Father. But Cardinal
Antonelli smiled blandly, and seemed not in the least surprised nor offended.

"Republicanism is an exceedingly vague term, Monsieur
Gouache," he said. "But with what other opinions do
you wish to reconcile your republicanism?"

"With those held by the Church. I am a good Catholic, and I desire to remain one—indeed I cannot help
remaining one."

"Christianity is not vague, at all events," answered the
Cardinal, who, to tell the truth, was somewhat astonished
at the artist's juxtaposition of two such principles. "In
the first place, allow me to observe, my friend, that Christianity is the purest form of a republic which the world
has ever seen, and that it therefore only depends upon
your good sense to reconcile in your own mind two ideas
which from the first have been indissolubly bound together."

It was Gouache's turn to be startled at the Cardinal's
confidence.

"I am afraid I must ask your Eminence for some further explanation," he said. "I had no idea that Christianity and republicanism were the same thing."

"Republicanism," returned the statesman, "is a vague
term, invented in an abortive attempt to define by one
word the mass of inextricable disorder arising in our times
from the fusion of socialistic ideas with ideas purely republican. If you mean to speak of this kind of thing,
you must define precisely your position in regard to
socialism, and in regard to the pure theory of a commonwealth. If you mean to speak of a real republic in any
known form, such as the ancient Roman, the Dutch, or
the American, I understand you without further explanation."

"I certainly mean to speak of the pure republic. I
believe that under a pure republic the partition of wealth
would take care of itself."

"Very good, my friend.   Now, with regard to the early
Christians, should you say that their communities were
monarchic, or aristocratic, or oligarchic ?"

"None of those three, I should think," said Gouache.

"There are only two systems left, then—democracy and
hierarchy.   You will probably say that the government of
the early Christians was of the latter kind—that they were
governed by priests, in fact.   But on the other hand, there
is no doubt that both those who governed, and those who
were governed by them, had all things in common, regarded
no man as naturally superior to another, and preached a
fraternity and equality at least as sincere as those incul-
cated by the first French Republic.   I do not see how you
can avoid calling such community a republic, seeing that
there was an equal partition of wealth; and defining it as
a democratic one, seeing that they all called each other
brethren."

"But the hierarchy — what became of it ?" inquired
Gouache.

"The hierarchy existed within the democracy, by common consent and for the public good, and formed a second
democracy of smaller extent but greater power.   Any man
might become a priest, any priest might become a bishop,
any bishop might become pope, as surely as any born
citizen of Rome could become consul, or any native of New
York may be elected President of the United States.
Now in theory this was beautiful, and in practice the
democratic spirit of the hierarchy, the smaller republic, has
survived in undiminished vigour to the present day.   In
the original Christian theory the whole world should now
be one vast republic, in which all Christians should call
each other brothers, and support each other in worldly as
well as spiritual matters.   Within this should exist the
smaller republic of the hierarchy, by common consent,—
an elective body, recruiting its numbers from the larger,
as it does now; choosing its head, the sovereign Pontiff,
as it does now, to be the head of both Church and State;
eminently fitted for that position, for the very simple reason
that in a community organised and maintained upon such

principles, in which, by virtue of the real and universal love of religion, the best men would find their way into the Church, and would ultimately find their way to the papal throne."

"Your Eminence states the case very convincingly," answered Gouache. "But why has the larger republic, which was to contain the smaller one, ceased to exist? or rather, why did it never come into existence?"

"Because man has not yet fulfilled his part in the great contract. The matter lies in a nutshell. The men who enter the Church are sufficiently intelligent and well educated to appreciate the advantages of Christian democracy, fellowship, solidarity, and brotherly love. The republic of the Church has therefore survived, and will survive for ever. The men who form the majority, on the other hand, have never had either the intelligence or the education to understand that democracy is the ultimate form of government: instead of forming themselves into a federation, they have divided themselves into hostile factions, calling themselves nations, and seeking every occasion for destroying and plundering each other, frequently even turning against the Church herself. The Church has committed faults in history, without doubt, but on the whole she has nobly fulfilled her contract, and reaps the fruits of fidelity in the vigour and unity she displays after eighteen centuries. Man, on the other hand, has failed to do his duty, and all races of men are consequently suffering for their misdeeds; the nations are divided against each other, and every nation is a house divided against itself, which sooner or later shall fall."

"But," objected Gouache, "allowing, as one easily may, that all this is true, your Eminence is always called reactionary in politics. Does that accord with these views?"

Gouache believed the question unanswerable, but as he put it he worked calmly on with his pencil, labouring hard to catch something of the Cardinal's striking expression in the rough drawing he was making.

"Nothing is easier, my friend," replied the statesman. "The republic of the Church is driven to bay. We are on

a war footing. For the sake of strength we are obliged to
hold together so firmly that for the time we can only think
of maintaining old traditions without dreaming of progress
or spending time in experiments. When we have weathered
the storm we shall have leisure for improving much that
needs improvement. Do not think that if I am alive
twenty years hence I shall advise what I advise now. We
are fighting now, and we have no time to think of the arts
of peace. We shall have peace some day. We shall lose
an ornament or two from our garments in the struggle, but
our body will not be injured, and in time of peace our
ornaments will be restored to us fourfold. But now there
is war and rumour of war. There is a vast difference between the ideal republic which I was speaking of, and the
real anarchy and confusion which would be brought about
by what is called republicanism."

"In other words, if the attack upon the Church were
suddenly abandoned, your Eminence would immediately
abandon your reactionary policy," said Gouache, "and
adopt progressive views?"

"Immediately," replied the Cardinal.

"I see," said Gouache. "A little more towards me—
just so that I can catch that eye. Thank you—that will
do."

CHAPTER XIX.

When Del Ferice was thought sufficiently recovered of
his wound to hear some of the news of the day, which was
about three weeks after the duel, he learned that Astrardente was dead, that the Duchessa had inherited all his
fortune, and that she was on the point of leaving Rome.
It would be hard to say how the information of her approaching departure had got abroad; it might be merely
a clever guess of the gossips, or it might be the report
gleaned from her maid by all the other maids in town.

Be that as it may, when Del Ferice heard it he ground his teeth as he lay upon his bed, and swore that if it were possible to prevent the Duchessa d'Astrardente from leaving town he would do it. In his judgment it would be a dangerous thing to let Corona and Giovanni part, and to allow Donna Tullia free play in her matrimonial designs. Of course Giovanni would never marry Madame Mayer, especially as he was now at liberty to marry the Astrardente; but Madame Mayer herself might become fatally interested in him, as she already seemed inclined to be, and this would be bad for Del Ferice's own prospects. It would not do to squander any of the advantages gained by the death of the old Duca. Giovanni must be hastened into a marriage with Corona; it would be time enough to think of revenge upon him afterwards for the ghastly wound that took so long to heal.

It was a pity that Del Ferice and Donna Tullia were not allies, for if Madame Mayer hated Corona d'Astrardente, Ugo del Ferice detested Giovanni with equal virulency, not only because he had been so terribly worsted by him in the duel his own vile conduct had made inevitable, but because Donna Tullia loved him and was doing her very best to marry him. Evidently the best thing to be done was to produce a misunderstanding between the two; but it would be dangerous to play any tricks with Giovanni, for he held Del Ferice in his power by his knowledge of that disagreeable scene behind the plants in the conservatory. Saracinesca was a great man in society and celebrated for his honesty; people would believe him rather than Del Ferice, if the story got abroad. This would not do. The next best thing was to endeavour to draw Giovanni and Corona together as quickly as possible, to precipitate their engagement, and thus to clear the field of a dangerous rival. Del Ferice was a very obstinate and a very intelligent man. He meant more than ever to marry Donna Tullia himself, and he would not be hindered in the accomplishment of his object by an insignificant scruple.

He was not allowed to speak much, lest the effort should

retard the healing of his throat; but in the long days and nights, when he lay silent in his quiet lodging, he had ample time to revolve many schemes in his brain. At last he no longer needed the care of the Sister of Mercy; his servant took charge of him, and the surgeon came twice a-day to dress his wound. He lay in bed one morning watching Temistocle, who moved noiselessly about the room.

"Temistocle," he said, "you are a youth of intelligence; you must use the gifts nature has given you."

Temistocle was at that time not more than five-and-twenty years of age. He had a muddy complexion, a sharp hooked nose, and a cast in one eye that gave him a singularly unpleasant expression. As his master addressed him, he stood still and listened with a sort of distorted smile in acknowledgment of the compliment made him.

"Temistocle, you must find out when the Duchessa d'Astrardente means to leave Rome, and where she is going. You know somebody in the house?"

"Yes, sir—the under-cook; he stood godfather with me for the baby of a cousin of mine—the young man who drives Prince Valdarno's private brougham : a clever fellow, too."

"And this under-cook," said Del Ferice, who was not above entering into details with his servant—"is he a discreet character?"   .

"Oh, for that, you may trust him. Only sometimes ——" Temistocle grinned, and made a gesture which signified drinking.

"And when he is drunk?" asked Del Ferice.

"When he is drunk he tells everything; but he never remembers anything he has been told, or has said. When he is drunk he is a dictionary; but the first draught of water washes out his memory like a slate."

"Well—give me my purse; it is under my pillow. Go. Here is a *scudo*, Temistocle. You can make him very drunk for that."

Temistocle hesitated, and looked at the money.

"Another couple of *pauls* would make it safer," he remarked.

"Well, there they are; but you must make him very drunk indeed. You must find out all he knows, and you must keep sober yourself."

"Leave that to me. I will make of him a sponge; he shall be squeezed dry, and sopped again and squeezed again. I will be his confessor."

"If you find out what I want, I will give you——" Del Ferice hesitated; he did not mean to give too much.

"The grey trousers?" asked Temistocle, with an avaricious light in the eye which did not wander.

"Yes," answered his master, rather regretfully; "I suppose you must have the grey trousers at last."

"For those grey trousers I will upset heaven and earth," returned Temistocle in great glee.

Nothing more was said on that day, but early on the following morning the man entered and opened the shutters, and removed the little oil-light that had burned all night. He kept one eye upon his master, who presently turned slowly and looked inquiringly at him.

"The Duchessa goes to Astrardente in the Sabines on the day after to-morrow," said Temistocle. "It is quite sure that she goes, because she has already sent out two pairs of horses, and several boxes of effects, besides the second housemaid and the butler and two grooms."

"Ah! that is very good. Temistocle, I think I will get up this morning and sit in the next room."

"And the grey trousers?"

"Take them, and wear them in honour of the most generous master living," said Del Ferice, impressively. "It is not every master who gives his servant a pair of grey trousers. Remember that."

"Heaven bless you, Signor Conte!" exclaimed Temistocle, devoutly.

Del Ferice lost no time. He was terribly weak still, and his wound was not entirely healed yet; but he set himself resolutely to his writing-table, and did not rise until he had written two letters. The first was carefully

written in a large round hand, such as is used by copyists
in Italy, resembling the Gothic.   It was impossible to connect the laboriously formed and conventional letters with
any particular person.   It was very short, as follows :—

"It may interest you to know that the Duchessa d'Astrardente is going to her castle in the Sabines on the day
after to-morrow."

This laconic epistle Del Ferice carefully directed to Don
Giovanni Saracinesca at his palace, and fastened a stamp
upon it; but he concealed the address from Temistocle.
The second letter was longer, and written in his own small
and ornate handwriting.   It was to Donna Tullia Mayer.
It ran thus :—

"You would forgive my importuning you with a letter,
most charming Donna Tullia, if you could conceive of my
desolation and loneliness.   For more than three weeks I
have been entirely deprived of the pleasure, the exquisite
delight, of conversing with her for whom I have suffered.
I still suffer so much.   Ah ! if my paper were a cloth of
gold, and my pen in moving traced characters of diamond
and pearl, yet any words which speak of you would be
ineffectually honoured by such transcription !   In the
miserable days and nights I have passed between life and
death, it is your image which has consoled me, the echo
of your delicate voice which has soothed my pain, the
remembrance of the last hours I spent with you which has
gilded the feverish dreams of my sickness.   You are the
guardian angel of a most unhappy man, Donna Tullia.
Do you know it ?   But for you I would have wooed death
as a comforter.   As it is, I have struggled desperately to
keep my grasp upon life, in the hope of once more seeing
your smile and hearing your happy laugh; perhaps—I
dare not expect it—I may receive from you some slight
word of sympathy, some little half-sighed hint that you do
not altogether regret having been in these long weeks the
unconscious comforter of my sorrowing spirit and tormented
body.   You would hardly know me, could you see me;
but saving for your sweet spiritual presence, which has

rescued me from the jaws of death, you would never have
seen me again. Is it presumption in me to write thus?
Have you ever given me a right to speak in these words?
I do not know. I do not care. Man has a right to be
grateful. It is the first and most divine right I possess,
to feel and to express my gratitude. For out of the store
of your kindness shown me when I was in the world,
strong and happy in the privilege of your society, I have
drawn healing medicine in my sickness, as tormented souls
in purgatory get refreshment from the prayers of good and
kind people who remember them on earth. So, therefore,
if I have said too much, forgive me, forgive the heartfelt
gratitude which prompts me; and believe still in the respectful and undying devotion of the humblest of your
servants,   UGO DEL FERICE."

Del Ferice read over what he had written with considerable satisfaction, and having addressed his letter to Donna
Tullia, he lost no time in despatching Temistocle with it,
instructing him to ask if there would be an answer. As
soon as the man was out of the house, Ugo rang for his
landlady, and sent for the porter's little boy, to whom he
delivered the letter for Don Giovanni, to be dropped into
the nearest post-box. Then he lay down, exhausted with
his morning's work. In the course of two hours Temistocle
returned from Donna Tullia's house with a little scented
note—too much scented, and the paper just a shade too
small. She took no notice of what he had said in his carefully penned epistle; but merely told him she was sincerely
glad that he was better, and asked him to call as soon as he
could. Ugo was not disappointed; he had expected no
compromising expression of interest in response to his own
effusions; and he was well pleased with the invitation, for
it showed that what he had written had produced the
desired result.

Don Giovanni Saracinesca received the anonymous note
late in the evening. He had, of course, together with his
father, deposited cards of condolence at the Palazzo Astrardente, and he had been alone to inquire if the Duchessa

would receive him. The porter had answered that, for the present, there were standing orders to admit no one; and as Giovanni could boast of no especial intimacy, and had no valid excuse to give, he was obliged to be satisfied. He had patiently waited in the Villa Borghese and by the band-stand on the Pincio, taking it for granted that sooner or later Corona's carriage would appear; but when at last he had seen her brougham, she had driven rapidly past him, thickly veiled, and he did not think she had even noticed him. He would have written to her, but he was still un-able to hold a pen; and he reflected that, after all, it would have been a hideous farce for him to offer condolences and sympathy, however much he might desire to hide from himself his secret satisfaction at her husband's death. Too proud to think of obtaining information through such base channels as Del Ferice was willing to use, he was wholly ignorant of Corona's intentions; and it was a brilliant proof of Ugo's astuteness that he had rightly judged Giovanni's position with regard to her, and justly estimated the value of the news conveyed by his anonymous note.

Saracinesca read the scrap of writing, and tossed it angrily into the fire. He hated underhand dealings, and scorned himself for the interest the note excited in him, wondering who could find advantage in informing him of the Duchessa's movements. But the note took effect, never-theless, although he was ashamed of it, and all night he pondered upon what it told him. The next day, at three o'clock, he went out alone, and walked rapidly towards the Palazzo Astrardente. He was unable to bear the suspense any longer; the thought that Corona was going away, apparently to shut herself up in the solitude of the ancient fortress, for any unknown number of months, and that he might not see her until the autumn, was intolerable. He knew that by the mere use of his name he could at least make sure that she should know he was at her door, and he determined to make the attempt. He waited a long time, pacing slowly the broad flagstones beneath the arch of the palace, while the porter himself went up with his card and message. The fellow had hesitated, but Don Giovanni

Saracinesca was not a man to be refused by a servant. At last the porter returned, and, bowing to the ground, said that the Signora Duchessa would receive him.

In five minutes he was waiting alone in the great drawing-room. It had cost Corona a struggle to allow him to be admitted. She hesitated long, for it seemed like a positive wrong to her husband's memory, but the woman in her yielded at last; she was going away on the following morning, and she could not refuse to see him for once. She hesitated again as she laid her hand upon the latch of the door, knowing that he was in the room beyond; then at last she entered.

Her face was very pale and very grave. Her simple gown of close-fitting black set off her height and figure, and flowed softly in harmony with her stately movements as she advanced towards Giovanni, who stood almost awestruck in the middle of the room. He could not realise that this dark sad princess was the same woman to whom less than a month ago he had spoken such passionate words, whom he had madly tried to take into his arms. Proud as he was, it seemed presumptuous in him to think of love in connection with so royal a woman; and yet he knew that he loved her better and more truly than he had done a month before. She held out her hand to him, and he raised it to his lips. Then they both sat down in silence.

"I had despaired of ever seeing you again," said Giovanni at last, speaking in a subdued voice. "I had wished for some opportunity of telling you how sincerely I sympathise with you in your great loss." It was a very formal speech, such as men make in such situations. It might have been better, but he was not eloquent; even his rough old father had a better command of language on ordinary occasions, though Giovanni could speak well enough when he was roused. But he felt constrained in the presence of the woman he adored. Corona herself hardly knew how to answer.

"You are very kind," she said, simply.

"I wish it were possible to be of any service to you," he answered. "I need not tell you that both my father

Q

and myself would hold it an honour to assist you in any
way." He mentioned his father from a feeling of delicacy;
he did not wish to put himself forward.

"You are very kind," repeated Corona, gravely. "I
have not had any annoyance. I have an excellent man of
business."

There was a moment's pause. Then she seemed to understand that he was embarrassed, and spoke again.

" I am glad to see that you are recovered," she said.

" It was nothing," answered Giovanni, with a glance at
his right arm, which was still confined in a bandage of
black silk, but was no longer in a sling.

" It was very wrong of you," returned Corona, looking
seriously into his eyes. " I do not know why you fought,
but it was wrong; it is a great sin."

Giovanni smiled a little.

" We all have to sin sometimes," he said. " Would you
have me stand quietly and see an abominable piece of base-
ness, and not lift a hand to punish the offender?"

" People who do base things always come to a bad end,"
answered the Duchessa.

" Perhaps. But we poor sinners are impatient to see
justice done at once. I am sorry to have done anything
you consider wrong," he added, with a shade of bitterness.
" Will you permit me to change the subject? Are you
thinking of remaining in Rome, or do you mean to go
away?"

" I am going up to Astrardente to-morrow," answered
Corona, readily. " I want to be alone and in the country."

Giovanni showed no surprise: his anonymous information had been accurate; Del Ferice had not parted with
the grey trousers in vain.

" I suppose you are right," he said. " But at this time
of year I should think the mountains would be very cold."

" The castle is comfortable. It has been recently fitted
up, and there are many warm rooms in it. I am fond of
the old place, and I need to be alone for a long time."

Giovanni thought the conversation was becoming op-
pressive. He thought of what had passed between them

at their last meeting in the conservatory of the Palazzo Frangipani.

"I shall myself pass the summer in Saracinesca," he said, suddenly. "You know it is not very far. May I hope that I may sometimes be permitted to see you?"

Corona had certainly had no thought of seeing Giovanni when she had determined to go to Astrardente; she had not been there often, and had not realised that it was within reach of the Saracinesca estate. She started slightly.

"Is it so near?" she asked.

"Half a day's ride over the hills," replied Giovanni.

"I did not know. Of course, if you come, you will not be denied hospitality."

"But you would rather not see me?" asked Saracinesca, in a tone of disappointment. He had hoped for something more encouraging. Corona answered courageously.

"I would rather not see you. Do not think me unkind," she added, her voice softening a little. "Why need there be any explanations? Do not try to see me. I wish you well; I wish you more—all happiness—but do not try to see me."

Giovanni's face grew grave and pale. He was disappointed, even humiliated; but something told him that it was not coldness which prompted her request.

"Your commands are my laws," he answered.

"I would rather that instead of regarding what I ask you as a command, you should feel that it ought to be the natural prompting of your own heart," replied Corona, somewhat coldly.

"Forgive me if my heart dictates what my obedience to you must effectually forbid," said Giovanni. "I beseech you to be satisfied that what you ask I will perform—blindly."

"Not blindly—you know all my reasons."

"There is that between you and me which annihilates reason," answered Giovanni, his voice trembling a little.

"There is that in my position which should command your respect," said Corona. She feared he was going too far, and yet this time she knew she had not said too much,

and that in bidding him avoid her, she was only doing
what was strictly necessary for her peace. "I am a
widow," she continued, very gravely; "I am a woman,
and I am alone. My only protection lies in the courtesy I
have a right to expect from men like you. You have expressed your sympathy; show it then by cheerfully fulfilling my request. I do not speak in riddles, but very plainly.
You recall to me a moment of great pain, and your presence,
the mere fact of my receiving you, seems a disloyalty to the
memory of my husband. I have given you no reason to
believe that I ever took a greater interest in you than such
as I might take in a friend. I hourly pray that this—this
too great interest you show in me, may pass quickly, and
leave you what you were before. You see I do not speak
darkly, and I do not mean to speak unkindly. Do not
answer me, I beseech you, but take this as my last word.
Forget me if you can——"

"I cannot," said Giovanni, deeply moved.

"Try. If you cannot, God help you! but I am sure
that if you try faithfully, you will succeed. And now you
must go," she said, in gentler tones. "You should not
have come—I should not have let you see me. But it is
best so. I am grateful for the sympathy you have expressed. I do not doubt that you will do as I have asked
you, and as you have promised. Good-bye."

Corona rose to her feet, her hands folded before her.
Giovanni had no choice. She let her eyes rest upon him,
not unkindly, but she did not extend her hand. He stood
one moment in hesitation, then bowed and left the room
without a word. Corona stood still, and her eyes followed
his retreating figure until at the door he turned once more
and bent his head and then was gone. Then she fell back
into her chair and gazed listlessly at the wall opposite.

"It is done," she said at last. "I hope it is well done
and wisely." Indeed it had been a hard thing to say;
but it was better to say it at once than to regret an ill-
timed indulgence when it should be too late. And yet it
had cost her less to send him away definitely than it had
cost her to resist his passionate appeal a month ago. She

seemed to have gained strength from her sorrows. So he was gone! She gave a sigh of relief, which was instantly followed by a sharp throb of pain, so sudden that she hardly understood it.

Her preparations were all made. She had at the last moment realised that it was not fitting for her, at her age, to travel alone, nor to live wholly alone in her widowhood. She had revolved the matter in her mind, and had decided that there was no woman of her acquaintance whom she could ask even for a short time to stay with her. She had no friends, no relations, none to turn to in such a need. It was not that she cared for company in her solitude; it was merely a question of propriety. To overcome the difficulty, she obtained permission to take with her one of the sisters of a charitable order of nuns, a lady in middle life, but broken down and in ill health from her untiring labours. The thing was easily managed; and the next morning, on leaving the palace, she stopped at the gate of the community and found Sister Gabrielle waiting with her modest box. The nun entered the huge travelling carriage, and the two ladies set out for Astrardente.

It was the first day of Carnival, and a memorably sad one for Giovanni Saracinesca. He would have been capable of leaving Rome at once, but that he had promised Corona not to attempt to see her. He would have gone to Saracinesca for the mere sake of being nearer to her, had he not reflected that he would be encouraging all manner of gossip by so doing. But he determined that so soon as Lent began, he would declare his intention of leaving the city for a year. No one ever went to Saracinesca, and by making a circuit he could reach the ancestral castle without creating suspicion. He might even go to Paris for a few days, and have it supposed that he was wandering about Europe, for he could trust his own servants implicitly; they were not of the type who would drink wine at a tavern with Temistocle or any of his class.

The old Prince came into his son's room in the morning and found him disconsolately looking over his guns, for the sake of an occupation.

"Well, Giovanni," he said, "you have time to reflect upon your future conduct. What! are you going upon a shooting expedition?"

"I wish I could. I wish I could find anything to do," answered Giovanni, laying down the breech-loader and looking out of the window. "The world is turned inside out like a beggar's pocket, and there is nothing in it."

"So the Astrardente is gone," remarked the Prince.

"Yes; gone to live within twenty miles of Saracinesca," replied Giovanni, with an angry intonation.

"Do not go there yet," said his father. "Leave her alone a while. Women become frantic in solitude."

"Do you think I am an idiot?" exclaimed Giovanni. "Of course I shall stay where I am till Carnival is over." He was not in a good humour.

"Why are you so petulant?" retorted the old man. "I merely gave you my advice."

"Well, I am going to follow it. It is good. When Carnival is over I will go away, and perhaps get to Saracinesca by a roundabout way, so that no one will know where I am. Will you not come too?"

"I daresay," answered the Prince, who was always pleased when his son expressed a desire for his company. "I wish we lived in the good old times."

"Why?"

"We would make small scruple of besieging Astrardente and carrying off the Duchessa for you, my boy," said the Prince, grimly.

Giovanni laughed. Perhaps the same idea had crossed his mind. He was not quite sure whether it was respectful to Corona to think of carrying her off in the way his father suggested; but there was a curious flavour of possibility in the suggestion, coming as it did from a man whose grandfather might have done such a thing, and whose great-grandfather was said to have done it. So strong are the instincts of barbaric domination in races where the traditions of violence exist in an unbroken chain, that both father and son smiled at the idea as if it were quite natural, although Giovanni had only the previous day promised that he would not even attempt to see Corona d'Astrardente without her permission. He did not tell his father of his promise, however, for his more delicate instinct made him sure that though he had acted rightly, his father would laugh at his scruples, and tell him that women liked to be wooed roughly.

Meanwhile Giovanni felt that Rome had become for him a vast solitude, and the smile soon faded from his face at the thought that he must go out into the world, and for Corona's sake act as though nothing had happened.

CHAPTER XX.

Poor Madame Mayer was in great anxiety of mind. She had not a great amount of pride, but she made up for it by a plentiful endowment of vanity, in which she suffered acutely. She was a good-natured woman enough, and by nature she was not vindictive; but she could not help being jealous, for she was in love. She felt how Giovanni every day evidently cared less and less for her society, and how, on the other hand, Del Ferice was quietly assuring his position, so that people already began to whisper that he had a chance of becoming her husband. She did not dislike Del Ferice; he was a convenient man of the world, whom she always found ready to help her when she needed help. But by dint of making use of him, she was beginning to feel in some way bound to consider him as an element in her life, and she did not like the position. The letter he had written her was of the kind a man might write to the woman he loved; it bordered upon the familiar, even while the writer expressed himself in terms of exaggerated respect. Perhaps if Del Ferice had been well, she would have simply taken 'no notice of what he had written, and would not even have sent an answer; but she had not the heart to repulse him altogether in his

present condition. There was a phrase cunningly introduced and ambiguously worded, which seemed to mean
that he had come by his wound in her cause. He spoke
of having suffered and of still suffering so much for her,—
did he mean to refer to pain of body or of mind? It was
not certain. Don Giovanni had assured her that she was
in no way concerned in the duel, and he was well known
for his honesty; nevertheless, out of delicacy, he might
have desired to conceal the truth from her. It seemed
like him. She longed for an opportunity of talking with
him and eliciting some explanation of his conduct. There
had been a time when he used to visit her, and always
spent some time in her society when they met in the
world — now, on the contrary, he seemed to avoid her
whenever he could; and in proportion as she noticed that
his manner cooled, her own jealousy against Corona d'Astrardente increased in force, until at last it seemed to
absorb her love for Giovanni into itself and turn it into
hate.

Love is a passion which, like certain powerful drugs,
acts differently upon each different constitution of temper;
love also acts more strongly when it is unreturned or
thwarted than when it is mutual and uneventful. If two
persons love each other truly, and there is no obstacle to
their union, it is probable that, without any violent emotion, their love will grow and become stronger by imperceptible degrees, without changing in its natural quality;
but if thwarted by untoward circumstances, the passion,
if true, attains suddenly to the dimensions which it would
otherwise need years to reach. It sometimes happens that
the nature in which this unforeseen and abnormal development takes place is unable to bear the precocious growth;
then, losing sight of its identity in the strange inward
confusion of heart and mind which ensues, it is driven to
madness, and, breaking every barrier, either attains its
object at a single bound, or is shivered and ruined in
dashing itself against the impenetrable wall of complete
impossibility. But again, in the last case, when love is
wholly unreturned, it dies a natural death of atrophy,

when it has existed in a person of common and average nature; or if the man or woman so afflicted be proud and of noble instincts, the passion becomes a kind of religion to the heart—sacred, and worthy to be guarded from the eyes of the world; or, finally, again, where it finds vanity the dominant characteristic of the being in whom it has grown, it draws a poisonous life from the unhealthy soil on which it is fed, and the tender seed of love shoots and puts forth evil leaves and blossoms, and grows to be a most venomous tree, which is the tree of hatred.

Donna Tullia was certainly a woman who belonged to the latter class of individuals. She had qualities which were perhaps good because not bad; but the mainspring of her being was an inordinate vanity; and it was in this characteristic that she was most deeply wounded, as she found herself gradually abandoned by Giovanni Saracinesca. She had been in the habit of thinking of him as a probable husband; the popular talk had fostered the idea, and occasional hints, and smiling questions concerning him, had made her feel that he could not long hang back. She had been in the habit of treating him familiarly; and he, tutored by his father to the belief that she was the best match for him, and reluctantly yielding to the force of circumstances, which seemed driving him into matrimony, had suffered himself to be ordered about and made use of with an indifference which, in Madame Mayer's eyes, had passed for consent. She had watched with growing fear and jealousy his devotion to the Astrardente, which all the world had noticed; and at last her anger had broken out at the affront she had received at the Frangipani ball. But even then she loved Giovanni in her own vain way. It was not till Corona was suddenly left a widow, that Donna Tullia began to realise the hopelessness of her position; and when she found how determinately Saracinesca avoided her wherever they met, the affection she had hitherto felt for him turned into a bitter hatred, stronger even than her jealousy against the Duchessa. There was no scene of explanation between them, no words passed, no dramatic situation, such as Donna Tullia loved; the change came in

a few days, and was complete. She had not even the
satisfaction of receiving some share of the attention Giovanni would have bestowed upon Corona if she had been
in town. Not only had he grown utterly indifferent to
her; he openly avoided her, and thereby inflicted upon
her vanity the cruellest wound she was capable of feeling.

With Donna Tullia to hate was to injure, to long for
revenge—not of the kind which is enjoyed in secret, and
known only to the person who suffers and the person who
causes the suffering. She did not care for that so much as
she desired some brilliant triumph over her enemies before
the world ; some startling instance of poetic justice, which
should at one blow do a mortal injury to Corona d'Astrardente, and bring Giovanni Saracinesca to her own feet by
force, repentant and crushed, to be dealt with as she saw
fit, according to his misdeeds. But she had chosen her
adversaries ill, and her heart misgave her. She had no hold
upon them, for they were very strong people, very powerful,
and very much respected by their fellows. It was not easy
to bring them into trouble ; it seemed impossible to humi-
liate them as she wished to do, and yet her hate was very
strong. She waited and pondered, and in the meanwhile,
when she met Giovanni, she began to treat him with
haughty coldness. But Giovanni smiled, and seemed well
satisfied that she should at last give over what was to him
very like a persecution. Her anger grew hotter from its
very impotence. The world saw it, and laughed.

The days of Carnival came and passed, much as they
usually pass, in a whirl of gaiety. Giovanni went everywhere, and showed his grave face ; but he talked little, and
of course every one said he was melancholy at the departure
of the Duchessa. Nevertheless he kept up an appearance
of interest in what was done, and as nobody cared to risk
asking him questions, people left him in peace. The hurry-
ing crowd of social life filled up the place occupied by old
Astrardente and the beautiful Duchessa, and they were soon
forgotten, for they had not had many intimate friends.

On the last night of Carnival, Del Ferice appeared
once more. He had not been able to resist the temptation

of getting one glimpse of the world he loved, before the wet blanket of Lent extinguished the lights of the ball-rooms and the jollity of the dancers. Every one was surprised to see him, and most people were pleased; he was such a useful man, that he had often been missed during the time of his illness. He was improved in appearance; for though he was very pale, he had grown also extremely thin, and his features had gained delicacy.

When Giovanni saw him, he went up to him, and the two men exchanged a formal salutation, while every one stood still for a moment to see the meeting. It was over in a moment, and society gave a little sigh of relief, as though a weight were removed from its mind. Then Del Ferice went to Donna Tullia's side. They were soon alone upon a small sofa in a small room, whither a couple strayed now and then to remain a few minutes before returning to the ball. A few people passed through, but for more than an hour they were not disturbed.

" I am very glad to see you," said Donna Tullia; " but I had hoped that the first time you went out you would have come to my house."

" This is the first time I have been out—you see I should not have found you at home, since I have found you here."

" Are you entirely recovered ? You still look ill."

" I am a little weak—but an hour with you will do me more good than all the doctors in the world."

"Thanks," said Donna Tullia, with a little laugh. " It was strange to see you shaking hands with Giovanni Saracinesca just now. I suppose men have to do that sort of thing."

" You may be sure I would not have done it unless it had been necessary," returned Del Ferice, bitterly.

" I should think not. What an arrogant man he is ! "

" You no longer like him ? " asked Del Ferice, innocently.

" Like him ! No ; I never liked him," replied Donna Tullia, quickly.

" Oh, I thought you did ; I used to wonder at it." Ugo grew thoughtful.

"I was always good to him," said Donna Tullia. "But of course I can never forgive him for what he did at the Frangipani ball."

"No; nor I," answered Del Ferice, readily. "I shall always hate him for that too."

"I do not say that I exactly hate him."

"You have every reason. It appears to me that since my illness we have another idea in common, another bond of sympathy." Del Ferice spoke almost tenderly; but he laughed immediately afterwards, as though not wishing his words to be interpreted too seriously. Donna Tullia smiled too; she was inclined to be very kind to him.

"You are very quick to jump at conclusions," she said, playing with her red fan and looking down.

"It is always easy to reach that pleasant conclusion—that you and I are in sympathy," he answered, with a tender glance, "even in regard to hating the same person. The bond would be close indeed, if it depended on the opposite of hate. And yet I sometimes think it does. Are you not the best friend I have in the world?"

"I do not know,—I am a good friend to you," she answered.

"Indeed you are; but do you not think it would be possible to cement our friendship even more closely yet?"

Donna Tullia looked up sharply; she had no idea of allowing him to propose to marry her. His face, however, was grave—unlike his usual expression when he meant to be tender, and which she knew very well.

"I do not know," she said, with a light laugh. "How do you mean?"

"If I could do you some great service—if I could by any means satisfy what is now your chief desire in life—would not that help to cement our friendship, as I said?"

"Perhaps," she answered, thoughtfully. "But then you do not know—you cannot guess even—what I most wish at this moment."

"I think I could," said Del Ferice, fixing his eyes upon her. "I am sure I could, but I will not. I should risk offending you."

"No; I will not be angry. You may guess if you please." Donna Tullia in her turn looked fixedly at her companion. They seemed trying to read each other's thoughts.

"Very well," said Ugo at last, " I will tell you. You would like to see the Astrardente dead and Giovanni Saracinesca profoundly humiliated."

Donna Tullia started. But indeed there was nothing strange in her companion's knowledge of her feelings. Many people, being asked what she felt, would very likely have said the same, for the world had seen her discomfiture and had laughed at it.

"You are a very singular man," she said, uneasily.

"In other words," replied Del Ferice, calmly, " I am perfectly right in my surmises. I see it in your face. Of course," he added, with a laugh, " it is mere jest. But the thing is quite possible. If I fulfilled your desire of just and poetic vengeance, what would you give me?"

Donna Tullia laughed in her turn, to conceal the extreme interest she felt in what he said.

"Whatever you like," she said. But even while the laugh was on her lips her eyes sought his uneasily.

"Would you marry me, for instance, as the enchanted princess in the fairy story marries the prince who frees her from the spell?" He seemed immensely amused at the idea.

"Why not?" she laughed.

"It would be the only just recompense," he answered. "See how impossible the thing appears. And yet a few pounds of dynamite would blow up the Great Pyramid. Giovanni Saracinesca is not so strong as he looks."

"Oh, I would not have him hurt!" exclaimed Donna Tullia in alarm.

"I do not mean physically, nor morally, but socially."

"How?"

"That is my secret," returned Del Ferice, quietly.

"It sounds as though you were pretending to know more than you really do," she answered.

"No; it is the plain truth," said Del Ferice, quietly.

"If you were in earnest I might be willing to tell you what the secret is, but for a mere jest I cannot. It is far too serious a matter."

His tone convinced Donna Tullia that he really possessed some weapon which he could use against Don Giovanni if he pleased. She wondered only why, if it were true, he did not use it, seeing that he must hate Saracinesca with all his heart. Del Ferice knew so much about people, so many strange and forgotten stories, he had so accurate a memory and so acute an intelligence, that it was by no means impossible that he was in possession of some secret connected with the Saracinesca. They were, or were thought to be, wild, unruly men, both father and son; there were endless stories about them both; and there was nothing more likely than that, in his numerous absences from home, Giovanni had at one time or another figured in some romantic affair, which he would be sorry to have had generally known. Del Ferice was wise enough to keep his own counsel; but now that his hatred was thoroughly roused, he might very likely make use of the knowledge he possessed. Donna Tullia's curiosity was excited to its highest pitch, and at the same time she had pleasant visions of the possible humiliation of the man by whom she felt herself so ill-used. It would be worth while making a sacrifice in order to learn Del Ferice's secret.

"This need not be a mere jest," she said, after a moment's silence.

"That is as you please," returned Del Ferice, seriously. "If you are willing to do your part, you may be sure that I will do mine."

"You cannot think I really meant what I said just now," replied Donna Tullia. "It would be madness."

"Why? Am I halt, am I lame, am I blind? Am I repulsively ugly? Am I a pauper, that I should care for your money? Have I not loved you—yes, loved you long and faithfully? Am I too old? Is there anything in the nature of things why I should not aspire to be your husband?"

It was strange. He spoke calmly, as though enumerating the advantages of a friend. Donna Tullia looked at him for a moment, and then laughed outright.

"No," she said; "all that is very true. You may aspire, as you call it. The question is, whether I shall aspire too. Of course, if we happened to agree in aspiring, we could be married to-morrow.'

"Precisely," answered Del Ferice, perfectly unmoved. "I am not proposing to marry you. I am arguing the case. There is this in the case which is perhaps outside the argument—this, that I am devotedly attached to you. The case is the stronger for that. I was only trying to demonstrate that the idea of our being married is not so unutterably absurd. You laughingly said you would marry me if I could accomplish something which would please you very much. I laughed also; but now I seriously repeat my proposition, because I am convinced that although at first sight it may appear extremely humorous, on a closer inspection it will be found exceedingly practical. In union is strength."

Donna Tullia was silent for a moment, and her face grew grave. There was reason in what he said. She did not care for him—she had never thought of marrying him; but she recognised the justice of what he said. It was clear that a man of his social position, received everywhere and intimate with all her associates, might think of marrying her. He looked positively handsome since he was wounded; he was accomplished and intelligent; he had sufficient means of support to prevent him from being suspected of marrying solely for money, and he had calmly stated that he loved her. Perhaps he did. It was flattering to Donna Tullia's vanity to believe him, and his acts had certainly not belied his words. He was by far the most thoughtful of all her admirers, and he affected to treat her always with a certain respect which she had never succeeded in obtaining from Valdarno and the rest. A woman who likes to be noisy, but is conscious of being a little vulgar, is always flattered when a man behaves towards her with profound reverence. It will even sometimes cure her of her vulgarity. Donna Tullia reflected seriously upon what Del Ferice had said.

"I never had such a proposition made to me in my life," she said. "Of course you cannot think I regard it as a possible one, even now. You cannot think I am so base as to sell myself for the sake of revenging an insult once offered me. If I am to regard this as a proposal of marriage, I must decline it with thanks. If it is merely a proposition for an alliance, I think the terms of the treaty are unequal."

Del Ferice smiled.

"I knew you well enough to know what your answer would be," he said. "I never insulted you by dreaming that you would accept such a proposition. But as a subject for speculation it is very pleasant. It is delightful to me to think of being your husband; it is equally delightful to you to think of the humiliation of an enemy. I took the liberty of uniting the two thoughts in one dream—a dream of unspeakable bliss for myself."

Donna Tullia's gay humour returned.

"You have certainly amused me very well for a quarter of an hour with your dreams," she answered. "I wish you would tell me what you know of Don Giovanni. It must be very interesting if it can really seriously influence his life."

"I cannot tell you. The secret is too valuable."

"But if the thing you know has such power, why do you not use it yourself? You must hate him far more than I do."

"I doubt that," answered Del Ferice, with a cunning smile. "I do not use it, I do not choose to strike the blow, because I do not care enough for retribution merely on my own account. I do not pretend to generosity, but I am not interested enough in him to harm him, though I dislike him exceedingly. We had a temporary settlement of our difficulties the other day, and we were both wounded. Poor Casalverde lost his head and did a foolish thing, and that cold-blooded villain Spicca killed him in consequence. It seems to me that there has been enough blood spilled

in our quarrel. I am prepared to leave him alone so far
as I am concerned. But for you, it would be different.
I could do something worse than kill him if I chose."

"For me?" said Donna Tullia. "What would you do
for me?" She smiled sweetly, willing to use all her persuasion to extract his secret.

"I could prevent Don Giovanni from marrying the
Astrardente, as he intends to do," he answered, looking
straight at his companion.

"How in the world could you do that?" she asked, in
great surprise.

"That, my dear friend, is my secret, as I said before.
I cannot reveal it to you at present."

"You are as dark as the Holy Office," said Donna
Tullia, a little impatiently. "What possible harm could
it do if you told me?"

"What possible good either?" asked Del Ferice, in
reply. "You could not use it as I could. You would
gain no advantage by knowing it. Of course," he added,
with a laugh, "if we entered into the alliance we were
jesting about, it would be different."

"You will not tell me unless I promise to marry you?"

"Frankly, no," he answered, still laughing.

It exasperated Donna Tullia beyond measure to feel that
he was in possession of what she so coveted, and to feel
that he was bargaining, half in earnest, for her life in
exchange for his secret. She was almost tempted for one
moment to assent, to say she would marry him, so great
was her curiosity; it would be easy to break her promise,
and laugh at him afterwards. But she was not a bad
woman, as women of her class are considered. She had
suffered a great disappointment, and her resentment was
in proportion to her vanity. But she was not prepared to
give a false promise for the sake of vengeance; she was
only bad enough to imagine such bad faith possible.

"But you said you never seriously thought I could
accept such an engagement," she objected, not knowing
what to say.

"I did," replied Del Ferice. "I might have added

R

that I never seriously contemplated parting with my secret."

"There is nothing to be got from you," said Donna Tullia, in a tone of disappointment. "I think that when you have nearly driven me mad with curiosity, you might really tell me something."

"Ah no, dear lady," answered her companion. "You may ask anything of me but that—anything. You may ask that too, if you will sign the treaty I propose."

"You will drive me into marrying you out of sheer curiosity," said Donna Tullia, with an impatient laugh.

"I wish that were possible. I wish I could see my way to telling you as it is, for the thing is so curious that it would have the most intense interest for you. But it is quite out of the question."

"You should never have told me anything about it," replied Madame Mayer.

"Well, I will think about it," said Del Ferice at last, as though suddenly resolving to make a sacrifice. "I will look over some papers I have, and I will think about it. I promise you that if I feel that I can conscientiously tell you something of the matter, you may be sure that I will."

Donna Tullia's manner changed again, from impatience to persuasion. The sudden hope he held out to her was delicious to contemplate. She could not realise that Del Ferice, having once thoroughly interested her, could play upon her moods as on the keys of an instrument. If she had been less anxious that the story he told should be true, she might have suspected that he was practising upon her credulity. But she seized the idea of obtaining some secret influence over the life of Giovanni, and it completely carried her away.

"You must tell me—I am sure you will," she said, letting her kindest glance rest upon her companion. "Come and dine with me,—do you fast? No—nor I. Come on Friday—will you?"

"I shall be delighted," answered Del Ferice, with a quiet smile of triumph.

"I will have the old lady, of course, so you cannot tell

me at dinner; but she will go to sleep soon afterwards—
she always does. Come at seven. Besides, she is deaf,
you know."

The old lady in question was the aged Countess whom
Donna Tullia affected as a companion in her solitary
magnificence.

"And now, will you take me back to the ball-room? I
have an idea that a partner is looking for me."

Del Ferice left her dancing, and went home in his little
coupé. He was desperately fatigued, for he was still very
weak, and he feared lest his imprudence in going out so
soon might bring on a relapse from his convalescence.
Nevertheless, before he went to bed he dismissed Temistocle, and opened a shabby-looking black box which stood
upon his writing-table. It was bound with iron, and was
fastened by a patent lock which had frequently defied
Temistocle's ingenuity. From this repository he took a
great number of papers, which were all neatly filed away
and marked in the owner's small and ornamented handwriting. Beneath many packages of letters he found what
he sought for, a long envelope containing several folded
documents.

He spread out the papers and read them carefully over.

"It is a very singular thing," he said to himself; "but
there can be no doubt about it. There it is."

He folded the papers again, returned them to their envelope, and replaced the latter deep among the letters in
his box. He then locked it, attached the key to a chain
he wore about his neck, and went to bed, worn out with
fatigue.

CHAPTER XXI.

Del Ferice had purposely excited Donna Tullia's curiosity,
and he meant before long to tell more than he had vouchsafed in his first confidence. But he himself trembled

before the magnitude of what he had suddenly thought of doing, for the fear of Giovanni was in his heart. The temptation to boast to Donna Tullia that he had the means of preventing Giovanni from marrying was too strong; but when it had come to telling her what those means were, prudence had restrained him. He desired that if the scheme were put into execution it might be by some one else; for, extraordinary as it was, he was not absolutely certain of its success. He was not sure of Donna Tullia's discretion, either, until by a judicious withholding of the secret he had given her a sufficient idea of its importance. But on mature reflection he came to the conclusion that, even if she possessed the information he was able to give, she would not dare to mention it, nor even to hint at it.

The grey light of Ash-Wednesday morning broke over Rome, and stole through the windows of Giovanni Saracinesca's bedroom. Giovanni had not slept much, but his restlessness was due rather to his gladness at having performed the last of his social duties than to any disturbance of mind. All night he lay planning what he should do,—how he might reach his place in the mountains by a circuitous route, leaving the general impression that he was abroad—and how, when at last he had got to Saracinesca unobserved, he would revel in the solitude and in the thought of being within half a day's journey of Corona d'Astrardente. He was willing to take a great deal of trouble, for he did not wish people to know his whereabouts; he would not have it said that he had gone into the country to be near Corona and to see her every day, as would certainly be said if his real movements were discovered. Accordingly, he fulfilled his programme to the letter. He left Rome on the afternoon of Ash-Wednesday for Florence; there he visited several acquaintances who, he knew, would write to their friends in Rome of his appearance; from Florence he went to Paris, and gave out that he was going upon a shooting expedition in the Arctic regions, as soon as the weather was warm enough. As he was well known for a sportsman and a traveller, this statement created no suspicion; and when he finally left Paris, the newspapers and the gossips all said he had gone to Copenhagen on his way to the far north. In due time the statement reached Rome, and it was supposed that society had lost sight of Giovanni Saracinesca for at least eight months. It was thought that he had acted with great delicacy in absenting himself; he would thus allow the first months of Corona's mourning to pass before formally presenting himself to society as her suitor. Considering the peculiar circumstances of the case, there would be nothing improper, from a social point of view, in his marrying Corona at the expiration of a year after her husband's death. Of course he would marry her; there was no doubt of that—he had been in love with her so long, and now she was both free and rich. No one suspected that Giovanni, instead of being in Scandinavia, was quietly established at Saracinesca, a day's journey from Rome, busying himself with the management of the estate, and momentarily satisfied in feeling himself so near the woman he loved.

Donna Tullia could hardly wait until the day when Del Ferice was coming to dinner: she was several times on the point of writing a note to ask him to come at once. But she wisely refrained, guessing that the more she pressed him the more difficulties he would make. At last he came, looking pale and worn — interesting, as Donna Tullia would have expressed it. The old countess talked a great deal during dinner; but as she was too deaf to hear more than a quarter of what was said by the others, the conversation was not interesting. When the meal was over, she established herself in a comfortable chair in the little sitting-room, and took a book. After a few minutes, Donna Tullia suggested to Del Ferice that they should go into the drawing-room. She had received some new waltz-music from Vienna which she wanted to look over, and Ugo might help her. She was not a musician, but was fond of a cheerful noise, and played upon the piano with the average skill of a well-educated young woman of the world. Of course the doors were left open between the drawing-room and the boudoir, where the Countess dozed over her book and presently fell asleep.

Donna Tullia sat at the grand piano, and made Del
Ferice sit beside her. She struck a few chords, and played
a fragment of dance-music.

"Of course you have heard that Don Giovanni is
gone?" she asked, carelessly. "I suppose he is gone to
Saracinesca; they say there is a very good road between
that and Astrardente."

"I should think he would have more decency than to
pursue the Duchessa in the first month of her mourning,"
answered Del Ferice, resting one arm upon the piano, and
supporting his pale face with his hand as he watched
Donna Tullia's fingers move upon the keys.

"Why? He does not care what people say—why
should he? He will marry her when the year is out.
Why should he care?"

"He never can marry her unless I choose to allow it,"
said Del Ferice, quietly.

"So you told me the other night," returned Donna
Tullia. "But you will allow him, of course. Besides, you
could not stop it, after all. I do not believe that you
could." She leaned far back in her chair, her hands resting upon the keys without striking them, and she looked
at Del Ferice with a sweet smile. There was a moment's
pause.

"I have decided to tell you something," he said at last,
"upon one condition."

"Why make conditions?" asked Donna Tullia, trying
to conceal her excitement.

"Only one, that of secrecy. Will you promise never to
mention what I am going to tell you without previously
consulting me? I do not mean a common promise; I
mean it to be an oath." He spoke very earnestly. "This
is a very serious matter. We are playing with fire and
with life and death. You must give me some guarantee
that you will be secret."

His manner impressed Donna Tullia; she had never
seen him so much in earnest in her life.

"I will promise in any way you please," she said.

"Then say this," he answered. "Say, 'I swear and

solemnly bind myself that I will faithfully keep the secret about to be committed to me; and that if I fail to keep it I will atone by immediately marrying Ugo del Ferice——'"

"That is absurd!" cried Donna Tullia, starting back from him. He did not heed her.

"'And I take to witness of this oath the blessed memory of my mother, the hope of the salvation of my soul, and this relic of the True Cross.'" He pointed to the locket she wore at her neck, which she had often told him contained the relic he mentioned.

"It is impossible!" she cried again. "I cannot swear so solemnly about such a matter. I cannot promise to marry you."

"Then it is because you cannot promise to keep my secret," he answered calmly. He knew her very well, and he believed that she would not break such an oath as he had dictated, under any circumstances. He did not choose to risk anything by her indiscretion. Donna Tullia hesitated, seeing that he was firm. She was tortured with curiosity beyond all endurance.

"I am only promising to marry you in case I reveal the secret?" she asked. He bowed assent. "So that I am really only promising to be silent? Well, I cannot understand why it should be solemn; but if you wish it so, I will do it. What are the words?"

He repeated them slowly, and she followed him. He watched her at every word, to be sure she overlooked nothing.

"I, Tullia Mayer, swear and solemnly bind myself that I will faithfully keep the secret about to be committed to me; and that if I fail to keep it, I will atone by immediately marrying Ugo del Ferice" — her voice trembled nervously: "and I take to witness of this oath the blessed memory of my mother, the hope of the salvation of my soul, and this relic of the True Cross." At the last words she took the locket in her fingers.

"You understand that you have promised to marry me if you reveal my secret? You fully understand that?" asked Del Ferice.

"I understand it," she answered hurriedly, as though ashamed of what she had done. "And now, the secret," she added eagerly, feeling that she had undergone a certain humiliation for the sake of what she so much coveted.

"Don Giovanni cannot marry the Duchessa d'Astrardente, because"—he paused a moment to give full weight to his statement—"because Don Giovanni Saracinesca is married already."

"What!" cried Donna Tullia, starting from her chair in amazement at the astounding news.

"It is quite true," said Del Ferice, with a quite smile. "Calm yourself; it is quite true. I know what you are thinking of—all Rome thought he was going to marry you."

Donna Tullia was overcome by the strangeness of the situation. She hid her face in her hands for a moment as she leaned forward over the piano. Then she suddenly looked up.

"What a hideous piece of villany!" she exclaimed, in a stifled voice. Then slowly recovering from the first shock of the intelligence, she looked at Del Ferice; she was almost as pale as he. "What proof have you?" she asked.

"I have the attested copy of the banns published by the priest who married them. That is evidence. Moreover, the real book of banns exists, and Giovanni's name is upon the parish register. I have also a copy of the certificate of the civil marriage, which is signed by Giovanni himself."

"Tell me more," said Donna Tullia, eagerly. "How did you find it?"

"It is very simple," answered Del Ferice. "You may go and see for yourself, if you do not mind making a short journey. Last summer I was wandering a little for my health's sake, as I often do, and I chanced to be in the town of Aquila—you know, the capital of the Abruzzi. One day I happened to go into the sacristy of one of the parish churches to see some pictures which are hung there. There had been a marriage service performed, and as the sacristan moved about explaining the pictures, he laid his hand upon an open book which looked like a register of some kind. I idly asked him what it was, and he showed it to me; it was amusing to look at the names of the people, and I turned over the leaves curiously. Suddenly my attention was arrested by a name I knew—'Giovanni Saracinesca,' written clearly across the page, and below it, 'Felice Baldi,'—the woman he had married. The date of the marriage was the 19th of June 1863. You remember, perhaps, that in that summer, in fact during the whole of that year, Don Giovanni was supposed to be absent upon his famous shooting expedition in Canada, about which he talks so much. It appears, then, that two years ago, instead of being in America, he was living in Aquila, married to Felice Baldi—probably some pretty peasant girl. I started at the sight of the names. I got permission to have an attested copy of it made by a notary. I found the priest who had married them, but he could not remember the couple. The man, he said, was dark, he was sure; the woman, he thought, had been fair. He married so many people in a year. These were not natives of Aquila; they had apparently come there from the country —perhaps had met. The banns—yes, he had the book of banns; he had also the register of marriages from which he sometimes issued certified extracts. He was a good old man, and seemed ready to oblige me; but his memory was very defective. He allowed me to take notary's copies of the banns and the entry in the list, as well as of the register. Then I went to the office of the Stato Civile. You know that people do not sign the register in the church themselves; the names are written down by the priest. I wanted to see the signatures, and the book of civil marriages was shown to me. The handwriting was Giovanni's, I am sure—larger, and a little less firm, but distinguishable at a glance. I took the copies for curiosity, and never said anything about it, but I have kept them. That is the history. Do you see how serious a matter it is?"

"Indeed, yes," answered Donna Tullia, who had listened

with intense interest to the story. "But what could have induced him to marry that woman?"

"One of those amiable eccentricities peculiar to his family," replied Del Ferice, shrugging his shoulders. "The interesting thing would be to discover what became of Felice Baldi—Donna Felice Saracinesca, as I suppose she has a right to be called."

"Let us find her—Giovanni's wife," exclaimed Donna Tullia, eagerly. "Where can she be?"

"Who knows?" ejaculated Del Ferice. "I would be curious to see her. The name of her native village is given, and the names of her parents. Giovanni described himself in the paper as 'of Naples, a landholder,' and omitted somehow the details of his parentage. Nothing could be more vague; everybody is a landholder, from the wretched peasant who cultivates one acre to their high-and-mightinesses the Princes of Saracinesca. Perhaps by going to the village mentioned some information might be obtained. He probably left her sufficiently provided for, and, departing on pretence of a day's journey, never returned. He is a perfectly unscrupulous man, and thinks no more of this mad scrape than of shooting a chamois in the Tyrol. He knows she can never find him—never guessed who he really was."

"Perhaps she is dead," suggested Donna Tullia, her face suddenly growing grave.

"Why? He would not have taken the trouble to kill her—a peasant girl in the Abruzzi! He would have had no difficulty in leaving her, and she is probably alive and well at the present moment, perhaps the mother of the future Prince Saracinesca—who can tell?"

"But do you not see," said Donna Tullia, "that unless you have proof that she is alive, we have no hold upon him? He may acknowledge the whole thing, and calmly inform us that she is dead."

"That is true; but even then he must show that she came to a natural end and was buried. Believe me, Giovanni would relinquish all intentions of marrying the Astrardente rather than have this scandalous story published."

"I would like to tax him with it in a point-blank question, and watch his face," said Donna Tullia, fiercely.

"Remember your oath," said Del Ferice. "But he is gone now. You will not meet him for some months."

"Tell me, how could you make use of this knowledge, if you really wanted to prevent his marriage with the Astrardente?"

"I would advise you to go to her and state the case. You need mention nobody. Any one who chooses may go to Aquila and examine the registers. I think that you could convey the information to her with as much command of language as would be necessary."

"I daresay I could," she answered, between her teeth. "What a strange chance it was that brought that register under your hand!"

"Heaven sends opportunities," said Del Ferice, devoutly; "it is for man to make good use of them. Who knows but what you may make a brilliant use of this?"

"I cannot, since I am bound by my promise," said Donna Tullia.

"No; I am sure you will not think of doing it. But then, we might perhaps agree that circumstances made it advisable to act. Many months must pass before he can think of offering himself to her. It will be time enough to consider the matter then—to consider whether we should be justified in raising such a terrible scandal, in causing so much unhappiness to an innocent woman like the Duchessa, and to a worthless man like Don Giovanni. Think what a disgrace it would be to the Saracinesca to have it made public that Giovanni was openly engaged to marry a great heiress while already secretly married to a peasant woman!"

"It would indeed be horrible," said Donna Tullia, with a disagreeable look in her blue eyes. "Perhaps we should not even think of it," she added, turning over the leaves of the music upon the piano. Then suddenly she added, "Do you know that you have put me in a dreadful position by exacting that promise from me?"

"No," said Del Ferice, quietly. "You wanted to hear

the secret. You have heard it. You have nothing to do
but to keep it to yourself."

"That is precisely——" She checked herself, and
struck a loud chord upon the instrument. She had turned
from Del Ferice, and could not see the smile upon his face,
which flickered across the pale features and vanished instantly.

"Think no more about it," he said pleasantly. "It is
so easy to forget such stories when one resolutely puts them
out of one's mind."

Donna Tullia smiled bitterly, and was silent. She began
playing from the sheet before her, with indifferent accuracy,
but with more than sufficient energy. Del Ferice sat
patiently by her side, turning over the leaves, and glancing
from time to time at her face, which he really admired
exceedingly. He belonged to the type of pale and somewhat phlegmatic men who frequently fall in love with
women of sanguine complexion and robust appearance.
Donna Tullia was a fine type of this class, and was called
handsome, though she did not compare well with women
of less pretension to beauty, but more delicacy and refinement. Del Ferice admired her greatly, however; and, as
has been said, he admired her fortune even more. He saw
himself gradually approaching the goal of his intentions,
and as he neared the desired end he grew more and more
cautious. He had played one of his strongest cards that
night, and he was content to wait and let matters develop
quietly, without any more pushing from him. The seed
would grow, there was no fear of that, and his position was
strong. He could wait quietly for the result.

At the end of half an hour he excused himself upon the
plea that he was still only convalescent, and was unable to
bear the fatigue of late hours. Donna Tullia did not press
him to stay, for she wished to be alone; and when he was
gone she sat long at the open piano, pondering upon what
she had done, and even more upon what she had escaped
doing. It was a hideous thought that if Giovanni, in all
that long winter, had asked her to be his wife, she would
readily have consented; it was fearful to think what her

position would have been towards Del Ferice, who would have been able by a mere word to annul her marriage by proving the previous one at Aquila. People do not trifle with such accusations, and he certainly knew what he was doing; she would have been bound hand and foot. Or supposing that Del Ferice had died of the wound he received in the duel, and his papers had been ransacked by his heirs, whoever they might be—these attested documents would have become public property. What a narrow escape Giovanni had had! And she herself, too, how nearly had she been involved in his ruin! She liked to think that he had almost offered himself to her; it flattered her, although she now hated him so cordially. She could not help admiring Del Ferice's wonderful discretion in so long concealing a piece of scandal that would have shaken Roman society to its foundations, and she trembled when she thought what would happen if she herself were ever tempted to reveal what she had heard. Del Ferice was certainly a man of genius—so quiet, and yet possessing such weapons; there was some generosity about him too, or he would have revenged himself for his wound by destroying Giovanni's reputation. She considered whether she could have kept her counsel so well in his place. After all, as he had said, the moment for using the documents had not yet come, for hitherto Giovanni had never proposed to marry any one. Perhaps this secret wedding in Aquila explained his celibacy; Del Ferice had perhaps misjudged him in saying that he was unscrupulous; he had perhaps left his peasant wife, repenting of his folly, but it was perhaps on her account that he had never proposed to marry Donna Tullia; he had, then, only been amusing himself with Corona. That all seemed likely enough—so likely, that it heightened the certainty of Del Ferice's information.

A few days later, as Giovanni had intended, news began to reach Rome that he had been in Florence, and was actually in Paris; then it was said that he was going upon a shooting expedition somewhere in the far north during the summer. It was like him, and in accordance with his tastes. He hated the quiet receptions at the great houses during Lent, to which, if he remained in Rome, he was obliged to go. He naturally escaped when he could. But there was no escape for Donna Tullia, and after all she managed to extract some amusement from these gatherings. She was the acknowledged centre of the more noisy set, and wherever she went, people who wanted to be amused, and were willing to amuse each other, congregated around her. On one of these occasions she met old Saracinesca. He did not go out much since his son had left; but he seemed cheerful enough, and as he liked Madame Mayer, for some inscrutable reason, she rather liked him. Moreover, her interest in Giovanni, though now the very reverse of affectionate, made her anxious to know something of his movements.

"You must be lonely since Don Giovanni has gone upon his travels again," she said.

"That is the reason I go out," said the Prince. "It is not very gay, but it is better than nothing. It suggests cold meat served up after the dessert; but when people are hungry, the order of their food is not of much importance."

"Is there any news, Prince? I want to be amused."

"News? No. The world is at peace, and consequently given over to sin, as it mostly is when it is resting from a fit of violence."

"You seem to be inclined to moralities this evening," said Donna Tullia, smiling, and gently swaying the red fan she always carried.

"Am I? Then I am growing old, I suppose. It is the privilege of old age to censure in others what it is no longer young enough to praise in itself. It is a bad thing to grow old, but it makes people good, or makes them think they are, which in their own eyes is precisely the same thing."

"How delightfully cynical!"

"Doggish?" inquired the Prince, with a laugh. "I have heard it said by scholars, that cynical means doggish in Greek. The fable of the dog in the horse's manger was invented to define the real cynic—the man who neither enjoys life himself nor will allow other people to enjoy it.

I am not such a man. I hope you, for instance, will enjoy everything that comes in your way."

"Even the cold meat after the dessert which you spoke of just now?" asked Donna Tullia. "Thank you—I will try; perhaps you can help me."

"My son despised it," said Saracinesca. "He is gone in search of fresh pastures of sweets."

"Leaving you behind."

"Somebody once said that the wisest thing a son could do was to get rid of his father as soon as possible——"

"Then Don Giovanni is a wise man," returned Donna Tullia.

"Perhaps. However, he asked me to accompany him."

"You refused?"

"Of course. Such expeditions are good enough for boys. I dislike Florence, I am not especially fond of Paris, and I detest the North Pole. I suppose you have seen from the papers that he is going in that direction? It is like him. He hankers after originality, I suppose. Being born in the south, he naturally goes to the extreme north."

"He will write you very interesting letters, I should think," remarked Donna Tullia. "Is he a good correspondent?"

"Remarkably, for he never gives one any trouble. He sends his address from time to time, and draws frequently on his banker. His letters are not so full of interest as might be thought, as they rarely extend over five lines; but on the other hand it does not take long to read them, which is a blessing."

"You seem to be an affectionate parent," said Donna Tullia, with a laugh.

"If you measure affection by the cost of postage-stamps, you have a right to be sarcastic. If you measure it in any other way, you are wrong. I could not help loving any one so like myself as my son. It would show a detestable lack of appreciation of my own gifts."

"I do not think Don Giovanni so very like you," said Donna Tullia, thoughtfully.

"Perhaps you do not know him so well as I do," remarked the Prince. "Where do you see the greatest difference?"

"I think you talk better, and I think you are more—not exactly more honest, perhaps, but more straightforward."

"I do not agree with you," said old Saracinesca, quickly. "There is no one alive who can say they ever knew Giovanni approach in the most innocent way to a distortion of truth. I daresay you have discovered, however, that he is reticent; he can hold his tongue; he is no chatterer, no parrot, my son."

"Indeed he is not," answered Donna Tullia, and the reply pacified the old man; but she herself was thinking what supreme reticence Giovanni had shown in the matter of his marriage, and she wondered whether the Prince had ever heard of it.

CHAPTER XXII.

Anastase Gouache worked hard at the Cardinal's portrait, and at the same time did his best to satisfy Donna Tullia. The latter, indeed, was not easily pleased, and Gouache found it hard to instil into his representation of her the precise amount of poetry she required, without doing violence to his own artistic sense of fitness. But the other picture progressed rapidly. The Cardinal was a restless man, and after the first two or three sittings, desired nothing so much as to be done with them altogether. Anastase amused him, it is true, and the statesman soon perceived that he had made a conquest of the young man's mind, and that, as Giovanni Saracinesca had predicted, he had helped Gouache to come to a decision. He was not prepared, however, for the practical turn that decision immediately took, and he was just beginning to wish the sittings at an end when Anastase surprised him by a very startling announcement.

As usual, they were in the Cardinal's study; the states-man was silent and thoughtful, and Gouache was working with all his might.

"I have made up my mind," said the latter, suddenly.

"Concerning what, my friend?" inquired the great man, rather absently.

"Concerning everything, Eminence," answered Gouache —"concerning politics, religion, life, death, and everything else which belongs to my career. I am going to enlist with the Zouaves."

The Cardinal looked at him for a moment, and then broke into a low laugh.

"*Extremis malis extrema remedia!*" he exclaimed.

"Precisely—*aux grands maux les grands remèdes*, as we say. I am going to join the Church militant. I am con-vinced that it is the best thing an honest man can do. I like fighting, and I like the Church—therefore I will fight for the Church."

"Very good logic, indeed," answered the Cardinal. But he looked at Anastase, and marking his delicate features and light frame, he almost wondered how the lad would look in the garb of a soldier. "Very good logic; but, my dear Monsieur Gouache, what is to become of your art?"

"I shall not be mounting guard all day, and the Zouaves are allowed to live in their own lodgings. I will live in my studio, and paint when I am not mounting guard."

"And my portrait?" inquired Cardinal Antonelli, much amused.

"Your Eminence will doubtless be kind enough to man-age that I may have liberty to finish it."

"You could not put off enlisting for a week, I suppose?"

Gouache looked annoyed; he hated the idea of waiting.

"I have taken too long to make up my mind already," he replied. "I must make the plunge at once. I am convinced — your Eminence has convinced me — that I have been very foolish."

"I certainly never intended to convince you of that," remarked the Cardinal, with a smile.

"Very foolish," repeated Gouache, not heeding the interruption. "I have talked great nonsense,—I scarcely know why—perhaps to try and find where the sense really lay. I have dreamed so many dreams, so long, that I sometimes think I am morbid. All artists are morbid, I suppose. It is better to do anything active than to lose one's self in the slums of a sickly imagination."

"I agree with you," answered the Cardinal; "but I do not think you suffered from a sickly imagination, — I should rather call it abundant than sickly. Frankly, I should be sorry to think that in following this new idea you were in any way injuring the great career which, I am sure, is before you; but, on the other hand, I cannot help wishing that a greater number of young men would follow your example."

"Your Eminence approves, then ? "

"Do you think you will make a good soldier ? "

"Other artists have been good soldiers. There was Cellini——"

"Benvenuto Cellini said he made a good soldier; he said it himself, but his reputation for veracity in other matters was doubtful, to say the least. If he did not shoot the Connétable de Bourbon, it is very certain that some one else did. Besides, a soldier in our times should be a very different kind of man from the self-armed citizen of the time of Clement the Eighth and the aforesaid Connétable. You will have to wear a uniform and sleep on boards in a guard-house; you will have to be up early to drill, and up late mounting guard, in wind and rain and cold. It is hard work; I do not believe you have the constitution for it. Nevertheless, the intention is good. You can try it, and if you fall ill I will see that you have no difficulty in returning to your artist life."

"I do not mean to give it up," replied Gouache, in a tone of conviction. "And as for my health, I am as strong as any one."

"Perhaps," said the Cardinal, doubtfully. "And when are you going to join the corps ? "

"In about an hour," said Gouache, quietly.

And he kept his word. But he had told no one, save
the Cardinal, of his intention; and for a day or two,
though he passed many acquaintances in the street, no
one recognised Anastase Gouache in the handsome young
soldier with his grey Turco uniform, a red sash round his
slender waist, and a small *képi* set jauntily upon one side.

It was one of the phenomena of those times. Foreigners
swarmed in Rome, and many of them joined the cosmopolitan corps—gentlemen, noblemen, artists, men of the
learned professions, adventurers, duellists driven from their
country in a temporary exile, enthusiasts, strolling Irish-
men, men of all sorts and conditions. But, take them all
in all, they were a fine set of fellows, who set no value
whatever on their lives, and who, as a whole, fought for an
idea, in the old crusading spirit. There were many who,
like Gouache, joined solely from conviction; and there
were few instances indeed of any who, having joined,
deserted. It often happened that a stranger came to
Rome for a mere visit, and at the end of a month surprised his friends by appearing in the grey uniform. You
had met him the night before at a ball in the ordinary
garb of civilisation, covered with cotillon favours, waltzing
like a madman; the next morning he entered the Café de
Rome in a braided jacket open at the throat, and told you
he was a soldier—a private soldier, who touched his cap
to every corporal of the French infantry, and was liable to
be locked up for twenty-four hours if he was late to
quarters.

Donna Tullia's portrait was not quite finished, and
Gouache had asked for one or two more sittings. Three
days after the artist had taken his great resolution, Madame
Mayer and Del Ferice entered his studio. He had had no
difficulty in being at liberty at the hour of the sitting, and
had merely exchanged his jacket for an old painting-coat,
not taking the trouble to divest himself of the remainder
of his uniform.

"Where have you been all this time?" asked Donna
Tullia, as she lifted the curtain and entered the studio.
He had kept out of her way during the past few days.

"Good heavens, Gouache!" cried Del Ferice, starting back, as he caught sight of the artist's grey trousers and yellow gaiters. "What is the meaning of this comedy?"

"What?" asked Gouache, coolly. Then, glancing at his legs, he answered, "Oh, nothing. I have turned Zouave—that is all. Will you sit down, Donna Tullia? I was waiting for you."

"Turned Zouave!" exclaimed Madame Mayer and Del Ferice in a breath. "Turned Zouave!"

"Well?" said Gouache, raising his eyebrows and enjoying their surprise. "Well—why not?"

Del Ferice struck a fine atitude, and, laying one hand upon Donna Tullia's arm, whispered hoarsely in her ear—

"*Siamo traditi*—we are betrayed!" he said. Whereupon Donna Tullia turned a little pale.

"Betrayed!" she repeated, "and by Gouache!"

Gouache laughed, as he drew out the battered old carved chair on which Madame Mayer was accustomed to sit when he painted.

"Calm yourself, Madame," he said. "I have not the least intention of betraying you. I have made a counter-revolution—but I am perfectly frank. I will not tell of the ferocious deeds I have heard discussed."

Del Ferice scowled and drew back, partly acting, partly in earnest. It lay in his schemes to make Donna Tullia believe herself involved in a genuine plot, and from this point of view he felt that he must pretend the greatest horror and surprise. On the other hand, he knew that Gouache had been painting the Cardinal's portrait, and guessed that the statesman had acquired a strong influence over the artist's mind—an influence which was already showing itself in a way that looked dangerous. It had never struck him until quite lately that Anastase, a republican by descent and by conviction, could suddenly step into the reactionary camp.

"Pardon me, Donna Tullia," said Ugo, in serious tones, "pardon me—but I think we should do well to leave Monsieur Gouache to the contemplation of his new career. This is no place for us—the company of traitors——"

"Look here, Del Ferice," said Gouache, suddenly going up to him and looking him in the face,—"do you seriously believe that anything you have ever said in this room is worth betraying? or, if you do, do you really think that I would betray it?"

"Bah!" exclaimed Donna Tullia, interposing, "it is nonsense! Gouache is a gentleman, of course—and besides, I mean to have my portrait, politics or no politics."

With this round statement Donna Tullia sat down, and Del Ferice had no choice but to follow her example. He was profoundly disgusted, but he saw at a glance that it would be hopeless to attempt to dissuade Madame Mayer when she had once made up her mind.

"And now you can tell us all about it," said Donna Tullia. "What, in the name of all that is senseless, has induced you to join the Zouaves? It really makes me very nervous to see you."

"That lends poetry to your expression," interrupted Gouache. "I wish you were always nervous. You really want to know why I am a Zouave? It is very simple. You must know that I always follow my impulses."

"Impulses!" ejaculated Del Ferice, moodily.

"Yes; because my impulses are always good,—whereas when I reflect much, my judgment is always bad. I felt a strong impulse to wear the grey uniform, so I walked into the recruiting office and wrote my name down."

"I feel a strong impulse to walk out of your studio, Monsieur Gouache," said Donna Tullia, with a rather nervous laugh.

"Then allow me to tell you that, whereas my impulses are good, yours are not," replied Anastase, quietly painting. "Because I have a new dress——"

"And new convictions," interrupted Del Ferice; "you who were always arguing about convictions!"

"I had none; that is the reason I argued about them. I have plenty now—I argue no longer."

"You are wise," retorted Ugo. "Those you have got will never bear discussion."

"Excuse me," answered Gouache; "if you will take the

trouble to be introduced to his Eminence Cardinal
Antonelli——"

Donna Tullia held up her hands in horror.

"That horrible man! That Mephistopheles!" she
cried.

"That Macchiavelli! That arch-enemy of our holy
Liberty!" exclaimed Del Ferice, in theatrical tones.

"Exactly," answered Gouache. "If he could be induced
to devote a quarter of an hour of his valuable time to talking with you, he would turn your convictions round his
finger."

"This is too much!" cried Del Ferice, angrily.

"I think it is very amusing," said Donna Tullia.
"What a pity that all Liberals are not artists, whom his
Eminence could engage to paint his portrait and be con-
verted at so much an hour!"

Gouache smiled quietly, and went on with his work.

"So he told you to go and turn Zouave," remarked
Donna Tullia, after a pause, "and you submitted like a
lamb."

"So far was the Cardinal from advising me to turn
soldier, that he expressed the greatest surprise when I
told him of my intention," returned Gouache, rather
coldly.

"Indeed it is enough to take away even a cardinal's
breath," answered Madame Mayer. "I was never, never
so surprised in my life!"

Gouache stood up to get a view of his work, and Donna
Tullia looked at him critically.

"*Tiens!*" she exclaimed, "it is rather becoming—what
small ankles you have, Gouache!"

Anastase laughed. It was impossible to be grave in
the face of such utterly frivolous inconsistency.

"You will allow your expression to change so often,
Donna Tullia! It is impossible to catch it."

"Like your convictions," murmured Del Ferice from
his corner. Indeed Ugo did not know what to make of
the scene. He had miscalculated the strength of Donna
Tullia's fears as compared with her longing to possess a

flattering portrait of herself. Rather than leave the picture unfinished, she exhibited a cynical indifference to danger which would have done honour to a better man than Del Ferice. Perhaps, too, she understood Gouache well enough to know that he might be trusted. Indeed any one would have trusted Gouache. Even Del Ferice was less disturbed at the possibility of the artist's repeating any of the trivial liberal talk which he had listened to, than at the indifference to discovery shown by Donna Tullia. To Del Ferice, the whole thing had been but a harmless play; but he wanted Madame Mayer to believe that it had all been in solemn earnest, and that she was really implicated in a dangerous plot; for it gave him a stronger hold upon her for his own ends.

"So you are going to fight for Pio Nono," remarked Ugo, scornfully, after another pause.

"I am," replied Gouache. "And, no offence to you, my friend, if I meet you in a red shirt among the Garibaldini, I will kill you. It would be very unpleasant, so I hope that you will not join them."

"Take care, Del Ferice," laughed Donna Tullia; "your life is in danger! You had better join the Zouaves instead."

"I cannot paint his Eminence's portrait," returned Ugo, with a sneer, "so there is no chance of that."

"You might assist him with wholesome advice, I should think," answered Gouache. "I have no doubt you could tell him much that would be very useful."

"And turn traitor to——"

"Hush! Do not be so silly, Del Ferice," interrupted Donna Tullia, who began to fear that Del Ferice's taunts would make trouble. She had a secret conviction that it would not be good to push the gentle Anastase too far. He was too quiet, too determined, and too serious not to be a little dangerous if roused.

"Do not be absurd," she repeated. "Whatever Gouache may choose to do, he is a gentleman, and I will not have you talk of traitors like that. He does not quarrel with you—why do you try to quarrel with him?"

"I think he has done quite enough to justify a quarrel, I am sure," replied Del Ferice, moodily.

"My dear sir," said Gouache, desisting from his work and turning towards Ugo, "Madame is quite right. I not only do not quarrel, but I refuse to be quarrelled with. You have my most solemn assurance that whatever has previously passed here, whatever I have heard said by you, by Donna Tullia, by Valdarno, by any of your friends, I regard as an inviolable secret. You formerly said I had no convictions, and you were right. I had none, and I listened to your exposition of your own with considerable interest. My case is changed. I need not tell you what I believe, for I wear the uniform of a Papal Zouave. When I put it on, I certainly did not contemplate offending you; I do not wish to offend you now—I only beg that you will refrain from offending me. For my part, I need only say that henceforth I do not desire to take a part in your councils. If Donna Tullia is satisfied with her portrait, there need be no further occasion for our meeting. If, on the contrary, we are to meet again, I beg that we may meet on a footing of courtesy and mutual respect."

It was impossible to say more; and Gouache's speech terminated the situation so far as Del Ferice was concerned. Donna Tullia smilingly expressed her approval.

"Quite right, Gouache," she said. "You know it would be impossible to leave the portrait as it is now. The mouth, you know—you promised to do something to it—just the expression, you know."

Gouache bowed his head a little, and set to work again without a word. Del Ferice did not speak again during the sitting, but sat moodily staring at the canvas, at Donna Tullia, and at the floor. It was not often that he was moved from his habitual suavity of manner, but Gouache's conduct had made him feel particularly uncomfortable.

The next time Donna Tullia came to sit, she brought her old countess, and Del Ferice did not appear. The portrait was ultimately finished to the satisfaction of all parties, and was hung in Donna Tullia's drawing-room, to be admired and criticised by all her friends. But Gouache rejoiced when the thing was finally removed from his studio, for he had grown to hate it, and had been almost willing to flatter it out of all likeness to Madame Mayer, for the sake of not being eternally confronted by the cold stare of her blue eyes. He finished the Cardinal's portrait too; and the statesman not only paid for it with unusual liberality, but gave the artist what he called a little memento of the long hours they had spent together. He opened one of the lockers in his study, and from a small drawer selected an ancient ring, in which was set a piece of crystal with a delicate intaglio of a figure of Victory. He took Gouache's hand and slipped the ring upon his finger. He had taken a singular liking to Anastase.

"Wear it as a little souvenir of me," he said kindly. "It is a Victory; you are a soldier now, so I pray that victory may go with you; and I give Victory herself into your hands."

"And I," said Gouache, "will pray that it may be a symbol in my hand of the real victories you are to win."

"Only a symbol," returned the Cardinal, thoughtfully. "Nothing but a symbol. I was not born to conquer, but to lead a forlorn-hope—to deceive vanquished men with a hope not real, and to deceive the victors with an unreal fear. Nevertheless, my friend," he added, grasping Gouache's hand, and fixing upon him his small bright eyes,— "nevertheless, let us fight, fight—fight to the very end!"

"We will fight to the end, Eminence," said Gouache. He was only a private of Zouaves, and the man whose hand he held was great and powerful; but the same spirit was in the hearts of both, the same courage, the same devotion to a failing cause—and both kept their words, each in his own way.

CHAPTER XXIII.

Astrardente was in some respects a picturesque place. The position of the little town gave it a view in both directions from where it stood; for it was built upon a precipitous eminence rising suddenly out of the midst of the narrow strip of fertile land, the long and rising valley which, from its lower extremity, conducted by many circuits to the Roman Campagna, and which ended above in the first rough passes of the lower Abruzzi. The base of the town extended into the vineyards and olive-orchards which surrounded the little hill on all sides; and the summit of it was crowned by the feudal palace-castle—an enormous building of solid stone, in the style of the fifteenth century. Upon the same spot had formerly stood a rugged fortress, but the magnificent ideas of the Astrardente pope had not tolerated such remains of barbarism; the ancient stronghold had been torn down, and on its foundations rose a gigantic mansion, consisting of a main palace, with great balconies and columned front, overlooking the town, and of two massive wings leading back like towers to the edge of the precipitous rock to northwards. Between these wings a great paved court formed a sort of terrace, open upon one side, and ornamented within with a few antique statues dug up upon the estates, and with numerous plants, which the old duke had caused to be carefully cultivated in vases, and which were only exposed upon the terrace during the warm summer months. The view from the court was to the north—that is to say, down the valley, comprehending ranges of hills that seemed to cross and recross into the extreme distance, their outlines being each time less clearly defined, as the masses in each succeeding range took a softer purple hue.

Within, the palace presented a great variety of apartments. There were suites of vaulted rooms upon the lower floor, frescoed in the good manner of the fifteenth century; there were other suites above, hung with ancient tapestry and furnished with old-fashioned marble tables, and mirrors in heavily gilt frames, and one entire wing had been lately

fitted up in the modern style. In this part of the house
Corona established herself with Sister Gabrielle, and began
to lead a life of regular occupations and profound retirement, which seemed to be rather a continuation of her
existence in the convent where she had been educated as
a girl, than to form any part in the life of the superb
Duchessa d'Astrardente, who for five years had been one
of the most conspicuous persons in society. Every morning
at eight o'clock the two ladies, always clad in deep black,
attended the Mass which was celebrated for them in the
palace chapel. Then Corona walked for an hour with her
companion upon the terrace, or, if it rained, beneath the
covered balconies upon the south side. The morning hours
she passed in solitude, reading such books of devotion and
serious matter as most suited the sad temper of her mind ;
precisely at mid-day she and Sister Gabrielle breakfasted
together in a sort of solemn state ; and at three o'clock the
great landau, with its black horses and mourning liveries,
stood under the inner gate. The two ladies appeared five
minutes later, and by a gesture Corona indicated whether
she would be driven up or down the valley. The dashing
equipage descended the long smooth road that wound
through the town, and returned invariably at the end of
two hours, again ascended the tortuous way, and disappeared beneath the dark entrance. At six o'clock dinner
was served, with the same solemn state as attended the
morning meal ; Corona and Sister Gabrielle remained together until ten, and the day was over. There was no more
variation in the routine of their lives than if they had been
moved by a machinery connected with the great castle clock
overhead, which chimed the hours and the quarters by day
and night, and regulated the doings of the town below.

But in spite of this unchanging sequence of similar
habit, the time passed pleasantly for Corona. She had had
too much of the brilliant lights and the buzzing din of society
for the last five years, too much noise, too much idle talk,
too much aimless movement ; she needed rest, too, from
the constant strain of her efforts to fulfil her self-imposed
duties towards her husband—most of all, perhaps, she re-

quired a respite from the sufferings she had undergone through her stifled love for Giovanni Saracinesca. All this she found in the magnificent calm of the life at Astrardente. She meditated long upon the memory of her husband, re-calling lovingly those things which had been most worthy in him, willingly forgetting his many follies and vanities and moments of petulance. She went over in her mind the many and varied scenes of the past, and learned to love the sweet and silent solitude of the present by comparison of it with all the useless and noisy activity of the world she had for a time abandoned. She had not expected to find anything more than a passive companion in Sister Gabrielle; but in the course of their daily converse she discovered in her a character of extreme refinement and quick perception, a depth of human sympathy and a breadth of experience which amazed her, and made her own views of things seem small. The Sister was devout and rigid in the observance of the institutions of her order, in so far as she was able to follow out the detail of religious regulation without interfering with the convenience of her companion; but in her conversation she showed an intimate knowledge of character which was a constant source of pleasure to Corona, who told the Sister long stories of people she had known for the sake of hearing her admirable comments upon social questions.

But besides her reading and her long hours of medita-tion and her talks with Sister Gabrielle, Corona found occupation in the state of the town below her residence. She attempted once or twice to visit the poor cottages, in the hope of doing some good; but she found that she was such an object of holy awe to the inmates that they were speechless in her presence, or became so nervous in their desire to answer her questions, that the information she was able to obtain concerning their troubles was too vague to be of any use.

The Italian peasant is not the same in all parts of the country, as is generally supposed; and although the Tuscan, who is constantly brought into familiar contact with his landlord, and acquires a certain pleasant faith in him, grows

eloquent upon the conditions of his being, the same is not
true of the rougher race that labours in the valleys of the
Sabine and the Samnite hills. The peasant of the Agro
Romano is indeed capable of civilisation, and he is able to
understand his superiors, provided that he is gradually
accustomed to seeing them : unfortunately this occurs but
rarely. Many of the great Roman landholders spend a
couple of months of every year upon their estates: old
Astrardente had in his later years gone to considerable expense in refitting and repairing the castle, but he had done
little for the town. Men like the Saracinesca, however,
were great exceptions at that time ; though they travelled
much abroad, they often remained for many months in
their rugged old fortress. They knew the inhabitants of
their lands far and wide, and were themselves not only
known but loved ; they spent their money in improving
the condition of their peasants, in increasing the area of
their forests, and in fostering the fertility of the soil, but
they cared nothing for adorning the grey stone walls of
their ancestors' stronghold. It had done well enough for a
thousand years, it would do well enough still ; it had stood
firm against fierce sieges in the dark ages of the Roman
baronry, it could afford to stand unchanged in its monu-
mental strength against the advancing sea of nineteenth-
century civilisation. They themselves, father and son,
were content with such practical improvements as they
could introduce for the good of their people and the en-
riching of their land ; a manly race, despising luxury, they
cared little whether their home was thought comfortable by
the few guests they occasionally invited to spend a week
with them. They saw much of the peasantry, and went
daily among them, understanding their wants, and wisely
promoting in their minds the belief that land cannot prosper
unless both landlord and tenant do their share.

But Astrardente was a holding of a very different kind,
and Corona, in her first attempts at understanding the state
of things, found herself stopped by a dead wall of silence,
beyond which she guessed that there lay an undiscovered
land of trouble. She knew next to nothing of the con-

dition of her people; she only imperfectly understood the
relations in which they actually stood to herself, the extent
of her power over them, and of their power over her. The
mysteries of *emphyteusis, emphyteuma*, and *emphyteuta* were
still hidden to her, though her steward spoke of them with
surprising loquacity and fluency. She laboured hard to
understand the system upon which her tenants held their
lands from her, and it was some time before she succeeded.
It is easier to explain the matter at once than to follow
Corona in her attempts to comprehend it.

To judge from the terms employed, the system of holdings common in the Pontifical States has descended without interruption from the time of the Romans to the present
day. As in old Roman law, *emphyteusis*, now spelt *emfiteuse*,
means the possession of rights over another person's land,
capable of transmission by inheritance; and to-day, as
under the Romans, the holder of such rights is called the
emphyteuta, or *emfiteuta*. How the Romans came to use
Greek words in their tenant-law does not belong to the
matter in hand; these words are the only ones now in use
in this part of Italy, and they are used precisely as they
were in remote times.

A tenant may acquire rights of *emfiteuse* directly from
the owner of the land, like an ordinary lease; or he may
acquire them by settlement—"squatting," as the popular
term is. Wherever land is lying waste, any one may
establish himself upon it and cultivate it, on condition of
paying to the owner a certain proportion of the yield of
the land—generally one quarter—either in kind or in
money. The landlord may, indeed, refuse the right of
settlement in the first instance, which would very rarely
occur, since most people who own barren tracts of rock and
heath are only too glad to promote any kind of cultivation.
But when the landlord has once allowed the right, the
right itself is constituted thereby into a possession of
which the peasant may dispose as he pleases, even by sell-
ing it to another. The law provides, however, that in case
of transfers by sale, the landlord shall receive one year's
rent in kind or in money in addition to the rent due, and

this bonus is paid jointly by the buyer and the seller according to agreement. Such holdings are inherited from father to son for many generations, and are considered to be perpetual leases. The landlord cannot expel a tenant except for non-payment of rent during three consecutive years. In actual fact, the right of the *emfiteuta* in the soil is far more important than that of the landlord; for the tenant can cheat his landlord as much as he pleases, whereas the injustice of the law provides that under no circumstance whatsoever shall the landlord cheat the tenant. In actual fact, also, the rents are universally paid in kind, and the peasant eats what remains of the produce, so that very little cash is seen in the land.

Corona discovered that the income she enjoyed from the lands of Astrardente was collected by the basketful from the threshing-floors, and by the barrel from the vineyards of some two hundred tenants. It was a serious matter to gather from two hundred threshing-floors precisely a quarter of the grain threshed, and from fifty or sixty vineyards precisely a quarter of the wine made in each. The peasants all made their wine at the same time, and all threshed their grain in the same week. If the agent was not on the spot during the threshing and the vintage, the peasant had no difficulty whatever in hiding a large quantity of his produce. As the rent was never fixed, but depended solely on the yield of the year, it was preeminently to the advantage of the tenant to throw dust in the eyes of the landlord whenever he got a chance. The landlord found the business of watching his tenants tedious and unprofitable, and naturally resorted to the crowning evil of agricultural evils—the employment of a rent-farmer. The latter, at all events, was willing to pay a fixed sum yearly; and if the sum paid was generally considerably below the real value of the rents, the arrangement at least assured a fixed income to the landlord, with the certainty of getting it without trouble to himself. The middleman then proceeded to grind the tenants at his leisure and discretion in order to make the best of his bargain. The result was, that while the tenant starved

and the landlord got less than his due in consideration of
being saved from annoyance, the middleman gradually
accumulated money.

Upon this system nine-tenths of the land in the Pontifical States was held, and much of the same land is so
held to-day, in spite of the modern tenant-law, for reasons
which will be clearly explained in another part of this
history. Corona saw and understood that the evil was
very great. She discussed the matter with her steward,
or *ministro* as he was called, who was none other than the
aforesaid middleman; and the more she discussed the
question, the more hopeless the question appeared. The
steward held a contract from her dead husband for a
number of years. He had regularly paid the yearly sums
agreed upon, and it would be impossible to remove him
for several years to come. He, of course, was strenuously
opposed to any change, and did his best to make himself
appear as an angel of mercy and justice, presiding over a
happy family of rejoicing peasants in the heart of a ter-
restrial paradise. Unfortunately for himself, however, he
had not at first understood the motive which prompted
Corona's inquiries. He supposed in the beginning that
she was not satisfied with the amount of rent he paid, and
that at the expiration of his contract she intended to raise
the sum; so that, on the first occasion when she sent for
him, he had drawn a piteous picture of the peasant's condition, and had expatiated with eloquence on his own
poverty, and on the extreme difficulty of collecting any
rents at all. It was not until he discovered that Corona's
chief preoccupation was for the welfare of her tenants that
he changed his tactics, and endeavoured to prove that all
was for the best upon the best of all possible estates.

Then, to his great astonishment, Corona informed him
that his contract would not be renewed, and that at the
expiration of his term she would collect her rents herself.
It had taken her long to understand the situation, but
when she had comprehended it, she made up her mind
that something must be done. If her fortune had depended solely upon the income she received from the

Astrardente lands, she would have made up her mind to reduce herself to penury rather than allow things to go on in the way they were going. Fortunately she was rich, and if she had not all the experience necessary to deal with such matters, she had plenty of goodwill, plenty of generosity, and plenty of money. In her simple theory of agrarian economy the best way to improve an estate seemed to be to spend the income arising from it directly upon its improvement, until she could take the whole management of it into her own hands. The trouble, as she thought, was that there was too little money among the peasants; the best way to help them was to put money within their reach. The only question was how to do this without demoralising them, and without increasing their liabilities towards the *ministro* or middleman.

Then she sent for the curate. From him she learned that the people did well enough in the summer, but that the winter was dreaded. She asked why. He answered that they were not provident; that the land system was bad; and that even if they saved anything the *ministro* would take it from them. She inquired whether he thought it possible to induce them to be more thrifty. He thought it might be done in ten years, but not in one.

" In that case," said Corona, " the only way to improve their condition is to give them work in the winter. I will make roads through the estate, and build large dwelling-houses in the town. There shall be work enough for everybody."

It was a simple plan, but it was destined to be carried into execution, and to change the face of the Astrardente domain in a few years. Corona sent to Rome for an engineer who was also a good architect, and she set herself to study the possibilities of the place, giving the man sufficient scope, and only insisting that there should be no labour and no material imported from beyond the limits of her lands. This provided her with an occupation whereby the time passed quickly enough.

The Lenten season ended, and Eastertide ran swiftly on to Pentecost. The early fruit-trees blossomed white, and

T

the flowers fell in a snow-shower to the ground, to give
place to the cherries and the almonds and the pears.   The
brown bramble-hedges turned leafy, and were alive with
little birds ; and the great green lizards shot across the
woodland paths upon the hillside, and caught the flies that
buzzed noisily in the spring sunshine.   The dried-up vines
put forth tiny leaves, and the maize shot suddenly up to
the sun out of the rich furrows, like myriads of brilliant
green poignards piercing the brown skin of the earth.   By
the roadside the grass grew high, and the broad shallow
brooks shrank to narrow rivulets, and disappeared in the
overgrowing rushes before the increasing heat of the climb-
ing sun.

Corona's daily round of life never changed, but as the
months wore on, a stealing thought came often and often
again—shy, as though fearing to be driven away ; silent at
first, as a shadow in a dream, but taking form and reality
from familiarity with its own self, and speaking intelligible
words, saying at last plainly, "Will he keep his promise ?
Will he never come ? "

But he came not as the fresh colours of spring deepened
with the rich maturity of summer ; and Corona, gazing
down the valley, saw the change that came over the fair
earth, and half guessed the change that was coming over
her own life.   She had sought solitude instinctively, but
she had not known what it would bring her.   She had
desired to honour her dead husband by withdrawing from
the world for a time and thinking of him and remembering
him.   She had done so, but the youth in her rebelled at last
against the constant memory of old age—of an old age, too,
which had passed away from her and was dead for ever.
It was right to dwell for a time upon the thought of her
widowhood, but the voice said it would not be always right.
The calm and noiseless tide of the old man's ceasing life
had ebbed slowly and reluctantly from her shore, and she
had followed the sad sea in her sorrow to the furthest verge
of its retreat ; but as she stood upon the edge of the stag-
nant waters, gazing far out and trying to follow even
further the slow subsiding ooze, the tide had turned upon

her unawares, the fresh seaward breeze sprang up and broke
the dead calm with the fresh motion of crisp ripples that
once more flowed gladly over the dreary sand, and the
waters of life plashed again and laughed gladly together
around her feet.

The thought of Giovanni—the one thought that again
and again kept recurring in her mind—grew very sweet,—
as sweet as it had once been bitter. There was nothing to
stop its growth now, and she let it have its way. What
did it matter, so long as he did not come near her—for the
present? Some day he would come; she wondered when,
and how long he would keep his promise. But meanwhile
she was not unhappy, and she went about her occupations
as before; only sometimes she would go alone at evening to
the balcony that faced the higher mountains, and there she
would stand for half an hour gazing southwards towards the
precipitous rocks that caught the red glare of the sinking
sun, and she asked herself if he were there, or whether, as
report had told her, he were in the far north. It was but
half a day's ride over the hills, he had said. But strain her
sight as she would, she could not pierce the heavy crags nor
see into the wooded dells beyond. He had said he would
pass the summer there; had he changed his mind?

But she was not unhappy. There was that in her which
forbade unhappiness, which would have broken out into
great joy if she would have let it; but yet she would not.
It was too soon yet to say aloud what she said in her heart
daily, that she loved Giovanni with a great love, and that
she knew she was free to love him. In that thought there
was enough of joy. But he might come if he would; her
anger would not be great if he broke his promise now, he
had kept it so long—six whole months. But by-and-by, as
the days passed, the first note of happiness was marred by
the discordant ring of a distant fear. What if she had too
effectually forbidden him to see her? What if he had gone
out disappointed of all hope, and was really in distant
Scandinavia, as the papers said, risking his life in mad
adventures?

But after all, that was not what she feared. He was

strong, young, brave—he had survived a thousand dangers, he would survive these also.   There arose between her and the thought of him an evil shadow, the image of a woman, and it took the shape of Donna Tullia so vividly that she could see the red lips move and almost hear the noisy laugh.   She was angry with herself at the idea, but it recurred continually and gave her pain, and the pain grew to an intolerable fear.   She began to feel that she must know where he was, at any cost, or she could have no peace.   She was restless and nervous, and began to be absent-minded in her conversation with Sister Gabrielle. The good woman saw it, and advised a little change—anything, an excursion of a day for instance.   Corona, she said, was too young to lead this life.

Her mind leaped at the idea.   It was but half a day's ride, he had said; she would climb those hills and look down upon Saracinesca—only once.   She might perhaps meet some peasant, and by a careless inquiry she would learn whether he was there — or would be there in the summer.   No one would know; and besides, Sister Gabrielle had said that an excursion would do Corona good. Sister Gabrielle had probably never heard that Saracinesca was so near, and she certainly would not guess that the Duchessa had any interest in its lord.   She announced her intention, and the Sister approved—she herself, she said, was too weak to undergo the fatigue.

On the following morning, Corona alone entered her carriage and was driven many miles up the southward hills, till the road was joined by a broad bridle-path that led eastwards towards the Abruzzi.   Here she was met by a party of horsemen, her own *guardiani*, or forest-keepers, as they are called, in rough dark-blue coats and leathern gaiters.   Each man wore upon his breast a round plate of chiselled silver, bearing the arms of the Astrardente; each had a long rifle slung behind him, and carried a holster at the bow of his huge saddle.   A couple of sturdy black-browed peasants held a mule by the bridle, heavily caparisoned in the old fashion, under a great red velvet Spanish saddle, with long tarnished trappings that had once been embroidered with silver. A little knot of peasants and ragged boys stood all around watching the preparations with interest, and commenting audibly upon the beauty of the great lady.

Corona mounted from a stone by the wayside, and the young men led her beast up the path. She smiled to herself, for she had never done such a thing before, but she was not uneasy in the company of her rough-looking escort. She knew well enough that she was as safe with them as in her own house.

As the bridle-path wound up from the road, the country grew more rugged, the vegetation more scanty, and the stones more plentiful. It was a wilderness of rocky desolation; as far as one could see there was no sign of humanity, not a soul upon the solitary road, not a living thing upon the desolate hills that rose on either side in jagged points to the sky. Corona talked a little with the head-keeper who rode beside her with a slack rein, letting his small mountain horse pick its own way over the rough path. He told her that few people ever passed that way. It was the short road to Saracinesca. The princes sometimes sent their carriage round by the longer way and rode over the hills; and in the vintage-time there was some traffic, as many of the smaller peasants carried grapes across the pass to the larger wine-presses, and sold them outright. It was not a dangerous road, for the very reason that it was so unfrequented. The Duchessa explained that she only wanted to see the valley beyond from the summit of the pass, and would then return. It was past mid-day when the party reached the highest point,—a depression between the crags just wide enough to admit one loaded mule. The keeper said she could see Saracinesca from the end of the narrow way, before the descent began. She uttered an exclamation of surprise as she reached the spot.

Scarcely a quarter of a mile to the right, at the extremity of a broad hill-road, she saw the huge towers of Saracinesca, grey and storm-beaten, rising out of a thick wood. The whole intervening space — and indeed the whole deep valley as far as she could see—was an unbroken forest of chestnut-trees. Here and there below the castle the houses of the town showed their tiled gables, but the mass of the buildings was hidden completely from sight. Corona had had no idea that she should find herself so near to the place, and she was seized with a sudden fear lest Giovanni should appear upon the long straight path that led into the trees. She drew back a little among her followers.

"Are the princes there now?" she asked of the head-keeper.

He did not know; but a moment later a peasant, riding astride of a bag of corn upon his donkey's back, passed along the straight road by the entrance to the bridle-path. The keeper hailed him, and put the question. Seeing Corona upon her mule, surrounded by armed men in livery, the man halted and pulled off his soft black-cloth hat.

Both the princes were in Saracinesca, he said. The young prince had been there ever since Easter. They were busy building an aqueduct which was to supply the whole town with water; it was to pass above, up there among the woods. The princes went almost every day to visit the works. Her Excellency might, perhaps, find them there now, or if not, they were at the castle.

But her Excellency had no intention of finding them. She gave the fellow a coin, and beat a somewhat hasty retreat. Her followers were silent men, accustomed to obey, and they followed her down the steep path without even exchanging a word among themselves. Beneath the shade of an overhanging rock she halted, and, dismounting from her mule, was served with the lunch that had been brought. She ate little, and then sat thoughtfully contemplating the bare stones, while the men at a little distance hastily disposed of the remains of her meal. She had experienced an extraordinary emotion on finding herself suddenly so near to Giovanni; it was almost as though she had seen him, and her heart beat fast, while a dark flush rose from time to time to her cheek. It would have been so natural that he should pass that way, just as she was halting at the entrance to the bridle-path. How unspeakably dreadful it would have been to be discovered thus spying out his dwelling-place when she had so strictly forbidden him to attempt to see her! The blush burned upon her cheeks—she had done a thing so undignified, so ill befitting her magnificent superiority. For a moment she was desperately ashamed. But for all that, she could not repress the glad delight she felt at knowing that he was there after all; that, if he had kept his word in avoiding her, he had, nevertheless, also fulfilled his intention of spending the summer in Saracinesca. He had even been there since Easter, and the story of his going to the North had been a mere invention of the newspapers. She could not understand his conduct, nor why he had gone to Paris—a fact attested by people who knew him. It had probably been for some matter of business—that excuse which, in a woman's mind, explains almost any sudden journey a man may undertake. But he was there in the castle now, and her heart was satisfied.

The men packed the things in the basket, and Corona was helped upon her mule. Slowly the party descended the steep path that grew broader and more practicable as they neared the bottom; there the carriage awaited her, and soon she was bowling along the smooth road towards home, leaving far behind her the mounted guards, the peasants, and her slow-paced mule. The sun was low when the carriage rolled under the archway of Astrardente. Sister Gabrielle said Corona looked much the better for her excursion, and she added that she must be very strong to bear such fatigue so well. And the next day—and for many days — the Sister noticed the change in her hostess's manner, and promised herself that if the Duchessa became uneasy again she would advise another day among the hills, so wonderful was the effect of a slight change from the ordinary routine of her life.

That night old Saracinesca and his son sat at dinner in a wide hall of their castle. The faithful Pasquale served them as solemnly as he was used to do in Rome. This evening he spoke again. He had ventured no remark since he had informed them of the Duca d'Astrardente's death.

"I beg your Excellencies' pardon," he began, adopting his usual formula of apologetic address.

"Well, Pasquale, what is it?" asked old Saracinesca.

"I did not know whether your Excellency was aware that the Duchessa d'Astrardente had been here to-day."

"What?" roared the Prince.

"You must be mad, Pasquale?" exclaimed Giovanni in a low voice.

"I beg your Excellencies' pardon if I am wrong, but this is how I know. Gigi Secchi, the peasant from Aquaviva in the lower forest, brought a bag of corn to the mill to-day, and he told the miller, and the miller told Ettore, and Ettore told Nino, and Nino told——"

"What the devil did he tell him?" interrupted old Saracinesca.

"Nino told the cook's boy," continued Pasquale unmoved, "and the cook's boy told me, your Excellency, that Gigi was passing along the road to Serveti coming here, when he was stopped by a number of *guardiani* who accompanied a beautiful dark lady in black, who rode upon a mule, and the *guardiani* asked him if your Excellencies were at Saracinesca; and when he said you were, the lady gave him a coin, and turned at once and rode down the bridle-path towards Astrardente, and he said the *guardiani* were those of the Astrardente, because he remembered to have seen one of them, who has a scar over his left eye, at the great fair at Genazzano last year. And that is how I heard."

"That is a remarkable narrative, Pasquale," answered the Prince, laughing loudly, "but it seems very credible. Go and send for Gigi Secchi if he is still in the neighbourhood, and bring him here, and let us have the story from his own lips."

When they were alone the two men looked at each other for a moment, and then old Saracinesca laughed again; but Giovanni looked very grave, and his face was pale. Presently his father became serious again.

"If this thing is true," he said, "I would advise you, Giovanni, to pay a visit to the other side of the hills. It is time."

Giovanni was silent for a moment. He was intensely interested in the situation, but he could not tell his father that he had promised Corona not to see her, and he had not yet explained to himself her sudden appearance so near Saracinesca.

"I think it would be better for you to go first," he said to his father. "But I am not at all sure this story is true."

"I? Oh, I will go when you please," returned the old man, with another laugh. He was always ready for anything active.

But Gigi Secchi could not be found. He had returned to Aquaviva at once, and it was not easy to send a message. Two days later, however, Giovanni took the trouble of going to the man's home. He was not altogether surprised when Gigi confirmed Pasquale's tale in every particular. Corona had actually been at Saracinesca to find out if Giovanni was there or not; and on hearing that he was at the castle, she had fled precipitately. Giovanni was naturally grave and of a melancholy temper; but during the last few months he had been more than usually taciturn, occupying himself with dogged obstinacy in the construction of his aqueduct, visiting the works in the day and spending hours in the evening over the plans. He was waiting. He believed that Corona cared for him, and he knew that he loved her, but for the present he must wait patiently, both for the sake of his promise and for the sake of a decent respect of her widowhood. In order to wait he felt the necessity of constant occupation, and to that end he had set himself resolutely to work with his father, whose ideal dream was to make Saracinesca the most complete and prosperous community in that part of the mountains.

"I think if you would go over," he said, at the end of a week, "it would be much better. I do not want to intrude myself upon her at present, and you could easily find out whether she would like to see me. After all, she may have been merely making an excursion for her amusement, and may have chanced upon us by accident. I have often noticed how suddenly one comes in view of the castle from that bridle-path."

"On the other hand," returned the Prince with a smile, "any one would tell her that the path leads nowhere except to Saracinesca. But I will go to-morrow," he added. "I will set your mind at rest in twenty-four hours."

"Thank you," said Giovanni.

CHAPTER XXIV.

Old Saracinesca kept his word, and on the following morning, eight days after Corona's excursion upon the hills, he rode down to Astrardente, reaching the palace at about mid-day. He sent in his card, and stood waiting beneath the great gate, beating the dust from his boots with his heavy whip. His face looked darker than ever, from constant exposure to the sun, and his close-cropped hair and short square beard had turned even whiter than before in the last six months, but his strong form was erect, and his step firm and elastic. He was a remarkable old man; many a boy of twenty might have envied his strength and energetic vitality.

Corona was at her mid-day breakfast with Sister Gabrielle, when the old Prince's card was brought. She started at the sight of the name; and though upon the bit of pasteboard she read plainly enough, "*Il Principe di Saracinesca,*" she hesitated, and asked the butler if it was really the Prince. He said it was.

"Would you mind seeing him?" she asked of Sister Gabrielle. "He is an old gentleman," she added, in explanation—"a near neighbour here in the mountains."

Sister Gabrielle had no objection. She even remarked that it would do the Duchessa good to see some one.

"Ask the Prince to come in, and put another place at the table," said Corona.

A moment later the old man entered, and Corona rose to receive him. There was something refreshing in the ring of his deep voice and the clank of his spurs as he crossed the marble floor.

"Signora Duchessa, you are very good to receive me. I did not know that this was your breakfast-hour. Ah!" he exclaimed, glancing at Sister Gabrielle, who had also risen to her feet, "good day, my Sister."

"Sister Gabrielle," said Corona, as an introduction; "she is good enough to be my companion in solitude."

To tell the truth, Corona felt uneasy; but the sensation was somehow rather pleasurable, although it crossed her mind that the Prince might have heard of her excursion, and had possibly come to find out why she had been so near to his place. She boldly faced the situation.

"I nearly came upon you the other day as unexpectedly as you have visited me," she said with a smile. "I had a fancy to look over into your valley, and when I reached the top of the hill I found I was almost in your house."

"I wish you had quite been there," returned the Prince. "Of course I heard that you had been seen, and we guessed you had stumbled upon us in some mountain excursion. My son rode all the way to Aquaviva to see the man who had spoken with you."

Saracinesca said this as though it were perfectly natural, helping himself to the dish the servant offered him. But when he looked up he saw that Corona blushed beneath her dark skin.

"It is such a very sudden view at that point," she said, nervously, "that I was startled."

"I wish you had preserved you equanimity to the extent of going a little further. Saracinesca has rarely been honoured with the visit of a Duchessa d'Astrardente. But since you have explained your visit—or the visit which you did not make—I ought to explain mine. You must know, in the first place, that I am not here by accident, but by intention, preconceived, well pondered, and finally executed to my own complete satisfaction. I came, not to get a glimpse of your valley nor a distant view of your palace, but to see you, yourself. Your hospitality in receiving me has therefore crowned and complemented the desire I had of seeing you."

Corona laughed a little.

"That is a very pretty speech,' she said.

"Which you would have lost if you had not received me," he answered, gaily. "I have not done yet. I have many pretty speeches for you. The sight of you induces beauty in language as the sun in May makes the flowers open."

"That is another," laughed Corona. "Do you spend your days in studying the poets at Saracinesca? Does Don Giovanni study with you?"

"Giovanni is a fact," returned the Prince; "I am a fable. Old men are always fables, for they represent, in a harmless form, the follies of all mankind; their end is always in itself a moral, and young people can learn much by studying them."

"Your comparison is witty," said Corona, who was much amused at old Saracinesca's conversation; "but I doubt whether you are so harmless as you represent. You are certainly not foolish, and I am not sure whether, as a study for the young——" she hesitated, and laughed.

"Whether extremely young persons would have the wit to comprehend virtue by the concealment of it—to say, as that witty old Roman said, that the images of Cassius and Brutus were more remarkable than those of any one else, for the very reason that they were nowhere to be seen— like my virtues? Giovanni, for instance, is the very reverse of me in that, though he has shown such singularly bad taste in resembling my outward man."

"One should never conceal virtues," said Sister Gabrielle, gently. "One should not hide one's light under a basket, you know."

"My Sister," replied the old Prince, his black eyes twinkling merrily, "if I had in my whole composition as much light as would enable you to read half-a-dozen words in your breviary, it should be at your disposal. I would set it in the midst of Piazza Colonna, and call it the most wonderful illumination on record. Unfortunately my light, like the lantern of a solitary miner, is only perceptible to myself, and dimly at that."

"You must not depreciate yourself so very much," said Corona.

"No; that is true. You will either believe I am speaking the truth, or you will not. I do not know which would be the worse fate. I will change the subject. My son Giovanni, Duchessa, desires to be remembered in your good graces."

"Thanks. How is he?"

"He is well, but the temper of him is marvellously melancholy. He is building an aqueduct, and so am I. The thing is accomplished by his working perpetually while I smoke cigarettes and read novels."

"The division of labour is to your advantage, I should say," remarked Corona.

"Immensely, I assure you. He promotes the natural advantages of my lands, and I encourage the traffic in tobacco and literature. He works from morning till night, is his own engineer, contractor, overseer, and master-mason. He does everything, and does it well. If we were less barbarous in our bachelor establishment I would ask you to come and see us—in earnest this time—and visit the work we are doing. It is well worth while. Perhaps you would consent as it is. We will vacate the castle for your benefit, and mount guard outside the gates all night."

Again Corona blushed. She would have given anything to go, but she felt that it was impossible.

"I would like to go," she said. "If one could come back the same day."

"You did before," remarked Saracinesca, bluntly.

"But it was late when I reached home, and I spent no time at all there."

"I know you did not," laughed the old man. "You gave Gigi Secchi some money, and then fled precipitately."

"Indeed I was afraid you would suddenly come upon me, and I ran away," answered Corona, laughing in her turn, as the dark blood rose to her olive cheeks.

"As my amiable ancestors did in the same place when

anybody passed with a full purse," suggested Saracinesca.
"But we have improved a little since then. We would
have asked you to breakfast. Will you come?"

"I do not like to go alone; I cannot, you see. Sister
Gabrielle could never ride up that hill on a mule."

"There is a road for carriages," said the Prince. "I
will propose something in the way of a compromise. I
will bring Giovanni down with me and our team of mountain horses. Those great beasts of yours cannot do this
kind of work. We will take you and Sister Gabrielle up
almost as fast as you could go by the bridle-path."

"And back on the same day?" asked Corona.

"No; on the next day."

"But I do not see where the compromise is," she replied.

"Sister Gabrielle is at once the compromise and the
cause that you will not be compromised. I beg her
pardon——"

Both ladies laughed.

"I will be very glad to go," said the Sister. "I do not
see that there is anything extraordinary in the Prince's
proposal."

"My Sister," returned Saracinesca, "you are on the way
to saintship; you already enjoy the beatific vision; you see
with a heavenly perspicuity."

"It is a charming proposition," said Corona; "but in
that case you will have to come down the day before."
She was a little embarrassed.

"We will not invade the cloister," answered the Prince.
"Giovanni and I will spend the night in concocting pretty
speeches, and will appear armed with them at dawn before
your gates."

"There is room in Astrardente," replied Corona. "You
shall not lack hospitality for a night. When will you come?"

"To-morrow evening, if you please. A good thing
should be done quickly, in order not to delay doing it
again."

"Do you think I would go again?"

Saracinesca fixed his black eyes on Corona's, and gazed
at her some seconds before he answered.

"Madam," he said at last, very gravely, "I trust you will come again and stay longer."

"You are very good," returned Corona, quietly. "At all events, I will go this first time."

"We will endeavour to show our gratitude by making you comfortable," answered the Prince, resuming his former tone. "You shall have a mass in the morning and a litany in the evening. We are godless fellows up there, but we have a priest."

"You seem to associate our comfort entirely with religious services," laughed Corona. "But you are very considerate." ·

"I see the most charming evidence of devotion at your side," he replied; "Sister Gabrielle is both the evidence of your piety and is in herself an exposition of the benefits of religion. There shall be other attractions, however, besides masses and litanies."

Breakfast being ended, Sister Gabrielle left the two together. They went from the dining-room to the great vaulted hall in the inner building. It was cool there, and there were great old arm-chairs ranged along the walls. The closed blinds admitted a soft green light from the hot noonday without. Corona loved to walk upon the cool marble floor;· she was a very strong and active woman, delighting in mere motion—not restless, but almost incapable of weariness; her movements not rapid, but full of grace and ease. Saracinesca walked by her side, smoking thoughtfully for some minutes.

"Duchessa," he said at last, glancing at her beautiful face, "things are greatly changed since we met last. You were angry with me then. I do not know whether you were so justly, but you were very angry for a few moments. I am going to return to the subject now; I trust you will not be offended with me."

Corona trembled for a moment, and was silent. She would have prevented him from going on, but before she could find the words she sought he continued.

"Things are much changed, in some respects; in others, not at all. It is but natural to suppose that in the course of time you will think of the possibility of marrying again. My son, Duchessa, loves you very truly. Pardon me, it is no disrespect to you, now, that he should have told me so. I am his father, and I have no one else to care for. He is too honest a gentleman to have spoken of his affection for you at an earlier period, but he has told me of it now."

Corona stood still in the midst of the great hall, and faced the old Prince. She had grown pale while he was speaking. Still she was silent.

"I have nothing more to say—that is all," said Saracinesca, gazing earnestly into the depths of her eyes. "I have nothing more to say."

"Do you then mean to repeat the warning you once gave me?" asked Corona, growing whiter still. "Do you mean to imply that there is danger to your son?"

"There is danger—great danger for him, unless you will avert it."

"And how?" asked Corona, in a low voice.

"Madam, by becoming his wife."

Corona started and turned away in great agitation. Saracinesca stood still while she slowly walked a few steps from him. She could not speak.

"I could say a great deal more, Duchessa," he said, as she came back towards him. "I could say that the marriage is not only fitting in every other way, but is also advantageous from a worldly point of view. You are sole mistress of Astrardente; my son will before long be sole master of Saracinesca. Our lands are near together—that is a great advantage, that question of fortune. Again, I would observe that, with your magnificent position, you could not condescend to accept a man of lower birth than the highest in the country. There is none higher than the Saracinesca—pardon my arrogance,—and among princes there is no braver, truer gentleman than my son Giovanni. I ask no pardon for saying that; I will maintain it against all comers. I forego all questions of advantage, and base my argument upon that. He is the best man I know, and he loves you devotedly."

"Is he aware that you are here for this purpose?" asked Corona, suddenly. She spoke with a great effort.

"No. He knows that I am here, and was glad that I came. He desired me to ascertain if you would see him. He would certainly not have thought of addressing you at present. I am an old man, and I feel that I must do things quickly. That is my excuse."

Corona was again silent. She was too truthful to give an evasive answer, and yet she hesitated to speak. The position was an embarrassing one; she was taken unawares, and was terrified at the emotion she felt. It had never entered her mind that the old Prince could appear on his son's behalf, and she did not know how to meet him.

"I have perhaps been too abrupt," said Saracinesca. " I love my son very dearly, and his happiness is more to me than what remains of my own. If from the first you regard my proposition as an impossible one, I would spare him the pain of a humiliation,—I fear I could not save him from the rest, from a suffering that might drive him mad. It is for this reason that I implore you, if you are able, to give me some answer, not that I may convey it to him, but in order that I may be guided in future. He cannot forget you; but he has not seen you for six months. To see you again if he must leave you for ever, would only inflict a fresh wound." He paused, while Corona slowly walked by his side.

"I do not see why I should conceal the truth from you,' she said at last. "I cannot conceal it from myself. I am not a child that I should be ashamed of it. There is nothing wrong in it—no reason why it should not be. You are honest, too—why should we try to deceive ourselves? I trust to your honour to be silent, and I own that I—that I love your son."

Corona stood still and turned her face away, as the burning blush rose to her cheeks. The answer she had given was characteristic of her, straightforward and honest. She was not ashamed of it, and yet the words were so new, so strange in their sound, and so strong in their meaning, that she blushed as she uttered them. Saracinesca was greatly

surprised too, for he had expected some evasive turn, some
hint that he might bring Giovanni. But his delight had
no bounds.

"Duchessa," he said, "the happiest day I can remember
was when I brought home my wife to Saracinesca. My
proudest day will be that on which my son enters the same
gates with you by his side."

He took her hand and raised it to his lips, with a
courteous gesture.

"It will be long before that—it must be very long,"
answered Corona.

"It shall be when you please, Madam, provided it is at
last. Meanwhile we will come down to-morrow, and take
you to our tower. Do you understand now why I said
that I hoped you would come again and stay longer? I
trust you have not changed your mind in regard to the
excursion."

"No. We will expect you to-morrow night. Remember, I have been honest with you—I trust to you to be
silent."

"You have my word. And now, with your permission,
I will return to Saracinesca. Believe me, the news that
you expect us will be good enough to tell Giovanni."

"You may greet him from me. But will you not rest
awhile before you ride back? You must be tired."

"No fear of that!" answered the Prince. "You have
put a new man into an old one. I shall never tire of
bearing the news of your greetings."

So the old man left her, and mounted his horse and
rode up the pass. But Corona remained for hours in the
vaulted hall, pacing up and down. It had come too soon
—far too soon. And yet, how she had longed for it! how
she had wondered whether it would ever come at all!

The situation was sufficiently strange, too. Giovanni
had once told her of his love, and she had silenced him.
He was to tell her again, and she was to accept what he
said. He was to ask her to marry him, and her answer
was a foregone conclusion. It seemed as though this
greatest event of her life were planned to the very smallest

details beforehand; as though she were to act a part which she had studied, and which was yet no comedy because it was the expression of her life's truth. The future had been, as it were, prophesied and completely foretold to her, and held no surprises; and yet it was more sweet to think of than all the past together. She wondered how he would say it, what his words would be, how he would look, whether he would again be as strangely violent as he had been that night at the Palazzo Frangipani. She wondered, most of all, how she would answer him. But it would be long yet. There would be many meetings, many happy days before that happiest day of all.

Sister Gabrielle saw a wonderful change in Corona's face that afternoon when they drove up the valley together, and she remarked what wonderful effect a little variety had upon her companion's spirits—she could not say upon her health, for Corona seemed made of velvet and steel, so smooth and dark, and yet so supple and strong. Corona smiled brightly as she looked far up at the beetling crags behind which Saracinesca was hidden.

"We shall be up there the day after to-morrow," she said. "How strange it will seem!" And leaning back, her deep eyes flashed, and she laughed happily.

On the following evening, again, they drove along the road that led up the valley. But they had not gone far when they saw in the distance a cloud of dust, from which in a few moments emerged a vehicle drawn by three strong horses, and driven by Giovanni Saracinesca himself. His father sat beside him in front, and a man in livery was seated at the back, with a long rifle between his knees. The vehicle was a kind of double cart, capable of holding four persons, and two servants at the back.

In a moment the two carriages met and stopped side by side. Giovanni sprang from his seat, throwing the reins to his father, who stood up hat in hand, and bowed from where he was. Corona held out her hand to Giovanni as he stood bareheaded in the road beside her. One long look told all the tale; there could be no words there before the Sister and the old Prince, but their eyes told all—the pain of past separation, the joy of two loving hearts that met at last without hindrance.

"Let your servant drive, and get in with us," said Corona, who could hardly speak in her excitement. Then she started slightly, and smiled in her embarrassment. She had continued to hold Giovanni's hand, unconsciously leaving her fingers in his.

The Prince's groom climbed into the front seat, and old Saracinesca got down and entered the landau. It was a strangely silent meeting, long expected by the two who so loved each other—long looked for, but hardly realised now that it had come. The Prince was the first to speak, as usual.

"You expected to meet us, Duchessa?" he said; "we expected to meet you. An expectation fulfilled is better than a surprise. Everything at Saracinesca is prepared for your reception. Don Angelo, our priest, has been warned of your coming, and the boy who serves mass has been washed. You may imagine that a great festivity is expected. Giovanni has turned the castle inside out, and had a room hung entirely with tapestries of my great-grandmother's own working. He says that since the place is so old, its antiquity should be carried into the smallest details.

Corona laughed gaily—she would have laughed at anything that day—and the old Prince's tone was fresh and sparkling and merry. He had relieved the first embarrassment of the situation.

"There have been preparations at Astrardente for your reception, too," answered the Duchessa. "There was a difficulty of choice, as there are about a hundred vacant rooms in the house. The butler proposed to give you a suite of sixteen to pass the night in, but I selected an airy little nook in one of the wings, where you need only go through ten to get to your bedroom."

"There is nothing like space," said the Prince; "it enlarges the ideas."

"I cannot imagine what my father would do if his ideas were extended," remarked Giovanni. "Everything

he imagines is colossal already. He talks about tun-
nelling the mountains for my aqueduct, as though it were
no more trouble than to run a stick through a piece of
paper."

"Your aqueduct, indeed!" exclaimed his father. "I
would like to know whose idea it was?"

"I hear you are working like an engineer yourself, Don
Giovanni," said Corona. "I have a man at work at Astrardente on some plans of roads. Perhaps some day you
could give us your advice."

Some day! How sweet the words sounded to Giovanni as he sat opposite the woman he loved, bowling
along through the rich vine lands in the cool of the summer evening!

CHAPTER XXV.

The opportunity which Giovanni sought of being alone
with Corona was long in coming. Sister Gabrielle retired
immediately after dinner, and the Duchessa was left alone
with the two men. Old Saracinesca would gladly have left
his son with the hostess, but the thing was evidently impossible. The manners of the time would not allow it, and
the result was that the Prince spent the evening in making
conversation for two rather indifferent listeners. He tried
to pick a friendly quarrel with Giovanni, but the latter was
too absent-minded even to be annoyed; he tried to excite
the Duchessa's interest, but she only smiled gently, making
a remark from time to time which was conspicuous for its
irrelevancy. But old Saracinesca was in a good humour,
and he bore up bravely until ten o'clock, when Corona gave
the signal for retiring. They were to start very early in
the morning, she said, and she must have rest.

When the two men were alone, the Prince turned upon
his son in semi-comic anger, and upbraided him with his
obstinate dulness during the evening. Giovanni only smiled

calmly, and shrugged his shoulders. There was nothing more to be said.

But on the following morning, soon after six o'clock, Giovanni had the supreme satisfaction of installing Corona beside him upon the driving-seat of his cart, while his father and Sister Gabrielle sat together behind him. The sun was not yet above the hills, and the mountain air was keen and fresh; the stamping of the horses sounded crisp and sharp, and their bells rang merrily as they shook their sturdy necks and pricked their short ears to catch Giovanni's voice.

"Have you forgotten nothing, Duchessa?" asked Giovanni, gathering the reins in his hand.

"Nothing, thanks. I have sent our things on mules— by the bridle-path." She smiled involuntarily as she recalled her adventure, and half turned her face away.

"Ah, yes—the bridle-path," repeated Giovanni, as he nodded to the groom to stand clear of the horses' heads. In a moment they were briskly descending the winding road through the town of Astrardente: the streets were quiet and cool, for the peasants had all gone to their occupations two hours before, and the children were not yet turned loose.

"I never hoped to have the honour of myself driving you to Saracinesca," said Giovanni. "It is a wild place enough, in its way. You will be able to fancy yourself in Switzerland."

"I would rather be in Italy," answered Corona. "I do not care for the Alps. Our own mountains are as beautiful, and are not infested by tourists."

"You are a tourist to-day," said Giovanni. "And it has pleased Heaven to make me your guide."

"I will listen to your explanations of the sights with interest."

"It is a reversal of the situation, is it not? When we last met, it was you who guided me, and I humbly followed your instructions. I did precisely as you told me."

"Had I doubted that you would do as I asked, I would not have spoken," answered Corona.

"There was one thing you advised me to do which I have not even attempted."

"What was that?"

"You told me to forget you. I have spent six months in constantly remembering you, and in looking forward to this moment. Was I wrong?"

"Of course," replied the Duchessa, with a little laugh. "You should by this time have forgotten my existence. They said you were gone to the North Pole—why did you change your mind?"

"I followed my load-star. It led me from Rome to Saracinesca by the way of Paris. I should have remained at Saracinesca—but you also changed your mind. I began to think you never would."

"How long do you think of staying up there?" asked Corona, to turn the conversation.

"Just so long as you stay at Astrardente," he answered. "You will not forbid me to follow you to Rome?"

"How can I prevent you if you choose to do it?"

"By a word, as you did before."

"Do you think I would speak that word?" she asked.

"I trust not. Why should you cause me needless pain and suffering? If it was right then, it is not right now. Besides, you know me too well to think that I would annoy you or thrust myself upon you. But I will do as you wish."

"Thank you," she said quietly. But she turned her dark face toward him, and looked at him for a moment very gently, almost lovingly. Where was the use of trying to conceal what would not be hidden? Every word he spoke told of his unchanged love, although the phrases were short and simple. Why should she conceal what she felt? She knew it was a foregone conclusion. They loved each other, and she would certainly marry him in the course of a year. The long pent up forces of her nature were beginning to assert themselves; she had conquered and fought down her natural being in the effort to be all things to her old husband, to quench her growing interest in Giovanni, to resist his declared love, to drive him from her in her

widowhood; but now it seemed as though all obstacles
were suddenly removed. She saw clearly how well she
loved him, and it seemed folly to try and conceal it. As
she sat by his side she was unboundedly happy, as she had
never been in her life before: the cool morning breeze
fanned her cheeks, and the music of his low voice soothed
her, while the delicious sense of rapid motion lent a thrill
of pleasure to every breath she drew. It was no matter
what she said; it was as though she spoke unconsciously.
All seemed predestined and foreplanned from all time, to
be acted out to the end. The past vanished slowly as a retreating landscape. The weary traveller, exhausted with
the heat of the scorching Campagna, slowly climbs the
ascent towards Tivoli, the haven of cool waters, and pausing now and then upon the path, looks back and sees how
the dreary waste of undulating hillocks beneath him seems
gradually to subside into a dim flat plain, while, in the far
distance, the mighty domes and towers of Rome dwindle to
an unreal mirage in the warm haze of the western sky;
then advancing again, he feels the breath of the mountains
upon him, and hears the fresh plunge of the cold cataract,
till at last, when his strength is almost failing, it is renewed
within him, and the dust and the heat of the day's journey
are forgotten in the fulness of refreshment. So Corona
d'Astrardente, wearied though not broken by the fatigues
and the troubles and the temptations of the past five years,
seemed suddenly to be taken up and borne swiftly through
the gardens of an earthly paradise, where there was neither
care nor temptation, and where, in the cool air of a new
life, the one voice she loved was ever murmuring gentle
things to her willing ear.

As the road began to ascend, sweeping round the base
of the mountain and upwards by even gradations upon its
southern flank, the sun rose higher in the heavens, and the
locusts broke into their summer song among the hedges
with that even, long-drawn, humming note, so sweet to
southern ears. But Corona did not feel the heat, nor
notice the dust upon the way; she was in a new state,
wherein such things could not trouble her. The first

embarrassment of a renewed intimacy was fast disappearing, and she talked easily to Giovanni of many things,
reviewing past scenes and speaking of mutual acquaintances, turning the conversation when it concerned Giovanni
or herself too directly, yet ever and again coming back to
that sweet ground which was no longer dangerous now.
At last, at a turn in the road, the grim towers of ancient
Saracinesca loomed in the distance, and the carriage entered
a vast forest of chestnut trees, shady and cool after the
sunny ascent. So they reached the castle, and the sturdy
horses sprang wildly forward up the last incline till their
hoofs struck noisily upon the flagstones of the bridge, and
with a rush and a plunge they dashed under the black
archway, and halted in the broad court beyond.

Corona was surprised at the size of the old fortress. It
seemed an endless irregular mass of towers and buildings,
all of rough grey stone, surrounded by battlements and
ramparts, kept in perfect repair, but destitute of any kind
of ornament whatever. It might have been even now a
military stronghold, and it was evident that there were
traditions of precision and obedience within its walls which
would have done credit to any barracks. The dominant
temper of the master made itself felt at every turn, and
the servants moved quickly and silently about their duties.
There was something intensely attractive to Corona in the
air of strength that pervaded the place, and Giovanni had
never seemed to her so manly and so much in his element
as under the grey walls of his ancestral home. The place,
too, was associated in history with so many events,—the
two men, Leone and Giovanni Saracinesca, stood there
beside her, where their ancestors of the same names had
stood nearly a thousand years before, their strong dark
faces having the same characteristics that for centuries had
marked their race, features familiar to Romans by countless
statues and pictures, as the stones of Rome themselves—
but for a detail of dress, it seemed to Corona as though she
had been suddenly transported back to the thirteenth century. The idea fascinated her. The two men led her
up the broad stone staircase, and ushered her and Sister

Gabrielle into the apartments of state which had been
prepared for them.

"We have done our best," said the Prince, "but it is
long since we have entertained ladies at Saracinesca."

"It is magnificent!" exclaimed Corona, as she entered
the ante-chamber. The walls were hung from end to end
with priceless tapestries, and the stone floor was covered
with long eastern carpets. Corona paused.

"You must show us all over the castle by-and-by," she
said.

"Giovanni will show you everything," answered the
Prince. "If it pleases you, we will breakfast in half-an-
hour." He turned away with his son, and left the two
ladies to refresh themselves before the mid-day meal.

Giovanni kept his word, and spared his guests no detail
of the vast stronghold, until at last poor Sister Gabrielle
could go no farther. Giovanni had anticipated that she
would be tired, and with the heartlessness of a lover seeking his opportunity, he had secretly longed for the moment
when she should be obliged to stop.

"You have not yet seen the view from the great tower,"
he said. "It is superb, and this is the very best hour for
it. Are you tired, Duchessa?"

"No—I am never tired," answered Corona.

"Why not go with Giovanni?" suggested the Prince.
"I will stay with Sister Gabrielle, who has nearly exhausted
herself with seeing our sights."

Corona hesitated. The idea of being alone with Giovanni for a quarter of an hour was delightful, but somehow
it did not seem altogether fitting for her to be wandering
over the castle with him. On the other hand, to refuse
would seem almost an affectation: she was not in Rome,
where her every movement was a subject for remark;
moreover, she was not only a married woman, but a
widow, and she had known Giovanni for years—it would
be ridiculous to refuse.

"Very well," said she. "Let us see the view before it
is too late."

Sister Gabrielle and old Saracinesca sat down on a stone

seat upon the rampart to wait, and the Duchessa disappeared with Giovanni through the low door that led into the great tower.

"What a wonderful woman you are!" exclaimed Giovanni, as they reached the top of the winding stair, which was indeed broader than the staircase of many great houses in Rome. "You seem to be never tired."

"No—I am very strong," answered Corona, with a smile. She was not even out of breath. "What a wonderful view!" she exclaimed, as they emerged upon the stone platform at the top of the tower. Giovanni was silent for a moment. The two stood together and looked far out at the purple mountains to eastward that caught the last rays of the sun high up above the shadows of the valley; and then looking down, they saw the Prince and the Sister a hundred feet below them upon the rampart.

Both were thinking of the same thing: three days ago, their meeting had seemed infinitely far off, a thing dreamed of and hoped for—and now they were standing alone upon the topmost turret of Giovanni's house, familiar with each other by a long day's conversation, feeling as though they had never been parted, feeling also that most certainly they would not be parted again.

"It is very strange," said Giovanni, "how things happen in this world, and how little we ever know of what is before us. Last week I wondered whether I should ever see you—now I cannot imagine not seeing you. Is it not strange?"

"Yes," answered Corona, in a low voice.

"That, yesterday, we should have seemed parted by an insurmountable barrier, and that to-day——" he stopped. "Oh, if to-day could only last for ever!" he exclaimed, suddenly.

Corona gazed out upon the purple hills in silence, but her face caught some of the radiance of the distant glow, and her dark eyes had strange lights in them. She could not have prevented him from speaking; she had loosed the bonds that had held her life so long; the anchor was up, and the breath of love fanned the sails, and gently bore the craft in which she trusted out to seaward over the fair water. In seeing him she had resigned herself to him, and she could not again get the mastery if she would. It had come too soon, but it was sweet.

"And why not?" he said, very softly. "Why should it not remain so for ever — till our last breath? Why will you not let it last?"

Still she was silent; but the tears gathered slowly in her eyes, and welled over and lay upon her velvet cheek like dewdrops on the leaves of a soft dark tulip. Giovanni saw them, and knew that they were the jewels which crowned his life.

"You will," he said, his broad brown hand gently covering her small fingers and taking them in his. "You will— I know that you will."

She said nothing, and though she at first made a slight movement—not of resistance, but of timid reluctance, utterly unlike herself—she suffered him to hold her hand. He drew closer to her, himself more diffident in the moment of success than he had ever been when he anticipated failure; she was so unlike any woman he had ever known before. Very gently he put his arm about her, and drew her to him.

"My beloved—at last," he whispered, as her head sank upon his shoulder.

Then with a sudden movement she sprang to her height, and for one instant gazed upon him. Her whole being was transfigured in the might of her passion: her dark face was luminously pale, her lips almost white, and from her eyes there seemed to flash a blazing fire. For one instant she gazed upon him, and then her arms went round his neck, and she clasped him fiercely to her breast.

"Ah, Giovanni," she cried, passionately, "you do not know what love means!"

A moment later her arms dropped from him; she turned and buried her face in her hands, leaning against the high stone parapet of the tower. She was not weeping, but her face was white, and her bosom heaved with quick and strong-drawn breath.

Giovanni went to her side and took her strongly in his right arm, and again her head rested upon his shoulder.

"It is too soon—too soon," she murmured. "But how can I help it? I love you so that there is no counting of time. It seems years since we met last night, and I thought it would be years before I told you. Oh, Giovanni, I am so happy! Is it possible that you love me as I love you?"

It is a marvellous thing to see how soon two people who love each other learn the gentle confidence that only love can bring. A few moments later Giovanni and Corona were slowly pacing the platform, and his arm was about her waist and her hand in his.

"Do you know," she was saying, "I used to wonder whether you would keep your word, and never try to see me. The days were so long at Astrardente."

"Not half so long as at Saracinesca," he answered. "I was going to call my aqueduct the Bridge of Sighs; I will christen it now the Spring of Love."

"I must go and see it to-morrow," said she.

"Or the next day——"

"The next day!" she exclaimed, with a happy laugh. "Do you think I am going to stay——"

"For ever," interrupted Giovanni. "We have a priest here, you know,—he can marry us to-morrow, and then you need never go away."

Corona's face grew grave.

"We must not talk of that yet," she said, gently, "even in jest."

"No; you are right. Forgive me," he answered; "I forget many things—it seems to me I have forgotten everything, except that I love you."

"Giovanni,"—she lingered on the name,—"Giovanni, we must tell your father at once."

"Are you willing I should?" he asked, eagerly.

"Of course—he ought to know; and Sister Gabrielle too. But no one else must be told. There must be no talk of this in Rome until—until next year."

"We will stay in the country until then, shall we not?" asked Giovanni, anxiously. "It seems to me so much better. We can meet here, and nobody will talk. I will go and live in the town at Astrardente, and play the engineer, and build your roads for you."

"I hardly know," said Corona, with a doubtful smile. "You could not do that. But you may come and spend the day once—in a week, perhaps."

"We will arrange all that," answered Giovanni, laughing. "If you think I can exist by only seeing you once a week—well, you do not know me."

"We shall see," returned Corona, laughing too. "By the bye, how long have we been here?"

"I do not know," said Giovanni; "but the view is magnificent, is it not?"

"Enchanting," she replied, looking into his eyes. Then suddenly the blood mounted to her cheeks. "Oh, Giovanni," she said, "how could I do it?"

"I should have died if you had not," he answered, and clasped her once more in his arms.

"Come," said she, "let us be going down. It is growing late."

When they reached the foot of the tower, they found the Prince walking the rampart alone. Sister Gabrielle was afraid of the evening air, and had retired into the house. Old Saracinesca faced them suddenly. He looked like an old lion, his thick white hair and beard bristling about his dark features.

"My father," said Giovanni, coming forward, "the Duchessa d'Astrardente has consented to be my wife. I crave your blessing."

The old man started, and then stood stock-still. His son had fairly taken his breath away, for he had not expected the news for three or four months to come. Then he advanced and took Corona's hand, and kissed it.

"Madam," he said, "you have done my son an honour which extends to myself and to every Saracinesca, dead, living, and to come."

Then he laid Corona's hand in Giovanni's, and held his own upon them both.

"God bless you," he said, solemnly; and as Corona

bent her proud head, he touched her forehead with his
lips. Then he embraced Giovanni, and his joy broke out
in wild enthusiasm.

"Ha, my children," he cried, " there has not been such
a couple as you are for generations—there has not been
such good news told in these old walls since they have
stood here. We will illuminate the castle, the whole
town, in your honour—we will ring the bells and have a
Te Deum sung—we will have such a festival as was never
seen before—we will go to Rome to-morrow and celebrate
the espousal—we will——"

"Softly, *padre mio*," interrupted Giovanni. "No one
must know as yet. You must consider——"

"Consider what? consider the marriage? Of course we
will consider it, as soon as you please. You shall have
such a wedding as was never heard of—you shall be married by the Cardinal Archpriest of Saint Peter's, by the
Holy Father himself. The whole country shall ring with
it."

It was with difficulty Giovanni succeeded in calming his
father's excitement, and in recalling to his mind the circumstances which made it necessary to conceal the engagement for the present. But at last the old man reluctantly
consented, and returned to a quieter humour. For some
time the three continued to pace the stone rampart.

"This is a case of arrant cruelty to a man of my temper," said the Prince. "To be expected to behave like an
ordinary creature, with grins and smiles and decent paces,
when I have just heard what I have longed to hear for
years. But I will revenge myself by making a noise about
it by-and-by. I will concoct schemes for your wedding,
and dream of nothing but illuminations and decorations.
You shall be Prince of Sant' Ilario, Giovanni, as I was
before my father died; and I will give you that estate
outright, and the palace in the Corso to live in."

"Perhaps we might live in my palace," suggested Corona. It seemed strange to her to be discussing her own
marriage, but it was necessary to humour the old Prince.

"Of course," he said. "I forgot all about it. You

have places enough to live in. One forgets that you will in the end be the richest couple in Italy. Ha!" he cried, in sudden enthusiasm, "the Saracinesca are not dead yet! They are greater than ever—and our lands here so near together, too. We will build a new road to Astrardente, and when you are married you shall be the first to drive over it from Astrardente here. We will do all kinds of things—we will tunnel the mountain!"

"I am sure you will do that in the end," said Giovanni, laughing.

"Well—let us go to dinner," answered his father. "It has grown quite dark since we have been talking, and we shall be falling over the edge if we are not careful."

"I will go and tell Sister Gabrielle before dinner," said Corona to Giovanni.

So they left her at the door of her apartment, and she went in. She found the Sister in an inner room, with a book of devotions in her hand.

"Pray for me, my sister," she said, quietly. "I have resolved upon a great step. I am going to be married again."

Sister Gabrielle looked up, and a quiet smile stole over her thin face.

"It is soon, my friend," she said. "It is soon to think of that. But perhaps you are right—is it the young Prince?"

"Yes," answered Corona, and sank into a deep tapestried chair. "It is soon, I know well. But it has been long— I have struggled hard—I love him very much—so much, you do not know!"

The Sister sighed faintly, and came and took her hand.

"It is right that you should marry," she said, gently. "You are too young, too famously beautiful, too richly endowed, to lead the life you have led at Astrardente these many months."

"It is not that," said Corona, an expression of strange beauty illuminating her lovely face. "Not that I am young, beautiful as you say, if it is so, or endowed with riches—those reasons are nothing. It is this that tells me," she whispered, pressing her left hand to her heart. "When one loves as I love, it is right."

"Indeed it is," assented the good Sister. "And I think you have chosen wisely. When will you be married?"

"Hardly before next summer—I can hardly think connectedly yet—it has been very sudden. I knew I should marry him in the end, but I never thought I could consent so soon. Oh, Sister Gabrielle, you are so good—were you never in love?"

The Sister was silent, and looked away.

"No—of course you cannot tell me," continued Corona; "but it is such a wonderful thing. It makes days seem like hundreds of years, or makes them pass in a flash of light, in a second. It oversets every idea of time, and plays with one's resolutions as the wind with a feather. If once it gets the mastery of one, it crowds a lifetime of pain and pleasure into one day; it never leaves one for a moment. I cannot explain love—it is a wonderful thing."

"My dear friend," said the Sister, "the explanation of love is life."

"But the end of it is not death. It cannot be," continued Corona, earnestly. "It must last for ever and ever. It must grow better and purer and stronger, until it is perfect in heaven at last: but where is the use of trying to express such things?"

"I think it is enough to feel them," said Sister Gabrielle.

CHAPTER XXVI.

The summer season ripened into autumn, and autumn again turned to winter, and Rome was once more full. The talk of society turned frequently upon the probability of the match between the Duchessa d'Astrardente and Gio-

vanni Saracinesca; and when at last, three weeks before
Lent, the engagement was made known, there was a general
murmur of approbation. It seemed as though the momen-
tous question of Corona's life, which had for years agitated
the gossips, were at last to be settled : every one had been
accustomed to regard her marriage with old Astrardente as
a temporary affair, seeing that he certainly could not live
long, and speculation in regard to her future had been
nearly as common during his lifetime as it was after his
death. One of the duties most congenial to society, and
one which it never fails to perform conscientiously, is that
judicial astrology, whereby it forecasts the issue of its
neighbour's doings. Everybody's social horoscope must be
cast by the circle of five-o'clock-tea-drinking astro-sociolo-
gists, and, generally speaking, their predictions are not far
short of the truth, for society knoweth its own bitterness,
and is uncommonly quick in the diagnosis of its own state
of health.

When it was announced that Corona was to marry
Giovanni after Easter, society looked and saw that the
arrangement was good. There was not one dissenting
voice heard in the universal applause. Corona had behaved with exemplary decency during the year of her
mourning—had lived a life of religious retirement upon
her estates in the sole company of a Sister of Charity, had
given no cause for scandal in any way. Everybody aspired
to like her—that is to say, to be noticed by her; but with
one exception, she had caused no jealousy nor ill-feeling by
her indifference, for no one had ever heard her say an unkind word concerning anybody she knew. Donna Tullia
had her own reasons for hating Corona, and perhaps the
world suspected them; but people did not connect the
noisy Donna Tullia, full of animal spirits and gay silly
talk, with the idea of serious hatred, much less with the
execution of any scheme of revenge.

Indeed Madame Mayer had not spent the summer and
autumn in nursing her wrath against Corona. She had
travelled with the old Countess, her companion, and several
times Ugo del Ferice had appeared suddenly at the water-

ing-places which she had selected for her temporary residence. From time to time he gave her news of mutual friends, which she repaid conscientiously with interesting accounts of the latest scandals. They were a congenial pair, and Ugo felt that by his constant attention to her wishes, and by her never-varying willingness to accept his service, he had obtained a hold upon her intimacy which, in the ensuing winter, would give him a decided advantage over all competitors in the field. She believed that she might have married half-a-dozen times, and that with her fortune she could easily have made a very brilliant match; she even thought that she could have married Valdarno, who was very good-natured : but her attachment to Giovanni, and the expectations she had so long entertained in regard to him, had prevented her from showing any marked preference for others ; and while she was hesitating, Del Ferice, by his superior skill, had succeeded in making himself indispensable to her—a success the more remarkable that, in spite of his gifts and the curious popularity he enjoyed, he was by far the least desirable man of her acquaintance from the matrimonial point of view.

But when Donna Tullia again met Giovanni in the world, the remembrance of her wrongs revived her anger against him, and the news of his engagement to the Astrardente brought matters to a climax. In the excitement of the moment, both her jealousy and her anger were illuminated by the light of a righteous wrath. She knew, or thought she knew, that Don Giovanni was already married. She had no proof that the peasant wife mentioned in the certificate was alive, but there was nothing either to show that she was dead. Even in the latter case it was a scandalous thing that he should marry again without informing Corona of the circumstances of his past life, and Donna Tullia felt an inner conviction that he had told the Duchessa nothing of the matter. The latter was such a proud woman, that she would be horrified at the idea of uniting herself to a man who had been the husband of a peasant.

Madame Mayer remembered her solemn promise to Del

Ferice, and feared to act without his consent. An hour after she had heard the news of the engagement, she sent for him to come to her immediately. To her astonishment and dismay, her servant brought back word that he had suddenly gone to Naples upon urgent business. This news made her pause; but while the messenger had been gone to Del Ferice's house, Donna Tullia had been anticipating and going over in her mind the scene which would ensue when she told Corona the secret. Donna Tullia was a very sanguine woman, and the idea of at last being revenged for all the slights she had received worked suddenly upon her brain, so that as she paced her drawing-room in expectation of the arrival of Del Ferice, she entirely acted out in her imagination the circumstances of the approaching crisis, the blood beat hotly in her temples, and she lost all sense of prudence in the delicious anticipation of violent words. Del Ferice had cruelly calculated upon her temperament, and he had hoped that in the excitement of the moment she would lose her head, and irrevocably commit herself to him by the betrayal of the secret. This was precisely what occurred. On being told that he was out of town, she could no longer contain herself, and with a sudden determination to risk anything blindly, rather than to forego the pleasure and the excitement she had been meditating, she ordered her carriage and drove to the Palazzo Astrardente.

Corona was surprised at the unexpected visit. She was herself on the point of going out, and was standing in her boudoir, drawing on her black gloves before the fire, while her furs lay upon a chair at her side. She wondered why Donna Tullia called, and it was in part her curiosity which induced her to receive her visit. Donna Tullia, armed to the teeth with the terrible news she was about to disclose, entered the room quickly, and remained standing before the Duchessa with a semi-tragic air that astonished Corona.

"How do you do, Donna Tullia?" said the latter, putting out her hand.

"I have come to speak to you upon a very serious matter," answered her visitor, without noticing the greeting.

Corona stared at her for a moment, but not being easily

disconcerted, she quietly motioned to Donna Tullia to sit down, and installed herself in a chair opposite to her.

"I have just heard the news that you are to marry Don Giovanni Saracinesca," said Madame Mayer. "You will pardon me the interest I take in you; but is it true?"

"It is quite true," answered Corona.

"It is in connection with your marriage that I wish to speak, Duchessa. I implore you to reconsider your decision."

"And why, if you please?" asked Corona, raising her black eyebrows, and fixing her haughty gaze upon her visitor.

"I could tell you—I would rather not," answered Donna Tullia, unabashed, for her blood was up. "I could tell you—but I beseech you not to ask me. Only consider the matter again, I beg you. It is very serious. Nothing but the great interest I feel in you, and my conviction——"

"Donna Tullia, your conduct is so extraordinary," interrupted Corona, looking at her curiously, "that I am tempted to believe you are mad. I must beg you to explain what you mean by your words."

"Ah, no," answered Madame Mayer. "You do me injustice. I am not mad, but I would save you from the most horrible danger."

"Again I say, what do you mean? I will not be trifled with in this way," said the Duchessa, who would have been more angry if she had been less astonished, but whose temper was rapidly rising.

"I am not trifling with you," returned Donna Tullia. "I am imploring you to think before you act, before you marry Don Giovanni. You cannot think that I would venture to intrude upon you without the strongest reasons. I am in earnest."

"Then, in heaven's name, speak out!" cried Corona, losing all patience. "I presume that if this is a warning, you have some grounds, you have some accusation to make against Don Giovanni. Have the goodness to state what you have to say, and be brief."

"I will," said Donna Tullia, and she paused a moment,

her face growing red with excitement, and her blue eyes sparkling disagreeably. "You cannot marry Don Giovanni," she said at length, "because there is an insurmountable impediment in the way."

"What is it?" asked Corona, controlling her anger.

"He is already married!" hissed Donna Tullia.

Corona turned a little pale, and started back. But in an instant her colour returned, and she broke into a low laugh.

"You are certainly insane," she said, eyeing Madame Mayer suspiciously. It was not an easy matter to shake her faith in the man she loved. Donna Tullia was disappointed at the effect she had produced. She was a clever woman in her way, but she did not understand how to make the best of the situation. She saw that she was simply an object of curiosity, and that Corona seriously believed her mind deranged. She was frightened, and, in order to help herself, she plunged deeper.

"You may call me mad, if you please," she replied, angrily. "I tell you it is true. Don Giovanni was married on the 19th of June 1863, at Aquila, in the Abruzzi, to a woman called Felice Baldi—whoever she may have been. The register is extant, and the duplicate of the marriage certificate. I have seen the copies attested by a notary. I tell you it is true," she continued, her voice rising to a harsh treble; "you are engaged to marry a man who has a wife—a peasant woman—somewhere in the mountains."

Corona rose from her seat and put out her hand to ring the bell. She was pale, but not excited. She believed Donna Tullia to be insane, perhaps dangerous, and she calmly proceeded to protect herself by calling for assistance.

"Either you are mad, or you mean what you say," she said, keeping her eyes upon the angry woman before her. "You will not leave this house except in charge of my physician, if you are mad; and if you mean what you say, you shall not go until you have repeated your words to Don Giovanni Saracinesca himself,—no, do not start or try to escape—it is of no use. I am very sudden and violent—beware!"

Donna Tullia bit her red lip. She was beginning to realise that she had got herself into trouble, and that it might be hard to get out of it. But she felt herself strong, and she wished she had with her those proofs which would make her case good. She was so sanguine by nature that she was willing to carry the fight to the end, and to take her chance for the result.

"You may send for Don Giovanni if you please," she said. "I have spoken the truth—if he denies it I can prove it. If I were you I would spare him the humiliation——"

A servant entered the room in answer to the bell, and Corona interrupted Donna Tullia's speech by giving the man her orders.

"Go at once to the Palazzo Saracinesca, and beg Don Giovanni to come here instantly with his father the Prince. Take the carriage—it is waiting below."

The man disappeared, and Corona quietly resumed her seat. Donna Tullia was silent for a few moments, attempting to control her anger in an assumption of dignity; but soon she broke out afresh, being rendered very nervous and uncomfortable by the Duchessa's calm manner and apparent indifference to consequences.

"I cannot see why you should expose yourself to such a scene," said Madame Mayer presently. "I honestly wished to save you from a terrible danger. It seems to me it would be quite sufficient if I proved the fact to you beyond dispute. I should think that instead of being angry, you would show some gratitude."

"I am not angry," answered Corona, quietly. "I am merely giving you an immediate opportunity of proving your assertion and your sanity."

"My sanity!" exclaimed Donna Tullia, angrily. "Do you seriously believe——"

"Nothing that you say," said Corona, completing the sentence.

Unable to bear the situation, Madame Mayer rose suddenly from her seat, and began to pace the small room with short, angry steps.

"You shall see," she said, fiercely—"you shall see that it is all true. You shall see this man's face when I accuse him—you shall see him humiliated, overthrown, exposed in his villany—the wretch! You shall see how——"

Corona's strong voice interrupted her enemy's invective in ringing tones.

"Be silent!" she cried. "In twenty minutes he will be here. But if you say one word against him before he comes, I will lock you into this room and leave you. I certainly will not hear you."

Donna Tullia reflected that the Duchessa was in her own house, and moreover that she was not a woman to be trifled with. She threw herself into a chair, and taking up a book that lay upon the table, she pretended to read.

Corona remained seated by the fireplace, glancing at her from time to time. She was strangely inclined to laugh at the whole situation, which seemed to her absurd in the extreme—for it never crossed her mind to believe that there was a word of truth in the accusation against Giovanni. Nevertheless she was puzzled to account for Donna Tullia's assurance, and especially for her readiness to face the man she so calumniated. A quarter of an hour elapsed in this armed silence—the two women glancing at each other from time to time, until the distant sound of wheels rolling under the great gate announced that the messenger had returned from the Palazzo Saracinesca, probably conveying Don Giovanni and his father.

"Then you have made up your mind to the humiliation of the man you love?" asked Donna Tullia, looking up from her book with a sneer on her face.

Corona vouchsafed no answer, but her eyes turned towards the door in expectation. Presently there were steps heard without. The servant entered, and announced Prince Saracinesca and Don Giovanni. Corona rose. The old man came in first, followed by his son.

"An unexpected pleasure," he said, gaily. "Such good luck! We were both at home. Ah, Donna Tullia," he cried, seeing Madame Mayer, "how are you?" Then seeing her face, he added, suddenly, "Is anything the matter?"

Meanwhile Giovanni had entered, and stood by Corona's side near the fireplace. He saw at once that something was wrong, and he looked anxiously from the Duchessa to Donna Tullia. Corona spoke at once.

"Donna Tullia," she said, quietly, "I have the honour to offer you an opportunity of explaining yourself."

Madame Mayer remained seated by the table, her face red with anger. She leaned back in her seat, and half closing her eyes with a disagreeable look of contempt, she addressed Giovanni.

"I am sorry to cause you such profound humiliation," she began, "but in the interest of the Duchessa d'Astrardente I feel bound to speak. Don Giovanni, do you remember Aquila?"

"Certainly," he replied, coolly—"I have often been there. What of it?"

Old Saracinesca stared from one to the other.

"What is this comedy?" he asked of Corona. But she nodded to him to be silent.

"Then you doubtless remember Felice Baldi — poor Felice Baldi," continued Donna Tullia, still gazing scornfully up at Giovanni from where she sat.

"I never heard the name, that I can remember," answered Giovanni, as though trying to recall some memory of the past. He could not imagine what she was leading to, but he was willing to answer her questions.

"You do not remember that you were married to her at Aquila on the 19th of June—— ?"

"I—married?" cried Giovanni, in blank astonishment.

"Signora Duchessa," said the Prince, bending his heavy brows, "what is the meaning of all this?"

"I will tell you the meaning of it," said Donna Tullia, in low hissing tones, and rising suddenly to her feet she assumed a somewhat theatrical attitude as she pointed to Giovanni. "I will tell what it means. It means that Don Giovanni Saracinesca was married in the church of

San Bernardino, at Aquila, on the 19th of June 1863, to the woman Felice Baldi—who is his lawful wife to-day, and for aught we know the mother of his children, while he is here in Rome attempting to marry the Duchessa d'Astrardente—can he deny it? Can he deny that his own signature is there, there in the office of the Stato Civile at Aquila, to testify against him? Can he——"

"Silence!" roared the Prince. "Silence, woman, or by God in heaven I will stop your talking for ever!" He made a step towards her, and there was a murderous red light in his black eyes. But Giovanni sprang forward and seized his father by the wrist.

"You cannot silence me," screamed Donna Tullia. "I will be heard, and by all Rome. I will cry it upon the housetops to all the world——"

"Then you will precipitate your confinement in the asylum of Santo Spirito," said Giovanni, in cold, calm tones. "You are clearly mad."

"So I said," assented Corona, who was nevertheless pale, and trembling with excitement.

"Allow me to speak with her," said Giovanni, who, like most dangerous men, seemed to grow cold as others grew hot. Donna Tullia leaned upon the table, breathing hard between her closed teeth, her face scarlet.

"Madame," said Giovanni, advancing a step and confronting her, "you say that I am married, and that I am contemplating a monstrous crime. Upon what do you base your extraordinary assertions?"

"Upon attested copies of your marriage certificate, of the civil register where your handwriting has been seen and recognised. What more would you have?"

"It is monstrous!" cried the Prince, advancing again. "It is the most abominable lie ever concocted! My son married without my knowledge, and to a peasant! Absurd!"

But Giovanni waved his father back, and kept his place before Donna Tullia.

"I give you the alternative of producing instantly those proofs you refer to," he said, "and which you certainly cannot produce, or of waiting in this house until a competent physician has decided whether you are sufficiently sane to be allowed to go home alone."

Donna Tullia hesitated. She was in a terrible position, for Del Ferice had left Rome suddenly, and though the papers were somewhere in his house, she knew not where, nor how to get at them. It was impossible to imagine a situation more desperate, and she felt it as she looked round and saw the pale dark faces of the three resolute persons whose anger she had thus roused. She believed that Giovanni was capable of anything, but she was astonished at his extraordinary calmness. She hesitated for a moment.

"That is perfectly just," said Corona. "If you have proofs, you can produce them. If you have none, you are insane."

"I have them, and I will produce them before this hour to-morrow," answered Donna Tullia, not knowing how she should get the papers, but knowing that she was lost if she failed to obtain them.

"Why not to-day — at once?" asked Giovanni, with some scorn.

"It will take twenty-four hours to forge them," growled his father.

"You have no right to insult me so grossly," cried Donna Tullia. "But beware—I have you in my power. By this time to-morrow you shall see with your own eyes that I speak the truth. Let me go," she cried, as the old Prince placed himself between her and the door.

"I will," said he. "But before you go, I beg you to observe that if between now and the time you show us these documents you breathe abroad one word of your accusations, I will have you arrested as a dangerous lunatic, and lodged in Santo Spirito; and if these papers are not authentic, you will be arrested to-morrow afternoon on a charge of forgery. You quite understand me?" He stood aside to let her pass. She laughed scornfully in his face, and went out.

When she was gone the three looked at each other, as

though trying to comprehend what had happened. Indeed, it was beyond their comprehension. Corona leaned against the chimneypiece, and her eyes rested lovingly upon Giovanni. No doubt had ever crossed her mind of his perfect honesty. Old Saracinesca looked from one to the other for a moment, and then, striking the palms of his hands together, turned and began to walk up and down the room.

"In the first place," said Giovanni, "at the time she mentions I was in Canada, upon a shooting expedition, with a party of Englishmen. It is easy to prove that, as they are all alive and well now, so far as I have heard. Donna Tullia is clearly out of her mind."

"The news of your engagement has driven her mad," said the old Prince, with a grim laugh. "It is a very interesting and romantic case."

Corona blushed a little, and her eyes sought Giovanni's, but her face was very grave. It was a terrible thing to see a person she had known so long becoming insane, and for the sake of the man she herself so loved. And yet she had not a doubt of Donna Tullia's madness. It was very sad.

"I wonder who could have put this idea into her head," said Giovanni, thoughtfully. "It does not look like a creation of her own brain. I wonder, too, what absurdities she will produce in the way of documents. Of course they must be forged."

"She will not bring them," returned his father, in a tone of certainty. "We shall hear to-morrow that she is raving in the delirium of a brain-fever."

"Poor thing!" exclaimed Corona. "It is dreadful to think of it."

"It is dreadful to think that she should have caused you all this trouble and annoyance," said Giovanni, warmly. "You must have had a terrible scene with her before we came. What did she say?"

"Just what she said to you. Then she began to rail against you; and I sent for you, and told her that unless she could be silent I would lock her up alone until you arrived. So she sat down in that chair, and pretended to read. But it was an immense relief when you came!"

"You did not once believe what she said might possibly be true?" asked Giovanni, with a loving look.

"I? How could you ever think it!" exclaimed Corona. Then she laughed, and added, "But of course you knew that I would not."

"Indeed yes," he answered. "It never entered. my head."

"By-the-bye," said old Saracinesca, glancing at the Duchessa's black bonnet and gloved hands, "you must have been just ready to go out when she came—we must not keep you. I suppose that when she said she would bring her proofs to-morrow at this hour, she meant she would bring them here. Shall we come to-morrow then?"

"Yes—by all means," she answered. "Come to break-fast at one o'clock. I am alone, you know, for Sister Gabrielle has insisted upon going back to her community. But what does it matter now?"

"What does it matter?" echoed the Prince. "You are to be married so soon. I really think we can do as we please." He generally did as he pleased.

The two men left her, and a few minutes later she descended the steps of the palace and entered her carriage, as though nothing had happened.

Six months had passed since she had given her troth to Giovanni upon the tower of Saracinesca, and she knew that she loved him better now than then. Little had happened of interest in the interval of time, and the days had seemed long. But until after Christmas she had remained at Astrardente, busying herself constantly with the improvements she had already begun, and aided by the counsels of Giovanni. He had taken a cottage of hers in the lower part of her village, and had fitted it up with the few comforts he judged necessary. In this lodging he had generally spent half the week, going daily to the palace upon the hill and remaining for long hours in Corona's society, studying her plans and visiting with her the works which grew beneath their joint direction. She had grown to know him as she had not known him before, and to understand more fully his manly character. He was a

very resolute man, and very much in earnest when he
chanced to be doing anything; but the strain of melancholy which he inherited from his mother made him often
inclined to a sort of contemplative idleness, during which
his mind seemed preoccupied with absorbing thoughts.
Many people called his fits of silence an affectation, or
part of his system for rendering himself interesting; but
Corona soon saw how real was his abstraction, and she saw
also that she alone was able to attract his attention and
interest him when the fit was upon him. Slowly, by a
gradual study of him, she learned what few had ever
guessed, namely, that beneath the experienced man of the
world, under his modest manner and his gentle ways, there
lay a powerful mainspring of ambition, a mine of strength,
which would one day exert itself and make itself felt upon
his surroundings. He had developed slowly, feeding upon
many experiences of the world in many countries, his quick
Italian intelligence comprehending often more than it
seemed to do, while the quiet dignity he got from his
Spanish blood made him appear often very cold. But now
and again, when under the influence of some large idea,
his tongue was loosed in the charm of Corona's presence,
and he spoke to her, as he had never spoken to any one,
of projects and plans which should make the world move.
She did not always understand him wholly, but she knew
that the man she loved was something more than the
world at large believed him to be, and there was a thrill
of pride in the thought which delighted her inmost soul.
She, too, was ambitious, but her ambition was all for him.
She felt that there was little room for common aspirations
in his position or in her own. All that high birth, and
wealth, and personal consideration could give, they both
had abundantly, beyond their utmost wishes; anything
they could desire beyond that must lie in a larger sphere
of action than mere society, in the world of political power.
She herself had had dreams, and entertained them still,
of founding some great institution of charity, of doing
something for her poorer fellows. But she learned by
degrees that Giovanni looked further than to such ordin-

ary means of employing power, and that there was in him a great ambition to bring great forces to bear upon great questions for the accomplishment of great results. The six months of her engagement to him had not only strengthened her love for him, already deep and strong, but had implanted in her an unchanging determination to second him in all his life, to omit nothing in her power which could assist him in the career he should choose for himself, and which she regarded as the ultimate field for his extraordinary powers. It was strange that, while granting him everything else, people had never thought of calling him a man of remarkable intelligence. But no one knew him as Corona knew him; no one suspected that there was in him anything more than the traditional temper of the Saracinesca, with sufficient mind to make him as fair a representative of his race as his father was.

There was more than mere love and devotion in the complete security she felt when she saw him attacked by Donna Tullia; there was already the certainty that he was born to be above small things, and to create a sphere of his own in which he would move as other men could not.

CHAPTER XXVII.

When Donna Tullia quitted the Palazzo Astrardente her head swam. She had utterly failed to do what she had expected; and from being the accuser, she felt that she was suddenly thrust into the position of the accused. Instead of inspiring terror in Corona, and causing Giovanni the terrible humiliation she had supposed he would feel at the exposure of his previous marriage, she had been coldly told that she was mad, and that her pretended proofs were forgeries. Though she herself felt no doubt whatever concerning the authenticity of the documents, it was very disappointing to find that the first mention of them produced no startling effect upon any one, least of all upon Giovanni himself. The man, she thought, was a most accomplished villain; since he was capable of showing such hardened indifference to her accusation, he was capable also of thwarting her in her demonstration of their truth—and she trembled at the thought of what she saw. Old Saracinesca was not a man to be trifled with, nor his son either: they were powerful, and would be revenged for the insult. But in the meanwhile she had promised to produce her proofs; and when she regained enough composure to consider the matter from all its points, she came to the conclusion that after all her game was not lost, seeing that attested documents are evidence not easily refuted, even by powerful men like Leone and Giovanni Saracinesca. She gradually convinced herself that their indifference was a pretence, and that they were accomplices in the matter, their object being to gain Corona with all her fortune for Giovanni's wife. But, at the same time, Donna Tullia felt in the depths of her heart a misgiving: she was clever enough to recognise, even in spite of herself, the difference between a liar and an honest man.

She must get possession of these papers—and immediately too; there must be no delay in showing them to Corona, and in convincing her that this was no mere fable, but an assertion founded upon very substantial evidence. Del Ferice was suddenly gone to Naples: obviously the only way to get at the papers was to bribe his servant to deliver them up. Ugo had once or twice mentioned Temistocle to her, and she judged from the few words he had let fall that the fellow was a scoundrel, who would sell his soul for money. Madame Mayer drove home, and put on the only dark-coloured gown she possessed, wound a thick veil about her head, provided herself with a number of bank-notes, which she thrust between the palm of her hand and her glove, left the house on foot, and took a cab. There was nothing to be done but to go herself, for she could trust no one. Her heart beat fast as she ascended the narrow stone steps of Del Ferice's lodging, and stopped upon the landing before the small green door, whereon she read his name. She pulled the bell, and Temistocle appeared in his shirt-sleeves.

"Does Count Del Ferice live here?" asked Donna Tullia, peering over the man's shoulder into the dark and narrow passage within.

"He lives here, but he is gone to Naples," answered Temistocle, promptly.

"When will he be back?" she inquired. The man raised his shoulders to his ears, and spread out the palms of his hands to signify that he did not know. Donna Tullia hesitated. She had never attempted to bribe anybody in her life, and hardly knew how to go about it. She thought that the sight of the money might produce an impression, and she withdrew a bank-note from the hollow of her hand, spreading it out between her fingers. Temistocle eyed it greedily.

"There are twenty-five scudi," she said. "If you will help me to find a piece of paper in your master's room, you shall have them."

Temistocle drew himself up with an air of mock pride. Madame Mayer looked at him.

"Impossible, signora," he said. Then she drew out another. Temistocle eyed the glove curiously to see if it contained more.

"Signora," he repeated, "it is impossible. My master would kill me. I cannot think of it." But his tone seemed to yield a little. Donna Tullia found another bank-note; there were now seventy-five scudi in her hand. She thought she saw Temistocle tremble with excitement. But still he hesitated.

"Signora, my conscience," he said, in a low voice of protestation.

"Come," said Madame Mayer, impatiently, "there is another—there are a hundred scudi—that is all I have got," she added, turning down her empty glove.

Suddenly Temistocle put out his hand and grasped the bank-notes eagerly. But instead of retiring to allow her to enter, he pushed roughly past her.

"You may go in," he said in a hoarse whisper, and

Y

turning quickly, fled precipitately down the narrow steps, in his shirt-sleeves as he was. Madame Mayer stood for a moment looking after him in surprise, even when he had already disappeared.

Then she turned and entered the door rather timidly; but before she had gone two steps in the dark passage, she uttered a cry of horror. Del Ferice stood in her way, wrapped in a loose dressing-gown, a curious expression upon his pale face, which from its whiteness was clearly distinguishable in the gloom. Temistocle had cheated her, had lied in telling her that his master was absent, had taken her bribe and had fled. He would easily find an excuse for having allowed her to enter; and with his quick varlet's instinct, he guessed that she would not confess to Del Ferice that she had bribed him. Ugo came forward a step and instantly recognised Madame Mayer.

"Donna Tullia!" he cried, "what are you doing? You must not be seen here."

A less clever man than Ugo would have pretended to be overjoyed at her coming. Del Ferice's fine instincts told him that for whatever cause she had come—and he guessed the cause well enough—he would get a firmer hold upon her consideration by appearing to be shocked at her imprudence. Donna Tullia was nearly fainting with fright, and stood leaning against the wall of the passage.

"I thought—I—I must see you at once," she stammered.

"Not here," he answered, quickly. "Go home at once; I will join you in five minutes. It will ruin you to have it known that you have been here."

Madame Mayer took courage at his tone.

"You must bring them—those papers," she said, hurriedly. "Something dreadful has happened. Promise me to come at once!"

"I will come at once, my dear lady," he said, gently pushing her towards the door. "I cannot even go downstairs with you—forgive me. You have your carriage of course?"

"I have a cab," replied Donna Tullia, faintly, submitting to be put out of the door. He seized her hand and kissed it passionately, or with a magnificent semblance of passion. With a startled look, Donna Tullia turned and went rapidly down the steps. Del Ferice smiled softly to himself when she was gone, and went in again to exchange his dressing-gown for a coat. He had her in his power at last. He had guessed that she would betray the secret— that after the engagement became known, she would not be able to refrain from communicating it to Corona d'Astrardente; and so soon as he heard the news, he had shut himself up in his lodging, pretending a sudden journey to Naples, determined not to set foot out of the house until he heard that Donna Tullia had committed herself. He knew that when she had once spoken she would make a desperate attempt to obtain the papers, for he knew that such an assertion as hers would need to be immediately proved, at the risk of her position in society. His plot had succeeded so far. His only anxiety was to know whether she had mentioned his name in connection with the subject, but he guessed, from his knowledge of her character, that she would not do so : she would respect her oath enough to conceal his name, even while breaking her promise; she would enjoy taking the sole credit of the discovery upon herself, and she would shun an avowal which would prove her to have discussed with any one else the means of preventing the marriage, because it would be a confession of jealousy, and consequently of personal interest in Don Giovanni. Del Ferice was a very clever fellow.

He put on his coat, and in five minutes was seated in a cab on his way to Donna Tullia's house, with a large envelope full of papers in his pocket. He found her as she had left him, her face still wrapped in a veil, walking up and down her drawing-room in great excitement. He advanced and saluted her courteously, maintaining a dignified gravity of bearing which he judged fitting for the occasion.

"And now, my dear lady," he said, gently, "will you tell me exactly what you have done ?"

"This morning," answered Madame Mayer, in a stifled voice, "I heard of the Astrardente's engagement to Don Giovanni. It seemed such a terrible thing!"

"Terrible, indeed," said Del Ferice, solemnly.

"I sent for you at once, to know what to do : they said you were gone to Naples. I thought, of course, that you would approve if you were here, because we ought to prevent such a dreadful crime—of course." She waited for some sign of assent, but Del Ferice's pale face expressed nothing but a sort of grave reproach.

"And then," she continued, "as I could not find you, I thought it was best to act at once, and so I went to see the Astrardente, feeling that you would entirely support me. There was a terrific scene. She sent for the two Saracinesca, and I—waited till they came, because I was determined to see justice done. I am sure I was right,—was I not ? "

"What did they say ? " asked Del Ferice, quietly watching her face.

"If you will believe it, that monster of villany, Don Giovanni, was as cold as stone, and denied the whole matter from beginning to end; but his father was very angry. Of course they demanded the proofs. I never saw anything like the brazen assurance of Don Giovanni."

"Did you mention me ? " inquired Del Ferice.

"No, I had not seen you : of course I did not want to implicate you. I said I would show them the papers to-morrow at the same hour."

"And then you came to see me," said Del Ferice. "That was very rash. You might have seriously compromised yourself. I would have come if you had sent for me."

"But they said you had gone to Naples. Your servant," continued Donna Tullia, blushing scarlet at the remembrance of her interview with Temistocle,—"your servant assured me in person that you had gone to Naples——"

"I see," replied Del Ferice, quietly. He did not wish to press her to a confession of having tried to get the papers in his absence. His object was to put her at her ease.

"My dear lady," he continued, gently, "you have done an exceedingly rash thing; but I will support you in every

way, by putting the documents in your possession at once.
It is unfortunate that you should have acted so suddenly,
for we do not know what has become of this Felice Baldi,
nor have we any immediate means of finding out. It
might have taken weeks to find her. Why were you so
rash? You could have waited till I returned, and we
could have discussed the matter carefully, and decided
whether it were really wise to make use of my information."

"You do not doubt that I did right?" asked Donna
Tullia, turning a little pale.

"I think you acted precipitately in speaking without
consulting me. All may yet be well. But in the first
place, as you did not ask my opinion, you will see the propriety of not mentioning my name, since you have not
done so already. It can do no good, for the papers speak
for themselves, and whatever value they may have is inherent in them. Do you see?"

"Of course, there is no need of mentioning you, unless
you wish to have a share in the exposure of this abominable wickedness."

"I am satisfied with my share," replied Del Ferice, with
a quiet smile.

"It is not an important one," returned Donna Tullia,
nervously.

"It is the lion's share," he answered. "Most adorable
of women, you have not, I am sure, forgotten the terms of
our agreement—terms so dear to me, that every word of
them is engraven for ever upon the tablet of my heart."

Madame Mayer started slightly. She had not realised
that her promise to marry Ugo was now due — she did
not believe that he would press it; he had exacted it to
frighten her, and besides, she had so persuaded herself
that he would approve of her conduct, that she had not
felt as though she were betraying his secret.

"You will not—you cannot hold me to that; you approve of telling the Astrardente, on the whole,—it is the
same as though I had consulted you——"

"Pardon me, my dear lady; you did not consult me,"

answered Del Ferice, soothingly. He sat near her by the
fire, his hat upon his knee, no longer watching her, but
gazing contemplatively at the burning logs. There was a
delicacy about his pale face since the wound he had received a year before which was rather attractive: from
having been a little inclined to stoutness, he had grown
slender and more graceful, partly because his health had
really been affected by his illness, and partly because he
had determined never again to risk being too fat.

"I tried to consult you," objected Donna Tullia. "It
is the same thing."

"It is not the same thing to me," he answered, "although you have not involved me in the affair. I would
have most distinctly advised you to say nothing about it
at present. You have acted rashly, have put yourself in
a most painful situation; and you have broken your promise to me—a very solemn promise, Donna Tullia, sworn
upon the memory of your mother and upon a holy relic.
One cannot make light of such promises as that."

"You made me give it in order to frighten me. The
Church does not bind us to oaths sworn under compulsion,"
she argued.

"Excuse me; there was no compulsion whatever. You
wanted to know my secret, and for the sake of knowing it
you bound yourself. That is not compulsion. I cannot
compel you. I could not think of presuming to compel
you to marry me now. But I can say to you that I am
devotedly attached to you, that to marry you is the aim
and object of my life, and if you refuse, I will tell you
that you are doing a great wrong, repudiating a solemn
contract——"

"If I refuse—well—but you would give me the papers?"
asked Donna Tullia, who was beginning to tremble for the
result of the interview. She had a vague suspicion that,
for the sake of obtaining them, she would even be willing
to promise to marry Del Ferice. It would be very wrong,
perhaps; but it would be for the sake of accomplishing
good, by preventing Corona from falling into the trap—
Corona, whom she hated! Still, it would be a generous

act to save her. The minds of women like Madame Mayer
are apt to be a little tortuous when they find themselves
hemmed in between their own jealousies, hatreds, and personal interests.

"If you refused—no; if you refused, I am afraid I could
not give you the papers," replied Del Ferice, musing as he
gazed at the fire. "I love you too much to lose that
chance of winning you, even for the sake of saving the
Duchessa d'Astrardente from her fate. Why do you refuse? why do you bargain?" he asked, suddenly turning
towards her. "Does all my devotion count for nothing—
all my love, my years of patient waiting? Oh, you cannot be so cruel as to snatch the cup from my very lips!
It is not for the sake of these miserable documents: what
is it to me whether Don Giovanni appears as the criminal
in a case of bigamy—whether he is ruined now, as by his
evil deeds he will be hereafter, or whether he goes on un-
harmed and unthwarted upon his career of wickedness?
He is nothing to me, nor his pale-faced bride either. It is
for you that I care, for you that I will do anything, bad or
good, to win you that I would risk my life and my soul.
Can you not see it? Have I not been faithful for very
long? Take pity on me—forget this whole business, forget that you have promised anything, forget all except
that I am here at your feet, a miserable man, unless you
speak the word, and turn all my wretchedness into joy!"

He slipped from his seat and knelt upon one knee before
her, clasping one of her hands passionately between both
his own. The scene was well planned and well executed;
his voice had a ring of emotion that sounded pleasantly in
Donna Tullia's ears, and his hands trembled with excitement. She did not repulse him, being a vain woman and
willing to believe in the reality of a passion so well simu-
lated. Perhaps, too, it was not wholly put on, for she was
a handsome, dashing woman, in the prime of youth, and
Del Ferice was a man who had always been susceptible to
charms of that kind. Donna Tullia hesitated, wondering
what more he could say. But he, on his part, knew the
danger of trusting too much to eloquence when not backed

by a greater strength than his, and he pressed her for an
answer.

"Be generous—trust me," he cried. "Believe that your
happiness is everything to me; believe that I will take no
unfair advantage of a hasty promise. Tell me that, of your
own free will, you will be my wife, and command me anything, that I may prove my devotion. It is so true, so
honest,—Tullia, I adore you, I live only for you! Speak
the word, and make me the happiest of men!"

He really looked handsome as he knelt before her, and
she felt the light, nervous pressure of his hand at every
word he spoke. After all, what did it matter? She might
accept him, and then—well, if she did not like the idea,
she could throw him over. It would only cost her a violent
scene, and a few moments of discomfort. Meanwhile she
would get the papers.

"But you would give me the papers, would you not, and
leave me to decide whether—— Really, Del Ferice," she
said, interrupting herself with a nervous laugh, "this is
very absurd."

"I implore you not to speak of the papers—it is not
absurd. It may seem so to you, but it is life or death to
me: death if you refuse me—life if you will speak the
word and be mine!"

Donna Tullia made up her mind. He would evidently
not give her what she wanted, except in return for a promise
of marriage. She had grown used to him, almost fond of
him, in the last year.

"Well, I do not know whether I am right," she said,
"but I am really very fond of you; and if you will do all I
say——"

"Everything, my dear lady; everything in the world I
will do, if you will make me so supremely happy," cried
Del Ferice, ardently.

"Then—yes; I will marry you. Only get up and sit
upon your chair like a reasonable being. No; you really
must be reasonable, or you must go away." Ugo was madly
kissing her hands. He was really a good actor, if it was
all acting. She could not but be moved by his pale delicate

face and passionate words. With a quick movement he sprang to his feet and stood before her, clasping his hands together and gazing into her face.

"Oh, I am the happiest man alive to-day!" he exclaimed, and the sense of triumph that he felt lent energy to his voice.

"Do sit ·down," said Donna Tullia, gaily, "and let us talk it all over. In the first place, what am I to do first?"

Del Ferice found it convenient to let his excitement subside, and as a preliminary he walked twice the length of the room.

"It is so hard to be calm!" he exclaimed; but nevertheless he presently sat down in his former seat, and seemed to collect his faculties with wonderful ease.

"What is to be done first?" asked Donna Tullia again.

"In the first place," answered Del Ferice, "here are those precious papers. As they are notary's copies themselves, and not the originals, it is of no importance whether Don Giovanni tears them up or not. It is easy to get others if he does. I have noted down all the names and dates. I wish we had some information about Felice Baldi. It is very unfortunate that we have not, but it would perhaps take a month to find her."

"I must act at once," said Donna Tullia, firmly; for she remembered old Saracinesca's threats, and was in a hurry.

"Of course. These documents speak for themselves. They bear the address of the notary who made the copies in Aquila. If the Saracinesca choose, they can themselves go there and see the originals."

"Could they not destroy those too?" asked Donna Tullia, nervously.

"No; they can only see one at a time, and the person who will show them will watch them. Besides, it is easy to write to the curate of the church of San Bernardino to be on his guard. We will do that in any case. The matter is perfectly plain. Your best course is to meet the Astrardente to-morrow at the appointed time, and simply present these papers for inspection. No one can deny their authenticity, for they bear the Government stamp and the notary's seal, as you see, here and here. If they ask you, as they certainly will, how you came by them, you can afford to answer, that, since you have them, it is not necessary to know whence they came; that they may go and verify the originals; and that in warning them of the fact, you have fulfilled a duty to society, and have done a service to the Astrardente, if not to Giovanni Saracinesca. You have them in your power, and you can afford to take the high hand in the matter. They must believe the evidence of their senses; and they must either allow that Giovanni's first wife is alive, or they must account for her death, and prove it. There is no denial possible in the face of these proofs."

Donna Tullia drew a long breath, for the case seemed perfectly clear; and the anticipation of her triumph already atoned for the sacrifice she had made.

"You are a wonderful man, Del Ferice!" she exclaimed. "I do not know whether I am wise in promising to marry you, but I have the greatest admiration for your intellect."

Del Ferice glanced at her and smiled. Then he made as though he would return the papers to his pocket. She sprang towards him, and seized him by the wrist.

"Do not be afraid!" she cried, "I will keep my promise."

"Solemnly?" he asked, still smiling, and holding the envelope firmly in his hand.

"Solemnly," she answered; and then added, with a quick laugh, "but you are so abominably clever, that I believe you could make me marry you against my will."

"Never!" said Del Ferice, earnestly; "I love you far too much." He had wonderfully clear instincts. "And now," he continued, "we have settled that matter; when shall the happy day be?"

"Oh, there is time enough to think of that," answered Donna Tullia, with a blush that might have passed for the result of a coy shyness, but which was in reality caused by a certain annoyance at being pressed.

"No," objected Del Ferice, "we must announce our en-

gagement at once. There is no reason for delay—to-day is
better than to-morrow."

"To-day?" repeated Donna Tullia, in some alarm.

"Why not? Why not, my dear lady, since you and I
are both in earnest?"

"I think it would be much better to let this affair pass
first."

"On the contrary," he argued, "from the moment we
are publicly engaged I become your natural protector. If
any one offers you any insult in this matter, I shall then
have an acknowledged right to avenge you—a right I dearly
covet. Do you think I would dread to meet Don Giovanni again? He wounded me, it is true, but he has the
marks of my sword upon his body also. Give me at once
the privilege of appearing as your champion, and you will
not regret it. But if you delay doing so, all sorts of circumstances may arise, all sorts of unpleasantness—who
could protect you? Of course, even in that case I would;
but you know the tongues of the gossips in Rome—it would
do you harm instead of good."

"That is true, and you are very brave and very kind.
But it seems almost too soon," objected Donna Tullia, who,
however, was fast learning to yield to his judgment.

"Those things cannot be done too soon. It gives us
liberty, and it gives the world satisfaction; it protects you,
and it will be an inestimable pleasure to me. Why delay
the inevitable? Let us appear at once as engaged to be
married, and you put a sword in my hand to defend you
and to enforce your position in this unfortunate affair with
the Astrardente."

"Well, you may announce it if you please," she answered,
reluctantly.

"Thank you, my dear lady," said Del Ferice. "And
here are the papers. Make the best use of them you can—
any use that you make of them will be good, I know. How
could it be otherwise?"

Donna Tullia's fingers closed upon the large envelope
with a grasping grip, as though she would never relinquish
that for which she had paid so dear a price. She had, in-

deed, at one time almost despaired of getting possession of them, and she had passed a terrible hour, besides having abased herself to the fruitless bribery she had practised upon Temistocle. But she had gained her end, even at the expense of permitting Del Ferice to publish her engagement to marry him. She felt that she could break it off if she decided at last that the union was too distasteful to her; but she foresaw that, from the point of worldly ambition, she would be no great loser by marrying a man of such cunning wit, who possessed such weapons against his enemies, and who, on the whole, as she believed, entirely sympathised with her view of life. She recognised that her chances of making a great match were diminishing rapidly; she could not tell precisely why, but she felt, to her mortification, that she had not made a good use of her rich widowhood: people did not respect her much, and as this touched her vanity, she was susceptible to their lack of deference. She had done no harm, but she knew that every one thought her an irresponsible woman, and the thrifty Romans feared her extravagance, though some of them perhaps courted her fortune: many had admired her, and had to some extent expressed their devotion, but no scion of all the great families had asked her to be his wife. The nearest approach to a proposal had been the doubtful attention she had received from Giovanni Saracinesca during the time when his headstrong father had almost persuaded him to marry her, and she thought of her disappointed hopes with much bitterness. To destroy Giovanni by the revelations she now proposed to make, to marry Del Ferice, and then to develop her position by means of the large fortune she had inherited from her first husband, seemed on the whole a wise plan. Del Ferice's title was not much, to be sure, but, on the other hand, he was intimate with every one she knew, and for a few thousand scudi she could buy some small estate with a good title attached to it. She would then change her mode of life, and assume the pose of a social power, which as a young widow she could not do. It was not so bad, after all, especially if she could celebrate the first day of her engagement by destroying the reputation of Giovanni Saracinesca, root and branch, and dealing a blow at Corona's happiness from which it would not recover.

As for Del Ferice, he regarded his triumph as complete. He cared little what became of Giovanni—whether he was able to refute the evidence brought against him or not. There had been nothing in the matter which was dishonest, and properly made out marriage-certificates are not easy things to annul. Giovanni might swim or sink—it was nothing to Ugo del Ferice, now that he had gained the great object of his life, and was at liberty to publish his engagement to Donna Tullia Mayer. He lost no time in telling his friends the good news, and before the evening was over a hundred people had congratulated him. Donna Tullia, too, appeared in more than usually gay attire, and smilingly received the expressions of good wishes which were showered upon her. She was not inclined to question the sincerity of those who spoke, for in her present mood the stimulus of a little popular noise was soothing to her nerves, which had been badly strained by the excitement of the day. When she closed her eyes she had evil visions of Temistocle retreating at full speed down the stairs with his unearned bribe, or of Del Ferice's calm, pale face, as he had sat in her house that afternoon grasping the precious documents in his hand until she promised to pay the price he asked, which was herself. But she smiled at each new congratulation readily enough, and said in her heart that she would yet become a great power in society, and make her house the centre of all attractions. And meanwhile she pondered on the title she should buy for her husband : she came of high blood herself, and she knew how such dignities as a "principe" or a "duca" were regarded when bought. There was nothing for it but to find some snug little marquisate — "marchese" sounded very well, though one could not be called "eccellenza" by one's servants ; still, as the daughter of a prince, she might manage even that. "Marchese" — yes, that would do. What a pity there were only four "canopy" marquises—"marchesi del baldacchino "—in Rome with the rank of princes! That was exactly the combination of dignities Donna Tullia required for her husband. But once a "marchese," if she was very charitable, and did something in the way of a public work, the Holy Father might condescend to make Del Ferice a "duca" in the ordinary course as a step in the nobility. Donna Tullia dreamed many things that night, and she afterwards accomplished most of them, to the surprise of everybody, and, if the truth were told, to her own considerable astonishment.

CHAPTER XXVIII.

"Giovanni, you are the victim of some outrageous plot," said old Saracinesca, entering his son's room on the following morning. "I have thought it all out in the night, and I am convinced of it."

Giovanni was extended upon a sofa, with a book in his hand and a cigar between his lips. He looked up quietly from his reading.

"I am not the victim yet, nor ever will be," he answered; "but it is evident that there is something at the bottom of this besides Madame Mayer's imagination. I will find out."

"What pleases me especially," remarked the old Prince, "is the wonderful originality of the idea. It would have been commonplace to make out that you had poisoned half-a-dozen wives, and buried their bodies in the vaults of Saracinesca; it would have been *banal* to say that you were not yourself, but some one else; or to assert that you were a revolutionary agent in disguise, and that the real Giovanni had been murdered by you, who had taken his place without my discovering it,—very commonplace all that. But to say that you actually have a living wife, and to try to prove it by documents, is an idea worthy of a great mind. It takes one's breath away."

Giovanni laughed.

"It will end in our having to go to Aquila in search of my supposed better half," he said. "Aquila, of all places! If she had said Paris—or even Florence—but why, in the name of geography, Aquila?"

"She probably looked for some out-of-the-way place upon an alphabetical list," laughed the prince. "Aquila stood first. We shall know in two hours—come along. It is time to be going."

They found Corona in her boudoir. She had passed an uneasy hour on the previous afternoon after they had left her, but her equanimity was now entirely restored. She had made up her mind that, however ingenious the concocted evidence might turn out to be, it was absolutely impossible to harm Giovanni by means of it. His position was beyond attack, as, in her mind, his character was above slander. Far from experiencing any sensation of anxiety as to the result of Donna Tullia's visit, what she most felt was curiosity to see what these fancied proofs would be like. She still believed that Madame Mayer was mad.

"I have been remarking to Giovanni upon Donna Tullia's originality," said old Saracinesca. "It is charming; it shows a talent for fiction which the world has been long in realising, which we have not even suspected—an amazing and transcendent genius for invention."

"It is pure insanity," answered Corona, in a tone of conviction. "The woman is mad."

"Mad as an Englishman," asseverated the Prince, using the most powerful simile in the Italian language. "We will have her in Santo Spirito before night, and she will puzzle the doctors."

"She is not mad," said Giovanni, quietly. "I do not even believe we shall find that her documents are forgeries."

"What?" cried his father. Corona looked quickly at Giovanni.

"You yourself," said the latter, turning to old Saracinesca, "were assuring me half an hour ago that I was the victim of a plot. Now, if anything of the kind is seriously attempted, you may be sure it will be well done. She has a good ally in the man to whom she is engaged. Del Ferice is no fool, and he hates me."

"Del Ferice!" exclaimed Corona, in surprise. As she went nowhere as yet, she had, of course, not heard the news which had been published on the previous evening. "You do not mean to say that she is going to marry Del Ferice?"

"Yes, indeed," said Giovanni. "They both appeared last night and announced the fact, and received everybody's congratulations. It is a most appropriate match."

"I agree with you—a beautiful triangular alliteration of wit, wealth, and wickedness," observed the Prince. "He has brains, she has money, and they are both as bad as possible."

"I thought you used to like Donna Tullia," said Corona, suppressing a smile.

"I did," said old Saracinesca, stoutly. "I wanted Giovanni to marry her. It has pleased Providence to avert that awful catastrophe. I liked Madame Mayer because she was rich and noisy and good-looking, and I thought that, as Giovanni's wife, she would make the house gay. We are such a pair of solemn bears together, that it seemed appropriate that somebody should make us dance. It was a foolish idea, I confess, though I thought it very beautiful at the time. It merely shows how liable we are to make mistakes. Imagine Giovanni married to a lunatic!"

"I repeat that she is not mad," said Giovanni. "I cannot tell how they have managed it, but I am sure it has been managed well, and will give us trouble. You will see."

"I do not understand at all how there can be any trouble about it," said Corona, proudly. "It is perfectly simple for us to tell the truth, and to show that what they say is a lie. You can prove easily enough that you were in Canada at the time. I wish it were time for her to come. Let us go to breakfast in the meanwhile."

The views taken by the three were characteristic of their various natures. The old Prince, who was violent of temper, and inclined always to despise an enemy in any shape, scoffed at the idea that there was anything to show; and though his natural wit suggested from time to time that there was a plot against his son, his general opinion was, that it was a singular case of madness. He hardly believed Donna Tullia would appear at all; and if she did, he expected some extraordinary outburst, some pitiable exhibition of insanity. Corona, on the other hand, maintained a proud indifference, scorning to suppose that anything could possibly injure Giovanni in any way, loving him too entirely to admit that he was vulnerable at all, still less that he could possibly have done anything to give colour to the accusation brought against him. Giovanni alone of all the three foresaw that there would be trouble, and dimly guessed how the thing had been done; for he did not fall into his father's error of despising an enemy, and he had seen too much of the world not to understand that danger is often greatest when the appearance of it is least.

Breakfast was hardly over when Donna Tullia was announced. All rose to meet her, and all looked at her with equal interest. She was calmer than on the previous day, and she carried a package of papers in her hand. Her red lips were compressed, and her eyes looked defiantly round upon all present. Whatever might be her faults, she was not a coward when brought face to face with danger. She was determined to carry the matter through, both because she knew that she had no other alternative, and because she believed herself to be doing a righteous act, which, at the same time, fully satisfied her desire for vengeance. She came forward boldly and stood beside the table in the midst of the room. Corona was upon one side of the fireplace, and the two Saracinesca upon the other. All three held their breath in expectation of what Donna Tullia was about to say; the sense of her importance impressed her, and her love of dramatic situations being satisfied, she assumed something of the air of a theatrical avenging angel, and her utterance was rhetorical.

" I come here," she said, " at your invitation, to exhibit to your eyes the evidence of what I yesterday asserted— the evidence of the monstrous crime of which I accuse that

z

man." Here she raised her finger with a gesture of scorn, and extending her whole arm, pointed towards Giovanni.

"Madam," interrupted the old Prince, "I will trouble you to select your epithets and expressions with more care. Pray be brief, and show what you have brought."

"I will show it, indeed," replied Donna Tullia, "and you shall tremble at what you see. When you have evidence of the truth of what I say, you may choose any language you please to define the action of your son. These documents," she said, holding up the package, "are attested copies made from the originals—the first two in the possession of the curate of the church of San Bernardino da Siena, at Aquila, the other in the office of the Stato Civile in the same city. As they are only copies, you need not think that you will gain anything by destroying them."

"Spare your comments upon our probable conduct," interrupted the Prince, roughly. Donna Tullia eyed him with a scornful glance, and her face began to grow red.

"You may destroy them if you please," she repeated; "but I advise you to observe that they bear the Government stamp and the notarial seal of Gianbattista Caldani, notary public in the city of Aquila, and that they are, consequently, beyond all doubt genuine copies of genuine documents."

Donna Tullia proceeded to open the envelope and withdraw the three papers it contained. Spreading them out, she took up the first, which contained the extract from the curate's book of banns. It set forth that upon the three Sundays preceding the 19th of June 1863, the said curate had published, in the parish church of San Bernardino da Siena, the banns of marriage between Giovanni Saracinesca and Felice Baldi. Donna Tullia read it aloud.

Giovanni could hardly suppress a laugh, it sounded so strangely. Corona herself turned pale, though she firmly believed the whole thing to be an imposture of some kind.

"Permit me, madam," said old Saracinesca, stepping forward and taking the paper from her hand. He carefully examined the seal and stamp. "It is very cleverly done," he said with a sneer; "but there should be only one letter *r* in the name Saracinesca—here it is spelt with two! Very clever, but a slight mistake! Observe," he said, showing the place to Donna Tullia.

"It is a mistake of the copyist," she said, scornfully. "The name is properly spelt in the other papers. Here is the copy of the marriage register. Shall I read it also?"

"Spare me the humiliation," said Giovanni, in quiet contempt. "Spare me the unutterable mortification of discovering that there is another Giovanni Saracinesca in the world!"

"I could not have believed that any one could be so hardened," said Donna Tullia. "But whether you are humiliated or not by the evidence of your misdeeds, I will spare you nothing. Here it is in full, and you may notice that your name is spelt properly too."

She held up the document and then read it out—the copy of the curate's register, stating that on the 19th of June 1863 Giovanni Saracinesca and Felice Baldi were united in holy matrimony in the church of San Bernardino da Siena. She handed the paper to the Prince, and then read the extract from the register of the Civil marriage and the notary's attestation to the signatures. She gave this also to old Saracinesca, and then folding her arms in a fine attitude, confronted the three.

"Are you satisfied that I spoke the truth?" she asked, defiantly.

"The thing is certainly remarkably well done," answered the old Prince, who scrutinised the papers with a puzzled air. Though he knew perfectly well that his son had been in Canada at the time of this pretended marriage, he confessed to himself that if such evidence had been brought against any other man, he would have believed it.

"It is a shameful fraud!" exclaimed Corona, looking at the papers over the old man's shoulder.

"That is a lie!" cried Donna Tullia, growing scarlet with anger.

"Do not forget your manners, or you will get into trouble," said Giovanni, sternly. "I see through the whole thing. There has been no fraud, and yet the de-

ductions are entirely untrue. In the first place, Donna
Tullia, how do you make the statements here given to
coincide with the fact that during the whole summer of
1863 and during the early part of 1864 I was in Canada
with a party of gentlemen, who are all alive to testify
to the fact?"

"I do not believe it," answered Madame Mayer, contemptuously. "I would not believe your friends if they
were here and swore to it. You will very likely produce
witnesses to prove that you were in the arctic regions
last summer, as the newspapers said, whereas every one
knows now that you were at Saracinesca. You are exceedingly clever at concealing your movements, as we all
know."

Giovanni did not lose his temper, but calmly proceeded
to demonstrate his theory.

"You will find that the courts of law will accept the
evidence of gentlemen upon oath," he replied, quietly.
"Moreover, as a further evidence, and a piece of very
singular proof, I can probably produce Giovanni Saracinesca and Felice Baldi themselves to witness against you. ·
And I apprehend that the said Giovanni Saracinesca will
vehemently protest that the said Felice Baldi is his wife,
and not mine."

"You speak in wonderful riddles, but you will not deceive me. Money will doubtless do much, but it will not
do what you expect."

"Certainly not," returned Giovanni, unmoved by her
reply. "Money will certainly not create out of nothing a
second Giovanni Saracinesca, nor his circle of acquaintances, nor the police registers concerning him which are
kept throughout the kingdom of Italy, very much as they
are kept here in the Pontifical States. Money will do
none of these things."

While he was speaking, his father and the Duchessa
listened with intense interest.

"Donna Tullia," continued Giovanni, "I am willing to
believe from your manner that you are really sure that I
am the man mentioned in your papers; but permit me to

inform you that you have been made the victim of a shallow trick, probably by the person who gave those same papers into your hands, and suggested to you the use you have made of them."

"I? I, the victim of a trick?" repeated Donna Tullia, frightened at last by his obstinately calm manner.

"Yes," he replied. "I know Aquila and the Abruzzi very well. It chances that although we, the Saracinesca of Rome, are not numerous, the name is not uncommon in that part of the country. It is the same with all our great names. There are Colonna, Orsini, Caetani all over the country—there are even many families bearing the name of the Medici, who are extinct. You know it as well as I, or you should know it, for I believe your mother was my father's cousin. Has it not struck you that this same Giovanni Saracinesca herein mentioned, is simply some low-born namesake of mine?"

" Donna Tullia had grown very pale, and she leaned upon the table as though she were faint. The others listened breathlessly.

"I do not believe it," said Madame Mayer, in a low and broken voice.

"Now I will tell you what I will do," continued Giovanni. "I will go to Aquila at once, and I daresay my father will accompany me——"

"Of course I will," broke in the old Prince.

"We will go, and in a fortnight's time we will produce the whole history of this Giovanni Saracinesca, together with his wife and himself in his own person, if they are both alive; we will bring them here, and they will assure you that you have been egregiously deceived, played upon and put in a false position by—by the person who furnished you with these documents. I wonder that any Roman of common-sense should not have seen at once the cause of this mistake."

"I cannot believe it," murmured Donna Tullia. Then raising her voice, she added, "Whatever may be the result of your inquiry, I cannot but feel that I have done my duty in this affair. I do not believe in your theory, nor in

you, and I shall not, until you produce this other man.   I
have done my duty———"

"An exceedingly painful one, no doubt," remarked old
Saracinesca.   Then he broke into a loud peal of laughter.

"And if you do not succeed in your search, it will be
my duty, in the interests of society, to put the matter in
the hands of the police.   Since you have the effrontery to
say that those papers are of no use, I demand them back."

"Not at all, madam," replied the Prince, whose laughter
subsided at the renewed boldness of her tone.   "I will not
give them back to you.   I intend to compare them with
the originals.   If there are no originals, they will serve very
well to commit the notary whose seal is on them, and yourself, upon a well-founded indictment for forgery, wilful cal-
umniation, and a whole list of crimes sufficient to send you
to the galleys for life.   If, on the other hand, the originals
exist, they can be of no possible value to you, as you can
send to Aquila and have fresh copies made whenever you
please, as you yourself informed me."

Things were taking a bad turn for Donna Tullia.   She
believed the papers to be genuine, but a fearful doubt crossed
her mind that Del Ferice might possibly have deceived her
by having them manufactured.   Anybody could buy Government paper, and it would be but a simple matter to have
a notary's seal engraved.   She was terrified at the idea, but
there was no possibility of getting the documents back from
the old Prince, who held them firmly in his broad brown
hand.   There was nothing to be done but to face the situation out to the end and go.

"As you please," she said.   "It is natural that you
should insult me, a defenceless woman trying to do what is
right.   It is worthy of your race and reputation.   I will
leave you to the consideration of the course you intend to
follow, and I advise you to omit nothing which can help to
prove the innocence of your son."

Donna Tullia bestowed one more glance of contemptuous defiance upon the group, and brushed angrily out of
the room.

"So much for her madness!" exclaimed Giovanni, when

she was gone. . "I think I have got to the bottom of that affair."

"It seems so simple, and yet I never thought of it," said Corona. "How clever you are, Giovanni!"

"There was not much cleverness needed to see through so shallow a trick," replied Giovanni. "I suspected it this morning; and when I saw that the documents were genuine and all in order, I was convinced of it. This thing has been done by Del Ferice, I suppose in order to revenge himself upon me for nearly killing him in fair fight. It was a noble plan. With a little more intelligence and a little more pains, he could have given me great trouble. Certificates like those he produced, if they had come from a remote French village in Canada, would have given us occupation for some time."

"I wish Donna Tullia joy of her husband," remarked the Prince. "He will spend her money in a year or two, and then leave her to the contemplation of his past extravagance. I wonder how he induced her to consent."

"Many people like Del Ferice," said Giovanni. "He is popular, and has attractions."

"How can you say that!" exclaimed Corona, ind'gnantly. "You should have a better opinion of women than to think any woman could find attractions in such a man."

"Nevertheless, Donna Tullia is going to marry him," returned Giovanni. "She must find him to her taste. I used to think she might have married Valdarno—he is so good-natured, you know!"

Giovanni spoke in a tone of reflection; the other two laughed.

"And now, Giovannino," said his father, "we must set out for Aquila, and find your namesake."

"You will not really go?" asked Corona, with a look of disappointment. She could not bear the thought of being separated even for a day from the man she loved.

"I do not see that we can do anything else," returned the Prince. "I must satisfy myself whether those papers are forgeries or not. If they are, that woman must go to prison for them."

"But she is our cousin—you cannot do that," objected Giovanni.

"Indeed I will. I am angry. Do not try to stop me. Do you suppose I care anything for the relationship in comparison with repaying her for all this trouble? You are not going to turn merciful, Giovanni? I should not recognise you."

There was a sort of mournful reproach about the old Prince's tone, as though he were reproving his son for having fallen from the paths of virtue. Corona laughed; she was not hard-hearted, but she was not so angelic of nature as to be beyond feeling deep and lasting resentment for injuries received. At that moment the idea of bringing Donna Tullia to justice was pleasant.

"Well," said Giovanni, "no human being can boast of having ever prevented you from doing whatever you were determined to do. The best thing that can happen will be, that you should find the papers genuine, and my namesake alive. I wish Aquila were Florence or Naples," he added, turning to Corona; "you might manage to go at the same time."

"That is impossible," she answered, sadly. "How long will you be gone, do you think?"

Giovanni did not believe that, if the papers were genuine, and if they had to search for the man mentioned in them, they could return in less than a fortnight.

"Why not send a detective — a *sbirro?*" suggested Corona.

"He could not accomplish anything," replied the Prince. "He would be at a great disadvantage there; we must go ourselves."

"Both?" asked Corona, regretfully, gazing at Giovanni's face.

"It is my business," replied the latter. "I can hardly ask my father to go alone."

"Absurd!" exclaimed the old Prince, resenting the idea that he needed any help to accomplish his mission. "Do you think I need some one to take care of me, like a baby in arms? I will go alone; you shall not come even if you wish it. Absurd, to talk of my needing anybody with me! I will show you what your father can do when his blood is up."

Protestations were useless after that. The old man grew angry at the opposition, and, regardless of all propriety, seized his hat and left the room, growling that he was as good as anybody, and a great deal better.

Corona and Giovanni looked at each other when he was gone, and smiled.

"I believe my father is the best man alive," said Giovanni. "He would go in a moment if I would let him. I will go after him and bring him back—I suppose I ought."

"I suppose so," answered Corona; but as they stood side by side, she passed her hand under his arm affectionately, and looked into his eyes. It was a very tender look, very loving and gentle—such a look as none but Giovanni had ever seen upon her face. He put his arm about her waist and drew her to him, and kissed her dark cheek.

"I cannot bear to go away and leave you, even for a day," he said, pressing her to his side.

"Why should you?" she murmured, looking up to him. "Why should he go, after all? This has been such a silly affair. I wonder if that woman thought that anything could ever come between you and me? That was what made me think she was really mad."

"And an excellent reason," he answered. "Anybody must be insane who dreams of parting us two. It seems as though a year ago I had not loved you at all."

"I am so glad," said Corona. "Do you remember, last summer, on the tower at Saracinesca, I told you that you did not know what love was?"

"It was true, Corona—I did not know. But I thought I did. I never imagined what the happiness of love was, nor how great it was, nor how it could enter into every thought."

"Into every thought? Into your great thoughts too?"

"If any thoughts of mine are great, they are so because you are the mainspring of them," he answered.

"Will it always be so?" she asked. "You will be a

very great man some day, Giovanni; will you always feel that I am something to you?"

"Always—more than anything to me, more than all of me together."

"I sometimes wonder," said Corona. "I think I understand you better than I used to do. I like to think that you feel how I understand you when you tell me anything. Of course I am not clever like you, but I love you so much that just while you are talking I seem to understand everything. It is like a flash of light in a dark room."

Giovanni kissed her again.

"What makes you think that I shall be great, Corona? Nobody ever thinks I am even clever. My father would laugh at you, and say it is quite enough greatness to be born a Saracinesca. What makes you think it?"

Corona stood up beside him and laid her delicate hand upon his thick, close-cut black hair, and gazed into his eyes.

"I know it," she said. "I know it, because I love you so. A man like you must be great. There is something in you that nobody guesses but I, that will amaze people some day—I know it."

"I wonder if you could tell me what it is? I wonder if it is really there at all?" said Giovanni.

"It is ambition," said Corona, gravely. "You are the most ambitious man I ever knew, and nobody has found it out."

"I believe it is true, Corona," said Giovanni, turning away and leaning upon the chimneypiece, his head supported on one hand. "I believe you are right. I am ambitious: if I only had the brains that some men have I would do great things."

"You are wrong, Giovanni. It is neither brains nor ambition nor strength that you lack—it is opportunity."

"They say that a man who has anything in him creates opportunities for himself," answered Giovanni, rather sadly. "I fear it is because I really have nothing in me that I can do nothing. It sometimes makes me very unhappy to think so. I suppose that is because my vanity is wounded."

"Do not talk like that," said Corona. "You have vanity, of course, but it is of the large kind, and I call it ambition. It is not only because I love you better than any man was ever loved before that I say that. It is that I know it instinctively. I have heard you say that these are unsettled times. Wait; your opportunity will come, as it came often to your forefathers in other centuries."

"I hardly think that their example is a good one," replied Giovanni, with a smile.

"They generally did something remarkable in remarkable times," said Corona. "You will do the same. Your father, for instance, would not."

"He is far more clever than I," objected Giovanni.

"Clever! It passes for cleverness. He is quick, active, a good talker, a man with a ready wit and a sharp answer—kind-hearted when the fancy takes him, cruel when he is so disposed—but not a man of great convictions or of great actions. You are very different from him."

"Will you draw my portrait, Corona?" asked Giovanni.

"As far as I know you. You are a man quick to think and slow to make a decision. You are not brilliant in conversation—you see I do not flatter you; I am just. You have the very remarkable quality of growing cold when others grow hot, and of keeping the full use of your faculties in any situation. When you have made a decision, you cannot be moved from it; but you are open to conviction in argument. You have a great repose of manner, which conceals a very restless brain. All your passions are very strong. You never forgive, never forget, and scarcely ever repent. Beneath all, you have an untamable ambition which has not yet found its proper field. Those are your qualities—and I love them all, and you more than them all."

Corona finished her speech by throwing her arms round his neck, and breaking into a happy laugh as she buried her face upon his shoulder. No one who saw her in the world would have believed her capable of those sudden and violent demonstrations—she was thought so very cold.

When Giovanni reached home, he was informed that his

father had left Rome an hour earlier by the train for Terni,
leaving word that he had gone to Aquila.

CHAPTER XXIX.

In those days the railroad did not extend beyond Terni
in the direction of Aquila, and it was necessary to perform
the journey of forty miles between those towns by diligence.
It was late in the afternoon of the next day before the
cumbrous coach rolled up to the door of the Locanda del
Sole in Aquila, and Prince Saracinesca found himself at his
destination.   The red evening sun gilded the snow of the
Gran Sasso d'Italia, the huge domed mountain that towers
above the city of Frederick.   The city itself had long been
in the shade, and the spring air was sharp and biting.   Saracinesca deposited his slender luggage with the portly landlord, said he would return for supper in half an hour, and
inquired the way to the church of San Bernardino da Siena.
There was no difficulty in finding it, at the end of the
Corso—the inevitable "Corso" of every Italian town.   The
old gentleman walked briskly along the broad, clean street,
and reached the door of the church just as the sacristan
was hoisting the heavy leathern curtain, preparatory to
locking up for the night.

"Where can I find the Padre Curato?" inquired the
Prince.   The man looked at him but made no answer, and
proceeded to close the doors with great care.   He was an
old man in a shabby cassock, with four days' beard on his
face, and he appeared to have taken snuff recently.

"Where is the Curato?" repeated the Prince, plucking
him by the sleeve.   But the man shook his head, and
began turning the ponderous key in the lock.   Two little
ragged boys were playing a game upon the church steps,
piling five chestnuts in a heap and then knocking them
down with a small stone.   One of them having upset the
heap, desisted and came near the Prince.

"That one is deaf," he said, pointing to the sacristan. Then running behind him he stood on tiptoe and screamed in his ear—"*Brutta bestia!*"

The sacristan did not hear, but caught sight of the urchin and made a lunge at him. He missed him, however, and nearly fell over.

"What education!—*che educazione!*" cried the old man, angrily.

Meanwhile the little boy took refuge behind Saracinesca, and pulling his coat asked for a *soldo*. The sacristan calmly withdrew the key from the lock, and went away without vouchsafing a look to the Prince.

"He is deaf," screamed the little boy, who was now joined by his companion, and both in great excitement danced round the fine gentleman.

"Give me a *soldo*," they yelled together.

"Show me the house of the Padre Curato," answered the Prince, "then I will give you each a *soldo*. *Lesti!* Quick!"

Whereupon both the boys begun turning cart-wheels on their feet and hands with marvellous dexterity. At last they subsided into a natural position, and led the way to the curate's house, not twenty yards from the church, in a narrow alley. The Prince pulled the bell by the long chain which hung beside the open street door, and gave the boys the promised coppers. They did not leave him, however, but stood by to see what would happen. An old woman looked out of an upper window, and after surveying the Prince with care, called down to him—

"What do you want?"

"Is the Padre Curato at home?"

"Of course he is at home," screamed the old woman. "At this hour!" she added, contemptuously.

"*Ebbene*—can I see him?"

"What! is the door shut?" returned the hag.

"No."

"Then why don't you come up without asking?" The old woman's head disappeared, and the window was shut with a clattering noise.

"She is a woman without education," remarked one of the ragged boys, making a face towards the closed window.

The Prince entered the door and stumbled up the dark stairs, and after some further palaver obtained admittance to the curate's lodging. The curate sat in a room which appeared to serve as dining-room, living-room, and study. A small table was spread with a clean cloth, upon which were arranged a plate, a loaf of bread, a battered spoon, a knife, and a small measure of thin-looking wine. A brass lamp with three wicks, one of which only was burning, shed a feeble light through the poor apartment. Against the wall stood a rough table with an inkstand and three or four mouldy books. Above this hung a little black cross bearing a brass Christ, and above this again a coloured print of San Bernardino of Siena. The walls were white-washed, and perfectly clean,—as indeed was everything else in the room,—and there was a sweet smell of flowers from a huge pot of pinks which had been taken in for the night, and stood upon the stone sill within the closed window.

The curate was a tall old man, with a singularly gentle face and soft brown eyes. He wore a threadbare cassock, carefully brushed; and from beneath his three-cornered black cap his thin hair hung in a straight grey fringe. As the Prince entered the room, the old woman called over his shoulder to the priest an uncertain formula of introduction.

"Don Paolo, c'è uno—there is one." Then she retired, grumbling audibly.

The priest removed his cap, and bowing politely, offered one of the two chairs to his visitor. With an apology, he replaced his cap upon his head, and seated himself opposite the Prince. There was much courteous simplicity in his manner.

"In what way can I serve you, Signore?" he asked.

"These papers," answered the Prince, drawing the famous envelope from his breast-pocket, "are copies of certain documents in your keeping, relating to the supposed marriage of one Giovanni Saracinesca. With your very kind permission, I desire to see the originals."

The old curate bowed, as though giving his assent, and looked steadily at his visitor for a moment before he answered.

"There is nothing simpler, my good sir. You will pardon me, however, if I venture to inquire your name, and to ask you for what purpose you desire to consult the documents?"

"I am Leone Saracinesca of Rome——"

The priest started uneasily.

"A relation of Giovanni Saracinesca?" he inquired. Then he added immediately, "Will you kindly excuse me for one moment?" and left the room abruptly. The Prince was considerably astonished, but he held his papers firmly in his hand, and did not move from his seat. The curate returned in a few seconds, bringing with him a little painted porcelain basket, much chipped and the worse for age, and which contained a collection of visiting-cards. There were not more than a score of them, turning brown with accumulated dust. The priest found one which was rather newer than the rest, and after carefully adjusting a pair of huge spectacles upon his nose, he went over to the lamp and examined it.

"'Il Conte del Ferice,'" he read slowly. "Do you happen to know that gentleman, my good sir?" he inquired, turning to the Prince, and looking keenly at him over his glasses.

"Certainly," answered Saracinesca, beginning to understand the situation. "I know him very well."

"Ah, that is good!" said the priest. "He was here two years ago, and had those same entries concerning Giovanni Saracinesca copied. Probably — certainly, indeed — the papers you have there are the very ones he took away with him. When he came to see me about it, he gave me this card."

"I wonder he did," answered Saracinesca.

"Indeed," replied the curate, after a moment's thought, "I remember that he came the next day—yes—and asked to have his card returned. But I could not find it for him. There was a hole in one of my pockets — it had slipped down. Carmela, my old servant, found it a day or two later in the lining of my cassock. I thought it strange that he should have asked for it."

"It was very natural. He wished you to forget his existence."

"He asked me many questions about Giovanni," said the priest, "but I could not answer him at that time."

"You could answer now?" inquired the Prince, eagerly.

"Excuse me, my good sir; what relation are you to Giovanni? You say you are from Rome?"

"Let us understand each other, Signor Curato," said Saracinesca. "I see I had better explain the position. I am Leone Saracinesca, the prince of that name, and the head of the family." The priest bowed respectfully at this intelligence. "My only son lives with me in Rome—he is now there—and his name is Giovanni Saracinesca. He is engaged to be married. When the engagement became known, an enemy of the family attempted to prove, by means of these papers, that he was married already to a certain Felice Baldi. Now I wish to know who this Giovanni Saracinesca is, where he is, and how he comes to have my son's name. I wish a certificate or some proof that he is not my son,—that he is alive, or that he is dead and buried."

The old priest burst into a genial laugh, and rubbed his hands together in delight.

"My dear sir — your Excellency, I mean — I baptised Felice Baldi's second baby a fortnight ago! There is nothing simpler——"

"I knew it!" cried the Prince, springing from his chair in great excitement; "I knew it! Where is that baby? Send and get the baby at once—the mother—the father— everybody!"

"*Subito!* At once—or come with me. I will show you the whole family together," said the curate, in innocent delight. "Splendid children they are, too. Carmela, my cloak—*sbrigati*, be quick!"

"One moment," objected Saracinesca, as though suddenly

recollecting something. "One moment, Signor Curato; who goes slowly goes safely. Where does this man come from, and how does he come by his name? I would like to know something about him before I see him."

"True," answered the priest, resuming his seat. "I had forgotten. Well, it is not a long story. Giovanni Saracinesca is from Naples. You know there was once a branch of your family in the Neapolitan kingdom—at least so Giovanni says, and he is an honest fellow. Their title was Marchese di San Giacinto; and if Giovanni liked to claim it, he has a right to the title still."

"But those Saracinesca were extinct fifty years ago," objected the Prince, who knew his family history very well.

"Giovanni says they were not. They were believed to be. The last Marchese di San Giacinto fought under Napoleon. He lost all he possessed—lands, money, everything—by confiscation, when Ferdinand was restored in 1815. He was a rough man; he dropped his title, married a peasant's only daughter, became a peasant himself, and died obscurely in a village near Salerno. He left a son who worked on the farm and inherited it from his mother, married a woman of the village of some education, and died of the cholera, leaving his son, the present Giovanni Saracinesca. This Giovanni received a better education than his father had before him, improved his farm, began to sell wine and oil for exportation, travelled as far as Aquila, and met Felice Baldi, the daughter of a man of some wealth, who has since established an inn here. Giovanni loved her. I married them. He went back to Naples, sold his farm for a good price last year, and returned to Aquila. He manages his father-in-law's inn, which is the second largest here, and drives a good business, having put his own capital into the enterprise. They have two children, the second one of which was born three weeks ago, and they are perfectly happy."

Saracinesca looked thoughtfully at Don Paolo, the old curate.

"Has this man any papers to prove the truth of this very singular story?" he inquired at last.

2 A

"*Altro!* That was all his grandfather left—a heap of parchments. They seem to be in order—he showed them to me when I married him."

"Why does he make no claim to have the attainder of his grandfather reversed?"

The curate shrugged his shoulders and spread out the palms of his hands, smiling incredulously.

"The lands, he says, have fallen into the hands of certain patriots. There is no chance of getting them back. It is of little use to be a Marchese without property. What he possesses is a modest competence; it is wealth, even, in his present position. For a nobleman it would be nothing. Besides, he is half a peasant by blood and tradition."

"He is not the only nobleman in that position," laughed Saracinesca. "But are you aware——"

He stopped short. He was going to say that if he himself and his son both died, the innkeeper of Aquila would become Prince Saracinesca. The idea shocked him, and he kept it to himself.

"After all," he continued, "the man is of my blood by direct descent. I would like to see him."

"Nothing easier. If you will come with me, I will present him to your Excellency," said the priest. "Do you still wish to see the documents?"

"It is useless. The mystery is solved. Let us go and see this new-found relation of mine."

Don Paolo wrapped his cloak around him, and ushering his guest from the room, led the way down-stairs. He carried a bit of wax taper, which he held low to the steps, frequently stopping and warning the Prince to be careful. It was night when they went out. The air was sharp and cold, and Saracinesca buttoned his greatcoat to his throat as he strode by the side of the old priest. The two walked on in silence for ten minutes, keeping straight down the Corso Vittorio Emmanuele. At last the curate stopped before a clean, new house, from the windows of which the bright light streamed into the street. Don Paolo motioned to the Prince to enter, and followed him in. A man in a white apron, with his arms full of plates, who was probably servant, butler, boots, and factotum to the establishment, came out of the dining-room, which was to the left of the entrance, and which, to judge by the noise, seemed to be full of people. He looked at the curate, and then at the Prince.

"Sorry to disappoint you, Don Paolo *mio*," he said, supposing the priest had brought a customer—"very sorry; there is not a bed in the house."

"That is no matter, Giacchino," answered the curate. "We want to see Sor Giovanni for a moment." The man disappeared, and a moment later Sor Giovanni himself came down the passage.

"*Favorisca*, dear Don Paolo. Come in." And he bowed to the Prince as he opened the door which led into a small sitting-room reserved for the innkeeper's family.

When they had entered, Saracinesca looked at his son's namesake. He saw before him a man whose face and figure he long remembered with an instinctive dislike. Giovanni the innkeeper was of a powerful build. Two generations of peasant blood had given renewed strength to the old race. He was large, with large bones, vast breadth of shoulder, and massive joints; lean withal, and brown of face, his high cheek-bones making his cheeks look hollow; clean shaved, his hair straight and black and neatly combed; piercing black eyes near together, the heavy eyebrows joining together in the midst of his forehead; thin and cruel lips, now parted in a smile and showing a formidable set of short, white, even teeth; a prominent square jaw, and a broad, strong nose, rather unnaturally pointed,—altogether a striking face, one that would be noticed in a crowd for its strength, but strangely cunning in expression, and not without ferocity. Years afterwards Saracinesca remembered his first meeting with Giovanni the innkeeper, and did not wonder that his first impulse had been to dislike the man. At present, however, he looked at him with considerable curiosity, and if he disliked him at first sight, he told himself that it was beneath him to show antipathy for an innkeeper.

"Sor Giovanni," said the curate, "this gentleman is desirous of making your acquaintance."

Giovanni, whose manners were above his station, bowed politely, and looked inquiringly at his visitor.

"Signor Saracinesca," said the Prince, "I am Leone Saracinesca of Rome. I have just heard of your existence. We have long believed your family to be extinct—I am delighted to find it still represented, and by one who seems likely to perpetuate the name."

The innkeeper fixed his piercing eyes on the speaker's face, and looked long before he answered.

"So you are Prince Saracinesca," he said, gravely.

"And you are the Marchese di San Giacinto," said the Prince, in the same tone, holding out his hand frankly.

"Pardon me,—I am Giovanni Saracinesca, the innkeeper of Aquila," returned the other. But he took the Prince's hand. Then they all sat down.

"As you please," said the Prince. "The title is none the less yours. If you had signed yourself with it when you married, you would have saved me a vast deal of trouble; but on the other hand, I should not have been so fortunate as to meet you."

"I do not understand," said Giovanni.

The Prince told his story in as few words as possible.

"Amazing! extraordinary! what a chance!" ejaculated the curate, nodding his old head from time to time while the Prince spoke, as though he had not heard it all before. The innkeeper said nothing until old Saracinesca had finished.

"I see how it was managed," he said at last. "When that gentleman was making inquiries, I was away. I had taken my wife back to Salerno, and my wife's father had not yet established himself in Aquila. Signor Del—what is his name?"

"Del Ferice."

"Del Ferice, exactly. He thought we had disappeared, and were not likely to come back. Or else he is a fool."

"He is not a fool," said Saracinesca. "He thought he was safe. It is all very clear now. Well, Signor Marchese, or Signor Saracinesca, I am very glad to have made your acquaintance. You have cleared up a very important question by returning to Aquila. It will always give me the greatest pleasure to serve you in any way I can."

"A thousand thanks. Anything I can do for you during your stay——"

"You are very kind. I will hire horses and return to Terni to-night. My business in Rome is urgent. There is some suspense there in my absence."

"You will drink a glass before going?" asked Giovanni; and without waiting for an answer, he strode from the room.

"And what does your Excellency think of your relation?" asked the curate, when he was alone with the Prince.

"A terrible-looking fellow! But——" The Prince made a face and a gesture indicating a question in regard to the innkeeper's character.

"Oh, do not be afraid," answered the priest. "He is the most honest man alive."

"Of course," returned the Prince, politely, "you have had many occasions of ascertaining that."

Giovanni, the innkeeper, returned with a bottle of wine and three glasses, which he placed upon the table, and proceeded to fill.

"By the by," said the Prince, "in the excitement I forgot to inquire for your Signora. She is well, I hope?"

"Thank you — she is very well," replied Giovanni, shortly.

"A boy, I have no doubt?"

"A splendid boy," answered the curate. "Sor Giovanni has a little girl, too. He is a very happy man."

"Your health," said the innkeeper, holding up his glass to the light.

"And yours," returned the Prince.

"And of all the Saracinesca family," said the curate, sipping his wine slowly. He rarely got a glass of old Lacrima, and he enjoyed it thoroughly.

"And now," said the Prince, "I must be off. Many thanks for your hospitality. I shall always remember with pleasure the day when I met an unknown relation."

"The Albergo di Napoli will not forget that Prince Sara-

cinesca has been its guest," replied Giovanni politely, a
smile upon his thin lips. He shook hands with both his
guests, and ushered them out to the door with a courteous
bow. Before they had gone twenty yards in the street, the
Prince looked back and caught a last glimpse of Giovanni's
towering figure, standing upon the steps with the bright
light falling upon it from within. He remembered that
impression long.

At the door of his own inn he took leave of the good
curate with many expressions of thanks, and with many
invitations to the Palazzo Saracinesca, in case the old man
ever visited Rome.

"I have never seen Rome, your Excellency," answered
the priest, rather sadly. "I am an old man—I shall never
see it now."

So they parted, and the Prince had a solitary supper of
pigeons and salad in the great dusky hall of the Locanda
del Sole, while his horses were being got ready for the long
night-journey.

The meeting and the whole clearing up of the curious
difficulty had produced a profound impression upon the
old Prince. He had not the slightest doubt but that the
story of the curate was perfectly accurate. It was all so
very probable, too. In the wild times between 1806 and
1815 the last of the Neapolitan branch of the Saracinesca
had disappeared, and the rich and powerful Roman princes
of the name had been quite willing to believe the Marchesi
di San Giacinto extinct. They had not even troubled
themselves to claim the title, for they possessed more than
fifty of their own, and there was no chance of recovering
the San Giacinto estate, already mortgaged, and more than
half squandered at the time of the confiscation. That the
rough soldier of fortune should have hidden himself in his
native country after the return of Ferdinand, his lawful
king, against whom he had fought, was natural enough; as
it was also natural that, with his rough nature, he should
accommodate himself to a peasant's life, and marry a peasant's only daughter, with her broad acres of orange and
olive and vine land; for peasants in the far south were

often rich, and their daughters were generally beautiful—a very different race from the starved tenants of the Roman Campagna.

The Prince decided that the story was perfectly true, and he reflected somewhat bitterly that unless his son had heirs after him, this herculean innkeeper of Aquila was the lawful successor to his own title, and to all the Saracinesca lands. He determined that Giovanni's marriage should not be delayed another day, and with his usual impetuosity he hastened back to Rome, hardly remembering that he had spent the previous night and all that day upon the road, and that he had another twenty-four hours of travel before him.

At dawn his carriage stopped at a little town not far from the papal frontier. Just as the vehicle was starting, a large man, muffled in a huge cloak, from the folds of which protruded the long brown barrel of a rifle, put his head into the window. The Prince started and grasped his revolver, which lay beside him on the seat.

"Good morning, Prince," said the man. "I hope you have slept well?"

"Sor Giovanni!" exclaimed the old gentleman. "Where did you drop from?"

"The roads are not very safe," returned the innkeeper. "So I thought it best to accompany you. Good-bye— *buon viaggio!*"

Before the Prince could answer, the carriage rolled off, the horses springing forward at a gallop. Saracinesca put his head out of the window, but his namesake had disappeared, and he rolled on towards Terni, wondering at the innkeeper's anxiety for his safety.

CHAPTER XXX.

Even old Saracinesca's iron strength was in need of rest when, at the end of forty-eight hours, he again entered his son's rooms, and threw himself upon the great divan.

"How is Corona?" was his first question.

"She is very anxious about you," returned Giovanni, who was himself considerably disturbed.

"We will go and set her mind at rest as soon as I have had something to eat," said his father.

"It is all right, then?" It was just as I said—a namesake?"

"Precisely. Only the namesake happens to be a cousin —the last of the San Giacinto, who keeps an inn in Aquila. I saw him, and shook hands with him."

"Impossible!" exclaimed Giovanni. "They are all extinct——"

"There has been a resurrection," returned the Prince. He told the whole story of his journey, graphically and quickly.

"That is a very extraordinary tale," remarked Giovanni, thoughtfully. "So, if I die without children the innkeeper will be prince."

"Precisely. And now, Giovanni, you must be married next week."

"As soon as you please—to-morrow if you like."

"What shall we do with Del Ferice?" asked the old Prince.

"Ask him to the wedding," answered Giovanni, magnanimously.

"The wedding will have to be a very quiet one, I suppose," remarked his father, thoughtfully. "The year is hardly over——"

"The more quiet the better, provided it is done quickly. Of course we must consult Corona at once."

"Do you suppose I am going to fix the wedding-day without consulting her?" asked the old man. "For heaven's sake order dinner, and let us be quick about it."

The Prince was evidently in a hurry, and moreover, he was tired and very hungry. An hour later, as both the men sat over the coffee in the dining-room, his mood was mellower. A dinner at home has a wonderful effect upon the temper of a man who has travelled and fared badly for eight-and-forty hours.

"Giovannino," said old Saracinesca, "have you any idea what the Cardinal thinks of your marriage?"

"No; and I do not care," answered the younger man. "He once advised me not to marry Donna Tullia. He has not seen me often since then."

"I have an idea that it will please him immensely," said the Prince.

"It would be very much the same if it displeased him."

"Very much the same. Have you seen Corona to-day?"

"Yes—of course," answered Giovanni.

"What is the use of my going with you this evening?" asked his father, suddenly. "I should think you could manage your own affairs without my help."

"I thought that as you have taken so much trouble, you would enjoy telling her the story yourself."

"Do you think I am a vain fool, sir, to be amused by a woman's praise? Nonsense! Go yourself."

"By all means," answered Giovanni. He was used to his father's habit of being quarrelsome over trifles, and he was much too happy to take any notice of it now.

"You are tired," he continued. "I am sure you have a right to be. You must want to go to bed."

"To bed indeed!" growled the old man. "Tired! You think I am good for nothing; I know you do. You look upon me as a doting old cripple. I tell you, boy, I can——"

"For heaven's sake, *padre mio*, do precisely as you are inclined. I never said——"

"Never said what? Why are you always quarrelling with me?" roared his father, who had not lost his temper for two days, and missed his favourite exercise.

"What day shall we fix upon?" asked Giovanni, unmoved.

"Day! Any day. What do I care? Oh!—well, since you speak of it, you might say a week from Sunday. To-day is Friday. But I do not care in the least."

"Very well—if Corona can get ready."

"She shall be ready—she must be ready!" answered the old gentleman, in a tone of conviction. "Why should she not be ready, I would like to know?"

"No reason whatever," said Giovanni, with unusual mildness.

"Of course not. There is never any reason in anything you say, you unreasonable boy."

"Never, of course." Giovanni rose to go, biting his lips to keep down a laugh.

"What the devil do you mean by always agreeing with me, you impertinent scapegrace? And you are laughing, too—laughing at me, sir, as I live! Upon my word!"

Giovanni turned his back and lighted a cigar. Then, without looking round, he walked towards the door.

"Giovannino," called the Prince.

"Well?"

"I feel better now. I wanted to abuse somebody. Look here—wait a moment." He rose quickly, and left the room.

Giovanni sat down and smoked rather impatiently, looking at his watch from time to time. In five minutes his father returned, bringing in his hand an old red morocco case.

"Give it to her with my compliments, my boy," he said. "They are some of your mother's diamonds—just a few of them. She shall have the rest on the wedding-day."

"Thank you," said Giovanni, and pressed his father's hand.

"And give her my love, and say I will call to-morrow at two o'clock," added the Prince, now perfectly serene.

With the diamonds under his arm, Giovanni went out. The sky was clear and frosty, and the stars shone brightly, high up between the tall houses of the narrow street. Giovanni had not ordered a carriage, and seeing how fine the night was, he decided to walk to his destination. It was not eight o'clock, and Corona would have scarcely finished dinner at that hour. He walked slowly. As he emerged into the Piazza di Venezia some one overtook him.

"Good evening, Prince." Giovanni turned, and recognised Anastase Gouache, the Zouave.

"Ah, Gouache—how are you?"

"I am going to pay you a visit," answered the Frenchman.

"I am very sorry—I have just left home," returned Giovanni, in some surprise.

"Not at your house," continued Anastase. "My company is ordered to the mountains. We leave to-morrow morning for Subiaco, and some of us are to be quartered at Saracinesca."

"I hope you will be among the number," said Giovanni. "I shall probably be married next week, and the Duchessa wishes to go at once to the mountains. We shall be delighted to see you."

"Thank you very much. I will not fail to do myself the honour. My homage to Madame la Duchesse. I must turn here. Good night."

"*Au revoir*," said Giovanni, and went on his way.

He found Corona in an inner sitting-room, reading beside a great wood-fire. There were soft shades of lilac mingled with the black of her dress. The year of mourning was past, and so soon as she could she modified her widow's weeds into something less solemnly black. It was impossible to wear funeral robes on the eve of her second marriage; and the world had declared that she had shown an extraordinary degree of virtue in mourning so long for a death which every one considered so highly appropriate. Corona, however, felt differently. To her, her dead husband and the man she now so wholly loved belonged to two totally distinct classes of men. Her love, her marriage with Giovanni, seemed so natural a consequence of her being left alone—so absolutely removed from her former life—that, on the eve of her wedding, she could almost wish that poor old Astrardente were alive to look as her friend upon her new-found happiness.

She welcomed Giovanni with a bright smile. She had not expected him that evening, for he had been with her all the afternoon. She sprang to her feet and came quickly

to meet him. She almost unconsciously took the morocco
case from his hands, not looking at it, and hardly noticing
what she did.

"My father has come back. It is all settled!" cried
Giovanni.

"So soon! He must have flown!" said she, making
him sit down.

"Yes, he has never rested, and he has found out all about
it. It is a most extraordinary story. By the by, he sends
you affectionate messages, and begs you to accept these
diamonds. They were my mother's," he added, his voice
softening and changing. Corona understood his tone, and
perhaps realised, too, how very short the time now was.
She opened the case carefully.

"They are very beautiful; your mother wore them, Giovanni?" She looked lovingly at him, and then bending
down kissed the splendid coronet as though in reverence
of the dead Spanish woman who had borne the man she
loved. Whereat Giovanni stole to her side, and kissed
her own dark hair very tenderly.

"I was to tell you that there are a great many more,"
he said, "which my father will offer you on the wedding-
day." Then he kneeled down beside her, and raising the
crown from its case, set it with both his hands upon her
diadem of braids.

"My princess!" he exclaimed. "How beautiful you
are!" He took the great necklace, and clasped it about
her white throat. "Of course," he said, "you have such
splendid jewels of your own, perhaps you hardly care for
these and the rest. But I like to see you with them—it
makes me feel that you are really mine."

Corona smiled happily, and gently took the coronet from
her head, returning it to its case. She let the necklace
remain about her throat.

"You have not told me about your father's discovery,"
she said, suddenly.

"Yes—I will tell you."

In a few minutes he communicated to her the details of
the journey. She listened with profound interest.

"It is very strange," she said. "And yet it is so very natural."

"You see it is all Del Ferice's doing," said Giovanni. "I suppose it was really an accident in the first place; but he managed to make a great deal of it. It is certainly very amusing to find that the last of.the other branch is an innkeeper in the Abruzzi. However, I daresay we shall never hear of him again. He does not seem inclined to claim his title. Corona *mia*, I have something much more serious to say to you to-night."

"What is it?" she asked, turning her great dark eyes rather wonderingly to his face.

"There is no reason why we should not be married, now——"

"Do you think I ever believed there was?" she asked, reproachfully.

"No, dear. Only — would you mind its being very soon?"

The dark blood rose slowly to her cheek, but she answered without any hesitation. She was too proud to hesitate.

"Whenever you please, Giovanni. Only it must be very quiet, and we will go straight to Saracinesca. If you agree to those two things, it shall be as soon as you please."

"Next week? A week from Sunday?" asked Giovanni, eagerly.

"Yes—a week from Sunday. I would rather not go through the ordeal of a long engagement. I cannot bear to have every one here, congratulating me from morning till night, as they insist upon doing."

"I will send the people out to Saracinesca to-morrow," said Giovanni, in great delight. "They have been at work all winter, making the place respectable."

"Not changing, I hope?" exclaimed Corona, who dearly loved the old grey walls.

"Only repairing the state apartments. By the by, I met Gouache this evening. He is going out with a company of Zouaves to hunt the brigands, if there really are any."

"I hope he will not come near us," answered Corona.

"I want to be all alone with you, Giovanni, for ever so long. Would you not rather be alone for a little while?" she asked, looking up suddenly with a timid smile. "Should I bore you very much?"

It is unnecessary to record Giovanni's answer. If Corona longed to be alone with him in the hills, Giovanni himself desired such a retreat still more. To be out of the world, even for a month, seemed to him the most delightful of prospects, for he was weary of the city, of society, of everything save the woman he was about to marry. Of her he could never tire; he could not imagine that in her company the days would ever seem long, even in old Saracinesca, among the grey rocks of the Sabines. The average man is gregarious, perhaps; but in strong minds there is often a great desire for solitude, or at least for retirement, in the society of one sympathetic soul. The instinct which bids such people leave the world for a time is never permanent, unless they become morbid. It is a natural feeling; and a strong brain gathers strength from communing with itself or with its natural mate. There are few great men who have not at one time or another withdrawn into solitude, and their retreat has generally been succeeded by a period of extraordinary activity. Strong minds are often, at some time or another, exposed to doubt and uncertainty incomprehensible to a smaller intellect—due, indeed, to that very breadth of view which contemplates the same idea from a vast number of sides. To a man so endowed, the casting-vote of some one whom he loves, and with whom he almost unconsciously sympathises, is sometimes necessary to produce action, to direct the faculties, to guide the overflowing flood of his thought into the mill-race of life's work. Without a certain amount of prejudice to determine the resultant of its forces, many a fine intellect would expend its power in burrowing among its own labyrinths, unrecognised, misunderstood, unheard by the working-day world without. For the working-day world never lacks prejudice to direct its working.

For some time Giovanni and Corona talked of their plans for the spring and summer. They would read, they would work togéther at the schemes for uniting and improving their estates; they would build that new road from Astrardente to Saracinesca, concerning which there had been so much discussion during the last year; they would visit every part of their lands together, and inquire into the condition of every peasant; they would especially devote their attention to extending the forest enclosures, in which Giovanni foresaw a source of wealth for his children; above all, they would talk to their hearts' content, and feel, as each day dawned upon their happiness, that they were free to go where they would, without being confronted at every turn by the troublesome duties of an exigent society.

At last the conversation turned again upon recent events, and especially upon the part Del Ferice and Donna Tullia had played in attempting to prevent the marriage. Corona asked what Giovanni intended to do about the matter.

"I do not see that there is much to be done," he answered. "I will go to Donna Tullia to-morrow, and explain that there has been a curious mistake—that I am exceedingly obliged to her for calling my attention to the existence of a distant relative, but that I trust she will not in future interfere in my affairs."

"Do you think she will marry Del Ferice after all?" asked Corona.

"Why not? Of course he gave her the papers. Very possibly he thought they really proved my former marriage. She will perhaps blame him for her failure, but he will defend himself, never fear; he will make her marry him."

"I wish they would marry and go away," said Corona, to whom the very name of Del Ferice was abhorrent, and who detested Donna Tullia almost as heartily. Corona was a very good and noble woman, but she was very far from that saintly superiority which forgets to resent injuries. Her passions were eminently human, and very strong. She had struggled bravely against her overwhelming love for Giovanni; and she had so far got the mastery of herself, that she would have endured to the end if her husband's death had not set her at liberty. Perhaps, too, while she felt the necessity of fighting against that love, she attained for a

time to an elevation of character which would have made
such personal injuries as Donna Tullia could inflict seem
insignificant in comparison with the great struggle she sustained against an even greater evil. But in the realisation
of her freedom, in suddenly giving the rein to her nature,
so long controlled by her resolute will, all passion seemed
to break out at once with renewed force; and the conviction that her anger against her two enemies was perfectly
just and righteous, added fuel to the fire. Her eyes gleamed
fiercely as she spoke of Del Ferice and his bride, and no
punishment seemed too severe for those who had so
treacherously tried to dash the cup of her happiness from
her very lips.

"I wish they would marry," she repeated, "and I wish
the Cardinal would turn them out of Rome the next day."

"That might be done," said Giovanni, who had himself
revolved more than one scheme of vengeance against the
evil-doers. "The trouble is, that the Cardinal despises Del
Ferice and his political dilettanteism. He does not care a
fig whether the fellow remains in Rome or goes away. I
confess it would be a great satisfaction to wring the villain's
neck."

"You must not fight him again, Giovanni," said Corona,
in sudden alarm. "You must not risk your life now—you
know it is mine now." She laid her hand tenderly on his,
and it trembled.

"No, dearest—I certainly will not. But my father is
very angry. I think we may safely leave the treatment of
Del Ferice in his hands. My father is a very sudden and
violent man."

"I know," replied Corona. "He is magnificent when
he is angry. I have no doubt he will settle Del Ferice's
affairs satisfactorily." She laughed almost fiercely. Giovanni looked at her anxiously, yet not without pride, as
he recognised in her strong anger something akin to
himself.

"How fierce you are!" he said, with a smile.

"Have I not cause to be? Have I not cause to wish
these people an evil end? Have they not nearly separated

us ! Nothing is bad enough for them—what is the use of
pretending not to feel ? You are calm, Giovanni ? Perhaps you are much stronger than I am. I do not think
you realise what they meant to do—to separate us—*us!*
As if any torture were bad enough for them ! "

Giovanni had never seen her so thoroughly roused. He
was angry himself, and more than angry, for his cheek
paled, and his stern features grew more hard, while his
voice dropped to a hoarser tone.

" Do not mistake me, Corona," he said. " Do not think
I am indifferent because I am quiet. Del Ferice shall
expiate all some day, and bitterly too."

" Indeed I hope so," answered Corona between her
teeth. Had Giovanni foreseen the long and bitter struggle
he would one day have to endure before that expiation was
complete, he would very likely have renounced his vengeance then and there, for his wife's sake. But we mortals
see but in a glass ; and when the mirror is darkened by
the master-passion of hate, we see not at all. Corona and
Giovanni, united, rich and powerful, might indeed appear
formidable to a wretch like Del Ferice, dependent upon a
system of daily treachery for the very bread he ate. But
in those days the wheel of fortune was beginning to turn,
and far-sighted men prophesied that many an obscure individual would one day be playing the part of a great
personage. Years would still elapse before the change,
but the change would surely come at last.

Giovanni was very thoughtful as he walked home that
night. He was happy, and he had cause to be, for the
long-desired day was at hand. He had nearly attained
the object of his life, and there was now no longer any
obstacle to be overcome. The relief he felt at his father's
return was very great ; for although he had known that
the impediment raised would be soon removed, any impediment whatever was exasperating, and he could not
calculate the trouble that might be caused by the further
machinations of Donna Tullia and her affianced husband.
All difficulties had, however, been overcome by his father's
energetic action, and at once Giovanni felt as though a

2 B

load had fallen from his shoulders, and a veil from his
eyes. He saw himself wedded to Corona in less than a
fortnight, removed from the sphere of society and of all
his troubles, living for a space alone with her in his ancestral home, calling her, at last, his wife. Nevertheless
he was thoughtful, and his expression was not one of un-
mingled gladness, as he threaded the streets on his way
home; for his mind reverted to Del Ferice and to Donna
Tullia, and Corona's fierce look was still before him. He
reflected that she had been nearly as much injured as himself, that her wrath was legitimate, and that it was his
duty to visit her sufferings as well as his own upon the
offenders. His melancholic nature easily fell to brooding
over any evil which was strong enough to break the barrier
of his indifference; and the annoyances which had sprung
originally from so small a cause had grown to gigantic
proportions, and had struck at the very roots of his
happiness.

He had begun by disliking Del Ferice in an indifferent
way whenever he chanced to cross his path. Del Ferice
had resented this haughty indifference as a personal insult,
and had set about injuring Giovanni, attempting to thwart
him whenever he could. Giovanni had caught Del Ferice
in a dastardly trick, and had been so far roused as to take
summary vengeance upon him in the duel which took
place after the Frangipani ball. The wound had entered
into Ugo's soul, and his hatred had grown the faster that
he found no opportunity of revenge. Then, at last, when
Giovanni's happiness had seemed complete, his enemy had
put forward his pretended proof of a former marriage;
knowing well enough that his weapons were not invincible
—were indeed very weak—but unable to resist any longer
the desire for vengeance. Once more Giovanni had triumphed easily, but with victory came the feeling that it
was his turn to punish his adversary. And now there
was a new and powerful motive added to Giovanni's just
resentment, in the anger his future wife felt, and had a
good right to feel, at the treachery which had been practised upon both. It had taken two years to rouse Gio-

vanni to energetic action against one whom he had in turn regarded with indifference, then despised, then honestly disliked, and finally hated. But his hatred had been doubled each time by a greater injury, and was not likely to be easily satisfied. Nothing short of Del Ferice's destruction would be enough, and his destruction must be brought about by legal means.

Giovanni had not far to seek for his weapons. He had long suspected Del Ferice of treasonable practices ; he did not doubt that with small exertion he could find evidence to convict him. He would, then, allow him to marry Donna Tullia; and on the day after the wedding, Del Ferice should be arrested and lodged in the prison of the Holy Office as a political delinquent of the meanest and most dangerous kind—as a political spy. The determination was soon reached. · It did not seem cruel to Giovanni, for he was in a relentless mood ; it would not have seemed cruel to Corona,—Del Ferice had deserved all that, and more also.

So Giovanni went home and slept the sleep of a man who has made up his mind upon an important matter. And in the morning he rose early and communicated his ideas to his father. The result was that they determined for the·present to avoid an interview with Donna Tullia, and to communicate to her by letter the result of old Saracinesca's rapid journey to Aquila.

CHAPTER XXXI.

When Donna Tullia received Saracinesca's note, explaining the existence of a second Giovanni, his pedigree and present circumstances, she almost fainted with disappointment. It seemed to her that she had compromised herself before the world, that all Rome knew the ridiculous part she had played in Del Ferice's comedy, and that her shame would never be forgotten. Suddenly she saw how

she had been led away by her hatred of Giovanni into believing blindly in a foolish tale which ought not to have
deceived a child. So soon as she learned the existence of
a second Giovanni Saracinesca, it seemed to her that she
must have been mad not to foresee such an explanation from
the first. She had been duped, she had been made a cat's-
paw, she had been abominably deceived by Del Ferice, who
had made use of this worthless bribe in order to extort from
her a promise of marriage. She felt very ill, as very vain
people often do when they feel that they have been made
ridiculous. She lay upon the sofa in her little boudoir,
where everything was in the worst possible taste—from the
gaudy velvet carpet and satin furniture to the gilt clock on
the chimney-piece—and she turned red and pale and red
again, and wished she were dead, or in Paris, or anywhere
save in Rome. If she went out she might meet one of the
Saracinesca at any turn of the street, or even Corona herself. How they would bow and smile sweetly at her, enjoying her discomfiture with the polite superiority of people
who cannot be hurt !

And she herself—she could not tell what she should do.
She had announced her engagement to Del Ferice, but she
could not marry him. She had been entrapped into making
him a promise, into swearing a terrible oath; but the Church
did not consider such oaths binding. She would go to
Padre Filippo and ask his advice.

But then, if she went to Padre Filippo, she would have
to confess all she had done, and she was not prepared to do
that. A few weeks would pass, and that time would be
sufficient to mellow and smooth the remembrance of her
revengeful projects into a less questionable shape. No—
she could not confess all that just yet. Surely such an
oath was not binding; at all events, she could not marry
Del Ferice, whether she broke her promise or not. In the
first place, she would send for him and vent her anger upon
him while it was hot.

Accordingly, in the space of three-quarters of an hour,
Ugo appeared, smiling, smooth and persuasive as usual.
Donna Tullia assumed a fine attitude of disdain as she

heard his step outside the door. She intended to impress
him with a full and sudden view of her just anger. He
did not seem much moved, and came forward as usual to
take her hand and kiss it. But she folded her arms and
stared at him with all the contempt she could concentrate
in the gaze of her blue eyes. It was a good comedy. Del
Ferice, who had noticed as soon as he entered the room
that something was wrong, and had already half guessed
the cause, affected to spring back in horror when she refused
to give her hand. His pale face expressed sufficiently well
a mixture of indignation and sorrow at the harsh treatment
he received. Still Donna Tullia's cold eye rested upon him
in a fixed stare.

"What is this? What have I done?" asked Del
Ferice in low tones.

"Can you ask? Wretch! Read that, and understand
what you have done," answered Donna Tullia, making a
step forward and thrusting Saracinesca's letter in his face.

Del Ferice had already seen the handwriting, and knew
what the contents were likely to be. He took the letter
in one hand, and without looking at it, still faced the
angry woman. His brows contracted into a heavy frown,
and his half-closed eyes gazed menacingly at her.

"It will be an evil day for any man who comes between
you and me," he said, in tragic tones.

Donna Tullia laughed harshly, and again drew herself up, watching his face, and expecting to witness his
utter confusion. But she was no match for the actor whom
she had promised to marry. Del Ferice began to read, and
as he read, his frown relaxed; gradually an ugly smile, intended to represent fiendish cunning, stole over his features, and when he had finished, he uttered a cry of triumph.

"Ha!" he said, "I guessed it! I hoped it—and it is
true! He is found at last! The very man—the real
Saracinesca! It is only a matter of time——"

Donna Tullia now stared in unfeigned surprise. Instead of crushing him to the ground as she had expected,
the letter seemed to fill him with boundless delight. He
paced the room in wild excitement, chattering like a mad-

man. In spite of herself, however, her own spirits rose, and her anger against Del Ferice softened. All was perhaps not lost—who could fathom the intricacy of his great schemes? Surely he was not the man to fall a victim to his own machinations.

"Will you please explain your extraordinary satisfaction at this news?" said Madame Mayer. Between her late anger, her revived hopes, and her newly roused curiosity, she was in a terrible state of suspense.

"Explain?" he cried. "Explain what, most adorable of women? Does it not explain itself? Have we not found the Marchese di San Giacinto, the real Saracinesca? Is not that enough?"

"I do not understand——"

Del Ferice was now by her side. He seemed hardly able to control himself for joy. As a matter of fact he was acting, and acting a desperate part too, suggested on the spur of the moment by the risk he ran of losing this woman and her fortune on the very eve of marriage. Now he seized her hand, and drawing her arm through his, led her quickly backwards and forwards, talking fast and earnestly. It would not do to hesitate, for by a moment's appearance of uncertainty all would be lost.

"No; of course you cannot understand the vast importance of this discovery. I must explain. I must enter into historic details, and I am so much overcome by this extraordinary turn of fortune that I can hardly speak. Remove all doubt from your mind, my dear lady, for we have already triumphed. This innkeeper, this Giovanni Saracinesca, this Marchese di San Giacinto, is the lawful and right Prince Saracinesca, the head of the house——"

"What!" screamed Donna Tullia, stopping short, and gripping his arm as in a vice.

"Indeed he is. I suspected it when I first found the signature at Aquila; but the man was gone, with his newly married wife, no one knew whither; and I could not find him, search as I might. He is now returned, and what is more, as this letter says, with all his papers proving his identity. This is how the matter lies. Listen, Tullia *mia.* The old Leone Saracinesca who last bore the title of Marquis——"

"The one mentioned here?" asked Donna Tullia, breathlessly.

"Yes—the one who took service under Murat, under Napoleon. Well, it is perfectly well known that he laid claim to the Roman title, and with perfect justice. Two generations before that, there had been an amicable arrangement—amicable, but totally illegal—whereby the elder brother, who was an unmarried invalid, transferred the Roman estates to his younger brother, who was married and had children, and, in exchange, took the Neapolitan estates and title, which had just fallen back to the main branch by the death of a childless Marchese di San Giacinto. Late in life this old recluse invalid married, contrary to all expectation—certainly contrary to his own previous intentions. However, a child was born—a boy. The old man found himself deprived by his own act of his principality, and the succession turned from his son to the son of his younger brother. He began a negotiation for again obtaining possession of the Roman title—at least so the family tradition goes—but his brother, who was firmly established in Rome, refused to listen to his demands. At this juncture the old man died, being legally, observe, still the head of the family of Saracinesca; his son should have succeeded him. But his wife, the young daughter of an obscure Neapolitan nobleman, was not more than eighteen years of age, and the child was only six months old. People married young in those days. She entered some kind of protest, which, however, was of no avail; and the boy grew up to be called the Marchese di San Giacinto. He learned the story of his birth from his mother, and protested in his turn. He ruined himself in trying to push his suit in the Neapolitan courts; and finally, in the days of Napoleon's success, he took service under Murat, receiving the solemn promise of the Emperor that he should be reinstated in his title. But the Emperor forgot his promise, or did not find it convenient to keep it, having perhaps reasons of his own for not quarrelling with

Pius the Seventh, who protected the Roman Saracinesca.
Then came 1815, the downfall of the Empire, the restora-
tion of Ferdinand IV. in Naples, the confiscation of property from all who had joined the Emperor, and the con-
sequent complete ruin of San Giacinto's hopes. He was
supposed to have been killed, or to have made away with
himself. Saracinesca himself acknowledges that his grand-
son is alive, and possesses all the family papers. Saracinesca himself has discovered, seen, and conversed with
the lawful head of his race, who, by the blessing of heaven
and the assistance of the courts, will before long turn him
out of house and home, and reign in his stead in all the
glories of the Palazzo Saracinesca, Prince of Rome, of the
Holy Roman Empire, grandee of Spain of the first class,
and all the rest of it. Do you wonder I rejoice, now that
I am sure of putting an innkeeper over my enemy's head?
Fancy the humiliation of old Saracinesca, of Giovanni, who
will have to take his wife's title for the sake of respecta-
bility, of the Astrardente herself, when she finds she has
married the penniless son of a penniless pretender!"

Del Ferice knew enough of the Saracinesca's family
history to know that something like what he had so
fluently detailed to Donna Tullia had actually occurred,
and he knew well enough that she would not remember
every detail of his rapidly told tale. Hating the family
as he did, he had diligently sought out all information
about them which he could obtain without gaining access
to their private archives. His ready wit helped him to
string the whole into a singularly plausible story. So
plausible, indeed, that it entirely upset all Donna Tullia's
determination to be angry at Del Ferice, and filled her
with something of the enthusiasm he showed. For himself he hoped that there was enough in his story to do
some palpable injury to the Saracinesca; but his more
immediate object was not to lose Donna Tullia by letting
her feel any disappointment at the discovery recently
made by the old Prince. Donna Tullia listened with
breathless interest until he had finished.

"What a man you are, Ugo! How you turn defeat

into victory! Is it all really true? Do you think we can do it?"

"If I were to die this instant," Del Ferice asseverated, solemnly raising his hand, "it is all perfectly true, so help me God!"

He hoped, for many reasons, that he was not perjuring himself.

"What shall we do, then?" asked Madame Mayer.

"Let them marry first, and then we shall be sure of humiliating them both," he answered. Unconsciously he repeated the very determination which Giovanni had formed against him the night before. "Meanwhile, you and I can consult the lawyers and see how this thing can best be accomplished quickly and surely," he added.

"You will have to send for the innkeeper——"

"I will go and see him. It will not be hard to persuade him to claim his lawful rights."

Del Ferice remained some time in conversation with Donna Tullia. The magnitude of the scheme fascinated her, and instead of thinking of breaking her promise to Ugo as she had intended doing, she so far fell under his influence as to name the wedding-day,—Easter Monday, they agreed, would exactly suit them and their plans. Indeed the idea of refusing to fulfil her engagement had been but the result of a transitory fit of anger; if she had had any fear of making a misalliance in marrying Del Ferice, the way in which the world received the news of the engagement removed all such apprehension from her mind. Del Ferice was already treated with increased respect—the very servants began to call him "Eccellenza," a distinction to which he neither had, nor could ever have, any kind of claim, but which pleased Donna Tullia's vain soul. The position which Ugo had obtained for himself by an assiduous attention to the social claims and prejudices of social lights and oracles, was suddenly assured to him, and rendered tenfold more brilliant by the news of his alliance with Donna Tullia. He excited no jealousies either; for Donna Tullia's peculiarities were of a kind which seemed to have interfered from the first with her matrimonial projects. As a young girl, a relation of the Saracinesca, whom she now so bitterly hated, she should have been regarded as marriageable by any of the young Roman nobles, from Valdarno down. But she had only a small dowry, and she was said to be extravagant—two objections then not so easily overcome as now. Moreover, she was considered to be somewhat flighty; and the social jury decided that when she was married, she would be excellent company, but would make a very poor wife. Almost before they had finished discussing her, however, she had found a husband, in the shape of the wealthy foreign contractor, Mayer, who wanted a wife from a good Roman house, and cared not at all for money. She treated him very well, but was speedily delivered from all her cares by his untimely death. Then, of all her fellow-citizens, none was found save the eccentric old Saracinesca, who believed that she would do for his son; wherein it appeared that Giovanni's father was the man of all others who least understood Giovanni's inclinations. But this match fell to the ground, owing to Giovanni's attachment to Corona, and Madame Mayer was left with the prospect of remaining a widow for the rest of her life, or of marrying a poor man. She chose the latter alternative, and fate threw into her way the cleverest poor man in Rome, as though desiring to compensate her for not having married one of the greatest nobles, in the person of Giovanni. Though she was always a centre of attraction, no one of those she most attracted wanted to marry her, and all expressed their unqualified approval of her ultimate choice. One said she was very generous to marry a penniless gentleman; another remarked that she showed wisdom in choosing a man who was in the way of making himself a good position under the Italian Government; a third observed that he was delighted, because he could enjoy her society without being suspected of wanting to marry her; and all agreed in praising her, and in treating Del Ferice with the respect due to a man highly favoured by fortune.

Donna Tullia named the wedding-day, and her affianced

husband departed in high spirits with himself, with her, and with his scheme. He felt still a little excited, and wanted to be alone. He hardly realised the magnitude of the plot he had undertaken, and needed time to reflect upon it; but with the true instinct of an intriguing genius he recognised at once that his new plan was the thing he had sought for long and ardently, and that it was worth all his other plans put together. Accordingly he went home, and proceeded to devote himself to the study of the question, sending a note to a friend of his—a young lawyer of doubtful reputation, but of brilliant parts, whom he at once selected as his chief counsellor in the important affair he had undertaken.

Before long he heard that the marriage of Don Giovanni Saracinesca to the Duchessa d'Astrardente was to take place the next week, in the chapel of the Palazzo Saracinesca. At least popular report said that the ceremony was to take place there; and that it was to be performed with great privacy was sufficiently evident from the fact that no invitations appeared to have been issued. Society did not fail to comment upon such exclusiveness, and it commented unfavourably, for it felt that it was being deprived of a long-anticipated spectacle. This state of things lasted for two days, when, upon the Sunday morning precisely a week before the wedding, all Rome was surprised by receiving an imposing invitation, setting forth that the marriage would be solemnised in the Basilica of the Santi Apostoli, and that it would be followed by a state reception at the Palazzo Saracinesca. It was soon known that the ceremony would be performed by the Cardinal Archpriest of St Peter's, that the united choirs of St Peter's and of the Sixtine Chapel would sing the High Mass, and that the whole occasion would be one of unprecedented solemnity and magnificence. This was the programme published by the 'Osservatore Romano,' and that newspaper proceeded to pronounce a eulogy of some length and considerable eloquence upon the happy pair. Rome was fairly taken off its feet; and although some malcontents were found, who said it was improper that Corona's marriage should be celebrated with such pomp so soon after her husband's death, the general verdict was that the whole proceeding was eminently proper and becoming to so important an event. So soon as every one had been invited, no one seemed to think it remarkable that the invitations should have been issued so late. It was not generally known that in the short time which elapsed between the naming of the day and the issuing of the cards, there had been several interviews between old Saracinesca and Cardinal Antonelli; that the former had explained Corona's natural wish that the marriage should be private, and that the latter had urged many reasons why so great an event ought to be public; that Saracinesca had said he did not care at all, and was only expressing the views of his son and of the bride; that the Cardinal had repeatedly asseverated that he wished to please everybody; that Corona had refused to be pleased by a public ceremony; and that, finally, the Cardinal, seeing himself hard pressed, had persuaded his Holiness himself to express a wish that the marriage should take place in the most solemn and public manner; wherefore Corona had reluctantly yielded the point, and the matter was arranged. The fact was that the Cardinal wished to make a sort of demonstration of the solidarity of the Roman nobility: it suited his aims to enter into every detail which could add to the importance of the Roman Court, and which could help to impress upon the foreign Ministers the belief that in all matters the Romans as one man would stand by each other and by the Vatican. No one knew better than he how the spectacle of a religious solemnity, at which the whole nobility would attend in a body, must strike the mind of a stranger in Rome; for in Roman ceremonies of that day there was a pomp and magnificence surpassing that found in any other Court of Europe. The whole marriage would become an event of which he could make an impressive use, and he was determined not to forego any advantages which might arise from it; for he was a man who of all men well understood the value of details in maintaining prestige.

But to the two principal actors in the day's doings the

affair was an unmitigated annoyance, and even their own great and true happiness could not lighten the excessive fatigue of the pompous ceremony and of the still more pompous reception which followed it. To describe that day would be to make out a catalogue of gorgeous equipages, gorgeous costumes, gorgeous decorations. Many pages would not suffice to enumerate the cardinals, the dignitaries, the ambassadors, the great nobles, whose magnificent coaches drove up in long file through the Piazza dei Santi Apostoli to the door of the Basilica. The columns of the ' Osservatore Romano ' were full of it for a week afterwards. There was no end to the descriptions of the costumes, from the white satin and diamonds of the bride to the festal uniforms of the Cardinal Archpriest's retinue. Not a personage of importance was overlooked in the newspaper account, not a diplomatist, not an officer of Zouaves. And society read the praise of itself, and found it much more interesting than the praise of the bride and bridegroom; and only one or two people were offended because the paper had made a mistake in naming the colours of the hammer-cloths upon their coaches: so that the affair was a great success.

But when at last the sun was low and the guests had departed from the Palazzo Saracinesca, Corona and Giovanni got into their travelling carriage under the great dark archway, and sighed a sigh of infinite relief. The old Prince put his arms tenderly around his new daughter and kissed her; and for the second time in the course of this history, it is to be recorded that two tears stole silently down his brown cheeks to his grey beard. Then he embraced Giovanni, whose face was pale and earnest.

"This is not the end of our living together, *padre mio*," he said. "We shall expect you before long at Saracinesca."

"Yes, my boy," returned the old man; "I will come and see you after Easter. But do not stay if it is too cold; I have a little business to attend to in Rome before I join you," he added, with a grim smile.

"I know," replied Giovanni, a savage light in his

black eyes.   "If you need help, send to me, or come yourself."

"No fear of that, Giovannino; I have got a terrible helper.   Now, be off.   The guards are growing impatient."

"Good-bye.   God bless you, *padre mio!*"

"God bless you both!"   So they drove off, and left old Saracinesca standing bareheaded and alone under the dim archway of his ancestral palace.   The great carriage rolled out, and the guard of mounted gendarmes, which the Cardinal had insisted upon sending with the young couple, half out of compliment, half for safety, fell in behind, and trotted down the narrow street, with a deafening clatter of hoofs and clang of scabbards.

But Giovanni held Corona's hand in his, and both were silent for a time.   Then they rolled under the low vault of the Porta San Lorenzo and out into the evening sunlight of the Campagna beyond.

"God be praised that it has come at last!" said Giovanni.

"Yes, it has come," answered Corona, her strong white fingers closing upon his brown hand almost convulsively; "and, come what may, you are mine, Giovanni, until we die!"

There was something fierce in the way those two loved each other; for they had fought many fights before they were united, and had overcome themselves, each alone, before they had overcome other obstacles together.

Relays of horses awaited them on their way, and relays of mounted guards.   Late that night they reached Saracinesca, all ablaze with torches and lanterns; and the young men took the horses from the coach and yoked themselves to it with ropes, and dragged the cumbrous carriage up the last hill with furious speed, shouting and singing like madmen in the cold mountain air.   Up the steep they rushed, and under the grand old gateway, made as bright as day with flaming torches; and then there went up a shout that struck the old vaults like a wild chord of fierce music, and Corona knew that her journey was ended.

So it was that Giovanni Saracinesca brought home his bride.

CHAPTER XXXII.

The old Prince was left alone, as he had often been left before, when Giovanni was gone to the ends of the earth in pursuit of his amusements. On such occasions old Saracinesca frequently packed up his traps and followed his son's example; but he rarely went further than Paris, where he had many friends, and where he generally succeeded in finding consolation for his solitude.

Now, however, he felt more than usually lonely. Giovanni had not gone far, it is true, for with good horses it was scarcely more than eight hours to the castle; but, for the first time in his life, old Saracinesca felt that if he had suddenly determined to follow his son, he would not be welcome. The boy was married at last, and must be left in peace for a few days with his bride. With the contrariety natural to him, old Saracinesca no sooner felt that his son was gone than he experienced the most ardent desire to be with him. He had often seen Giovanni leave the house at twenty-four hours' notice on his way to some distant capital, and had not cared to accompany him, simply because he knew he might do so if he pleased; but now he felt that some one else had taken his place, and that, for a time at least, he was forcibly excluded from Giovanni's society. It is very likely that but for the business which detained him in Rome he would have astonished the happy pair by riding into the gateway of the old castle on the day after the wedding: that business, however, was urgent, secret, and, moreover, very congenial to the old man's present temper.

He had discussed the matter fully with Giovanni, and
they had agreed upon the course to be pursued. There
was, nevertheless, much to be done before the end they
both so earnestly desired could be attained. It seemed a
simple plan to go to Cardinal Antonelli and to demand the
arrest of Del Ferice for his misdeeds; but as yet those
misdeeds were undefined, and it was necessary to define
them. The Cardinal rarely resorted to such measures except when the case was urgent, and Saracinesca knew perfectly well that it would be hard to prove anything more
serious against Del Ferice than the crime of joining in the
silly talk of Valdarno and his set. Giovanni had told his
father plainly that he was sure Del Ferice derived his living from some illicit source, but he was wholly unable to
show what that source was. Most people believed the
story that Del Ferice had inherited money from an obscure relative; most people thought he was clever and
astute, but were so far deceived by his frank and un-
affected manner as to feel sure that he always said everything that came into his head; most people are so much
delighted when an unusually clever man deigns to talk to
them, that they cannot, for vanity's sake, suspect him of
deceiving them. Saracinesca did not doubt that the mere
statement of his own belief in regard to Del Ferice would
have considerable weight with the Cardinal, for he was
used to power of a certain kind, and was accustomed to
see his judgment treated with deference; but he knew the
Cardinal to be a cautious man, hating despotic measures,
because by his use of them he had made himself so bitterly hated—loth always to do by force what might be
accomplished by skill, and in the end far more likely to
attempt the conversion of Del Ferice to the reactionary
view, than to order his expulsion because his views were
over liberal. Even if old Saracinesca had possessed a
vastly greater diplomatic instinct than he did, coupled
with an unscrupulous mendacity which he certainly had
not, he would have found it hard to persuade the Cardinal
against his will; but Saracinesca was, of all men, a man
violent in action and averse to reflection before or after the

fact. That he should ultimately be revenged upon Del Ferice and Donna Tullia for the part they had lately played, was a matter which it never entered his head to doubt; but when he endeavoured to find means which should persuade the Cardinal to assist him, he seemed fenced in on all sides by impossibilities. One thing only helped him—namely, the conviction that if the statesman could be induced to examine Del Ferice's conduct seriously, the latter would prove to be not only an enemy to the State, but a bitter enemy to the Cardinal himself.

The more Saracinesca thought of the matter, the more convinced he was that he should go boldly to the Cardinal and state his belief that Del Ferice was a dangerous traitor, who ought to be summarily dealt with. If the Cardinal argued the case, the Prince would asseverate, after his manner, and some sort of result was sure to follow. As he thus determined upon his course, his doubts seemed to vanish, as they generally do in the mind of a strong man, when action becomes imminent, and the confidence the old man had exhibited to his son very soon became genuine. It was almost intolerable to have to wait so long, however, before doing anything. Giovanni and he had decided to allow Del Ferice's marriage to take place before producing the explosion, in order the more certainly to strike both the offenders; now it seemed best to strike at once. Supposing, he argued with himself, that Donna Tullia and her husband chose to leave Rome for Paris the day after their wedding, half the triumph would be lost; for half the triumph was to consist in Del Ferice's being imprisoned for a spy in Rome, whereas if he once crossed the frontier, he could at most be forbidden to return, which would be but a small satisfaction to Saracinesca, or to Giovanni.

A week passed by, and the gaiety of Carnival was again at its height; and again a week elapsed, and Lent was come. Saracinesca went everywhere and saw everybody as usual, and then after Ash-Wednesday he occasionally showed himself at some of those quiet evening receptions which his son so much detested. But he was restless and discontented. He longed to begin the fight, and could not sleep for thinking of it. Like Giovanni, he was strong and revengeful; but Giovanni had from his mother a certain slowness of temperament, which often deterred him from action just long enough to give him time for reflection, whereas the father, when roused, and he was roused easily, loved to strike at once. It chanced one evening, in a great house, that Saracinesca came upon the Cardinal standing alone in an outer room. He was on his way into the reception; but he had stopped, attracted by a beautiful crystal cup of old workmanship, which stood, among other objects of the kind, upon a marble table in one of the drawing-rooms through which he had to pass. The cup itself, of deeply carved rock crystal, was set in chiselled silver, and if not the work of Cellini himself, must have been made by one of his pupils. Saracinesca stopped by the great man's side.

"Good evening, Eminence," he said.

"Good evening, Prince," returned the Cardinal, who recognised Saracinesca's voice without looking up. "Have you ever seen this marvellous piece of work? I have been admiring it for a quarter of an hour." He loved all objects of the kind, and understood them with rare knowledge.

"It is indeed exceedingly beautiful," answered Saracinesca, who longed to take advantage of the opportunity of speaking to Cardinal Antonelli upon the subject nearest to his heart.

"Yes—yes," returned the Cardinal rather vaguely, and made as though he would go on. He saw from Saracinesca's commonplace praise, that he knew nothing of the subject. The old Prince saw his opportunity slipping from him, and lost his head. He did not recollect that he could see the Cardinal alone whenever he pleased, by merely asking for an interview. Fate had thrust the Cardinal in his path, and fate was responsible.

"If your Eminence will allow me, I would like a word with you," he said suddenly.

"As many as you please," answered the statesman, blandly. "Let us sit down in that corner—no one will disturb us for a while."

He seemed unusually affable, as he sat himself down by Saracinesca's side, gathering the skirt of his scarlet mantle across his knee, and folding his delicate hands together in an attitude of restful attention.

"You know, I daresay, a certain Del Ferice, Eminence?" began the Prince.

"Very well—the *deus ex machinâ* who has appeared to carry off Donna Tullia Mayer. Yes, I know him."

"Precisely, and they will match very well together; the world cannot help applauding the union of the flesh and the devil."

The Cardinal smiled.

"The metaphor is apt," he said; "but what about them?"

"I will tell you in two words," replied Saracinesca. "Del Ferice is a scoundrel of the first water——"

"A jewel among scoundrels," interrupted the Cardinal, "for being a scoundrel he is yet harmless—a stage villain."

"I believe your Eminence is deceived in him."

"That may easily be," answered the statesman. "I am much more often deceived than people imagine." He spoke very mildly, but his small black eyes turned keenly upon Saracinesca. "What has he been doing?" he asked, after a short pause.

"He has been trying to do a great deal of harm to my son and to my son's wife. I suspect him strongly of doing harm to you."

Whether Saracinesca was strictly honest in saying "you" to the Cardinal, when he meant the whole State as represented by the prime minister, is a matter not easily decided. There is a Latin saying, to the effect that a man who is feared by many should himself fear many, and the saying is true. The Cardinal was personally a brave man; but he knew his danger, and the memory of the murdered Rossi was fresh in his mind. Nevertheless, he smiled blandly as he answered—

"That is rather vague, my friend. How is he doing me harm, if I may ask?"

"I argue in this way," returned Saracinesca, thus pressed.

"The fellow found a most ingenious way of attacking my son—he searched the whole country till he found that a man called Giovanni Saracinesca had been married some time ago in Aquila. He copied the certificates, and produced them as pretended proof that my son was already married. If I had not found the man myself, there would have been trouble. Now besides this, Del Ferice is known to hold Liberal views——"

"Of the feeblest kind," interrupted the statesman, who nevertheless became very grave.

"Those he exhibits are of the feeblest kind, and he takes no trouble to hide them. But a fellow so ingenious as to imagine the scheme he practised against us is not a fool."

"I understand, my good friend," said the Cardinal. "You have been injured by this fellow, and you would like me to revenge the injury by locking him up. Is that it?"

"Precisely," answered Saracinesca, laughing at his own simplicity. "I might as well have said so from the first."

"Much better. You would make a poor diplomatist, Prince. But what in the world shall I gain by revenging your wrongs upon that creature?"

"Nothing—unless when you have taken the trouble to examine his conduct, you find that he is really dangerous. In that case your Eminence will be obliged to look to your own safety. If you find him innocent, you will let him go."

"And in that case, what will you do?" asked the Cardinal with a smile.

"I will cut his throat," answered Saracinesca, unmoved.

"Murder him?"

"No—call him out and kill him like a gentleman, which is a great deal better than he deserves."

"I have no doubt you would," said the Cardinal, gravely. "I think your proposition reasonable, however. If this man is really dangerous, I will look to him myself. But I must really beg you not to do anything rash. I have determined that this duelling shall stop, and I warn you that neither you nor any one else will escape imprisonment if you are involved in any more of these personal encounters."

Saracinesca suppressed a smile at the Cardinal's threat; but he perceived that he had gained his point, and was pleased accordingly. He had, he felt sure, sown in the statesman's mind a germ of suspicion which would before long bring forth fruit. In those days danger was plentiful, and people could not afford to overlook it, no matter in what form it presented itself, least of all such people as the Cardinal himself, who, while sustaining an unequal combat against superior forces outside the State, felt that his every step was encompassed by perils from within. That he had long despised Del Ferice as an idle chatterer did not prevent him from understanding that he might have been deceived, as Saracinesca suggested. He had caused Ugo to be watched, it is true, but only from time to time, and by men whose only duty was to follow him and to see whether he frequented suspicious society. The little nest of talkers at Gouache's studio in the Via San Basilio was soon discovered, and proved to be harmless enough. Del Ferice was then allowed to go on his way unobserved. But the half-dozen words in which Saracinesca had described Ugo's scheme for hindering Giovanni's marriage had set the Cardinal thinking, and the Cardinal seldom wasted time in thinking in vain. His interview with Saracinesca ended very soon, and the Prince and the statesman entered the crowded drawing-room and mixed in the throng. It was long before they met again in private.

The Cardinal on the following day gave orders that Del Ferice's letters were to be stopped—by no means an uncommon proceeding in those times, nor so rare in our own day as is supposed. The post-office was then in the hands of a private individual so far as all management was concerned, and the Cardinal's word was law. Del Ferice's letters were regularly opened and examined.

The first thing that was discovered was that they frequently contained money, generally in the shape of small drafts on London signed by a Florentine banker, and that the envelopes which contained money never contained anything else. They were all posted in Florence. With regard to the letters, they appeared to be very innocent communications from all sorts of people, rarely referring to politics, and then only in the most general terms. If Del Ferice had expected to have his correspondence examined, he could not have arranged matters better for his own safety. To trace the drafts to the person who sent them was not an easy business; it was impossible to introduce a spy into the banking-house in Florence, and among the many drafts daily bought and sold, it was almost impossible to identify, without the aid of the banker's books, the person who chanced to buy any particular one. The addresses were, it is true, uniformly written by the same hand; but the writing was in no way peculiar, and was certainly not that of any prominent person whose autograph the Cardinal possessed.

The next step was to get possession of some letter written by Del Ferice himself, and, if possible, to intercept everything he wrote. But although the letters containing the drafts were regularly opened, and, after having been examined and sealed again, were regularly transmitted through the post-office to Ugo's address, the expert persons set to catch the letters he himself wrote were obliged to own, after three weeks' careful watching, that he never seemed to write any letters at all, and that he certainly never posted any. They acknowledged their failure to the Cardinal with timid anxiety, expecting to be reprimanded for their carelessness. But the Cardinal merely told them not to relax their attention, and dismissed them with a bland smile. He knew, now, that he was on the track of mischief; for a man who never writes any letters at all, while he receives many, might reasonably be suspected of having a secret post-office of his own. For some days Del Ferice's movements were narrowly watched, but with no result whatever. Then the Cardinal sent for the police register of the district where Del Ferice lived, and in which the name, nationality, and residence of every individual in the " Rione " or quarter were carefully inscribed, as they still are.

Running his eye down the list, the Cardinal came upon the name of " Temistocle Fattorusso, of Naples,

servant to Ugo dei Conti del Ferice:" an idea struck
him.

"His servant is a Neapolitan," he reflected. "He probably sends his letters by way of Naples."

Accordingly Temistocle was watched instead of his
master. It was found that he frequented the society of
other Neapolitans, and especially that he was in the habit
of going from time to time to the Ripa Grande, the port
of the Tiber, where he seemed to have numerous acquaintances among the Neapolitan boatmen who constantly came
up the coast in their "martingane"—heavy, sea-going,
lateen-rigged vessels, bringing cargoes of oranges and
lemons to the Roman market. The mystery was now
solved. One day Temistocle was actually seen giving a
letter into the hands of a huge fellow in a red woollen cap.
The *sbirro* who saw him do it marked the sailor and his
vessel, and never lost sight of him till he hoisted his jib
and floated away down stream. Then the spy took horse
and galloped down to Fiumicino, where he waited for the
little vessel, boarded her from a boat, escorted by a couple
of gendarmes, and had no difficulty in taking the letter
from the terrified seaman, who was glad enough to escape
without detention. During the next fortnight several
letters were stopped in this way, carried by different sailors,
and the whole correspondence went straight to the Cardinal.
It was not often that he troubled himself to play the detective in person, but when he did so, he was not easily
baffled. And now he observed that about a week after the
interception of the first letter the small drafts which used
to come so frequently to Del Ferice's address from Florence
suddenly ceased, proving beyond a doubt that each letter
was paid for according to its value so soon as it was received.

With regard to the contents of these epistles little need
be said. So sure was Del Ferice of his means of transmission that he did not even use a cipher, though he, of
course, never signed any of his writings. The matter was
invariably a detailed chronicle of Roman sayings and
doings, a record as minute as Del Ferice could make it,

of everything that took place, and even the Cardinal himself was astonished at the accuracy of the information thus
conveyed.   His own appearances in public—the names of
those with whom he talked—even fragments of his conversation—were given with annoying exactness.   The statesman
learned with infinite disgust that he had for some time
past been subjected to a system of espionage at least as
complete as any of his own invention; and, what was still
more annoying to his vanity, the spy was the man of all
others whom he had most despised, calling him harmless
and weak, because he cunningly affected weakness.   Where
or how Del Ferice procured so much information the
Cardinal cared little enough, for he determined there and
then that he should procure no more.   That there were
other traitors in the camp was more than likely, and that
they had aided Del Ferice with their counsels; but though
by prolonging the situation it might be possible to track
them down, such delay would be valuable to enemies abroad.
Moreover, if Del Ferice began to find out, as he soon must,
that his private correspondence was being overhauled at the
Vatican, he was not a man to hesitate about attempting his
escape; and he would certainly not be an easy man to catch,
if he could once succeed in putting a few miles of Campagna between himself and Rome.   There was no knowing
what disguise he might not find in which to slip over the
frontier; and indeed, as he afterwards proved, he was well
prepared for such an emergency.

The Cardinal did not hesitate.   He had just received
the fourth letter, and if he waited any longer Del Ferice
would take alarm, and slip through his fingers.   He wrote
with his own hand a note to the chief of police, ordering
the immediate arrest of Ugo dei Conti del Ferice, with instructions that he should be taken in his own house, without any publicity, and conveyed in a private carriage to the
Sant' Uffizio by men in plain clothes.   It was six o'clock
in the evening when he wrote the order, and delivered it to
his private servant to be taken to its destination.   The
man lost no time, and within twenty minutes the chief of
police was in possession of his orders, which he hastened to

execute with all possible speed. Before seven o'clock two respectable-looking citizens were seated in the chief's own carriage, driving rapidly in the direction of Del Ferice's house. In less than half an hour the man who had caused so much trouble would be safely lodged in the prisons of the Holy Office, to be judged for his sins as a political spy. In a fortnight he was to have been married to Donna Tullia Mayer,—and her trousseau had just arrived from Paris.

It can hardly be said that the Cardinal's conduct was unjustifiable, though many will say that Del Ferice's secret doings were easily defensible on the ground of his patriotism. Cardinal Antonelli had precisely defined the situation in his talk with Anastase Gouache by saying that the temporal power was driven to bay. To all appearances Europe was at peace, but as a matter of fact the peace was but an armed neutrality. An amount of interest was concentrated upon the situation of the Papal States which has rarely been excited by events of much greater apparent importance than the occupation of a small principality by foreign troops. All Europe was arming. In a few months Austria was to sustain one of the most sudden and overwhelming defeats recorded in military history. In a few years the greatest military power in the world was to be overtaken by an even more appalling disaster. And these events, then close at hand, were to deal the death-blow to papal independence. The papacy was driven to bay, and those to whom the last defence was confided were certainly justified in employing every means in their power for strengthening their position. That Rome herself was riddled with rotten conspiracies, and turned into a hunting-ground for political spies, while the support she received from Louis Napoleon had been already partially withdrawn, proves only how hard was the task of that man who, against such odds, maintained so gallant a fight. It is no wonder that he hunted down spies, and signed orders forcing suspicious characters to leave the city at a day's notice; for the city was practically in a state of siege, and any relaxation of the iron discipline by which the great Cardinal governed would at any moment in those twenty years have proved disastrous. He was hated and feared; more than once he was in imminent danger of his life, but he did his duty in his post. Had his authority fallen, it is impossible to say what evil might have ensued to the city and its inhabitants—evils vastly more to be feared than the entrance of an orderly Italian army through the Porta Pia. For the recollections of Count Rossi's murder, and of the short and lawless Republic of 1848, were fresh in the minds of the people, and before they had faded there were dangerous rumours of a rising even less truly Republican in theory, and far more fatal in the practical social anarchy which must have resulted from its success. Giuseppe Mazzini had survived his arch-enemy, the great Cavour, and his influence was incalculable.

But my business is not to write the history of those uncertain days, though no one who considers the social life of Rome, either then or now, can afford to overlook the influence of political events upon the everyday doings of men and women. We must follow the private carriage containing the two respectable citizens who were on their way to Del Ferice's house.

CHAPTER XXXIII.

Now it chanced that Del Ferice was not at home at the hour when the carriage containing the detectives drew up at his door. Indeed he was rarely to be found at that time, for when he was not engaged elsewhere, he dined with Donna Tullia and her old countess, accompanying them afterwards to any of the quiet Lenten receptions to which they desired to go. Temistocle was also out, for it was his hour for supper, a meal which he generally ate in a small *osteria* opposite his master's lodging. There he sat now, finishing his dish of beans and oil, and debating whether he should indulge himself in another *mezza fogli-*

etta of his favourite white wine. He was installed upon
the wooden bench against the wall, behind the narrow
table on which was spread a dirty napkin with the remains
of his unctuous meal. The light from the solitary oil-
lamp that hung from the black ceiling was not brilliant,
and he could see well enough through the panes of the
glass door that the carriage which had just stopped on the
opposite side of the street was not a cab. Suspecting that
some one had called at that unusual hour in search of his
master, he rose from his seat and went out.

He stood looking at the carriage. It did not please him.
It had that peculiar look which used to mark the equipages of the Vatican, and which to this day distinguishes
them from all others in the eyes of a born Roman. The
vehicle was of rather antiquated shape, the horses were
black, the coachman wore a plain black coat, with a somewhat old-fashioned hat; withal, the turnout was respectable
enough, and well kept. But it did not please Temistocle.
Drawing his hat over his eyes, he passed behind it, and
having ascertained that the occupants, if there had been
any, had already entered the house, he himself went in.
The narrow staircase was dimly lighted by small oil-lamps.
Temistocle ascended the steps on tiptoe, for he could already
hear the men ringing the bell, and talking together in a low
voice. The Neapolitan crept nearer. Again and again the
bell was rung, and the men began to grow impatient.

" He has escaped," said one angrily.

" Perhaps—or he has gone out to dinner—much more
likely."

" We had better go away and come later," suggested the
first.

" He is sure to come home. We had better wait. The
orders are to take him in his lodgings."

" We might go into the *osteria* opposite and drink a
foglietta."

" No," said the other, who seemed to be the one in
authority. " We must wait here, if we wait till midnight.
Those are the orders."

The second detective grumbled something not clearly

audible, and silence ensued. But Temistocle had heard
quite enough. He was a quick-witted fellow, as has been
seen, much more anxious for his own interests than for his
master's, though he had hitherto found it easy to consult
both. Indeed, in a certain way he was faithful to Del
Ferice, and admired him as a soldier admires his general.
The resolution he now formed did honour to his loyalty to
Ugo and to his thievish instincts. He determined to save
his master if he could, and to rob him at his leisure afterwards. If Del Ferice failed to escape, he would probably
reward Temistocle for having done his best to help him;
if, on the other hand, he got away, Temistocle had the key
of his lodgings, and would help himself. But there was
one difficulty in the way. Del Ferice was in evening dress
at the house of Donna Tullia. In such a costume he
would have no chance of passing the gates, which in those
days were closed and guarded all night. Del Ferice was a
cautious man, and, like many another in those days, kept
in his rooms a couple of disguises which might serve if he
was hard pressed. His ready money he always carried
with him, because he frequently went into the club before
coming home, and played a game of écarté, in which he
was usually lucky. The question was how to enter the
lodgings, to get possession of the necessary clothes, and
to go out again, without exciting the suspicions of the
detectives.

Temistocle's mind was soon made up. He crept softly
down the stairs, so as not to appear to have been too near,
and then, making as much noise as he could, ascended
boldly, drawing the key of the lodging from his pocket as
he reached the landing where the two men stood under the
little oil-lamp.

"*Buona sera, signori,*" he said, politely, thrusting the
key into the lock without hesitation. "Did you wish to
see the Conte del Ferice?"

"Yes," answered the elder man, affecting an urbane
manner. "Is the Count at home?"

"I do not think so," returned the Neapolitan. "But
I will see. Come in, gentlemen. He will not be long—

sempre verso quest'ora—he always comes home about this time."

"Thank you," said the detective. "If you will allow us to wait——"

"*Altro*—what? Should I leave the *padrone's* friends on the stairs? Come in, gentlemen—sit down. It is dark. I will light the lamp." And striking a match, Temistocle lit a couple of candles and placed them upon the table of the small sitting-room. The two men sat down, holding their hats upon their knees.

"If you will excuse me," said Temistocle, "I will go and make the signore's coffee. He dines at the restaurant, and always comes home for his coffee. Perhaps the signori will also take a cup? It is the same to make three as one."

But the men thanked Temistocle, and said they wanted none, which was just as well, since Temistocle had no idea of giving them any. He retired, however, to the small kitchen which belongs to every Roman lodging, and made a great clattering with the coffee-pot. Presently he slipped into Del Ferice's bedroom, and extracted from a dark corner a shabby black bag, which he took back with him into the kitchen. From the kitchen window ran the usual iron wire to the well in the small court, bearing an iron traveller with a rope for drawing water. Temistocle, clattering loudly, hooked the bag to the traveller and let it run down noisily; then he tied the rope and went out. He had carefully closed the door of the sitting-room, but he had been careful to leave the door which opened upon the stairs unlatched. He crept noiselessly out, and leaving the door still open, rushed down-stairs, turned into the little court, unhooked his bag from the rope, and taking it in his hand, passed quietly out into the street. The coachman was dozing upon the box of the carriage which still waited before the door, and would not have noticed Temistocle had he been awake. In a moment more the Neapolitan was beyond pursuit. In the Piazza di Spagna he hailed a cab and drove rapidly to Donna Tullia's house, where he paid the man and sent him away. The servants knew him well enough, for scarcely a day passed without his bringing some note or message from his master to Madame Mayer. He sent in to say that he must speak to his master on business. Del Ferice came out hastily in considerable agitation, which was by no means diminished by the sight of the well-known shabby black bag.

Temistocle glanced round the hall to see that they were alone.

"The *forza*—the police," he whispered, "are in the house, Eccellenza. Here is the bag. Save yourself, for the love of heaven!"

Del Ferice turned ghastly pale, and his face twitched nervously.

"But——" he began, and then staggering back leaned against the wall.

"Quick—fly!" urged Temistocle, shaking him roughly by the arm. "It is the Holy Office—you have time. I told them you would be back, and they are waiting quietly —they will wait all night. Here is your overcoat," he added, almost forcing his master into the garment—"and your hat—here! Come along, there is no time to lose. I will take you to a place where you can dress."

Del Ferice submitted almost blindly. By especial good fortune the footman did not come out into the hall. Donna Tullia and her guests had finished dinner, and the servants had retired to theirs; indeed the footman had complained to Temistocle of being called away from his meal to open the door. The Neapolitan pushed his master out upon the stairs, urging him to use all speed. As the two men hurried along the dark street they conversed in low tones. Del Ferice was trembling in every joint.

"But Donna Tullia," he almost whined. "I cannot leave her so—she must know——"

"Save your own skin from the Holy Office, master," answered Temistocle, dragging him along as fast as he could. "I will go back and tell your lady, never fear. She will leave Rome to-morrow. Of course you will go to Naples. She will follow you. She will be there before you."

Del Ferice mumbled an unintelligible answer. His

teeth were chattering with cold and fear ; but as he began to realise his extreme peril, terror lent wings to his heels, and he almost outstripped the nimble Temistocle in the race for safety. They reached at last the ruined part of the city near the Porta Maggiore, and in the shadow of the deep archway where the road branches to the right towards Santa Croce in Gerusalemme, Temistocle halted.

"Here," he said, shortly. Del Ferice said never a word, but began to undress himself in the dark. It was a gloomy and lowering night, the roads were muddy, and from time to time a few drops of cold rain fell silently, portending a coming storm. In a few moments the transformation was complete, and Del Ferice stood by his servant's side in the shabby brown cowl and rope-girdle of a Capuchin monk.

"Now comes the hard part," said Temistocle, producing a razor and a pair of scissors from the bottom of the bag. Del Ferice had too often contemplated the possibility of flight to have omitted so important a detail.

"You cannot see—you will cut my throat," he murmured plaintively.

But the fellow was equal to the emergency. Retiring deeper into the recess of the arch, he lit a cigar, and holding it between his teeth, puffed violently at it, producing a feeble light by which he could just see his master's face. He was in the habit of shaving him, and had no difficulty in removing the fair moustache from his upper lip. Then, making him hold his head down, and puffing harder than ever, he cropped his thin hair, and managed to make a tolerably respectable tonsure. But the whole operation had consumed half an hour at the least, and Del Ferice was trembling still. Temistocle thrust the clothes into his bag.

"My watch !" objected the unfortunate man, "and my pearl studs—give them to me—what? You villain ! you thief ! you——"

"No *chiacchiere*, no talk, *padrone*," interrupted Temistocle, snapping the lock of the bag. "If you chance to be searched, it would ill become a mendicant friar to be carry-

ing gold watches and pearl studs. I will give them to
Donna Tullia this very evening. You have money—you
can say you are taking that to your convent."

"Swear to give the watch to Donna Tullia," said Del
Ferice. Whereupon Temistocle swore a terrible oath, which
he did not fail to break, of course. But his master had to
be satisfied, and when all was completed the two parted
company.

"I will ask Donna Tullia to take me to Naples on her
passport," said the Neapolitan.

"Take care of my things, Temistocle. Burn all the
papers if you can—though I suppose the *sbirri* have got
them by this time. Bring my clothes—if you steal anything, remember there are knives in Rome, and I know
where to write to have them used." Whereat Temistocle
broke into a torrent of protestations. How could his
master think that, after saving him at such risk, his faithful servant would plunder him?

"Well," said Del Ferice, thoughtfully, "you are a great
scoundrel, you know. But you have saved me, as you say.
There is a scudo for you."

Temistocle never refused anything. He took the coin,
kissed his master's hand as a final exhibition of servility,
and turned back towards the city without another word.
Del Ferice shuddered, and drew his heavy cowl over his
head as he began to walk quickly towards the Porta Maggiore. Then he took the inside road, skirting the walls
through the mud to the Porta San Lorenzo. He was perfectly safe in his disguise. He had dined abundantly, he
had money in his pocket, and he had escaped the clutches
of the Holy Office. A barefooted friar might walk for
days unchallenged through the Roman Campagna and the
neighbouring hills, and it was not far to the south-eastern
frontier. He did not know the way beyond Tivoli, but he
could inquire without exciting the least suspicion. There
are few disguises more complete than the garb of a Capuchin monk, and Del Ferice had long contemplated playing
the part, for it was one which eminently suited him. His
face, much thinner now than formerly, was yet naturally

round, and without his moustache would certainly pass for a harmless clerical visage. He had received an excellent education, and knew vastly more Latin than the majority of mendicant monks. As a good Roman he was well acquainted with every convent in the city, and knew the names of all the chief dignitaries of the Capuchin order. When a lad he had frequently served at Mass, and was acquainted with most of the ordinary details of monastic life. The worst that could happen to him might be to be called upon in the course of his travels to hear the dying confession of some poor wretch who had been stabbed after a game of *mora*. His case was altogether not so bad as might seem, considering the far greater evils he had escaped.

At the Porta San Lorenzo the gates were closed as usual, but the dozing watchman let Del Ferice out of the small door without remark. Any one might leave the city, though it required a pass to gain admittance during the night. The heavily-ironed oak clanged behind the fugitive, and he breathed more freely as he stepped upon the road to Tivoli. In an hour he had crossed the Ponte Mammolo, shuddering as he looked down through the deep gloom at the white foam of the Teverone, swollen with the winter rains. But the fear of the Holy Office was behind him, and he hurried on his lonely way, walking painfully in the sandals he had been obliged to put on [to] complete his disguise, sinking occasionally ankle-deep [in] mud, and then trudging over a long stretch of broken ones where the road had been mended; but not noticing [o]r caring for pain and fatigue, while he felt that every [m]inute took him nearer to the frontier hills where he [w]ould be safe from pursuit. And so he toiled on, till he [s]melled the fetid air of the sulphur springs full fourteen [m]iles from Rome; and at last, as the road began to rise [to]wards Hadrian's Villa, he sat down upon a stone by the [w]ayside to rest a little. He had walked five hours through [th]e darkness, seeing but a few yards of the broad road [be]fore him as he went. He was weary and footsore, and [th]e night was growing wilder with gathering wind and

2 D

rain as the storm swept down the mountains and through
the deep gorge of Tivoli on its way to the desolate black
Campagna. He felt that if he did not die of exposure he
was safe, and to a man in his condition bad weather is the
least of evils.

His reflections were not sweet. Five hours earlier he
had been dressed as a fine gentleman should be, seated
at a luxurious table in the company of a handsome and
amusing woman who was to be his wife. He could still
almost taste the delicate *chaud froid*, the tender woodcock,
the dry champagne; he could still almost hear Donna
Tullia's last noisy sally ringing in his ears—and behold,
he was now sitting by the roadside in the rain, in the
wretched garb of a begging monk, five hours' journey from
Rome. He had left his affianced bride without a word of
warning, had abandoned all his possessions to Temistocle
—that scoundrelly thief Temistocle!—and he was utterly
alone.

But as he rested himself, drawing his monk's hood
closely over his head and trying to warm his freezing
feet with the skirts of his rough brown frock, he reflected
that if he ever got safely across the frontier he would be
treated as a patriot, as a man who had suffered for the
cause, and certainly as a man who deserved to be rewarded.
He reflected that Donna Tullia was a woman who had a
theatrical taste for romance, and that his present position
was in theory highly romantic, however uncomfortable it
might be in the practice. When he was safe his story
would be told in the newspapers, and he would himself
take care that it was made interesting. Donna Tullia
would read it, would be fascinated by the tale of his
sufferings, and would follow him. His marriage with her
would then add immense importance to his own position.
He would play his cards well, and with her wealth at his
disposal he might aspire to any distinction he coveted.
He only wished the situation could have been prolonged
for three weeks, till he was actually married. Meanwhile
he must take courage and push on, beyond the reach of
pursuit. If once he could gain Subiaco, he could be over

the frontier in twelve hours. From Tivoli there were *vetture* up the valley, cheap conveyances for the country people, in which a barefooted friar could travel unnoticed. He knew that he must cross the boundary by Trevi and the Serra di Sant' Antonio. He would inquire the way from Subiaco.

While Del Ferice was thus making his way across the Campagna, Temistocle was taking measures for his own advantage and safety. He had the bag with his master's clothes, the valuable watch and chain, and the pearl studs. He had also the key to Del Ferice's lodgings, of which he promised himself to make some use, as soon as he should be sure that the detectives had left the house. In the first place he made up his mind to leave Donna Tullia in ignorance of his master's sudden departure. There was nothing to be gained by telling her the news, for she would probably in her rash way go to Del Ferice's house herself, as she had done once before, and on finding he was actually gone she would take charge of his effects, whereby Temistocle would be the loser. As he walked briskly away from the ruinous district near the Porta Maggiore, and began to see the lights of the city gleaming before him, his courage rose in his breast. He remembered how easily he had eluded the detectives an hour and a half before, and he determined to cheat them again.

But he had reckoned unwisely. Before he had been gone ten minutes the two men suspected, from the prolonged silence, that something was wrong, and after searching the lodging perceived that the polite servant who had offered them coffee had left the house without taking leave. One of the two immediately drove to the house of his chief and asked for instructions. The order to arrest the servant if he appeared again came back at once. The consequence was that when Temistocle boldly opened the door with a ready framed excuse for his absence, he was suddenly pinioned by four strong arms, dragged into the sitting-room, and told to hold his tongue in the name of the law. And that is the last that was heard of Temistocle for some time. But when the day dawned the men knew that Del Ferice had escaped them.

The affair had not been well managed. The Cardinal was a good detective, but a bad policeman. In his haste he had made the mistake of ordering Del Ferice to be arrested instantly and in his lodgings. Had the statesman simply told the chief of police to secure Ugo as soon as possible without any scandal, he could not have escaped. But the officer interpreted the Cardinal's note to mean that Del Ferice was actually at his lodgings when the order was given. The Cardinal was supposed to be omniscient by his subordinates, and no one ever thought of giving any interpretation not perfectly literal to his commands. Of course the Cardinal was at once informed, and telegrams and mounted detectives were despatched in all directions. But Del Ferice's disguise was good, and when just after sunrise a gendarme galloped into Tivoli, he did not suspect that the travel-stained and pale-faced friar, who stood telling his beads before the shrine just outside the Roman gate, was the political delinquent whom he was sent to overtake.

Donna Tullia spent an anxious night. She sent down to Del Ferice's lodgings, as Temistocle had anticipated, and the servant brought back word that he had not seen the Neapolitan, and that the house was held in possession by strangers, who refused him admittance. Madame Mayer understood well enough what had happened, and began to tremble for herself. Indeed she began to think of packing together her own valuables, in case she should be ordered to leave Rome, for she did not doubt that the Holy Office was in pursuit of Del Ferice, in consequence of some discovery relating to her little club of malcontents. She trembled for Ugo with an anxiety more genuine than any feeling of hers had been for many a day, not knowing whether he had escaped or not. But on the following evening she was partially reassured by hearing from Valdarno that the police had offered a large reward for Del Ferice's apprehension. Valdarno declared his intention of leaving Rome at once. His life, he said, was not safe for a moment. That villain Gouache,

who had turned Zouave, had betrayed them all, and they
might be lodged in the Sant' Uffizio any day. As a matter
of fact, after he discovered how egregiously he had been
deceived by Del Ferice, the Cardinal grew more suspicious,
and his emissaries were more busy than they had been
before. But Valdarno had never manifested enough wisdom, nor enough folly, to make him a cause of anxiety to
the Prime Minister. Nevertheless he actually left Rome
and spent a long time in Paris before he was induced to
believe that he might safely return to his home.

Roman society was shaken to its foundations by the
news of the attempted arrest, and Donna Tullia found some
slight compensation in becoming for a time the centre of
interest. She felt, indeed, great anxiety for the man she
was engaged to marry; but for the first time in her life she
felt also that she was living in an element of real romance,
of which she had long dreamed, but of which she had never
found the smallest realisation. Society saw, and speculated,
and gossiped, after its fashion; but its gossip was more
subdued than of yore, for men began to ask who was safe,
since the harmless Del Ferice had been proscribed. Old
Saracinesca said little. He would have gone to see the
Cardinal and to offer him his congratulations, since it would
not be decent to offer his thanks; but the Cardinal was not
in a position to be congratulated. If he had caught Del
Ferice he would have thanked the Prince instead of waiting
for any expressions of gratitude; but he did not catch Del
Ferice, for certain very good reasons which will appear in
the last scene of this comedy.

Three days after Ugo's disappearance, the old Prince got
into his carriage and drove out to Saracinesca. More than
a month had elapsed since the marriage, and he felt that he
must see his son, even at the risk of interrupting the honeymoon. On the whole, he felt that his revenge had been
inadequate. Del Ferice had escaped the Holy Office, no
one knew how; and Donna Tullia, instead of being profoundly humiliated, as she would have been had Del Ferice
been tried as a common spy, was become a centre of attraction and interest, because her affianced husband had for

some unknown cause incurred the displeasure of the great
Cardinal, almost on the eve of her marriage—a state of
things significant as regards the tone of Roman society.
Indeed the whole circumstance, which was soon bruited
about among all classes with the most lively adornment
and exaggeration, tended greatly to increase the fear and
hatred which high and low alike felt for Cardinal Antonelli
—the man who was always accused and never heard in his
own defence.

CHAPTER XXXIV.

People wondered that Giovanni and Corona should have
chosen to retire into the country for their honeymoon, instead of travelling to France and England, and ending their
wedding-trip in Switzerland. The hills were so very cold
at that early season, and besides, they would be utterly
alone. People could not understand why Corona did not
take advantage of the termination of her widowhood to
mix at once with the world, and indemnify herself for the
year of mourning by a year of unusual gaiety. But there
were many, on the other hand, who loudly applauded the
action, which, it was maintained, showed a wise spirit of
economy, and contrasted very favourably with the extravagance recently exhibited by young couples who in reality
had far more cause to be careful of their money. Those
who held this view belonged to the old, patriarchal class,
the still flourishing remnant of the last generation, who
prided themselves upon good management, good morals,
and ascetic living; the class of people in whose marriage-
contracts it was stipulated that the wife was to have meat
twice a-day, excepting on fast days, a drive—the *trottata,*
as it used to be called—daily, and two new gowns every
year. Even in our times, when most of that generation
are dead, these clauses are often introduced; in the first
half of the century they were universal. A little earlier

it used to be stipulated that the "meat" was not to be *capra*, goat's-flesh, which was considered to be food fit only for servants. But the patriarchal generation were a fine old class in spite of their economy, and they loudly applauded Giovanni's conduct.

No one, however, understood that the solitude of Saracinesca was really the greatest luxury the newly-married couple could desire. They wanted to be left alone, and they got their wish. No one had known of the preparations Giovanni had made for his wife's reception, and had any idea of the changes in the castle reached the ears of the aforesaid patriarchs, they would probably have changed their minds in regard to Giovanni's economy. The Saracinesca were not ostentatious, but they spent their money royally in their own quiet way, and the interior of the old stronghold had undergone a complete transformation, while the ancient gray stones of the outer walls and towers frowned as gloomily as ever upon the valley. Vast halls had been decorated and furnished in a style suited to the antiquity of the fortress, small sunny rooms had been fitted up with the more refined luxury which was beginning to be appreciated in Italy twenty years ago. A great conservatory had been built out upon the southern battlement. The aqueduct had been completed successfully, and fountains now played in the courts. The old-fashioned fireplaces had been again put into use, and huge logs burned upon huge fire-dogs in the halls, shedding a ruddy glow upon the trophies of old armour, the polished floors, and the heavy curtains. Quantities of magnificent tapestry, some of which had been produced when Corona first visited the castle, were now hung upon the stairs and in the corridors. The great *baldacchino*, the canopy which Roman princes are privileged to display in their ante-chambers, was draped above the quartered arms of Saracinesca and Astrardente, and the same armorial bearings appeared in rich stained glass in the window of the grand staircase. The solidity and rare strength of the ancient stronghold seemed to grow even more imposing under the decorations and improvements of a later age, and for the first time Giovanni felt

that justice had been done to the splendour of his ancestral
home.

Here he and his dark bride dwelt in perfect unity and
happiness, in the midst of their own lands, surrounded by
their own people, and wholly devoted to each other. But
though much of the day was passed in that unceasing conversation and exchange of ideas which seem to belong ex-
clusively to happily-wedded man and wife, the hours were
not wholly idle. Daily the two mounted their horses and
rode along the level stretch towards Aquaviva till they
came to the turning from which Corona had first caught
sight of Saracinesca. Here a broad road was already
broken out; the construction was so far advanced that two
miles at least were already serviceable, the gentle grade
winding backwards and forwards, crossing and recrossing
the old bridle-path as it descended to the valley below;
and now from the furthest point completed Corona could
distinguish in the dim distance the great square palace of
Astrardente crowning the hills above the town. Thither
the two rode daily, pushing on the work, consulting with
the engineer they employed, and often looking forward to
the day when for the first time their carriage should roll
smoothly down from Saracinesca to Astrardente without
making the vast detour which the old road followed as it
skirted the mountain. There was an inexpressible pleasure
in watching the growth of the work they had so long contemplated, in speculating on the advantages they would
obtain by so uniting their respective villages, and in feeling
that, being at last one, they were working together for the
good of their people. For the men who did the work were
without exception their own peasants, who were unemployed
during the winter time, and who, but for the timely occupation provided for them, would have spent the cold months
in that state of half-starved torpor peculiar to the indigent
agricultural labourer when he has nothing to do—at that
bitter season when father and mother and shivering little
ones watch wistfully the ever-dwindling sack of maize, as
day by day two or three handfuls are ground between the
stones of the hand-mill and kneaded into a thick unwhole-

some dough, the only food of the poorer peasants in the winter. But now every man who could handle pickaxe and bore, and sledge-hammer and spade, was out upon the road from dawn to dark, and every Saturday night each man took home a silver scudo in his pocket; and where people are sober and do not drink their wages, a silver scudo goes a long way further than nothing. Yet many a lean and swarthy fellow there would have felt that he was cheated if besides his money he had not carried home daily the remembrance of that tall dark lady's face and kindly eyes and encouraging voice, and they used to watch for the coming of the "*gran principessa*" as anxiously as they expected the coming of the steward with the money-bags on a Saturday evening. Often, too, the wives and daughters of the rough workers would bring the men their dinners at noonday, rather than let them carry away their food with them in the morning, just for the sake of catching a sight of Corona, and of her broad-shouldered manly husband. And the men worked with a right good will, for the story had gone abroad that for years to come there would be no lack of work for willing hands.

So the days sped, and were not interrupted by any incident for several weeks. One day Gouache, the artist Zouave, called at the castle. He had been quartered at Subiaco with a part of his company, but had not been sent on at once to Saracinesca as he had expected. Now, however, he had arrived with a small detachment of half-a-dozen men, with instructions to watch the pass. There was nothing extraordinary in his being sent in that direction, for Saracinesca was very near the frontier, and lay on one of the direct routes to the Serra di Sant' Antonio, which was the shortest hill-route into the kingdom of Naples; the country around was thought to be particularly liable to disturbance, and though no one had seen a brigand there for some years, the mountain-paths were supposed to be infested with robbers. As a matter of fact there was a great deal of smuggling carried on through the pass, and from time to time some political refugee found his way across the frontier at that point.

Gouache was received very well by Giovanni, and rather coldly by Corona, who knew him but slightly.

"I congratulate you," said Giovanni, noticing the stripes on the young man's sleeve; "I see that you have risen in grade."

"Yes. I hold an important command of six men. I spend much time in studying the strategy of Condé and Napoleon. By the bye, I am here on a very important mission."

"Indeed!"

"I suppose you give yourselves the luxury of never reading the papers in this delightful retreat. The day before yesterday the Cardinal attempted to arrest our friend Del Ferice—have you heard that?"

"No—what—has he escaped?" asked Giovanni and Corona in a breath. But their tones were different. Giovanni had anticipated the news, and was disgusted at the idea that the fellow·had got off. Corona was merely surprised.

"Yes. Heaven knows how — he has escaped. I am here to cut him off if he tries to get to the Serra di Sant' Antonio."

Giovanni laughed.

"He will scarcely try to come this way—under the very walls of my house," he said.

"He may do anything. He is a slippery fellow." Gouache proceeded to tell all he knew of the circumstances.

"That is very strange," said Corona, thoughtfully. Then after a pause, she added, "We are going to visit our road, Monsieur Gouache. Will you not come with us? My husband will give you a horse."

Gouache was charmed. He preferred talking to Giovanni and looking at Corona's face to returning to his six Zouaves, or patrolling the hills in search of Del Ferice. In a few minutes the three were mounted, and riding slowly along the level stretch towards the works. As they entered the new road Giovanni and Corona unconsciously fell into conversation, as usual, about what they were doing, and forgot their visitor. Gouache dropped behind, watching the pair and admiring them with true artistic appreciation. He had a Parisian's love of luxury and perfect appointments as well as an artist's love of beauty, and his eyes rested with unmitigated pleasure on the riders and their horses, losing no detail of their dress, their simple English accoutrements, their firm seats and graceful carriage. But at a turn of the grade the two riders suddenly slipped from his field of vision, and his attention was attracted to the marvellous beauty of the landscape, as looking down the valley towards Astrardente he saw range on range of purple hills rising in a deep perspective, crowned with jagged rocks or sharply defined brown villages, ruddy in the lowering sun. He stopped his horse and sat motionless, drinking in the loveliness before him. So it is that accidents in nature make accidents in the lives of men.

But Giovanni and Corona rode slowly down the gentle incline, hardly noticing that Gouache had stopped behind, and talking of the work. As they again turned a curve of the grade Corona, who was on the inside, looked up and caught sight of Gouache's motionless figure at the opposite extremity of the gradient they had just descended. Giovanni looked straight before him, and was aware of a pale-faced Capuchin friar who with downcast eyes was toiling up the road, seemingly exhausted; a particularly weather-stained and dilapidated friar even for those wild mountains.

"Gouache is studying geography," remarked Corona.

"Another of those Capuccini!" exclaimed Giovanni, instinctively feeling in his pocket for coppers. Then with a sudden movement he seized his wife's arm. She was close to him as they rode slowly along side by side.

"Good God! Corona," he cried, "it is Del Ferice!" Corona looked quickly at the monk. His cowl was raised enough to show his features; but she would, perhaps, not have recognised his smooth shaven face had Giovanni not called her attention to it.

Del Ferice had recognised them too, and, horror-struck, he paused, trembling and uncertain what to do. He had taken the wrong turn from the main road below; unaccustomed to the dialect of the hills, he had misunderstood the peasant who had told him especially not to take the bridle-path if he wished to avoid Saracinesca. He stopped, hesitated, and then, pulling his cowl over his face, walked steadily on. Giovanni glanced up and saw that Gouache was slowly descending the road, still absorbed in contemplating the landscape.

"Let him take his chance," muttered Saracinesca. "What should I care?"

"No—no! Save him, Giovanni,—he looks so miserable," cried Corona, with ready sympathy. She was pale with excitement.

Giovanni looked at her one moment and hesitated, but her pleading eyes were not to be refused.

"Then gallop back, darling. Tell Gouache it is cold in the valley—anything. Make him go back with you—I will save him since you wish it."

Corona wheeled her horse without a word and cantered up the hill again. The monk had continued his slow walk, and was now almost at Giovanni's saddle-bow. The latter drew rein, staring hard at the pale features under the cowl.

"If you go on you are lost," he said, in low distinct tones. "The Zouaves are waiting for you. Stop, I say!" he exclaimed, as the monk attempted to pass on. Leaping to the ground Giovanni seized his arm and held him tightly. Then Del Ferice broke down.

"You will not give me up—for the love of Christ!" he whined. "Oh, if you have any pity—let me go—I never meant to harm you——"

"Look here," said Giovanni. "I would just as soon give you up to the Holy Office as not; but my wife asked me to save you——"

"God bless her! Oh, the saints bless her! God render her kindness!" blubbered Del Ferice, who, between fear and exhaustion, was by this time half idiotic.

"Silence!" said Giovanni, sternly. "You may thank her if you ever have a chance. Come with me quietly. I will send one of the workmen round the hill with you. You must sleep at Trevi, and then get over the Serra as best you can." He ran his arm through the bridle of his horse and walked by his enemy's side.

"You will not give me up," moaned the wretched man. "For the love of heaven do not betray me—I have come so far—I am so tired."

"The wolves may make a meal of you, for all I care," returned Giovanni. "I will not. I give you my word that I will send you safely on, if you will stop this whining and behave like a man."

At that moment Del Ferice was past taking offence, but for many a year afterwards the rough words rankled in his heart. Giovanni was brutal for once; he longed to wring the fellow's neck, or to give him up to Gouache and the Zouaves. The tones of Ugo's voice reminded him of injuries not so old as to be yet forgotten. But he smothered his wrath and strode on, having promised his wife to save the wretch, much against his will. It was a quarter of an hour before they reached the works, the longest quarter of an hour Del Ferice remembered in his whole life. Neither spoke a word. Giovanni hailed a sturdy-looking fellow who was breaking stones by the roadside.

"Get up, Carluccio," he said. "This good monk has lost his way. You must take him round the mountain, above Ponza to Arcinazzo, and show him the road to Trevi. It is a long way, but the road is good enough after Ponza —it is shorter than to go round by Saracinesca, and the good friar is in a hurry."

Carluccio started up with alacrity. He greatly preferred roaming about the hills to breaking stones, provided he was paid for it. He picked up his torn jacket and threw it over one shoulder, setting his battered hat jauntily on his thick black curls.

"Give us a benediction, *padre mio*, and let us be off— *non è mica un passo*—it is a good walk to Trevi."

Del Ferice hesitated. He hardly knew what to do or say, and even if he had wished to speak he was scarcely able to control his voice. Giovanni cut the situation short by turning on his heel and mounting his horse. A moment later he was cantering up the road again, to the

www.ingramcontent.com/pod-product-compliance
Lightning Source LLC
Chambersburg PA
CBHW071357050326
40689CB00010B/1678